GW01607816

WESTMORLAND HERITAGE

Popular Edition

It is fourteen years since Wainwright's Westmorland Heritage was published as a numbered and signed edition of 1000 copies. Continual demand from Wainwright's many followers has persuaded the publishers that this beautiful book should now become more widely available. The Westmorland Gazette has therefore decided to issue this 'popular' edition of Westmorland Heritage which will enable those whose roots have remained firmly in the old county of Westmorland to become more intimately acquainted with its many facets.

WESTMORLAND HERITAGE

A BOOK FOR THOSE
WHO HAVE THEIR ROOTS
IN WESTMORLAND

And long may it continue!

To Jill

love from Colin - Xmas 1989.

WESTMORLAND HERITAGE

A. Wainwright

PUBLISHED BY
WESTMORLAND GAZETTE, KENDAL
1988

ISBN 0 902272 74 8

PRINTED BY Titus Wilson and Son Ltd., Kendal

INTRODUCTION

Whenever I see a book prefaced by an apology from the author for having written it, as so many are in these days of prolific literary output, I always think that it should never have been written at all. I make no apology for this book on Westmorland, feeling it to be overdue, but concede a regret that it has not come from the pen of someone born and bred in the county. I, an offcomer, was introduced to it only in middle life.

This is the time, more than any other, when Westmorland deserves a book. 31st. March 1974 was a fateful day in local history. Whitehall decreed that on this day Westmorland should officially cease to be a separate entity and be incorporated in the newly-formed county of Cumbria, a decision that, being statutory, had to be accepted. Many, and probably most, Westmorland people regretted this enforced loss of identity. They liked the county as it was: a distinctive region of fields and farms, fells and mountains, everywhere pleasant, free from heavy industry, independent, and having little in common with neighbouring areas into whose company they were thrust. They liked the name, too. They liked to be able to call Westmorland their very own.

This book tries to describe the Westmorland we know and love, and in simple terms. One can know and love without a background of scholarship, and the book has no pretensions to be a learned treatise on every aspect of the county. It is strictly an amateur effort written by a non-specialist for non-specialists, by a wandering observer, not a tutor. It is a guide only in restricted degree. It touches on history, geology, architecture and archaeology, but briefly, not going beyond the rudiments of these subjects. Its references to topography and landscape are mainly based on a detailed exploration of the county over many happy years.

The book is nothing more than an illustrated catalogue of the buildings and landmarks and natural scenes of special merit or unique character that I have found personally interesting and particularly the treasures of architecture that have been preserved through the centuries and the distinctive landscapes that are peculiar to Westmorland and not found elsewhere. It is representative but not comprehensive. The book could have been twice the size and not exhausted the material worthy of inclusion.

When reading the book it is important to bear in mind that it is descriptive of Westmorland as the county was on the last day of its existence and makes no mention of the changes in administration that have taken place since, with which I have little sympathy. It is a 'dated' book and the date is 31st March 1974.

In compiling the book I have been greatly helped by my wife, who has not only done much research but chauffered me over every road in the county and walked with me into the remotest corners; who has assisted me over stiles and gates (at which I was never adept), supplied sustenance, kept me buttoned up against the weather, guided my apprehensive steps in farmyards, and generally had sympathetic regard for my advanced years (without ever mentioning them, which would have annoyed me). To the many others who have provided information I am also grateful.

To supplement my patchy knowledge I have referred to and freely quoted from the authoritative writings of others, and pay tribute gladly to the help provided by the following publications:

- First and foremost, AN INVENTORY OF THE HISTORICAL MONUMENTS IN WESTMORLAND (1936), prepared by the Royal Commission on Historical Monuments — a classical work, beautifully designed and written;
- HISTORY, TOPOGRAPHY, AND DIRECTORY OF WESTMORELAND (1885), edited by T. F. Bulmer — an admirable survey, all the more valuable for having been compiled nearly a century ago;
- KELLY'S DIRECTORY OF CUMBERLAND AND WESTMORLAND (1906) — also a mine of information;
- THE CASTLES AND FORTIFIED TOWERS OF CUMBERLAND, WESTMORLAND AND LANCASHIRE NORTH-OF-THE-SANDS (1913), by John F. Curwen;
- HISTORIC FARMHOUSES IN AND AROUND WESTMORLAND (1944), written by J. H. Palmer and revised by W. T. McIntire;
- INDUSTRIAL ARCHAEOLOGY OF THE LAKE COUNTIES (1969), by J. D. Marshall and M. Davies-Shiel — a fascinating account of the old industries;
- SOME WESTMORLAND VILLAGES (1957) — aspects of social life;
- and a miscellany of 'official' guidebooks, brochures, leaflets and other published literature, including my favourite reading: THE MAPS OF THE ORDNANCE SURVEY.

All the books individually mentioned are excellent, but most of the older volumes are out of print. Which is a pity, for they too are part of Westmorland's heritage....

JUNE 1975

CONTENTS *(in alphabetical order of parishes)*

CONTENTS *continued*

CONTENTS *continued*

MAP SYMBOLS

A map of each parish accompanies the text.
In every case the top of the map is north.
The adjoining parishes are named in CAPITALS.

Parish boundary

County boundary

Public roads A.b M.b

Public path

Active railway

Dismantled railway

Buildings

Parish church +

Cairn ▲

Stream

River

Surface limestone

Woodlands and plantations

Crags

AMBLESIDE

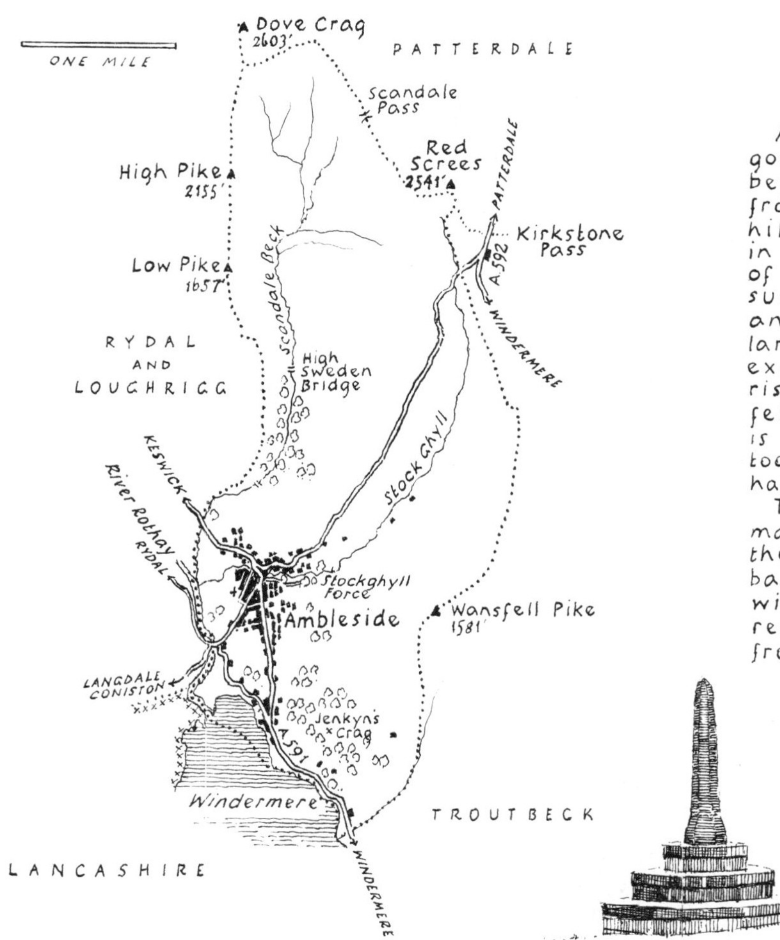

Ambleside is a small Lakeland town that, by the good fortune of a favourable location, is known far beyond the district and even internationally. Apart from a huddle of picturesque old buildings on the hillside rising from the main street, the town is not in itself particularly attractive and has few items of architectural merit. Its great appeal lies in the surrounding romantic landscape of valley and fell and woodland, in its fine position at the head of the largest lake in the country. It is the scenery that excites, not the town. On three sides the mountains rise abruptly and invitingly: friendly and colourful fells reached by much-trodden paths, for Ambleside is a popular base for walkers. On the lower slopes, too, are many charming natural features. Ambleside has been well described as the hub of a wheel of beauty.

The town is long founded, obtaining a charter for a market in 1650. Its appearance has changed little in the present century: each year pilgrims in boots come back to familiar and well loved scenes, confident they will not be shocked by garish re-development. New residences there are but they are mainly out of sight from the main streets. Nothing offends. A housing estate off the Rydal road deservedly won an award for site layout and design.

Tourism is the big local industry. Hotels and boarding houses are numerous, but in summer accommodation is severely strained. When the Romans stayed here as early visitors they built their own quarters at Waterhead.

The parish boundary extends high into the mountains, enclosing the valleys of Stock Ghyll and Scandale and exceeding 2500' in altitude on Dove Crag and Red Screes.

Market Cross (medieval shaft; modern base)

Ambleside

In old Ambleside:

1 : Bridge House
2 : Smithy Brow
3 : Peggy Hill
4 : A typical cottage
5 : Old corn mill, Stock Ghyll
6 : Old bark mill, Bridge Street

2

5

3

1

4

6

Ambleside

Old Ambleside occupied Chapel Hill (the How), up which the Kirkstone road winds steeply from the town centre. A remarkable cluster of old buildings crowns this hill and flanks its tortuous byways. Here is the church of St. Anne, overlooking a complex of rough stone cottages and one-time farmhouses set higgledy-piggledy in a lack of pattern no modern planner could approve. Here is a ready-made site museum. The most interesting of these properties, How Head, is pictured above: it has 16th and 17th century features and was recently restored.

In early days the turnpike road through the town climbed North Road from the market cross and then descended Smithy Brow, passing the Unicorn and Golden Rule inns. The present direct road was non-existent (constructed 1833), the site being part of the garden of the Old House in Smithy Brow, and the so-called Bridge House spanning the beck, and now isolated, was a summerhouse within the garden.

Ambleside

When Ambleside was a hamlet centred on the How its place of worship was an Elizabethan chapel situated in its midst, hence the name Chapel Hill. The chapel was replaced by St Anne's Church on the same site in 1812. St Anne's in turn became inadequate and, with the trend of new building moving to the foot of the hill in the meadows of the Rothay, St Mary's was built in 1854 to cater for the needs of the growing town, being more conveniently sited in Rothay Park; and when Ambleside was created a separate parish in 1863 St Mary's became the parish church. Designed by Sir Gilbert Scott, it is an elegant edifice but subject to the criticism that its style is out of character in the Lake District and more appropriate to a city suburb. Among its internal features of interest is a large mural depicting the traditional festival of rush-bearing.

St Anne's has been de-consecrated, and is now a church hall.

In Wansfell Road is a Roman Catholic church notable for a beautiful interior and in Millans Park is a Methodist church of good proportions.

St Anne's Church

Ambleside Churches

The church of St Mary the Virgin

High Sweden Bridge

Stockghyll Force

Ambleside

Ambleside has not escaped involvement in the great postwar problem of Lakeland — that of controlling increased traffic on narrow winding roads that were not built to contain the summer invasion of cars, nor for speedy travel. The authorities propose to cut a new bypass through Rothay Park to ease congestion in the main street. The objectors to this plan contend that it would be irretrievable sacrilege in a landscape so precious and is unnecessary, alternative remedies being available.

Ambleside, from Low Gale

1 : Crinkle Crags
2 : Bowfell
3 : Esk Pike
4 : Great End
5 : Loft Crag
6 : Pike O' Stickle
7 : Harrison Stickle
8 : Lingmoor Fell

The Langdale Fells, from Jenkyn's Crag

Jenkyn's (or Jenkin or Jenkin's) Crag is a platform of bare rock in Skelghyll Wood, occurring where a break in the trees permits an open view of Windermere and the fells beyond. The crag is National Trust property. The popular walk to it coincides with a nature trail.

Waterhead, one mile south of the town centre, is Ambleside's foothold on Windermere. From the pier here the lake steamers ply; there is fishing, boating, yachting, water-skiing; in Borrans Park, along the lake side, are several delightful bays much in use for family picnics. The summer scene at Waterhead is animated and colourful. Ranging along the foreshore is a large concentration of hotels, indicative of the popularity of Ambleside's "harbour."

The Romans came to Waterhead and established themselves, not for the water sports, but for the purpose of constructing and maintaining a fort, known as Galava, on the fields at the head of the lake. This fort was linked by roads with others at Brougham and Ravenglass and Kendal, the first two roads entailing spectacular crossings of the mountains. The present name of the site, Borrans Field, suggests that when it was so named by the Norsemen who came later, the collapsed walls of the fort were still to be seen but today the remains, in the form of a series of grassed earthworks enclosed by a fence, are disappointing.

The boat landings, Waterhead

Galava today

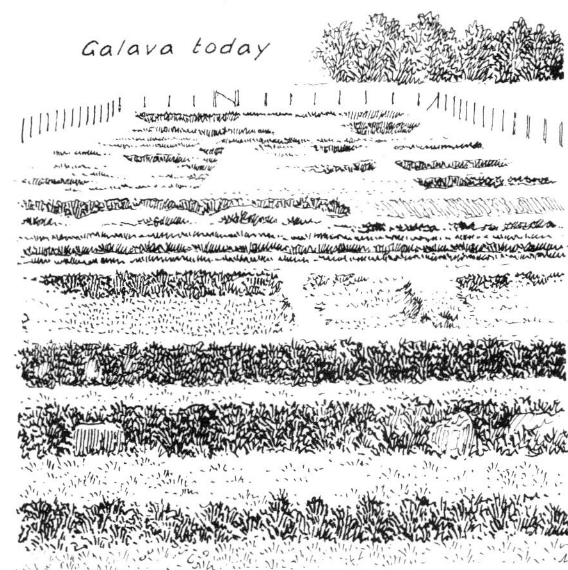

APPLEBY

COUNTY TOWN OF WESTMORLAND

The Latin inscription on the town's Coat of Arms, translated, is a defiant echo of the past:
NEITHER BY FIRE NOR SWORD

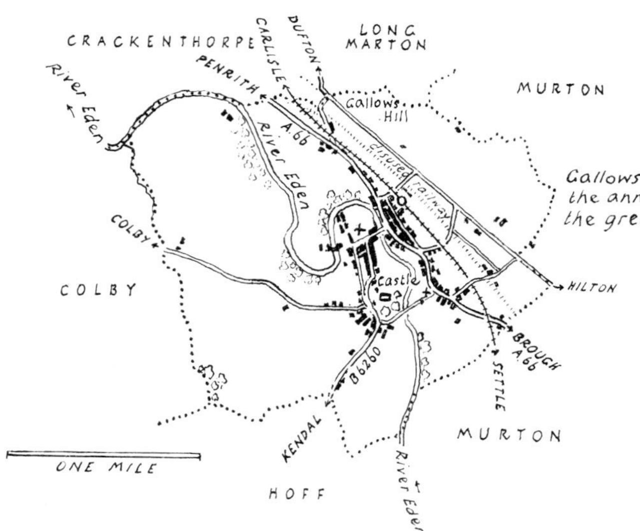

Gallows Hill is the venue of the annual Appleby Horse Fair, the great local event of the year.

The ancient borough of Appleby, honoured by a succession of Royal Charters dating from 1179, has an eventful history, recorded from the 10th century when Danish settlers founded a community; before their coming, but not documented, were occupations by the Celts and the Anglo-Saxons, and the Romans had camps nearby. At the time of the Normans the area was part of the Scottish kingdom. Choice of site may have been influenced by considerations of defence, for the town lies within a great loop of the River Eden and is further protected by the hill on which the castle stands. These natural defences were, however, of no avail against raids from over the Border, which ravaged the town in the 12th century and laid it waste in the 14th.

Appleby, prior to this later misfortune, had become a place of great importance, with a population twice that of today, but never fully recovered its proud status, and, suffering further from the 1598 plague and defeat in the Civil War, when it supported the Royalist cause, sadly declined in influence, although remaining the county town and the centre of traditional ceremonies. The older part of the town has retained its quiet dignity and pleasing appearance and escaped disturbance caused by the coming of the railway and heavy road traffic. Two railways, each with a station, followed parallel courses along the hillside east of the river and above the main Carlisle-Scotch Corner road: it was in this vicinity, across the river from the old town, that development, residential and commercial, took place in Victorian times and has mainly continued since. The Eden proves more effective today than ever it did in the past: it preserves the best of Appleby in a tranquil backwater.

Appleby

The church of St Lawrence

The entrance to St Lawrence's Church

The church of St Michael

The church of St Lawrence stands behind a cloister screen at the lower end of Boroughgate. Twice it was devastated in Scots raids and rebuilt; parts of the fabric are the 12th century restoration, notably the bottom part of the tower, which was strongly built as a refuge. There are many later additions and alterations, some undertaken by Lady Anne Clifford, whose elaborate tomb within was constructed in her lifetime. The attractive cloister was built in 1811. Upon a recent merger of ecclesiastical parishes the church of St Lawrence became the parish church of Appleby.

St Michael's Church, situated in Bongate, and previously also a parish church, is believed to be an even older foundation, possibly occupying the site of a Saxon church, as some interesting fragments suggest. St Michael's was reconstructed in the 17th century under the direction of Lady Anne Clifford. The present tower was added in 1885 during a further reconstruction.

Appleby

Low Cross, the Moot Hall and Boroughgate, from the Cloisters

The main street of Appleby is not the busiest — happily, for its comparative quiet is appropriate to its elegant grace and dignity. This is Boroughgate, Westmorland's finest street. Lined with trees and grass verges, Boroughgate is a wide rising avenue between the parish church by the river and the castle on the hill, and is flanked by buildings of differing period and style, many of them of great interest. At the top of the street, near the castle gates and on the site of an earlier market, is High Cross, a 17th century column bearing the inscription RETAIN YOUR LOYALTY, PRESERVE YOUR RIGHTS. At the foot of the hill is Low Cross, a later counterpart, and here a cloister-like arcade terminates the street. Nearby, on an 'island' site, is the ancient Moot Hall (1596).

Appleby

Appleby

The castle keep, known as Caesar's Tower

The splendid castle keep is 12th century Norman, and although besieged and attacked and later restored and altered internally from time to time it retains its original commanding appearance, standing in isolation away from the main castle buildings, which are of later date.

Appleby Castle

The castle occupies a fine position on the crest of a hill overlooking the Eden. It dates from the 11th century and was first of the motte and bailey type but later extended on several occasions. It suffered severely from Scottish raids, which left it in a ruinous condition, in the 14th century, but was subsequently rebuilt and restored, notably by Lady Anne Clifford in the 17th century. For many generations the castle was the home of the Cliffords and latterly of a descendant, Lord Hothfield. Recently it was sold and is at present a private residence, not open to the public.

The castle, from the riverside

The Hospital of St. Anne

Lady Anne Clifford

Appleby's medieval history is closely interwoven with the name of the early owners of the castle, the Cliffords, an illustrious family distinguished by long service to the Crown. The last of the line was Lady Anne, born at Skipton Castle in 1589, who became Countess of Pembroke by marriage. She was a woman of remarkable determination, a fervent loyalist, who left an indelible impression on the affairs of North Westmorland by dedicating her long life to the restoration of the castles and churches and bridges and to the welfare of the people living within her large estates. Her benefactions were many, one example being the pleasant arrangement of almshouses for widows situated in Boroughgate and known as St. Anne's Hospital. She died in 1675 and was interred in a tomb in St. Lawrence's Church. Three hundred years later it is still true to say that no other person has done more to influence the social history of Westmorland.

Appleby

By the time the Eden reaches Appleby it has developed into a wide river, and in the vicinity of the town has the confidence and beauty and grace of maturity, its wooded banks affording delightful walks both up-river and down. In many places the underlying red sandstone of the area is exposed in colourful rocks.

Bongate Mill

Pleasantly situated in a sheltered hollow by the riverside at the foot of Mill Brow is the plain but impressive building of Bongate Mill. This was a corn mill until the last war and has since served for a time as a store but is largely derelict. It seems a pity that the opportunity to re-furbish it with machinery and replace the water-wheel, as a site for educational and industrial study, has not been taken; failing that, it is good to know that the building is to be preserved and converted to residential accommodation.

Appleby Bridge (over the Eden), built in 1889. Originally a Norman bridge spanned the river at this point.

ARNSIDE

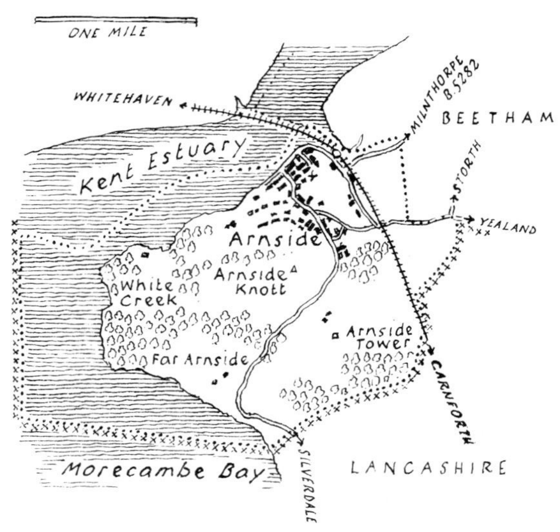

Westmorland is an inland county but has a footing on the coast on both sides of the Kent Estuary, notably where the promontory of Arnside thrusts far into Morecambe Bay. The village and its environs are places of quiet delight, with a lengthy frontage to the estuary and a wide view beyond to the hills of southern Lakeland, while on the shore are interesting evidences of small fishing and boat-building activities, and, for ornithologists, a rare pageant of bird life on the sands and mudflats at low tide, when the River Kent can be seen running along its channel until submerged; high tides here can be spectacular and dangerous. Behind the promenade and its row of shops rises the eminence of Arnside Knott, a splendid viewpoint. All this is limestone terrain with the charms inherent in such, outcrops occurring in the native woodlands of oak, hazel and birch with which the promontory is richly endowed and through which wind many enchanting paths.

In the old days the village was busily occupied with industries of shipping, fishing and boat-building and had little intervention from outside, but two developments have since radically changed both its economics and way of life. First was the coming of a railway in the middle of last century, and secondly and more recently, the coming of the motor car. The quiet seclusion of Arnside and its picturesque charms were thus brought to the notice of many people for the first time and it has developed into a holiday resort, happily without damage to its amenities or appearance, and into a desirable residential retreat.

It seems an anomaly that the parish of Arnside should be included within the county of Westmorland, the obvious natural boundary with Lancashire being the estuary of the Kent, and it is surprising that the position was not corrected in the 1974 revision of county boundaries. Arnside's status as a parish is, however, comparatively recent, the area formerly being part of the ancient parish of Beetham, which has a closer affinity with Westmorland.

"Delightful Arnside! If any man loves the beautiful in nature – if he be a geologist, or a botanist, or an invalid in search of peaceful restoration, let him wander about Arnside." Edwin Waugh

Arnside

In times past Arnside benefitted from its withdrawn position on a remote headland, escaping the military campaigns and raids that beset many communities on or near the main highways. Its one great contribution to the history of Westmorland is the massive pele of Arnside Tower on a green hill conspicuously seen from the road to Silverdale. Built in 1375 for both defensive and residential purposes, the Tower has been ruinous for more than two centuries, but the outer walls are still mainly intact and of sufficiently imposing proportions to convey to visitors a good impression of the original structure. The walls, 4½' thick, are faced with blocks of squared and coursed limestone and rise to a height of 50'. The overall dimensions are 45' x 31½' plus a projection, and there were four floors (five in the projection).

The Tower suffered a severe fire in 1602, but was subsequently rebuilt and occupied until 1690. Today it is but a shell. The interior has been completely dismantled or destroyed, the south-west corner wall collapsed in a hurricane in 1884 and other parts of the outer fabric have since fallen. The building is not kept in safe repair — explorers should enter with caution.

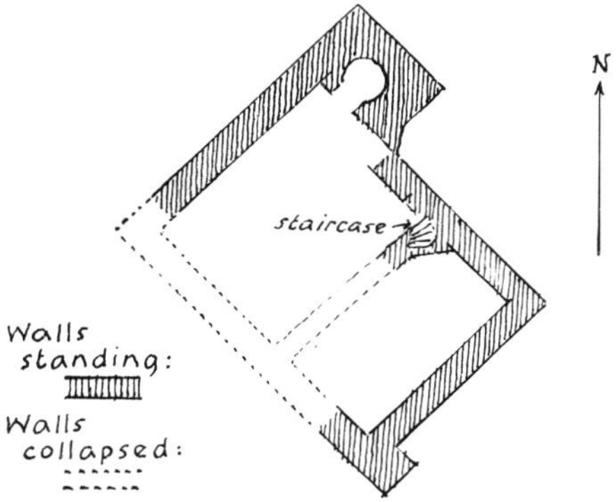

Arnside Tower

Arnside

The Kent Estuary,
from the view indicator on Arnside Knott

Summit of Arnside Knott

Blackstone Point

This yew provided the name for Yew Tree Cottage and is reputedly the oldest tree in the village.

Trees in Arnside

The "knotted trees" by the path on Arnside Knott are a curiosity, a human interference with natural growth. Some time early last century four young saplings (larch) were knotted together in pairs by bending two over to their partners, and from each pair one trunk only continued upwards to maturity. The trees have been dead for many years and one has broken off just above the knot. A romantic legend attributes this outrage to a lover and his lass; another, more credible, to two seamen from a ship moored at the quarry on Blackstone Point.

ASBY

Asby is a large parish, sparsely populated and, although in the heart of the county, bypassed by the principal channels of communication and served only by a few quiet country roads. Lying hidden in a shallow valley, the village of Great Asby seems remote from worldly and even urban affairs. Formerly two mills operated here but today it is the centre of a farming community, with much of its area overlaid with surface limestone: in the south of the parish particularly the whole landscape is a desert of outcropping rocks. Here is the ancient British settlement of Castle Folds, a remarkable ruin: this and other earthworks and burial cairns tell of man's early occupation of the district. In the village the most notable buildings are the Rectory, the north wing being a converted pele tower, and Asby Hall, now a farmhouse. Elsewhere both Gaythorn Hall and Grange Hall have interesting features. Of botanical appeal is the profuse *primula farinosa*, the best habitat being the roadside on Little Asby Scar. But it is the limestone landscape that one associates most of all with the parish of Asby.

Asby

The church of St Peter, rebuilt 1866.

Asby Hall, now a farmhouse, bears the heraldic arms of the Musgrave family with the initials E.M. and the date 1694 on a stone panel over the front door.

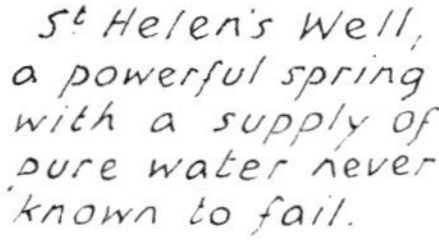

St Helen's Well, a powerful spring with a supply of pure water never known to fail.

In the village of Great Asby.

A rustic 17th century footbridge.

The north wing of the Rectory is a 17th century reconstruction of a 14th century pele tower.

Gaythorn Hall

Gaythorn Hall, beautifully situated in the remote valley of Scale Beck, is an imposing house of unusual appearance and design, being a perfect square in plan but with a projection on each wall, two being staircase wings, the others porches. It was built in the late 16th century, the back part being rebuilt in the 18th. Amongst many interesting features it bears the shield of the Bellingham family, but has long been occupied as a farmhouse.

Asby

Castle Folds

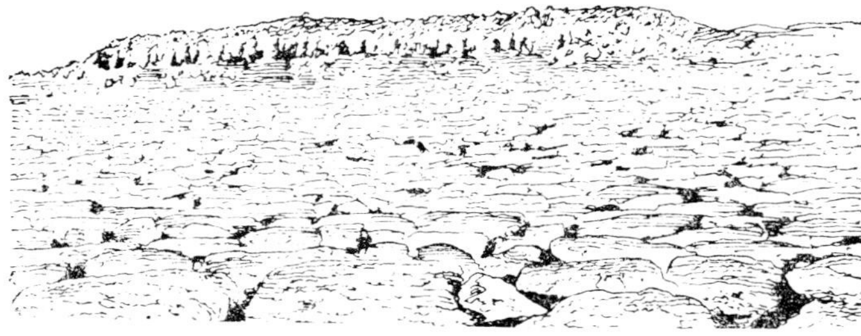

There are several ancient settlements and tumuli in remote parts of the parish in ruinous condition, the best preserved being the British settlement at Castle Folds, spectacularly sited at 1300′ on a knoll defended by a crevassed limestone pavement: here the boundary walls are still clearly seen although now crumbled and there are traces of hut circles within the enclosed area of 1¼ acres.

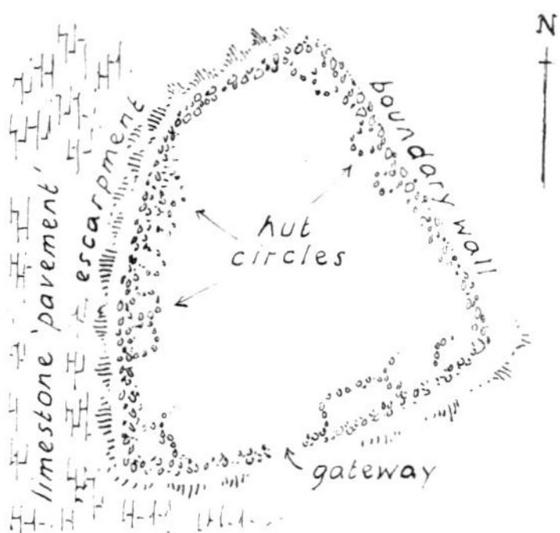

The largest of the many tumuli within the parish is Hollin Stump Cairn, 70′ in diameter. Excavated last century, it was found to contain human bones in a cist and the skull of a horse.

The boundary wall, Castle Folds

The summit of High Pike

Clapper bridge
at Water Houses

Pate Hole Mouth

Except for those in the parish of Casterton there are few limestone caves in the county, the largest being Pate Hole, a mile upstream of Great Asby. The low entrance admits to a passage with pools, a flood channel, which becomes impenetrable after 500 yards.

Little Asby

Little Asby is a remote hamlet at a quiet road-end, and is in decline. A few generations ago it had a larger population served by a chapel (St Leonard's), destroyed and replaced in 1889 by another that has also ceased to function as such. In a field nearby are ancient earthworks. The terrain around, where not pastoral, is open limestone upland.

The earthworks at Little Asby, in a field behind the chapel, have survived the centuries without disturbance and are in almost pristine condition. They consist of grassed mounds, having the appearance of long barrows but probably serving as defensive ramparts, on three sides of a rectangle. Thus enclosed is a smaller circular mound and a well that provided the water for Little Asby before a piped supply was brought to the hamlet.

Chapel Farm,
Little Asby

ASKHAM

General consensus of opinion, rarely questioned or disputed, awards to Askham the title of Westmorland's loveliest village. The single wide street has ample verges and noble trees and is flanked by a charming disarray of picturesque cottages set at different angles and elevations: it forms an attractive avenue extending from the River Lowther uphill to open moorland. Down by the river, which marks the eastern boundary of the parish, are the church and Askham Hall, set in wooded surroundings; on the further side is the great estate of Lowther Park.

Nor is the village alone attractive. The parish stretches southwest to the mountains and comes within sight of Ullswater, crossing the plateau of Moor Divock, an antiquarian site of great interest, coinciding in places with the High Street of the Romans, and rising to the limestone escarpment of Heughscar Hill. The only other community in the parish is Helton, a cluster of cottages giving access to Heltondale, where water is gathered and tunnelled to Haweswater.

A wide variety of scenery, between extremes of bare fell and sylvan woodland, makes Askham a favoured parish.

Village street Helton

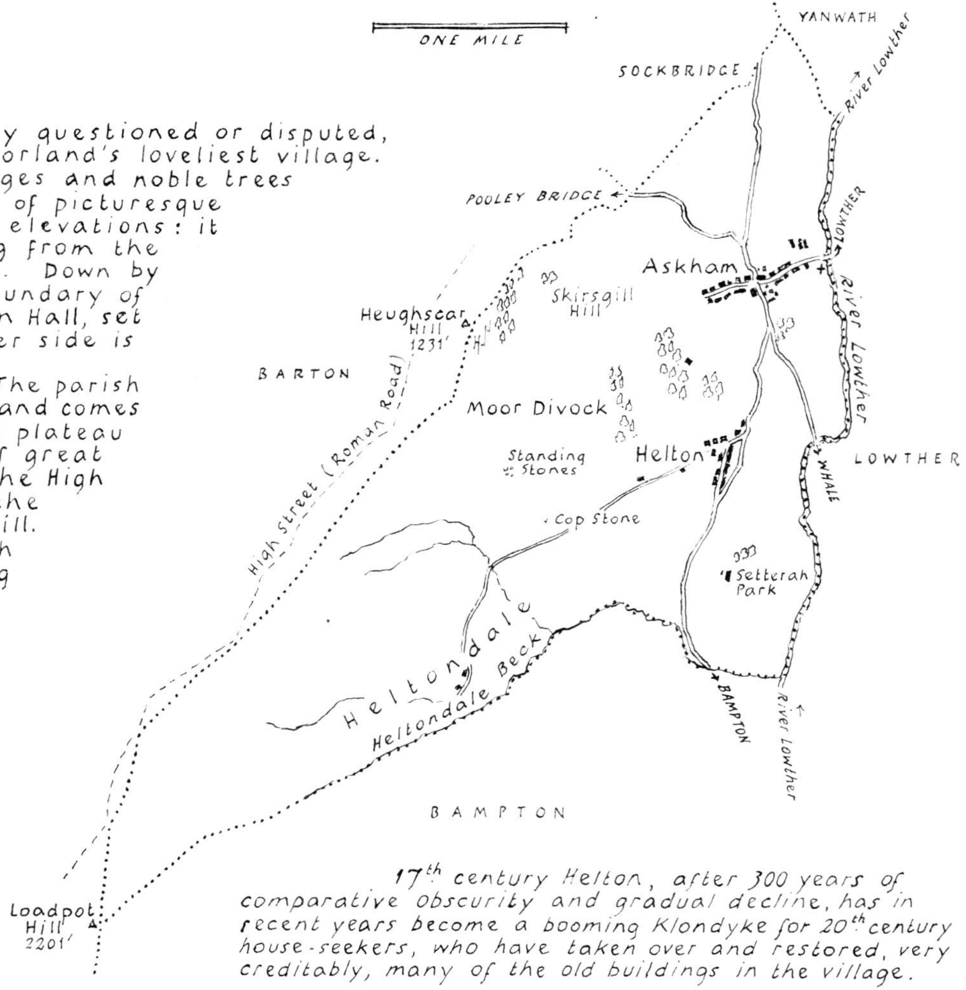

17th century Helton, after 300 years of comparative obscurity and gradual decline, has in recent years become a booming Klondyke for 20th century house-seekers, who have taken over and restored, very creditably, many of the old buildings in the village.

Askham

The Green,
Askham

Askham

The massive defence tower of Askham Hall dates from the 14th century.

Askham Hall, the ancient manor house of the Lowther estate, has been the seat of the Earl of Lonsdale since the recent dismantling of Lowther Castle. First occupied in 1375, the Hall has been subject to many later additions and alterations, mainly by the Sandford family whose home it was until 1680.

The Church of St Peter, Askham (formerly St Columba) was rebuilt in 1832 by the architect who designed Lowther Castle.

Askham

Marked on Ordnance maps as "Standing Stones" this small circle of boulders indicates a burial mound from which evidences of cremation and a food vessel were excavated in 1866.

The moor southwest of Askham village has many relics of the prehistoric inhabitants of the area. On Skirsgill Hill are the remains of an ancient settlement. On Moor Divock, a happy hunting ground for antiquarians, is a miscellany of tumuli and standing stones. More recent are the monoliths marking the parish boundary and often inscribed. Also of interest is a double series of crater-like hollows or shakeholes: a natural formation. Just over the Barton parish boundary is the Roman High Street and a stone circle.

The Cop Stone, 5 feet high, stands isolated, the sole survivor of a stone circle of which few traces today remain.

Boundary stone Heughscar Hill

BAMPTON

The River Lowther descends from the bare hills of Shap to reach gentler and greener pastures at Keld, thereafter proceeding pleasantly along a broad valley with lofty fells rising to the west and a limestone escarpment to the east. At the point where the Lowther is joined by the outflow from Haweswater is the village of Bampton, in two parts, attractively sited but not unduly disturbed by tourist traffic. The church is at Bampton Grange, and the parish it serves is very extensive. Butterwick and Knipe were the only other small communities until Haweswater was made into a reservoir, since when the workmen's camp at Burn Banks has grown into a residential area for the reservoir staff. More than half of the area of the parish, southwest of a straight line between Carhullan and the dam, is entirely without habitations, although, in pre-reservoir days, the banks of the lake were populated. Elsewhere, farmsteads are scattered on the fellsides. There are many remains of old native settlements within the parish (the reservoir having contributed to their number!)

The Parish Church of St Patrick, rebuilt 1726, restored 1884

Bampton

Halfa Bridge, over Haweswater Beck

Thornthwaite Hall, near Burn Banks, was built for the Curwen family in the 16th century; now it is occupied as a farmhouse. The south-east block (on the right in the drawing) was an embattled tower originally.

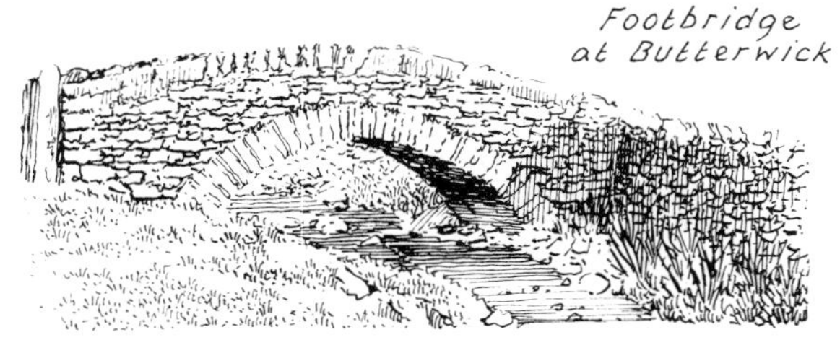

Footbridge at Butterwick

Footbridge over Cawdale Beck

Roadbridge, Bampton

Bampton

The western boundary of the parish is coincident with a mountain ridge: a long spur along which the Romans made their most spectacular road. The ridge rises to four distinct summits, Kidsty Pike being the most shapely, High Raise at 2634' the loftiest, and Wether Hill and Loadpot Hill the least exciting, although the top of the latter was distinguished, until recently, by a shooting lodge with stables, now quite ruinous. The grassy slopes are grazed by fell ponies and the Martindale deer.

The summits of High Raise (above) and Kidsty Pike (left)

The Haweswater dam (construction completed in 1941) measures 1540' in length. It was the first hollow-arch dam to be built within the United Kingdom.

Measand sacrificed a bridge, a road and a settlement in the conversion of Haweswater to a reservoir but is still a place of popular resort by virtue of its waterfalls, the Forces, which display a pretty picture near the lakeside path. In its higher reaches, among the hills, Measand Beck has other falls (shown above) but these are rarely visited.

Bampton

Ancient Monuments of Bampton

Two standing stones on Bampton Common, at 1600', occur in an area of ancient cairns, near a ruined enclosure, and command a view of Mardale Head.

Most remarkable of the monuments in Bampton parish is the British hill fort perched high above Haweswater on the top of the steep Castle Crag and difficult of access. A tumbled wall, still visible, rims the crag top and two artificial ditches protect the site from an approach via the fellside behind.

Towtop Kirk is a circular earthwork on a headland near Cawdale Beck. Few stones remain to be seen but the site is definable.

This tumulus on Low Raise, at 2465', is the highest in the county. The cairn is a recent addition by visitors.

A Ministry of Works notice marks a stone circle on Knipe Moor: this is overgrown and in bad condition.

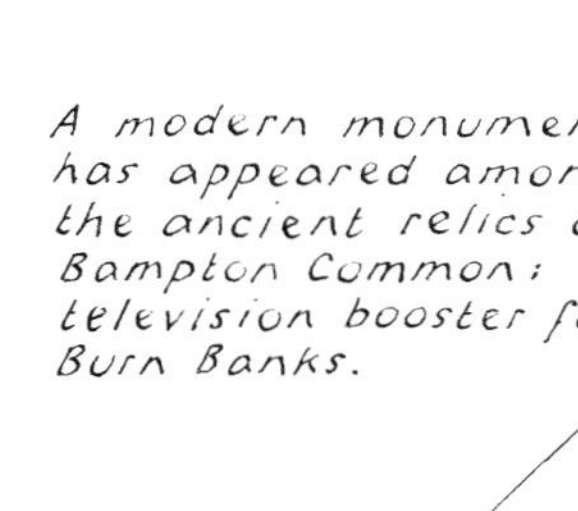

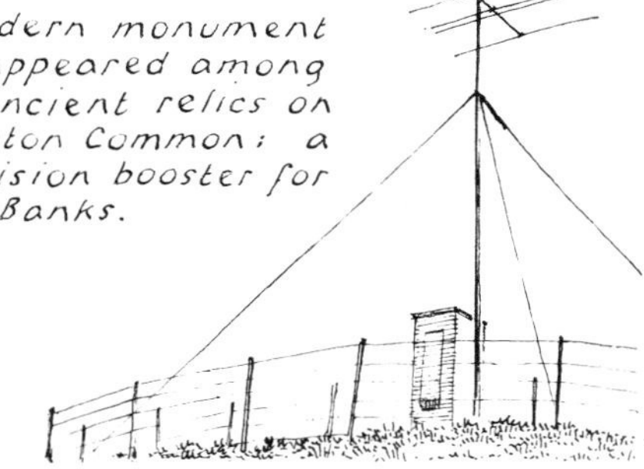

A modern monument has appeared among the ancient relics on Bampton Common: a television booster for Burn Banks.

BARBON

Bypassed by the A.683 linking Kirkby Lonsdale and Sedbergh is a church and an inn and a cluster of cared-for cottages at the foot of a long line of rough fells. This is Barbon, through which the Romans passed and later a railway line with a station, but these invaders having departed the village enjoys a rural tranquillity, disturbed only by the new invaders, motor cars, on summer weekends, and, on one day each year, by crowds attending a Hill Climb (for vehicles), on the drive of Barbon Manor, the home of Roger Fulford, the historian.

The weekend traffic is due to the deep valley of Barbondale carved out of the fells behind, which not only provides picnic places as yet unspoiled but carries a picturesque road through to Dent.

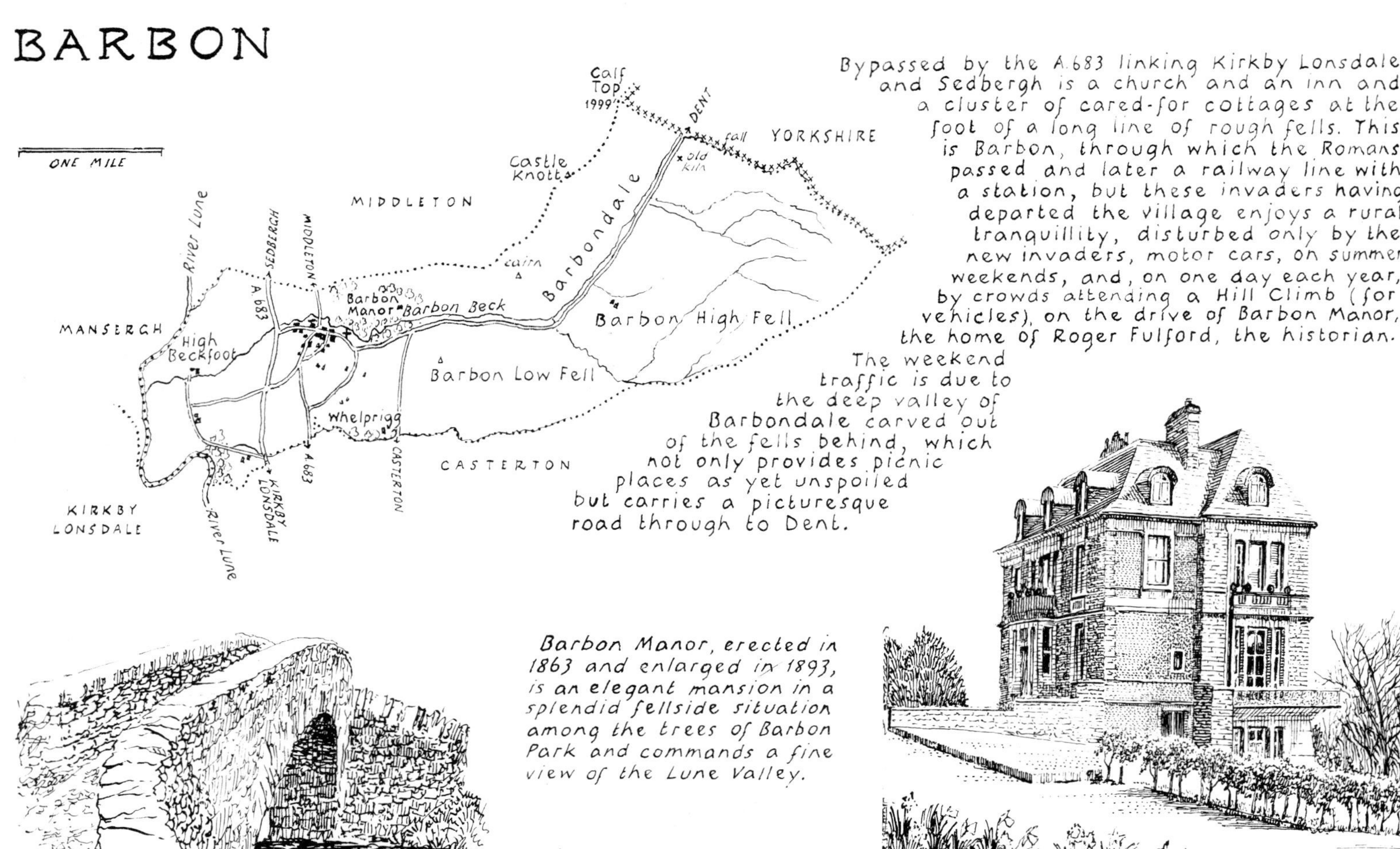

Barbon Manor, erected in 1863 and enlarged in 1893, is an elegant mansion in a splendid fellside situation among the trees of Barbon Park and commands a fine view of the Lune Valley.

17th century packhorse bridge at High Beckfoot.

Barbon

The parish church of St Bartholomew, built in 1893, replaced an earlier building (a chapel served by Kirkby Lonsdale) on a nearby site.

Barbon village

Barbon

Cairn on Castle Knott above Barbondale

Short Gill Waterfall, on the county boundary

Barbon was one of the six statutory beacon sites in Westmorland in a list dated 1468. The site is believed to be on Barbon Low Fell, above the village.

This splendid shelter-cairn, 12 feet high, within the wall of the Barbon Manor Estate, is known as Josse Pike after the gamekeeper (Joseph Parrington) who built it in the 1870's as a place from which he could watch the grouse moor on Barbon High Fell, as a shelter for himself and on top of which a poll-trap could be set for birds of prey; today it is a monument to craftsmanship. Recently it has been damaged by trespassers: the public should bear in mind, please, that this interesting landmark is on private property.

Hodge Bridge, carrying the A.683 over Barbon Beck, is probably 16th century. The stone roadsign alongside, of a type not in favour with modern highways engineers, is itself a quaint antiquity, a reminder of days gone by, that should be preserved.

BARTON

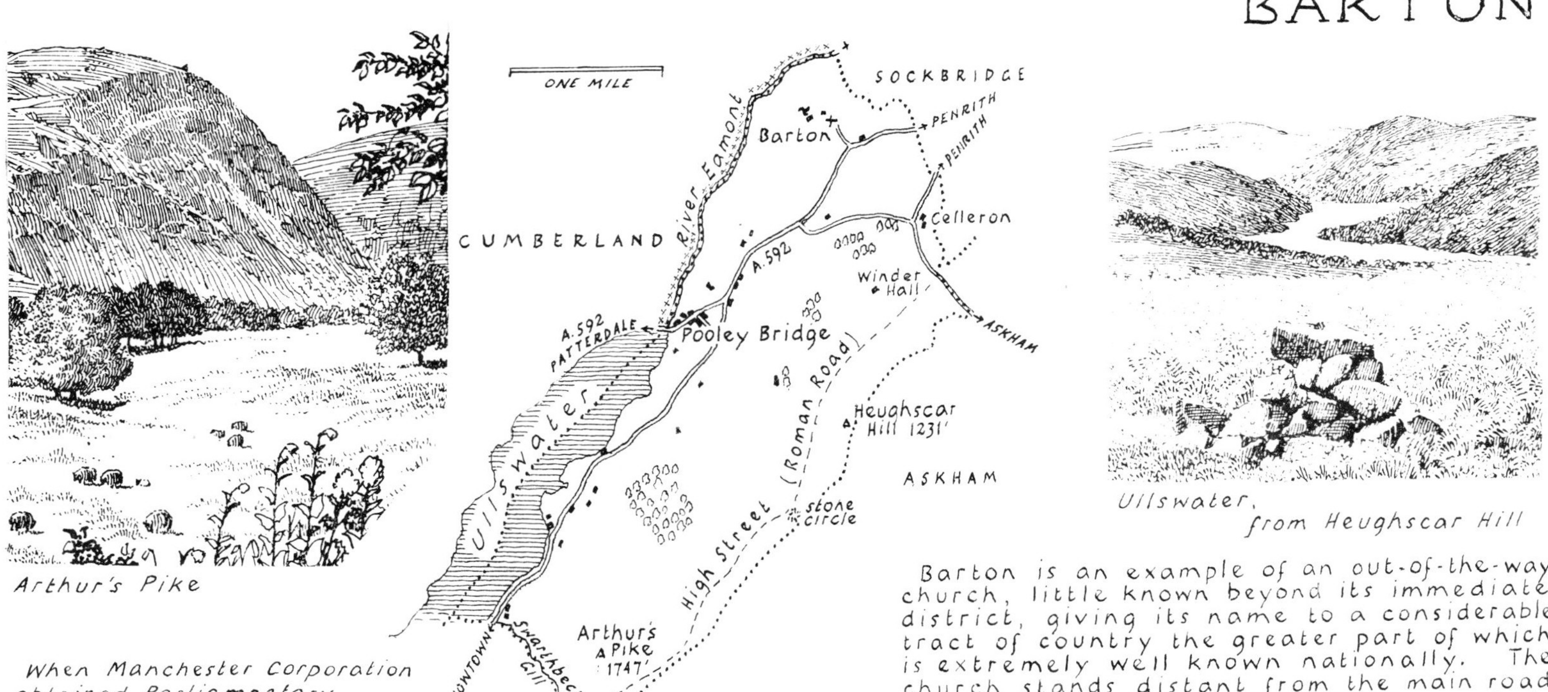

Arthur's Pike

Ullswater, from Heughscar Hill

When Manchester Corporation obtained Parliamentary approval to the extraction of water supplies from Ullswater, after many years of spirited opposition first led by Lord Birkett, stringent conditions regarding the water-level of the lake and concealment of the works were imposed and have been most scrupulously observed, the place of intake being unobtrusive and the works built underground in Barton parish.

Barton is an example of an out-of-the-way church, little known beyond its immediate district, giving its name to a considerable tract of country the greater part of which is extremely well known nationally. The church stands distant from the main road and the few farms around hardly constitute a hamlet, yet the parish includes not only the tourist resort of Pooley Bridge but also much of the east shore of popular Ullswater, extending to the moorland traversed by the Roman High Street and earlier inhabited by primitive settlers who left behind an array of prehistoric relics and monuments. The splendid church, however, fully justifies its distinction as the ecclesiastical centre. The River Eamont, issuing from Ullswater, forms with the lake a natural parish boundary.

Barton

Old farmhouses near the church

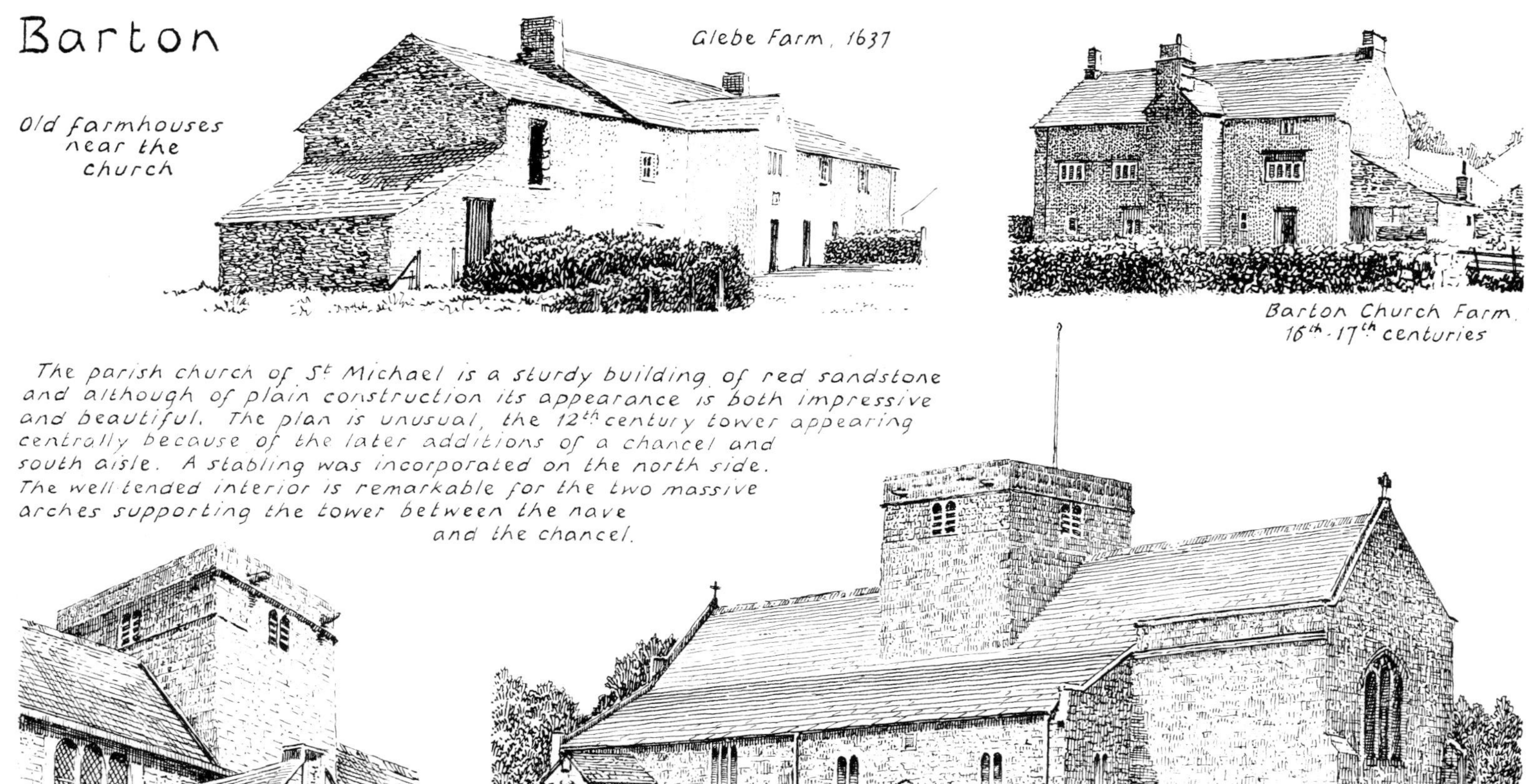

Glebe Farm, 1637

Barton Church Farm. 16th-17th centuries

The parish church of St Michael is a sturdy building of red sandstone and although of plain construction its appearance is both impressive and beautiful. The plan is unusual, the 12th century tower appearing centrally because of the later additions of a chancel and south aisle. A stabling was incorporated on the north side. The well-tended interior is remarkable for the two massive arches supporting the tower between the nave and the chancel.

Barton

On the main road A.592 near the junction to the church stands the picturesque medieval formhouse of Kirkbarrow, largely rebuilt in the 16th century but retaining the evidences of crutch-construction. Notable are the rugged walls and the quaint two-storey porch with its effigy and other ornamentation.

The stone circle on Moor Divock at a height of 1060' is known as the Cockpit and thought to have been a primitive ring wall 30 yards in diameter. The Roman High Street passes alongside.

Porch details, Kirkbarrow

There is another stone circle within the parish, near the source of Swarth Beck.

BEETHAM

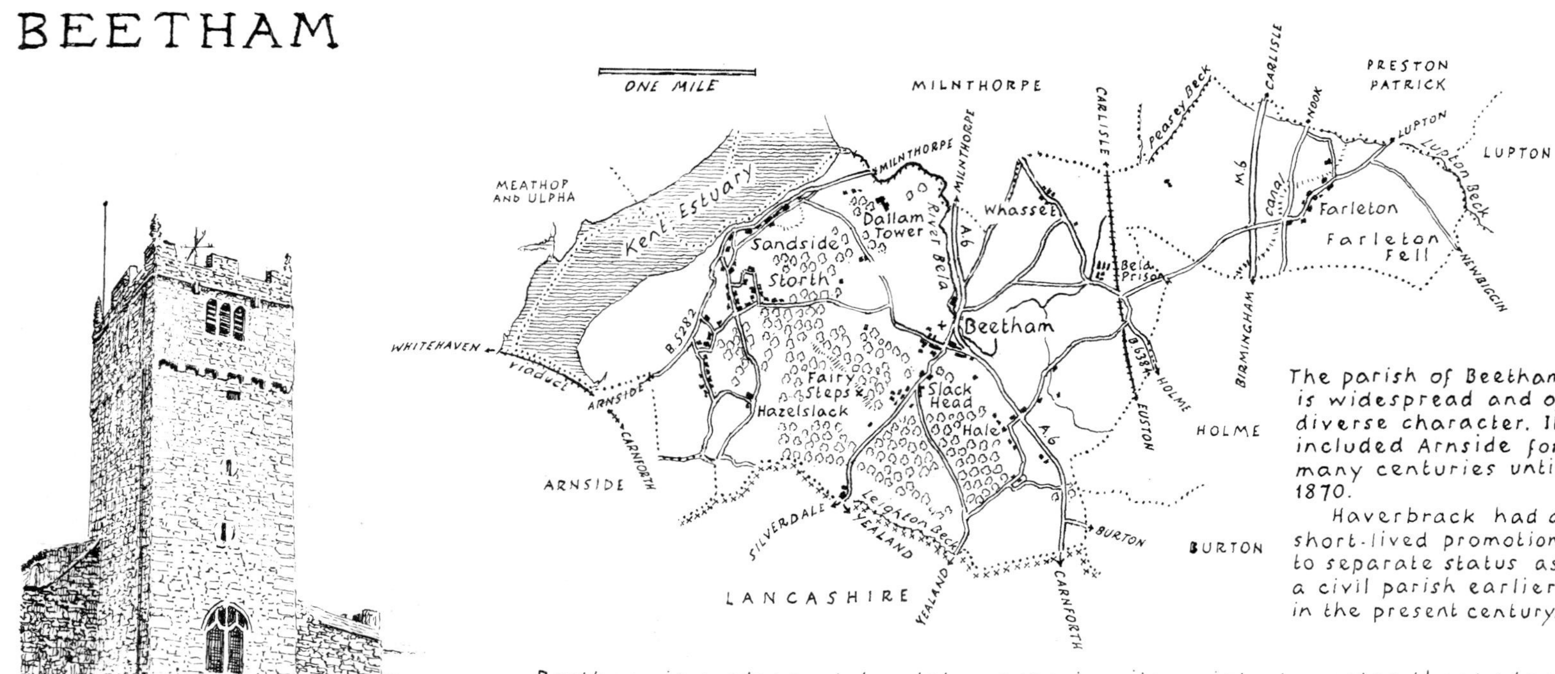

The parish of Beetham is widespread and of diverse character. It included Arnside for many centuries until 1870.

Haverbrack had a short-lived promotion to separate status as a civil parish earlier in the present century.

Beetham's lovely parish church of St Michael, reached under a rose pergola, is an old Norman foundation. The west tower of unbuttressed random limestone, pictured above, is 12th century below the bell-chamber (16th c.).

Beetham is a pleasant hamlet preserving its quiet character thanks to a merciful bypass that takes the busy A.6 traffic out of its narrow streets. The A.6 bisects the parish and also marks a pronounced division in the nature of the scenery. To the west is a delightful region of low limestone hills where outcrops and escarpments occur under a rich canopy of natural woodlands, a place of nooks and crannies, a joy to explore: here are the communities of Sandside, on the edge of the Kent Estuary and once the port of Milnthorpe but now dominated by a huge quarry; and Storth, fast losing its rural aspect because of much new residential development; and **Hazelslack, with its pele; and Haverbrack, embowered in trees; and Dallam Tower, a gracious house in a beautiful deer park. East of the A.6 is open country of rolling pastures, crossed by a main railway, a motorway, and a disused canal, with the township of Farleton and an open prison accounting for most of its sparse population and Farleton Fell overlooking the scene.**

Beetham

Beetham: Parish Church and War Memorial

Hazelslack Tower

The 14th century pele tower at Hazelslack is in a ruinous condition although the outer walls, 42' high, are largely intact. There were four storeys. There is evidence on the east wall that the tower, now standing detached, was adjoined by another building, of which only the arched fireplace remains to be seen.

Beetham

The present Beetham Hall is an attractive 17th century farmhouse, but the main interest is centred on the substantial ruins of a 14th century fortified manor house adjoining. Of almost castle-like proportions, the manor house is, even in decay, a most impressive edifice, having domestic quarters, a Great Hall and a private chapel, in a big courtyard enclosed by a strong curtain wall, the whole being a fine example of a medieval mansion constructed for defensive and domestic purposes.

Beetham Hall

Dallam Tower, as it appears today, dates from 1720-22, when it was entirely rebuilt on the site of a former residence; the pillared entrance and pavilion wings were added in 1826. This handsome and elegant mansion, the home of the Wilson family, is situated in a spacious park crossed by a public road and public footpaths. Here, in a lovely setting, a herd of fallow deer, a delight to see, finds perfect sanctuary.

Dallam Tower

A visit to Fairy Steps is one of the joys of life for the children of South Westmorland, and is a pleasure that persists into old age. In lovely surroundings, a steep limestone escarpment between Hazelslack and Slack Head is cleft by a narrow fissure, and negotiable by a flight of rough steps. Once used as a regular way to Beetham Church, this delightful spot has long been known as Fairy Steps.

Farleton Fell, from Town End, Farleton.

The social pattern of the rural communities has changed radically in the last generation. Gone is the introspective close-knit fellowship, partly because the motor-car has made the country people far more mobile but largely because of the demand by outsiders for cottages and barns in rural areas for use as weekend and holiday homes, a practice that tends to deprive local agricultural workers of accommodation. To their credit, however, the 'off-comers' almost invariably produce commendable conversions and have saved many derelict buildings from decay.

This barn conversion at Farleton won a Civic Trust award in 1971.

BOLTON

Bolton is a small village high on the west bank of the River Eden, which hereabouts is pleasantly wooded, and is surrounded by a countryside of rich pastures, farming being the only industry in the parish. Being distant from main roads it has preserved a quiet rural atmosphere, a fact appreciated by discerning newcomers who have built homes in the village in recent years, but not in sufficient numbers to mar its tranquil character. There is parkland around the mansion of Eden Grove, now a school, but all else is farmed.

The joy of Bolton is its quaint and lovely church. Of historic interest is the unkempt ruin of Bewley Castle, hidden in a wooded dell on the southern perimeter of the parish.

Bolton does not lack neighbours. No fewer than eight other parishes adjoin its boundaries.

Bolton Bridge is the only road-crossing of the Eden on a seven-mile stretch of the river north of Appleby.

BROUGHAM
TEMPLE SOWERBY
KIRKBY THORE
CLIBURN
River Lyvennet
TEMPLE SOWERBY
ONE MILE
CLIBURN
River Eden
CRACKENTHORPE
River Lyvennet
Eden Grove
Bolton Hall
MORLAND
APPLEBY
Bolton Bridge
Bolton
MORLAND
KINGS MEABURN
Bolton Lodge
KING'S MEABURN
New Bewley
COLBY
Bewley Castle
COLBY

Bolton Bridge

There must be many interesting and now-forgotten stories behind the fixing of the parish boundaries: it is not easy to understand the reason for the erratic course followed by some of them. For example, the River Eden seems to be a natural and obvious border to the parish of Bolton, but the parish boundary does not adopt it throughout, making slight deviations at several points, and doing the same with the River Lyvennet, on the west flank. These are not aberrations, the probable explanation in such cases being that farm boundaries, which may extend to both banks of a river, are generally to be preferred for administrative purposes.

Bolton

The parish church of All Saints, formerly a chapel of Morland, has retained features of its 12th century origin, the base of the tower, nave, chancel and two Norman doorways being of this period. The bell-turret dates from 1693. Built into the outer walls are the effigy of a woman and other carved figures, the interior also displaying many interesting items.

Now a forlorn ruin and quite neglected, Bewley Castle occupies a remote and secluded site on the north bank of a wooded stream, Sweetmilk Sike. Originally of three storeys, the fragmentary remains include south and east walls with good windows, all else being derelict.

The castle replaced an earlier building in the 14th century and was occupied as a residence by successive Bishops of Carlisle.

BOWNESS ON WINDERMERE

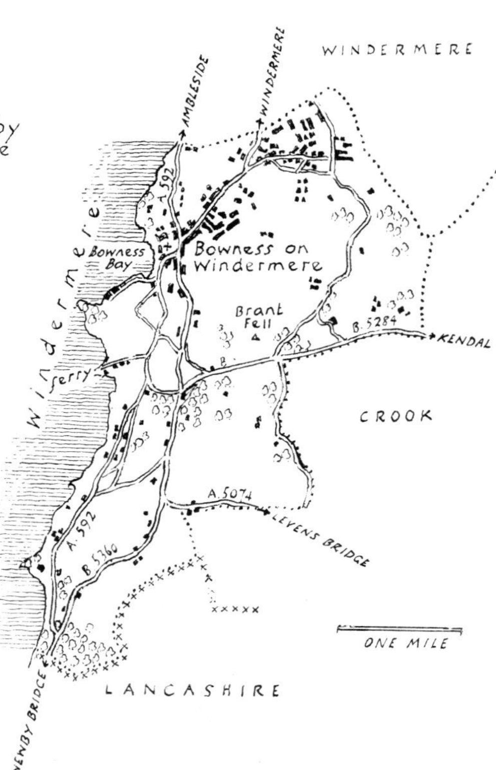

The few remaining buildings of 17th and 18th century Bowness are swamped by Victorian development in the form of palatial hotels, arcades of shops, large mansions and terraces of stone houses, the rapid growth of this one-time small lakeside community into a busy holiday resort being remarkable.

The main attraction is Bowness Bay on Windermere, offering sailing and other aquatic sports in a lovely environment and presenting an animated and colourful scene throughout the summer. It is a popular venue for coach parties and crowds throng the lake front. The atmosphere is alien to Westmorland and more akin to the Lancashire coast. This is not the Westmorland most visitors know and love.

Yet the scenery of Bowness has charm, and the prospect over the lake from the higher ground bordering the bay is beautiful. There are pleasant rambles to be enjoyed and the rocky crest of Brant Fell is a superb viewpoint. A car ferry and cruises give a more intimate appreciation of the lake, the largest in England.

Bowness was created a civil parish in 1894 and is administered by Windermere Urban District Council, this latter authority owning all the bed of the lake although more than three-quarters of its shore is within the county of Lancashire.

Bowness Bay

Bowness on Windermere

Two familiar objects on Lake Road are The Bath House (above) and The Memorial to M. J. B. Baddeley (left)

The parish church of St Martin dates from 1483 and was built on the foundations of an earlier structure, believed to have been burnt down, traces of which exist under the arches of the nave. A restoration, with additions to the tower and the chancel, was undertaken in 1870. An unusual feature of the exterior is the roof covering of lead sheets. This is the parish church of Windermere.

Bowness on Windermere

right:
Matson Ground

bottom right:
Summit rocks of Brant Fell

below:
The Rectory

BROUGH

Brough, sometimes referred to as Brough-under-Stainmore and a strategic outpost in Roman and medieval times, is today a straggling village astride the busy A.66 highway at the foot of the long climb over the bleak, exposed upland of Stainmore Forest, notorious for winter storms, and although it may be a welcome refuge for travellers after the ordeal of a snowy crossing the irregular buildings bordering the road have no special interest for the ordinary summer visitor. But away from the main road there is interest in profusion centred in the pleasant suburb known as Church Brough, where, in addition to the old parish church, there stand the gaunt remains of Brough Castle superimposed on the earthworks of the Roman Fort of Verterae, both of considerable archaeological importance.

Almost encompassed by lofty hills, the parish is situated on the fringe of the Eden Valley.

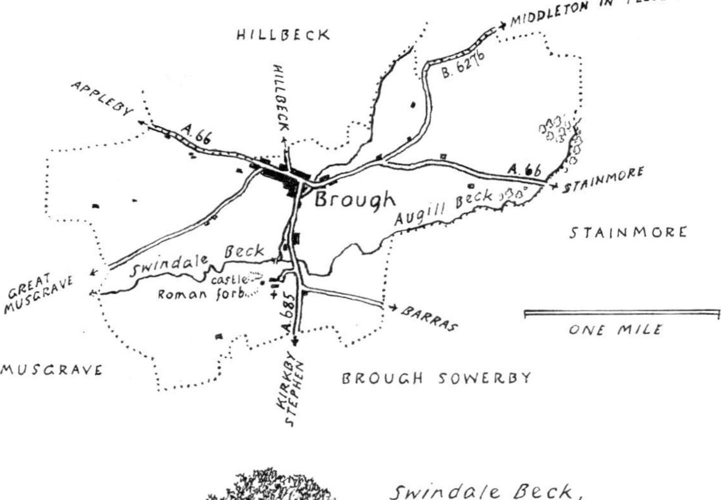

Market Street, Brough.
The clock tower was erected in 1911.

Brough's ancient and once-proud market cross is in disgrace, having been removed to a depot from its former site in the street because of traffic hazards. Local folk would like it restored, on a safer site. This should most certainly be done — it is a matter of dignity.

Swindale Beck, in Brough

Brough

The Parish Church of St Michael

Less conspicuously sited than most parish churches, St Michael's is in a wooded hollow below the castle and out of sight of the village. It is a long, squat building, parts of the nave being of 12th century construction; extensions, including the tower (1513), are of later date. The church was restored in 1880.

Verterae

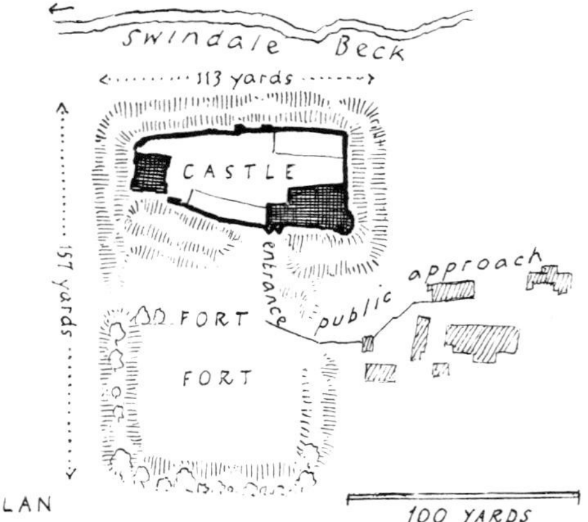

The Roman fort of Verterae served as a midway station on the Maiden Way between Bowes and Kirkby Thore, occupying a hillock overlooking the route. It was laid out to the customary rectangular plan and surrounded entirely by a ditch, the earthworks of which are still clearly visible although not completely in their original condition. The site appealed to the builders of the castle almost a thousand years later and their structure was wholly superimposed on the northern part of the fort enclosure: traces of Roman buildings have been found beneath the floor of the keep. The southern part of the fort has been disturbed by later cultivation, but the outline of the ditch, now marked by trees and fenced, is distinct. The site has not been fully excavated and there are no buildings or masonry to be seen above ground, nevertheless there have been many finds of Roman artifacts, some in the bed of Swindale Beck, some in the castle precincts and in the ditch.

1 o----o 2 ------ 3 o------ o 4

1: Brougham
2: Kirkby Thore
3: Brough
4: Bowes

Brough Castle

The Keep

The south-east corner

The origins of Brough Castle date from the late 11th century but the first edifice was largely destroyed in a Scottish raid in 1174, being afterwards rebuilt and, following further damage by fire, restored by Lady Anne Clifford in the 17th century. The keep, now a sad ruin, is the oldest part of the fabric. A rounded south-east tower, with much of the masonry still in good condition, is attributed to Lady Anne and known as Clifford's Tower. The Castle occupies a commanding position on the site of the Roman fort, the prominent earthworks on the south side being mainly Roman. It is in the care of the Ministry of Works and open to the public.

BROUGHAM

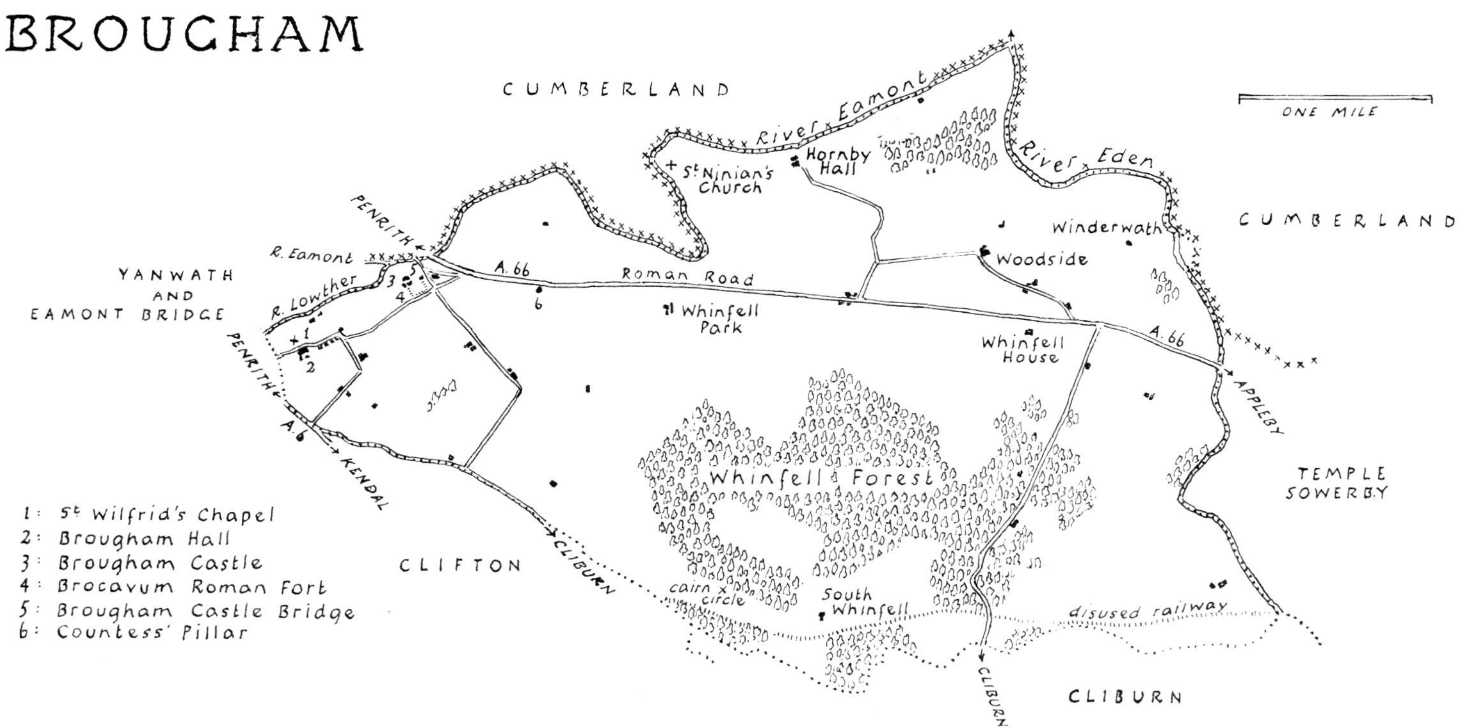

The parish of Brougham comprises an extensive area of pasture and woodland and forest to the south of the River Eamont: a quiet and pleasant countryside although bisected by the busy A.66. A few scattered farms and houses are the only habitations, yet, in its day, Brougham was a place of considerable importance; the western salient is, in fact, almost crowded with the remains of former occupations, the relics and ruins of which attract many visitors. Here is Brougham Castle, a noble edifice still, of much interest, with the Roman fort of Brocavum (which gave Brougham its name) adjoining. Not far away is the quaint chapel of St Wilfrid and the gaunt walls of the short-lived Brougham Hall. The Countess' Pillar, standing by the side of the A.66, which hereabouts is laid on the foundations of a Roman road, is a monument of note. Rather unexpectedly, the parish church (St Ninian's) is situated in a lonely and remote dell in a loop of the Eamont. A railway (Clifton Junction - Appleby and beyond) formerly crossed the southern parts of the parish and had a station, but it was Cliburn's, not Brougham's. To the north is Cumberland.

The south-west tower and Norman keep

Brougham Castle

Brougham Castle is a ruin, but still a handsome structure with massive red sandstone walls, surrounded by a moat, rising proudly almost to the original height and having a commanding view over the Eamont flowing alongside. It is an impressive sight, even in decay: enough remains to confirm the authoritative opinion that this medieval stronghold was the most extensive and important fortification in the county. The Keep was built in the 12th century and stood at first in isolation, the two gatehouses and a complex of other buildings being of later date. In the Civil War the Castle suffered great damage, but was restored by Lady Anne Clifford, the then owner, in 1651-2. The site was earlier favoured by the Romans, whose fort Brocavum occupies a field abutting on the south.

The Castle is in the care of the Ministry of Works, and open to the public.

Brougham

The Parish Church of St Ninian, locally named Ninekirks, was entirely rebuilt by Lady Anne Clifford in 1660. The humble exterior matches its rural setting and internally its appearance is almost primitive, the plain furniture and fittings having remained unchanged. The porch only is a later addition. The church is isolated, and reached only by a rough lane or a footpath. Services are now held infrequently in the summer months.

The Chapel of St Wilfrid stands on a mound, within sight of the A.6. In its present form it is 17th century, having been rebuilt by Lady Anne Clifford in 1658 and structurally is typical of that period. although some restoration was undertaken in the mid-19th. A special feature is the extravagant interior woodwork, notably the carved screen across the nave, much of it being of Continental origin.

Brougham Hall, rebuilt in 1829-40 and notable for a magnificent interior, was demolished in 1934 except for the outbuildings and walls flanking the road opposite St Wilfrid's Chapel.

Brougham Castle Bridge, over the Eamont, carried the A.66 until a recent bypass relieved it of this burden.

Brougham

Brocavum

The Roman fort of Brocavum, founded by Agricola at a junction of important military roads, adjoins Brougham Castle to the south. In the absence of a complete excavation the site is identifiable only by its outline and a surrounding ditch, the northern section of which appears to have been adapted and enlarged to serve as the castle moat. Several relics and coins of the Roman occupation have been found and some inscribed stones are on display in the Castle gateway.

PLAN OF CASTLE AND ROMAN FORT

River Eamont
Brougham Castle Bridge
CASTLE
Castle Farm
moat
100 YARDS
ROMAN FORT
ditch

Cairn circle, South Whinfell

Long before the coming of the Romans, there were settlers in these parts, evidence of their existence being found at South Whinfell, where a barrow (named 'cairn circle' on Ordnance maps) in a ring of stones revealed upon excavation traces of cremation and burial urns of the Bronze Age.

In commemoration of her last parting from her mother in 1616 Lady Anne Clifford 40 years later erected this pillar, since known as the Countess' Pillar. It stands by the side of the road that is now the A.66, is 14 feet high and decorated with shields-of-arms, sundials and a memorial tablet providing for a distribution of charity annually to the poor of Brougham upon the slab nearby.

Hornby Hall, in a quiet setting on the south bank of the Eamont, is an attractive house built by the Birkbeck family in the middle of the 16th century. A west extension is more recent. The older part retains many original features. A door lintel dated 1602 is thought to be the earliest in the county. A range of farm buildings was added later.

BROUGH SOWERBY

Brough Sowerby is a small township of no great importance except to the few people who live in it and patrons of the local inn but in former years was considered worthy of separate status as a parish which it has retained although little more than a suburb of Brough, a mile away along the A.685. Recent road surgery has radically changed the appearance of its one street and cut through the heart of the tiny community quite savagely. The two sharp corners round which travellers once threaded a cautious way have gone and been replaced by a wide swathe of tarmac with grass verges, and motorists on this new speedway hasten through the hamlet with no more than a momentary glance. Other features have gone or been replaced, too. The single-arch bridge over the River Belah, which forms the southern boundary of the parish, is now obsolete, having been bypassed by a modern substitute much less attractive.

Brough Sowerby has lost its character.

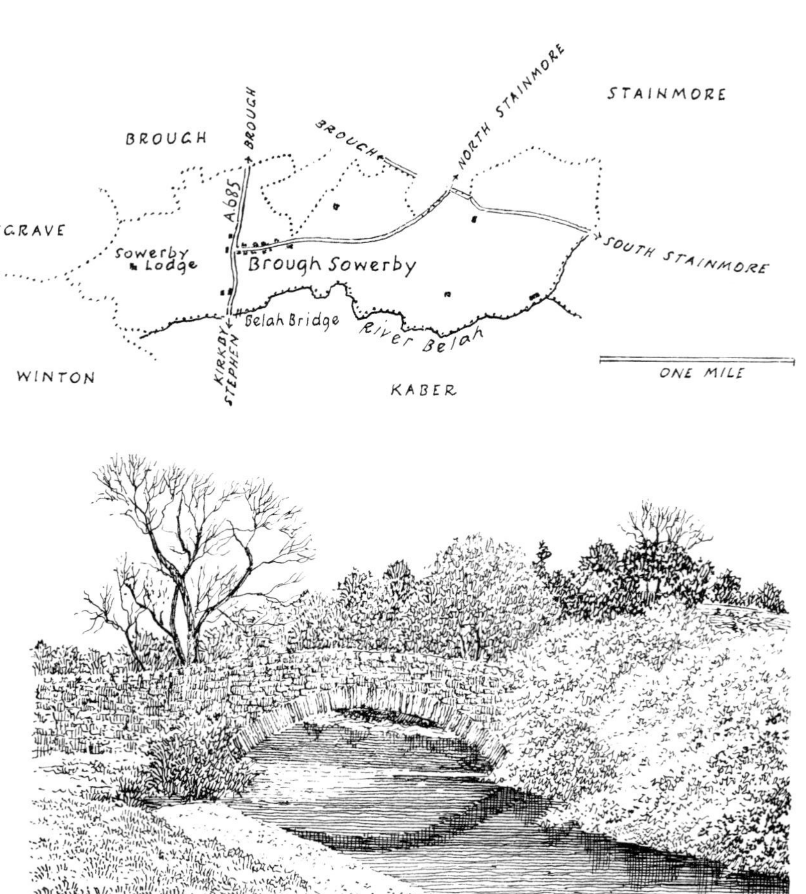

Belah Bridge

The new road makes a double curve to avoid Belahbridge House, rebuilt in 1783 and incorporating two inscribed stones from an earlier building.

BURTON

Burton, formerly named Burton-in-Kendal to distinguish it from Burton-in-Lonsdale, is a village with a main street that has the appearance and atmosphere, and more than the usual appeal and attractiveness, of a small town centre. Along this thoroughfare are ranged buildings of individual style and character, hardly two alike, which have a wealth of historical and archaeological interest and present a scene that has changed little since the road was an important turnpike. Leading off the main street are alleyways and yards that have retained an old-world charm. Even the most fleeting visitor is immediately aware that Burton must, in times past, have played an important role in the life and communications of the district, and it was in fact a main coaching halt and held a market charter long before the coming of the railways; today it rests more quietly on its many laurels, its importance to travellers diminished but its visual attraction enhanced by the passing of the years. The weight of modern traffic along the old turnpike road, now the A.6070, has posed a succession of problems that first the railway, then the A.6, and latterly the motorway have greatly relieved, yet the village remains active and busy with local affairs.

There are many fine houses here and in the vicinity, but it is the ancient parish church, standing a little remote, that has most to tell of the proud history of Burton.

The area of the parish is relatively small. The west part, although predominantly farmland, is carved up by arteries of communication, the old canal and the new motorway providing a sharp contrast in standards of locomotion. Seekers of rural quiet will prefer the limestone uplands above the hamlet of Clawthorpe.

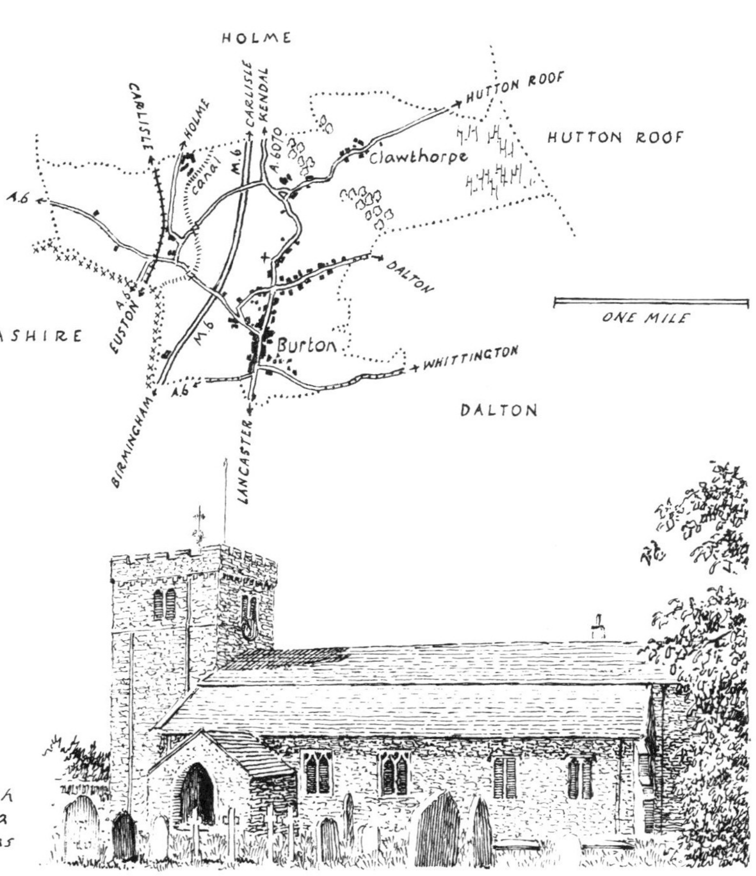

Apart from restorations in 1844 and 1872 the parish church of St James has changed little since the 16th century, when a succession of additions to the original Norman structure was completed. The oldest part is the 12th century bell-tower.

Burton

Street scenes

Burton

Burton House
(18th century)

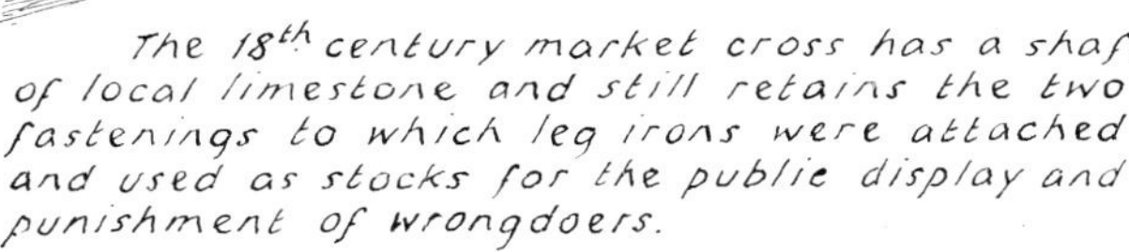

The 18th century market cross has a shaft of local limestone and still retains the two fastenings to which leg irons were attached and used as stocks for the public display and punishment of wrongdoers.

Clawthorpe Hall
(17th century)

CASTERTON

Casterton, as its name implies, has associations with the Roman occupation, a road linking the forts at Burrow and Low Borrow Bridge passing through the district, but few traces remain and the hamlet today is much better known for the school that was established here in 1833, has since developed into a large academy and is now the dominant influence in the community. This school, originally for daughters of the clergy, was founded in 1823 by the Rev. William Carus Wilson, M.A. in nearby Cowan Bridge, where its most illustrious pupils were the Brontë sisters, but removed, ten years later, to more suitable and commodious premises, since supplemented by extra classrooms and dormitories, at Casterton. The former qualification for acceptance into the school has been relaxed and it has a wide reputation for its scholastic attainments.

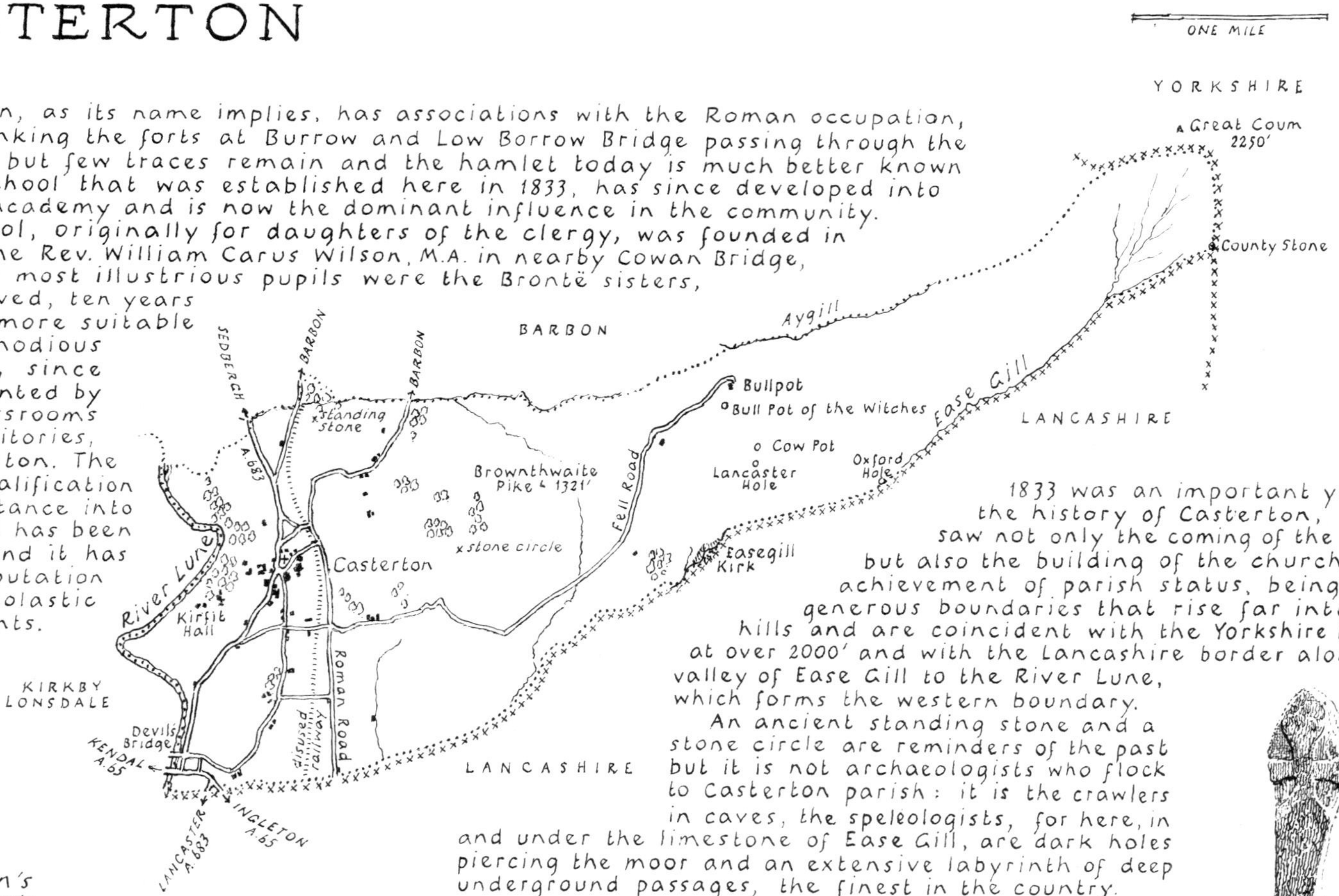

1833 was an important year in the history of Casterton, for it saw not only the coming of the school but also the building of the church and achievement of parish status, being given generous boundaries that rise far into the hills and are coincident with the Yorkshire border at over 2000′ and with the Lancashire border along the valley of Ease Gill to the River Lune, which forms the western boundary.

An ancient standing stone and a stone circle are reminders of the past but it is not archaeologists who flock to Casterton parish: it is the crawlers in caves, the speleologists, for here, in and under the limestone of Ease Gill, are dark holes piercing the moor and an extensive labyrinth of deep underground passages, the finest in the country.

Casterton's Stone Circle, near a wall on the lower slopes of Brownthwaite Pike, consists of twenty small embedded stones projecting only slightly from the ground.

The Standing Stone, 4 feet high, bears the carving of a cross. It stands on the line of the Roman road and is thought to be 14th or 15th century.

Casterton

The origin of the church of Holy Trinity is unusual: it was built to serve the needs of the Girls School, the cost of erection being borne by the founder of the school. It is used also for public services. The exterior, of coursed limestone, is neat and pleasing; the internal decorations, which include wall paintings, are notable.

The old toll house on the Kirkby Lonsdale road

Kirfit Hall

Architecturally the most interesting building in Casterton parish, the 17th century Kirfit Hall, with a four-storey tower, is backed by woodlands and has open fields alongside the River Lune. It features in 'Ruskin's view.'

Casterton

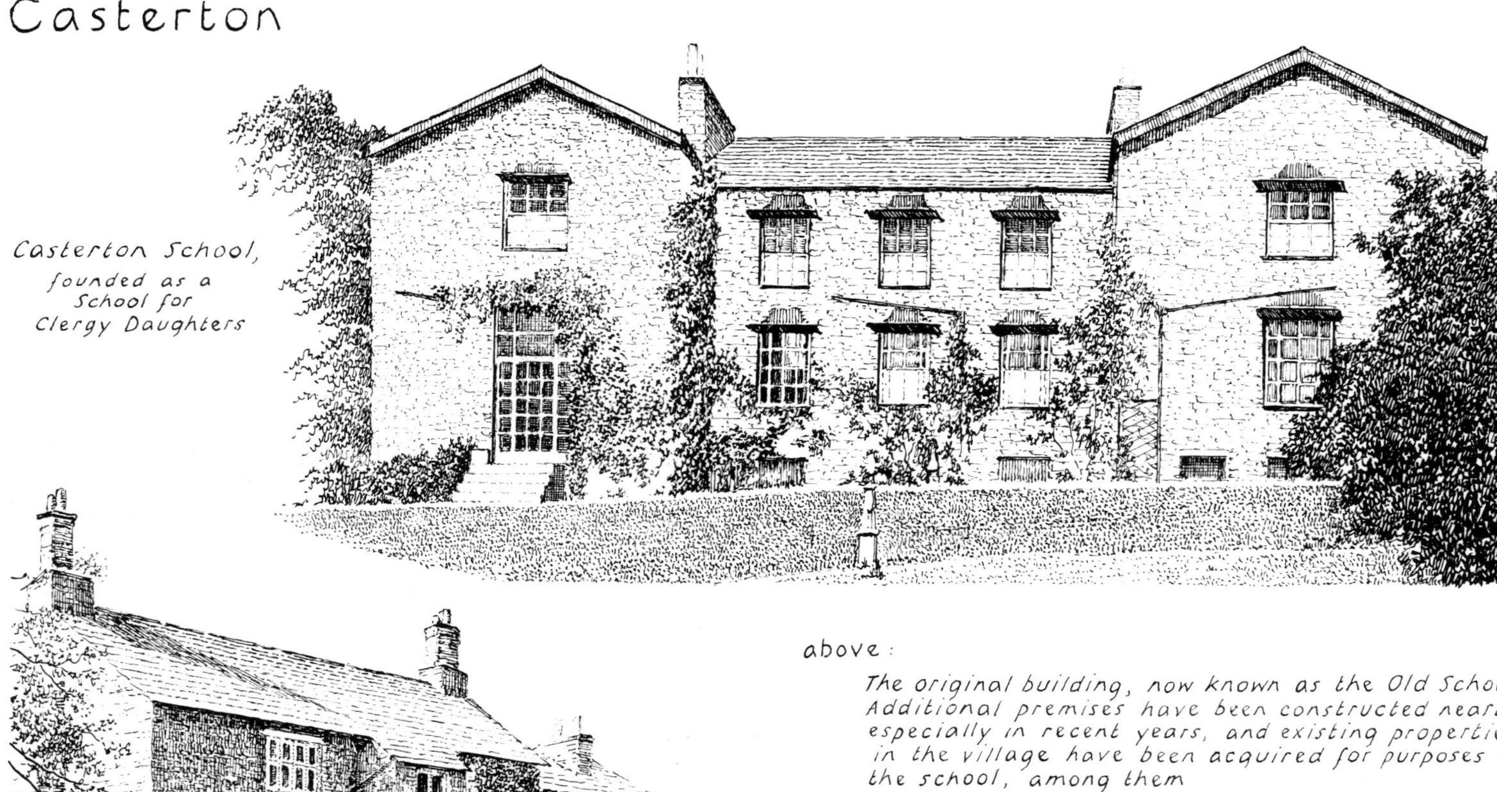

Casterton School, founded as a School for Clergy Daughters

above:

The original building, now known as the Old School. Additional premises have been constructed nearby, especially in recent years, and existing properties in the village have been acquired for purposes of the school, among them

left:

The Old Hall, a 17th century residence built for the Wilson family and still retaining fittings and furniture of that period and incorporating even earlier features. The twin chimney stacks and the mullioned and transomed stone windows on the south front are also original.

Ease Gill

Casterton

On Casterton's fells:

near right: *The cairn on Brownthwaite Pike*

centre right: *Bullpot Farm, occupied by the Red Rose Cave and Pothole Club*

far right: *The County Stone*

The County Stone is a huge boulder sited precisely (by accident or design) at the meeting point of the boundary walls of Westmorland, Lancashire and Yorkshire. It bears the inscribed date 1832.

Casterton's Limestone Underground

The more obvious potholes on Casterton Fell were known to farmers and shepherds long before modern adventurers came to explore them, but the most significant of all, Lancaster Hole, was discovered as recently as 1946 and found to be the key to an extensive underground system of caves containing rare and beautiful limestone formations, where continuing exploration has already accounted for six miles of passages, with alternative entrances from the stream bed in Ease Gill. The discovery of Lancaster Hole was a 'chance' find — a potholer resting nearby noticed a single clump of grass quivering as if agitated by a breeze although the day was calm, and, curiosity leading to investigation, he encountered a strong draught issuing from a tiny hole in the ground; this was subsequently enlarged a little to permit entrance to a vertical shaft 110 feet in depth, at the bottom of which access was gained to a vast series of wonderful caverns — a fantastic underworld of fairy grottoes with delicate calcite traceries, of lofty halls with columns of massive stalagmites, of ceilings formed of myriads of fine opalescent stalactites, of floors and shelves littered with cave pearls and crystals, the whole a store of supreme beauty that has been slowly developing through countless ages and only now is revealed to man. The evidences below ground, in the size and nature of the formations and the superimposed layers of old stalagmitic deposits, suggest that this is the oldest cave system in the country. Certainly it is Westmorland's greatest natural treasure. And the most secret. Few have seen it. Few will ever see it.

Lancaster Hole

The entrance is closed by a manhole lid

Bull Pot of the Witches

Ease Gill

Ease Gill is ordinary — until it leaves the peaty moorland on which it has its beginnings and encounters limestone, whereupon its behaviour becomes quite extraordinary. Here its course is interrupted by huge rock steps in a steep-sided ravine made colourful by bracken, heather and rowans and a profusion of flowers: a lovely place, but eerily silent because the wide bouldery stream normally carries no surface water, the bed being drained dry. The ravine has three sections: (a) upper Ease Gill, above the double waterfall of Cow Holes, deeply enclosed by sheer cliffs, where the stream flows gently down from Great Coum, reaches the limestone, and sinks in rock crevices; (b) the middle reach, less dramatic but of great interest, and (c) the spectacular Easegill Kirk, a chasm with impending wooded walls and many caves and pools, at the end of which the subterranean stream returns to daylight at the powerful resurgence of Leck Beck Head. In times of flood, however, the scene changes: the 'sinks' fill rapidly to the brim and cannot take more, the valley is pounded by a raging surface torrent, and, where there was silence, there is tumult.

Ease Gill is the most interesting watercourse in the county: this is true even when there is no water to be seen. Westmorland cannot claim exclusive ownership, however, for the south-east bank is wholly in Lancashire. But the greatest marvel in this limestone wonderland is Lancaster Hole, and this, despite its name, is in Westmorland.

far right: Cow Holes

right: in Easegill Kirk

below: Leck Beck Head

The stream bed at the top of Cow Holes is a wonderful example of naked limestone carved by the action of water: a very beautiful and impressive natural sculpturing, a work of art on a massive scale, one of Westmorland's unknown marvels.

CLIBURN

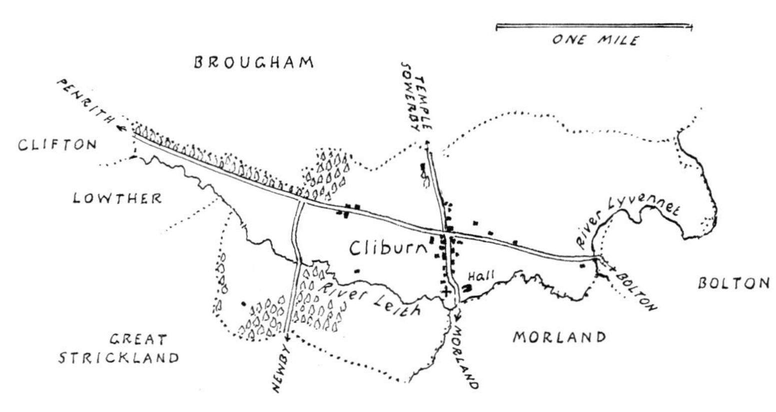

Cliburn Hall

As the result of a drastic modernisation, Cliburn Hall today bears little resemblance to its appearance up to a few years ago. Until then it was a dour and rugged structure, almost forbidding, but the stone-mullioned windows have been replaced, buttressing outbuildings have been taken down and the grim stone walls have been masked by pebbledash. Gone are the peletower and battlements, and its long history is suggested now externally only by an inscribed panel dated 1567, happily preserved.

Cliburn is a quiet and pleasant village, a backwater away from the main streams of traffic and with an air of remoteness: the sort of place where nothing of more than local importance is expected to happen and nothing does. From its crossroads inn, buildings line a wide street irregularly and lead down to the ancient church, a neat edifice of red sandstone, on a mound by Cliburn's river, the Leith, and opposite to the 16th century hall. Unusually, a small section of the parish, the Winderwath estate of 406 acres, is completely detached from the rest and 3 miles distant. Cliburn formerly had a railway station, but this and the railway line, now disused, were situated in the adjacent parish of Brougham.

The 12th century parish church of St Cuthbert, built in the Norman style and retaining some original features, owes its present appearance largely to a restoration and partial rebuilding, with extensions, in 1887. Incorporated in the porch are two inscribed Roman stones found during the restoration.

CLIFTON

Clifton has long been known to travellers between north and south. It is a village at a meeting of railways, one of which is defunct, and lies astride the main highway, the A.6, and alongside a motorway, the M.6, that has appeared within the last decade. Many of the cottages retain rural characteristics but the unending chorus of sound one hears is not that of the countryside — it is the drone of traffic. At the north end of the village 'street' are the church, defiantly impeding a dangerous corner on the A.6, and the medieval pele tower of Clifton Hall, built as a defence against the Scots and now incongruously finding itself overlooking a modern motorway. Clifton claims the distinction of staging the last pitched battle on English soil, in 1745, the scene being the then open moor, now patterned by fields, in the south of the parish, and the combatants the retreating Jacobite forces of Bonnie Prince Charlie and an English army under the Duke of Cumberland. There are relics of times more distant in an ancient earthwork in fields east of the church and two standing stones to the south. An old-established and well-known pottery at Wetheriggs has an interesting disused kiln.
Clifton survives the weight of its traffic but has suffered permanent scars in doing so.

Clifton Tower, built around 1500, stands in isolation, but was originally attached to a Hall, since demolished.

Old pottery kiln, Wetheriggs

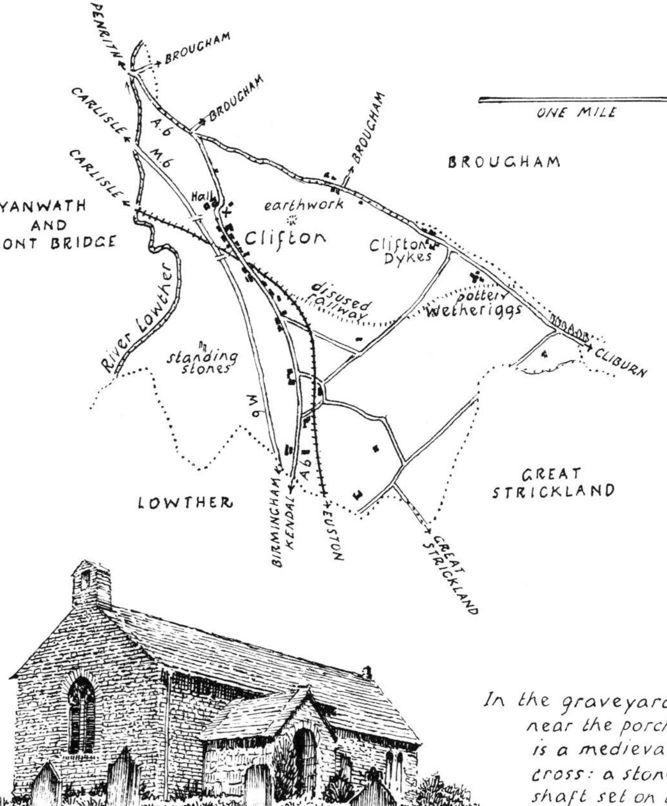

The parish church of St Cuthbert. Parts of the structure date from the 12th and 13th centuries.

In the graveyard, near the porch, is a medieval cross: a stone shaft set on a square stepped base.

COLBY

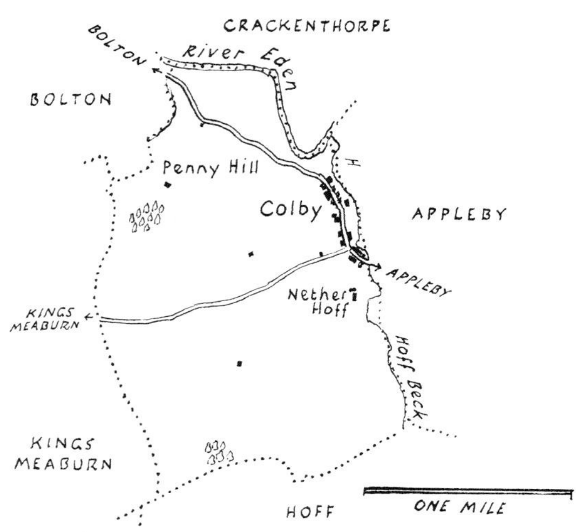

Colby straggles a narrow country road and enjoys the rural benefits of a quiet environment and a pleasant outlook in close proximity to a delightful stretch of the River Eden, but recent encroachment by new houses on the green belt separating it from Appleby threatens to turn it into a suburb of the county town. Colby is a civil parish, being so formed in 1894 from a rural part of Appleby. There is a small iron church, and two residences worthy of special mention, both 17th century: Colby Hall, hidden from the road, and Nether Hoff, prominently in view; these are now occupied as farmhouses.

Nether Hoff, built 1683

Cottages at Colby

CRACKENTHORPE

In the days of horses and carts Crackenthorpe was a picturesque wayside hamlet far enough removed from Appleby to have a separate identity as a civil parish (since 1894), and content with an inn, no church, an open view over good farmland to the Pennines and an intimate association with the River Eden. Then, with the development of modern road transport and the designation of the Crackenthorpe highway as a main artery, the A.66, peace was shattered and life was less tolerable, but the travail of the little community ceased abruptly with the building of two bypasses that restored tranquillity, and once again the hamlet enjoys a quiet existence although now bereft of its inn. Also bypassed is the entrance to Crackenthorpe Hall, a handsome residence in wooded grounds. Disturbed by the bypass is the site of an ancient chapel, St Giles, which still gives the names to Chapel Hill and Chapel Wood although nothing remains of it. Nor is there much left to see of the Roman camp, historically the most important monument in the parish.

KIRKBY THORE
PENRITH
River Eden
LONG MARTON
BOLTON
Roman camp
disused railway
Roman road
A66
BOLTON
LONG MARTON
Crackenthorpe
Hall
CARLISLE
DUFTON and LONG MARTON
River Eden
SETTLE
APPLEBY
COLBY
APPLEBY
ONE MILE

In contrast to the sinuous western boundary to the parish provided by the River Eden, the eastern, shared with Long Marton, adopts the line of the Roman road and is perfectly straight.

A dismantled railway (Clifton Junction – Appleby and beyond) runs through the parish, and an active one (Carlisle - Settle) cuts across the south-east corner.

Crackenthorpe Hall

Formerly the residence of the Machell family, the Hall is an elegant 17th century mansion with later major additions.

The Roman Camp

The Roman camp at Crackenthorpe had no great military significance, being provided as a temporary halting place, probably not fortified, for soldiers marching along the road between Brough and Kirkby Thore. The site is bisected by both the A66 and the road to Long Marton and Powis Cottages are built upon it. Its outline is distinct in parts only, the ramparts having been levelled and the ditches filled in by later farming operations. The old railway was laid on the Roman road.

CROOK

The parish boundary, surprisingly, does not include all the properties in the hamlet of Crook. Some are within the neighbouring parish of Strickland Ketel.

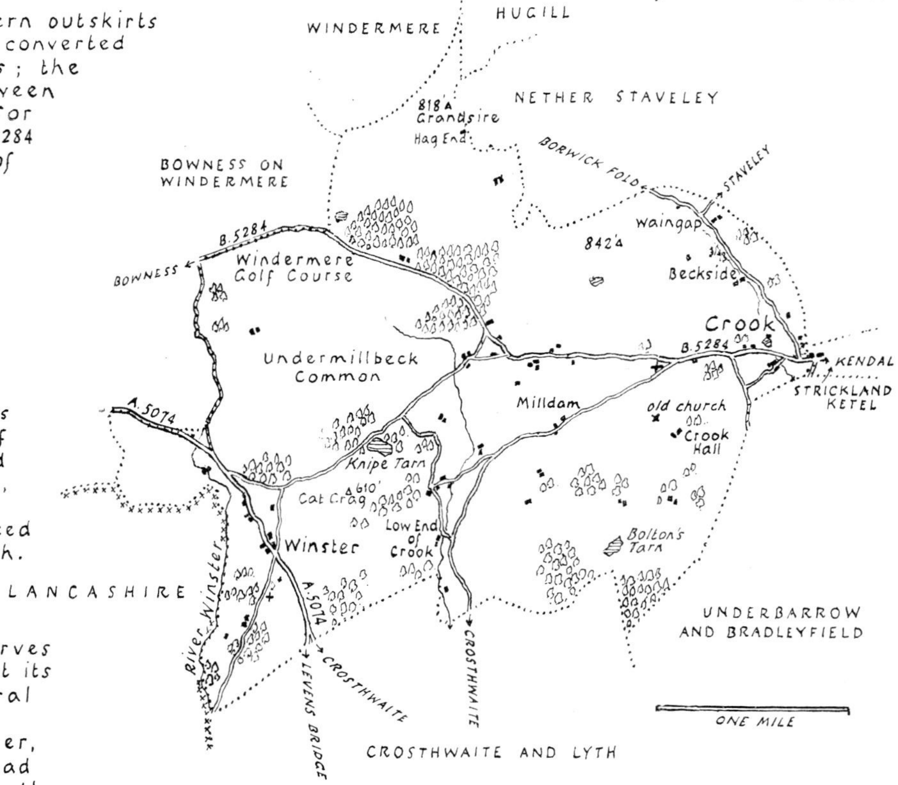

Two roads lead to Windermere from the western outskirts of Kendal. The main highway is the A.591, now converted into a wide racetrack with featureless verges; the secondary road, B.5284, is a leafy avenue between fragrant hedges. One is for speed, the other for pleasure. And one of the pleasures of the B.5284 is the sudden sight, on coming over the brow of a hill, of the terraces of trim white cottages of the hamlet of Crook, facing south to the sun, their tiny gardens bedecked with flowers.

There are other clusters of houses in the parish, not less attractive, some being conversions of the five mill properties that once found employment for the men and women of the community in the manufacture of bobbins and woollens and the grinding of corn.

The landscape hereabouts is lovely, forming an undulating labyrinth of hillocks and hollows at the head of the flat Lyth Valley, a place of farmsteads nestling in sheltered seclusion and an occasional expanse of uncultivated common, of green pastures and woodland plantations, the ups and downs being sufficiently pronounced to prohibit any comprehensive view of the parish. It is a region of curves and corners, inclines and declines, of tinkling becks, with patches of copse and conifer and a popular golf course. A scene so delightful deserves a rustic church to match: this it once had, but its modern replacement lacks the charm of the rural surroundings.

Within the parish is the sweet hamlet of Winster, which has the misfortune to straggle a main road that brings motorists to Windermere from the south and gives its name to a quiet valley that was recently threatened, happily abortively, with a large reservoir.

The best-remembered personality of Crook is Robert Philipson, who lived at Thwatterden Hall (since rebuilt as Crook Hall) and was known for his exploits as 'Robin the Devil'. He it was who, as a Royalist sympathiser, rode on horseback into Kendal Parish Church to do battle with soldiers of Cromwell's army.

Crook

The present parish church of St Catherine, built in 1887, is a plain, austere structure, as indeed may befit a House of God. Unlike most of the country churches built centuries earlier by medieval craftsmen, richly embellished and adorned with buttresses, carvings and battlements, it does not excite admiration; the beholder is even deprived of the joy of stonework by a coating of roughcast. St Catherine's is prose.

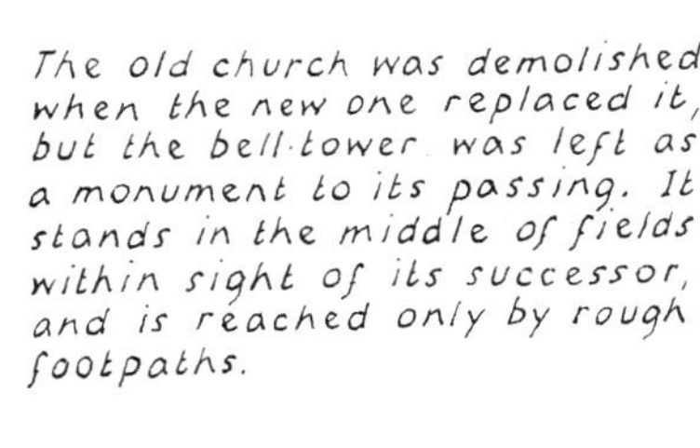

The old church was demolished when the new one replaced it, but the bell-tower was left as a monument to its passing. It stands in the middle of fields within sight of its successor, and is reached only by rough footpaths.

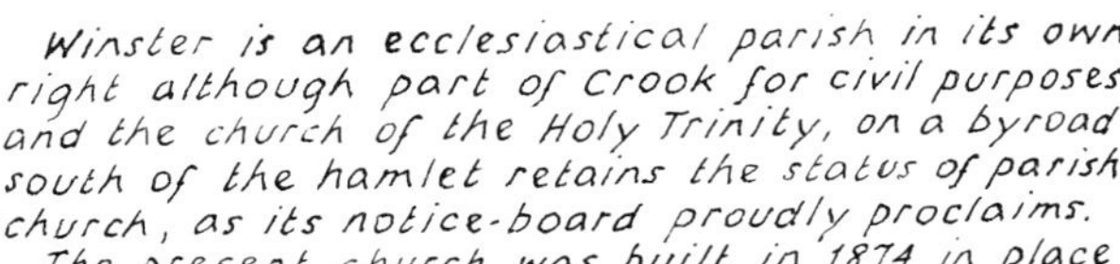

Winster is an ecclesiastical parish in its own right although part of Crook for civil purposes and the church of the Holy Trinity, on a byroad south of the hamlet retains the status of parish church, as its notice-board proudly proclaims.

The present church was built in 1874 in place of an earlier one, from which five wood tablets inscribed with texts and dated 1796 were saved for incorporation in the new church.

Crook

Cottages at Crook

Crook

Knipe Tarn

Footbridge, River Winster

Gilpin Mill, where bobbins were once made, is today in a ruinous condition but retains in situ one of the few remaining waterwheels.

Post Office, Winster

CROSBY GARRETT

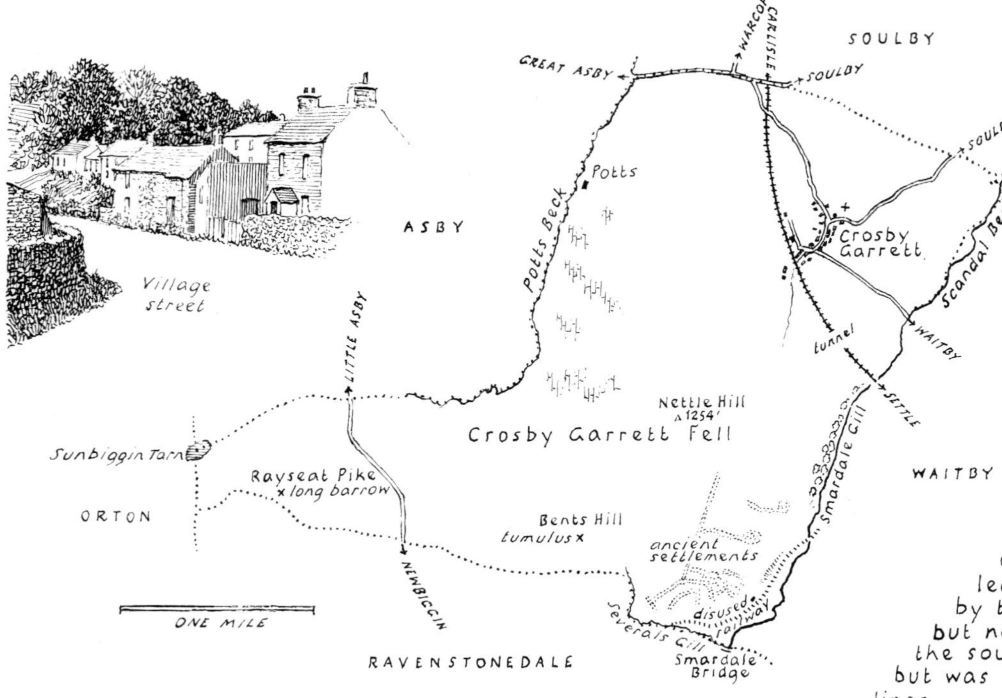

The village of Crosby Garrett lies in a sequestered hollow reached only by quiet roads that are little more than country lanes, and is a *cul-de-sac* for those who come to it on wheels. It is remote from the routes of tourists, a hidden community that is rarely visited by curious strangers. The old church, crowning a steep hill, dominates the scene and enjoys a superb view of the Eden Valley and the Pennines.

The peaceful seclusion of the village was sadly disturbed for a time around 1870-5 when an army of labourers and engineers camped here to construct a section of the Settle-Carlisle railway in terrain that made their task arduous and the results spectacular, the track running high above the cottages on a viaduct between a tunnel and a deep cutting: a drastic intrusion of man in a natural landscape. The village was given a station, defunct since 1952 although the line, despite forebodings of closure, remains active. Crosby has learnt to live with a stillness punctuated by the screams of trains. A less important but no less exciting railway formerly crossed the southern part of the parish along Smardale but was an early casualty in the closure of rural lines.

Most of the area is a wild limestone upland, not well known and infrequently visited yet splendid territory for walking, crossed by a few old tracks and without a habitation. In this lonely setting, before the dawn of history, early man formed an extensive village complex, regarded as one of the most important sites in the country, and elsewhere in the vicinity there are many other indications of primitive occupation.

Tumulus on Bents Hill

Excavated in 1873, this burial mound was found to contain the burnt bones of a body, interred with some artifacts, the latter being removed to the British Museum.

Crosby Garrett

The village of Crosby Garrett, as seen from the church

Crosby Garrett

The parish church of St Andrew, an ancient edifice of quaint and rugged appearance, occupies a site fit for a castle on the crest of a steep hill overlooking the village of Crosby Garrett. The fabric is mainly 12th century, with a later chancel, but contains evidences of a pre-Norman structure on the same site.

Crosby Garrett

Crosby Garrett Fell is a gently undulating plateau over a thousand feet in elevation; on the west it is defined by the deep cutting of Potts Beck, an interesting hidden valley with surface limestone exhibited in large slabs and cliffs and boulders: a perfect sanctuary for bird and beast, unspoilt and unfrequented. The beck forms a common parish boundary with Asby.

The valley of Potts Beck

The construction of the Settle-Carlisle railway was an engineering triumph, the track being laid through very difficult country where the contours were unfavourable. In the vicinity of Crosby Garrett three viaducts were necessary to cross deep valleys, the middle one, 55 feet high, giving a sudden aerial view of the village: a highlight of the journey.

Railway viaduct, Crosby Garrett

Crosby Garrett

Long Barrow on Rayseat Pike

Dimensions: 179 feet in length; width tapering from 62 to 36 feet.

The long barrow on Rayseat Pike, near Sunbiggin Tarn, is one of the best relics of its kind and possibly the earliest of all evidences of Westmorland's prehistory. It was excavated, examined and measured in 1875, the search revealing the remains of both adults and children. A discovery not expected was a cremation trench that contained burnt bones, a feature causing speculation about the age of this ancient burial ground.

Village Settlement at Severals (160 acres)

The Royal Commission on Ancient Monuments, in their inventory for Westmorland published 1935, included references to a complex of prehistoric villages comprising stone-walled fields, hutments, dykes and pathways on the south-east slope of the fellside above Smardale, describing this as a key site and one of the most remarkable in Britain.

The remains are fragmentary, and a trained eye and a learned mind are attributes necessary to piece together the story of these primitive ruins and earthworks: the parapets are foundations of former walls marking boundaries and enclosures, the sunken ways were farm tracks and the small patterned areas are the traces of stone huts.

Men lived here as a community where no men now live and few men today ever come. A gap in our knowledge of the early settlers in the district might well be bridged by expert excavation of the site.

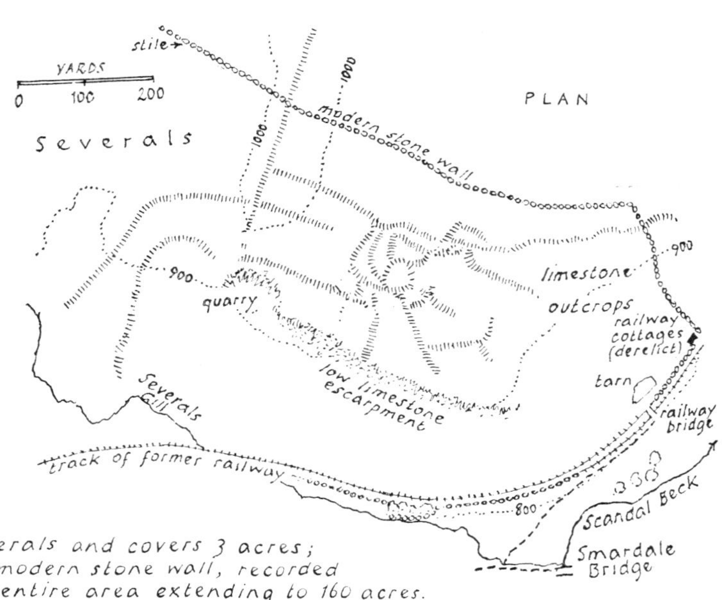

The principal settlement (plan on right) is known as Severals and covers 3 acres; there are two others immediately to the north, beyond a modern stone wall, recorded officially as Intake 1 (1¼ acres) and Intake 2 (1 acre), the entire area extending to 160 acres.

CROSBY RAVENSWORTH

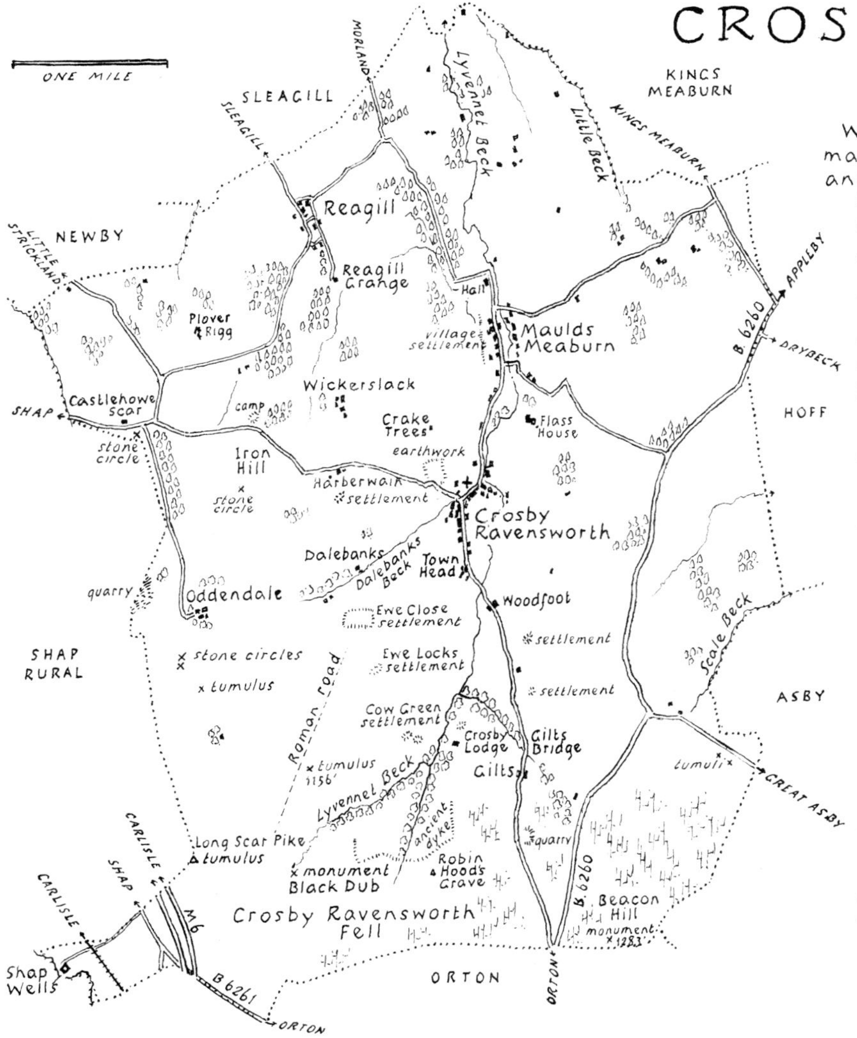

Westmorland is a county of diverse scenery, with marked variations of landscape between one region and another, yet all areas share in common a sweet beauty uninterrupted by industrial scars and by crowded centres of population. It is perhaps the fairest of all English counties, predominantly of a rural character but having wild expanses of mountain and moorland. Parts are well known to tourists and visitors, but most is relatively unknown and gains in attractiveness because of its freedom from commercial enterprise. Such a place is the Vale of Lyvennet, far removed from tourist penetration and without a fast road: it is a shallow depression in an elevated plateau, unseen and unsuspected by speeding travellers. Its river gently meanders from an upland of bare limestone to the richer pastures and woods on a bedrock of red sandstone, overlooked by a sparse scattering of farmsteads and hamlets. A sleepy quiet and an undisturbed tranquillity pervade in this delightful sanctuary.

Crosby Ravensworth is the capital of Lyvennet, although but a small village, and gives its name to an extensive parish that includes nothing not fair to look upon. Within its boundaries are two other little communities, Maulds Meaburn and Reagill, and a network of country lanes.

Men have long regarded this district as a good place to live and work. The remains of old British settlements are remarkably profuse: enclosures, hut dwellings, stone circles, burial mounds with cairns, are numerous. The Romans laid a roadway along the valley. Armies have marched through it. But modern road engineers have, happily, ignored these ancient highways and the railway builders also sought easier terrain. Crosby Ravensworth is bypassed by fast communications. Hence its charm.

Crosby Ravensworth

The parish church of St Lawrence, beautifully situated amongst fine trees, is, in its present form, the result of many centuries of extension and alteration starting in the 12th century, when an earlier church on the site was adapted. It contains many interesting features, and the graveyard has a medieval cross and several ornate and decorative carvings.

Jubilee Monument (1887), Beacon Hill, Orton Scar

Memorial to the local-born Lancelot Addison, Dean of Lichfield and father of Joseph Addison, the distinguished essayist, at Hill Top, Maulds Meaburn.

Crosby Ravensworth

Gilts — a 17th century farmhouse

Vicarage Bridge

Gilts Bridge, if not unique, is quite extraordinary in construction. Built of mortared limestone blocks, roughcut and massive, the channel through it is a narrow vertical slit, just big enough to admit a man upright — an unusual form of construction for which the purpose is obscure. According to a local legend the bridge was erected by the Devil himself — which might explain it.

Cottages at Woodfoot

Crosby Ravensworth

Stone tablet built into the outside wall of the former blacksmith's shop — one of many inscribed panels in the building.

Maulds Meaburn

Maulds Meaburn is a village most delightfully situated in a fertile hollow threaded by the Lyvennet Beck, its scattered buildings lining an open green fringed by noble trees. Time has left the place unscathed and it is reached only by quiet country lanes; the closure of its rural activities — the smithy, the sawmill and others — and the advent of weekend "off-comers" to some of the old cottages, has made its sleepy tranquillity even more profound. At the rear of the buildings on the west side of the green are the fragmentary earthworks of an ancient village settlement, its history unknown. Also in the vicinity are elegant residences and pleasant farmhouses, but it is the Arcadian setting of Maulds Meaburn that appeals most of all.

Meaburn Hall

Much of the glory of Meaburn Hall has departed, for it was an early seat of the Lowther family and furnished with a deer park, pleasure grounds and a bowling green; the latter amenity, with two summerhouses, can still be seen in the field adjoining. But the Hall itself, mellowed with age, is no less charming. It was built in the 16th century, with later additions, being an adaptation of a former manor house. Today, as a tenanted farmstead, it retains an air of Elizabethan grace and dignity.

Crosby Ravensworth

Reagill

Reagill, formerly known as **Renegill**, is a quiet hamlet on a slight eminence in surroundings once wholly pastoral but now severely encroached upon by forestry plantations. An almost-forgotten Roman road passed this way. Here is a splendid Grange, remote from the cottages, and an old school with inscribed stones and a 15th century window from the parish church, but for the few visitors to the hamlet the great surprise is a walled garden containing a wonderful collection of statuary and carved stones.

The Image Garden

The garden of statues has an amazing variety of ornamental stone carvings and sculptures of considerable merit, featuring many eminent men, with lions and dogs as embellishments. The sculptor was a self-taught local farmer's son, Thomas Bland. In its heyday, a century ago, the Image Garden, as it was named, was a place of popular resort, with tea-parties and brass bands; today, although forlorn, it remains a striking memorial to a remarkable man. Thomas also made the three monuments in the parish illustrated in this chapter.

Reagill Grange

Reagill Grange is an imposing 16th century building, its sturdiness exemplified by large cylindrical chimney shafts and a two-storeyed porch. It is occupied as a farmhouse and sited in a sequestered hollow sheltered by woodlands and plantations. Nearby are the scanty remains of an ancient chapel, once a dependency of Shap Abbey.

Crosby Ravensworth

The antiquities of
Crosby Ravensworth Fell

Monument at Black Dub

This bears the following inscription:

HERE AT BLACK DUB
THE SOURCE OF THE LIVENNET
KING CHARLES THE II
REGALED HIS ARMY
AND DRANK OF THE WATER
ON HIS MARCH FROM SCOTLAND
AUGUST 8 1651

The obelisk was erected in 1843.

Although difficult to believe today, the 'road' from London to Scotland formerly passed this lonely spot (pre-Shap).

There are many erratic boulders of Shap granite resting on the basic limestone of the fell.

Stone circles at Oddendale

There are traces of an ancient dyke over a two-mile length within the intake wall on the fell. This is believed to be the boundary of a former deer park.

Robin Hood's Grave

Most ancient cairns occur on hillsides and uplands. The cairn in the illustration stands in the bottom of a dry limestone valley and is probably not an antiquity. It has long been known as Robin Hood's Grave —— a name not to be interpreted literally.

Crosby Ravensworth

Monk's Bridge, Crosby Ravensworth

Flass ("the house by the water"), at Maulds Meaburn, is a Victorian mansion, the former residence of a High Sheriff of Westmorland.

The ancient settlements

There are the remains of eleven village settlements within the parish and innumerable other traces of early communities. Of these, the extensive settlement at Ewe Close, a complex group of huts and walled enclosures, is regarded as the most important, but its condition is so decayed that its arrangement is no longer clearly discernible. The date of the settlement is obscure, but the Roman road between Low Borrow Bridge and Kirkby Thore, which crossed the moor hereabouts (but has disappeared as the result of later cultivation) is thought to have deviated from a straight course to avoid the settlement, which suggests that it was in existence at the time of the Roman occupation.

Perimeter stones, Ewe Close

At the neighbouring settlement of Ewe Locks many groups of stones, the relics of huts and small enclosures, are still to be seen.

Stone circle, Iron Hill

Crosby Ravensworth has many scattered boulders, some of them erratics of Shap granite. Six have the name of Thunder Stone — and all these, curiously, occur on the parish boundary.

CROSTHWAITE AND LYTH

The Lyth Valley has a national renown for its beauty and when viewed from the limestone escarpments around lives up to its reputation. Yet the floor of the valley, several miles in length and two in width, is possibly the least attractive in Lakeland, being an alluvial flat, a natural reclamation of an inlet of the sea, drained by the sluggish River Gilpin and artificially irrigated to provide pasture. It is a valley plain, lacking trees and so uniformly flat that even at its head, far inland, the ground is no more than a few feet above sea level. For its attraction it depends on the surroundings of limestone cliffs, pretty clusters of homesteads and rich woodlands around the fringe, and only when seen in conjunction with these, and especially with the mountain skyline of Lakeland as a background, does the scene become wellnigh perfect. The farms are the fruit gardens of Westmorland, almost every one having an orchard of damsons that endow them with a garland of snowy blossom in springtime: these orchards are traditional in Lyth; they 'go with the farms' but are quite incidental to the main industry of rearing sheep and cattle.

The valley is shared by four parishes, that of Crosthwaite and Lyth occupying the western side. At the head occur undulations of landscape: hillocks and hollows on and in which are scattered farmhouses, some elevated and some snugly hidden, and a maze of narrow country lanes radiating from the village of Crosthwaite, which comprises the two colonies of Crosthwaite Green and Church Town, the latter having the parish church. Bowland Bridge, on the River Winster, and Row and Howe, on the northern slopes of Whitbarrow, are other small communities of great charm.

Whitbarrow is an abrupt limestone hill accounting for half the acreage of the parish and dominating the whole. Despite an unsightly quarry eating into its south-east corner, Whitbarrow affords a most delightful high-level promenade with superb views. The summit, Lord's Seat, was selected for its botanical and geological interest as the site for a memorial to the founder of the Lake District Naturalists' Trust. The eastern slopes are extensively wooded.

In the south the parish is crossed by the busy road linking Levens Bridge and West Cumberland and terminates on the shore of the Kent estuary.

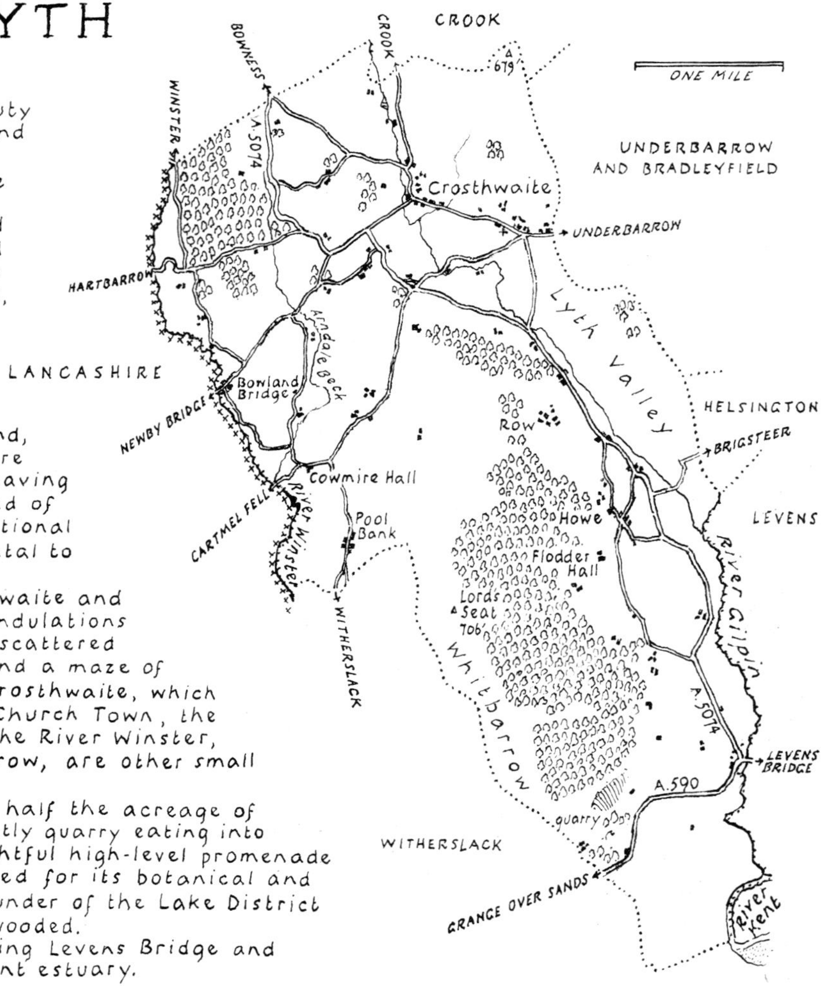

Crosthwaite and Lyth

The parish church of St Mary has twice been rebuilt, in 1813 and in 1878-85, on the site of an earlier church.

A clapper bridge at Crosthwaite Green

Blossom time, Lyth Valley

"When I went down to Winster
  Full fifty years ago
The vale was filled with blossom,
  Wild cherry and the sloe,
But the grace of all its graces
  And the charm of all its charms
Was the snowy damson blossom
  Around the fellside farms."

Crosthwaite and Lyth

Flodder Hall is of rugged construction, sturdily buttressed by outbuildings and having massive round chimney shafts. The interior retains many original features. Built in the 17th century, it incorporates parts of an earlier structure. The porch, added in 1865, displays an old tablet with a Latin inscription, translated as " If you wish to be a wise man, observe these six things .... what you say, and where, of whom, to whom, how and when."

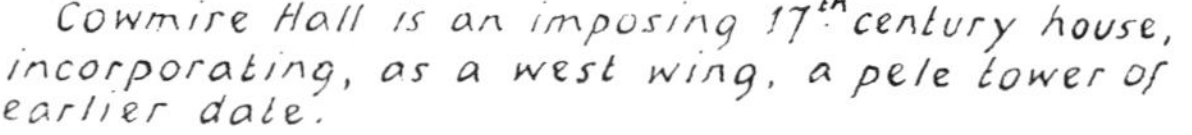

Cowmire Hall is an imposing 17th century house, incorporating, as a west wing, a pele tower of earlier date.

Bowland Bridge

Crosthwaite and Lyth

Whitbarrow

Whitbarrow is an abrupt ridge of limestone on a north-south axis soaring boldly above the flat marshes and mosses of the Kent Estuary and is a parallel counterpart to the long cliff of Scout Scar across the alluvial valley of Lyth. Rich woodlands clothe the lower slopes and in the east pine plantations climb almost to the summit. To the west a four-mile escarpment extends along the crest like a castle wall and is repeated on a smaller scale at the highest limits of the eastern forests. But the spine of the ridge is bare, although 'bare' is an inapt word for the wealth of heather and bracken, juniper and saplings that form so colourful a carpet. In places this carpet has worn thin, revealing a naked surface of patchy scree and outcrops of dazzling whiteness.

Whitbarrow's delights of plant and wild life have been recognised by the recent adoption of its summit plateau as a nature reserve, and there is nowhere a more attractive landscape in which to enjoy the manifold pleasures of a natural environment allied to a far-reaching and very lovely panorama.

Lord's Seat, the summit of Whitbarrow

The Nature Reserve

The Lake District Naturalists' Trust was formed in 1962 largely as a result of the efforts of Canon G.A.K. Hervey, and after his death in 1967 a proposal to acquire the walled enclosure known as Flodder Allotment on the top of Whitbarrow, and including Lord's Seat, as a memorial to him was brought to fruition. The area was declared a nature reserve in 1969, a visible recognition of the Canon's services to the Trust being provided by a stone tablet built into a fine new cairn on Lord's Seat, inscribed as follows:

This Reserve
Commemorates
CANON G.A.K. HERVEY
1893-1967
Founder of the
Lake District Naturalists' Trust

The emblem of the Trust

The memorial cairn

DALTON

Dalton is a rural parish adjoining Burton, and was, until 1896, within the county of Lancashire and the ecclesiastical parish of Warton. Centred away from through motor roads and having no known attractions for passing travellers, it is rarely visited. Scattered farms, a cluster of forestry houses and a very new Hall (replacing a Victorian mansion) constitute the few habitations; there is no church, no building for public use. Natural woodlands are supplemented by coniferous plantations and an extensive area is laid out as private parkland. On the face of it, there is little to see at Dalton.

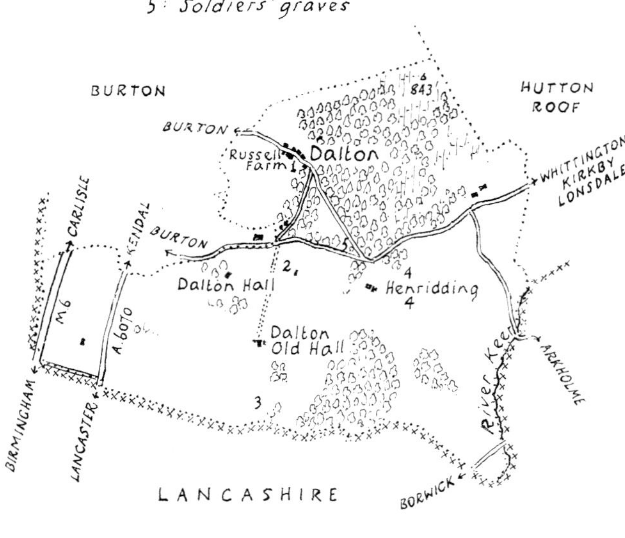

It may be that Dalton's sheltered seclusion in the lee of a limestone hill and a sleepy atmosphere suggesting that nothing ever happens here to catch the headlines are the reasons why its history has gone unrecorded and escaped general recognition. Only recently has the attention of archaeologists been directed to several features that warrant close investigation. There are many surface indications of forgotten communities, some so clear on the ground that their omission from the records of ancient monuments is quite surprising. Other earthworks are less well defined and call for expert appraisal. It is a place of legends, of wisps of information passed down from father to son: these tell of a decimation of the population by the Plague, of a battle that took place locally between Roundheads and Royalists, leaving nineteen corpses buried in graves marked by nineteen trees that can still be seen. The clearance of a village in the 17th century is better authenticated and there are distinct traces, enough to indicate its arrangement, visible in fields now used for grazing. There is some evidence that a Roman road passed through the parish; and the obvious remains of an iron age settlement and burial cairns. But the most remarkable relic, and clearly to be seen, is an ancient settlement patterned by limestone boulders in a farm paddock, revealed on inspection as a walled enclosure serviced by defined lanes, the existence of which seems to have escaped notice through the centuries since it was occupied, probably in early medieval times.

The fascinating story of Dalton's past is waiting to be researched and unfolded. It will make interesting reading.

Dalton

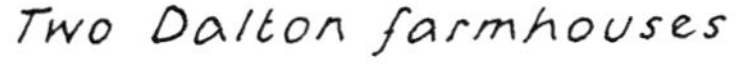

Two Dalton farmhouses

Henridding, an early 18th century farmstead, is thought to be the scene of a battle, possibly legendary, the action of which took place in the field immediately east of the buildings. Nearby is a breached dam, which may originally have been connected with a former use of the land.

The opinion has been expressed that Dalton Old Hall and its farmlands together comprise the most interesting agricultural unit in the county — but for historical and archaeological reasons unconnected with farming. The Hall, which has a date-panel 1666, has a cylindrical flue and other original features; alongside are the foundations and fragmentary remains of a pele tower. The farmlands include (1) the site of the cleared village, (2) the settlement at Quamps and the related burial mound and cairn and (3) many traces of early roads and dykes, of which some may be Roman. Several artifacts of Roman origin have been found in the fields.

Dalton

Dalton's Vanished Village

In a rising field south of the Burton-Kirkby Lonsdale road and alongside the access lane to Dalton Old Hall are indications of a former community, the foundations of buildings and terraced roads being traceable on the hillside, where a solitary apple tree still bears fruit and clumps of garden flowers continue to flourish despite the present use of the land as a pasture.

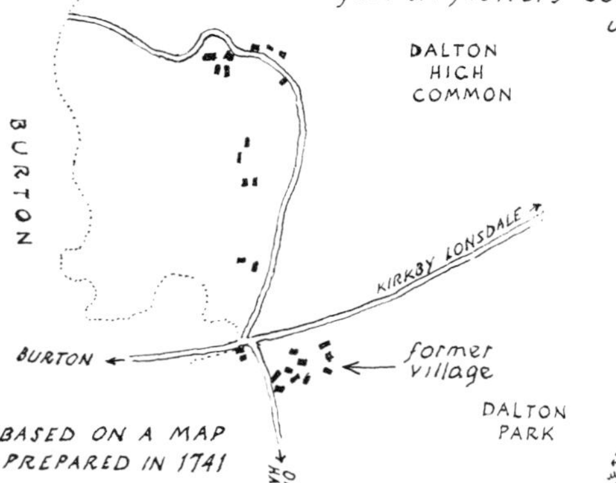

The existence of a village here is confirmed by a map drawn in 1741 (now in the archives of the County Hall, Kendal), the clearance of the buildings possibly being due to the subsequent development of estate grounds for the new Dalton Hall.

An isolated dwelling of the long-house type (illustrated below) remains in a derelict condition at the top of the village site and was occupied until a few decades ago. Encroaching trees and head-high undergrowth make access to it difficult.

This copse of nineteen trees at the junction of the Burton-Kirkby Lonsdale road and the local road is reputed to mark the burial place of nineteen men killed in a nearby battle between the Roundhead and Royalist soldiers.

In a hilltop field known as Quamps remains of parapet walls mark the boundary of an ancient settlement, which has been confirmed as of the iron age period by discoveries on the site.

Dalton

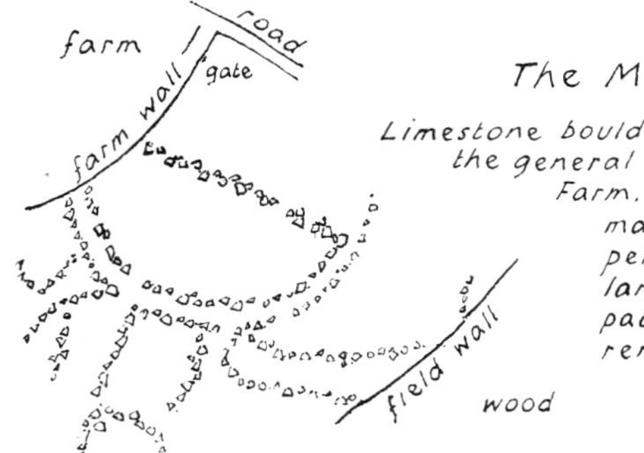

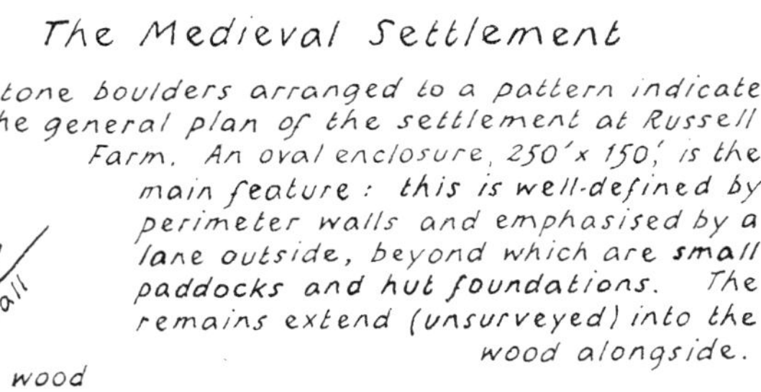

The Medieval Settlement

Limestone boulders arranged to a pattern indicate the general plan of the settlement at Russell Farm. An oval enclosure, 250' x 150', is the main feature : this is **well-defined** *by perimeter walls and emphasised by a lane outside, beyond which are* **small paddocks and hut foundations.** *The remains extend (unsurveyed) into the wood alongside.*

left : the perimeter wall
below : the lane

Historical and archaeological information in this chapter was kindly provided by Mr. John Marsh of Kendal

DILLICAR

Few northbound travellers along the railway or the motorway know that when they turn the curve into the Lune Gorge they are in the parish of Dillicar: it is not a name well known even to Westmorland people, there being no village or hamlet so called, and it is insignificant in ecclesiastical and civil matters. There is no parish church; merely a huddle of cottages at Beck Foot, a terrace of railway houses and a converted school at Lowgill, and a few farms. Lowgill was formerly a railway junction and achieved a small measure of fame as a well-kept station, but this has now vanished and a jungle of weeds has replaced the neat gardens. An impressive and obsolete viaduct at Beck Foot is the most striking feature in the parish, but its greatest joy is the old Crook of Lune Bridge and the lovely river scenery nearby.

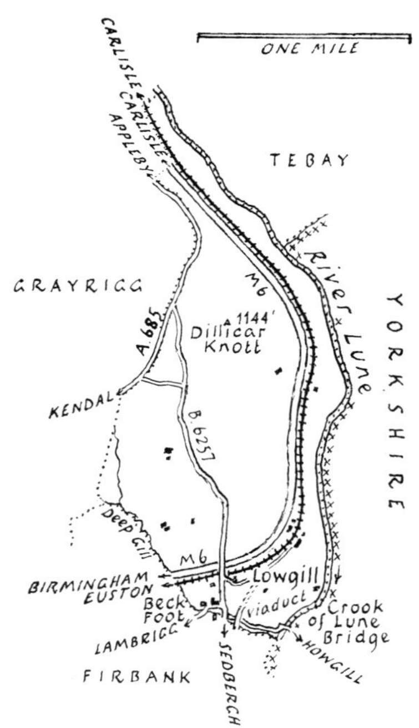

Railway houses, Lowgill

Beck Foot

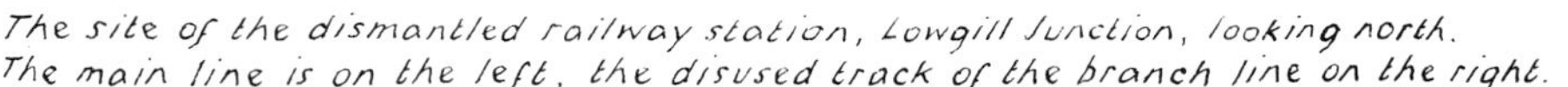

The site of the dismantled railway station, Lowgill Junction, looking north. The main line is on the left, the disused track of the branch line on the right.

Lowgill Viaduct

Even the motorists who scrape their cars against the narrow parapets of Crook of Lune Bridge (as many do) must concede (as do all who see it) that it is, despite its hazards, a picturesque and elegant structure. Its date is uncertain but probably early 16th century.

Looking from Crook of Lune Bridge up-river to Fell Head, Howgill Fells

DOCKER

Docker is a parish of farms, mainly 17th century, serviced by access roads from narrow country lanes. There is no church, no school, no inn, no shop, no hamlet. An undulating landscape of pastures, with some plantations, rises to a moorland on the southern boundary. The parish is crossed by the A.685 Kendal-Appleby road and the railway, which is carried on a viaduct over Flodder Beck.

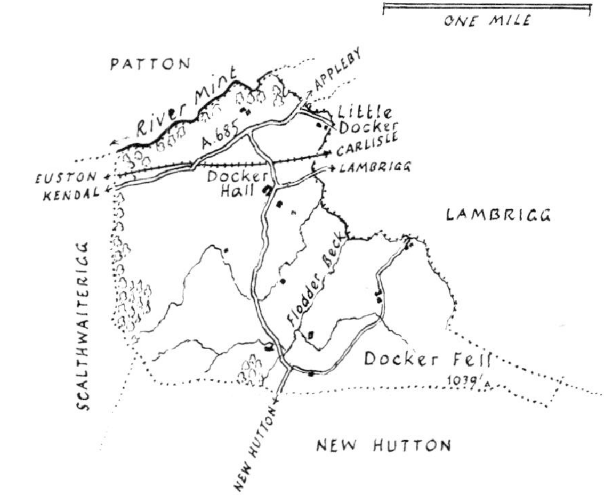

a Docker landscape

Railway viaduct and Flodder Beck

two Docker farmsteads

Haygarth

Hollins

DUFTON

Since the opening in 1965 of the popular long-distance footpath, the Pennine Way, the village of Dufton has lost much of its insularity and is now nationally known as an important stage of the journey; and, as the approach is across an inhospitable wilderness of many weary miles, it is reached with relief and remembered with affection. Dufton is an admirable halting place, the pleasant surroundings providing welcome contrast to the desolation of the moors. Visitors other than walkers are no less appreciative. The village is delightfully arranged around a tree-lined green.

The parish is very extensive, most of it being a dreary plateau of peat mosses, an upland desert with barren summits exceeding 2500′ in altitude. This vast wasteland is uninhabited except for two lonely outposts, and unfrequented away from the track of the Pennine Way; indeed, part of the area is a target range for the Army, used for gun practice, and therefore out of bounds, and much of the remainder is a nature reserve from which the public is also excluded. The parish (and county) boundary in this wild region is not determined, as might be expected, by the Pennine watershed but by the River Tees after a long decline to the east. Durham thus gets the benefit of rainfall in Westmorland. Yorkshire, too, comes alongside for a few miles. This area is the loneliest part of Westmorland although scattered with the remains of old mines where men once laboured for little reward; yet it has certain attractive natural features: High Cup takes pride of place in the landscape and the cataract of Caldron Snout is of high renown; less impressive but having a peculiar beauty is the dimpled limestone bed of the upper reaches of Maize Beck.

Dufton is one of the places occasionally ravaged by the phenomenon known as the Helm Wind, which sweeps down from the hills with great force, but normally is a scene of tranquil pastures and woodlands, a point of vantage overlooking the lovely Eden Valley. And in this wide and pleasing panorama nothing is more fair than Dufton village.

The fountain, Dufton Green

Cottages at Dufton Green

Dufton

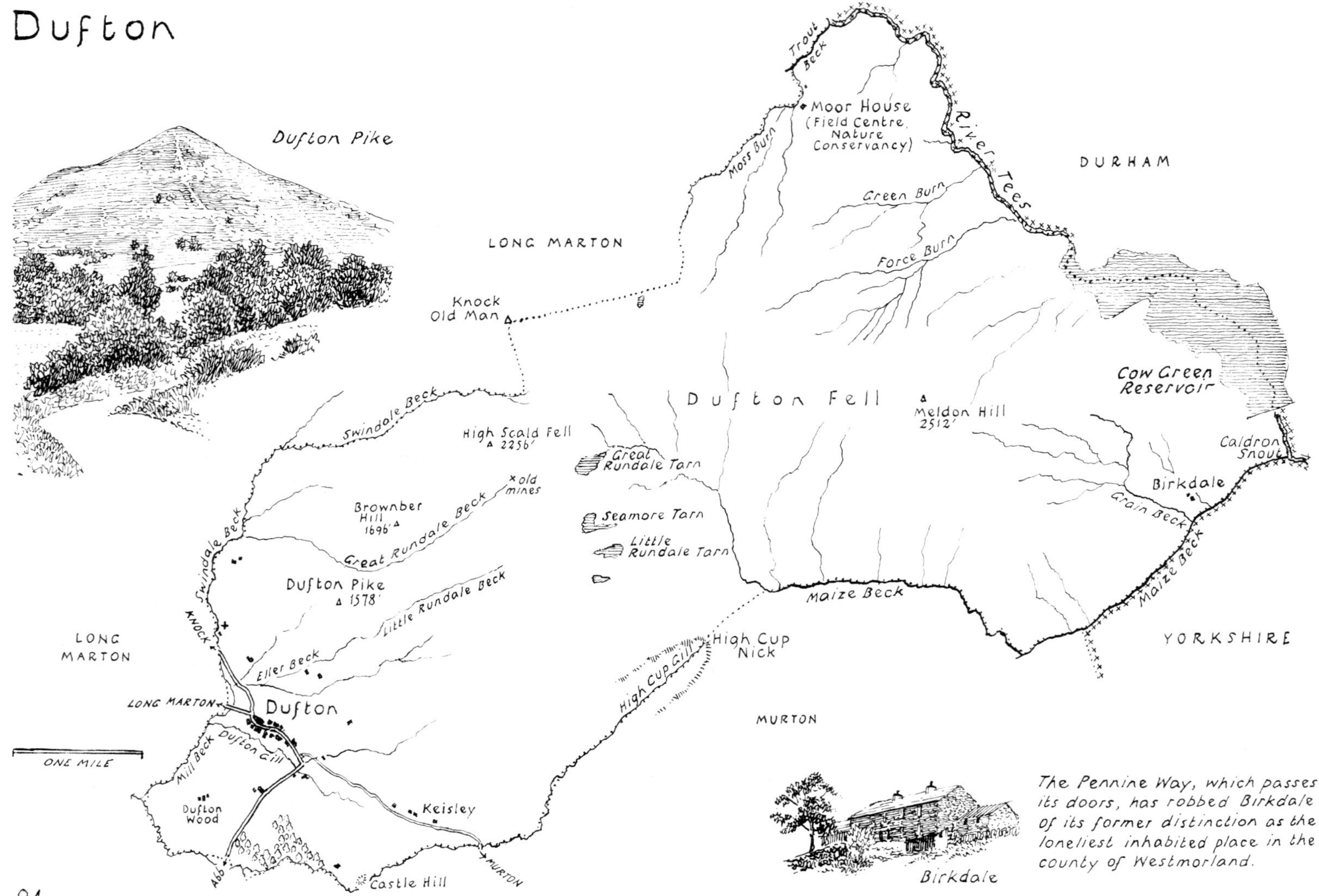

The Pennine Way, which passes its doors, has robbed Birkdale of its former distinction as the loneliest inhabited place in the county of Westmorland.

Dufton

The central block of Dufton Hall was rebuilt in 1779; the north wing is older, probably 16th century. Part of the interior was left unfinished (owing to a lack of funds) during the rebuilding and has remained so. The Hall is now used as three residences.

Cottages at Dufton

The parish church of St Cuthbert is in fields a mile from Dufton village on the road to Knock. An earlier church on the site was rebuilt in 1784, some features of 12th century masonry being incorporated.

Footbridge, Great Rundale Beck

High Cup

Approached from the east, High Cup is reached suddenly, without warning, and after many miles of uneventful tramping at a high level the effect is awesome. A profound depression opens dramatically at one's feet and in the course of only a few paces is fully revealed as a massive symmetrical bowl rimmed by a formation of columnar basalt crags maintaining a remarkably even contour, below which fall steep slopes of tumbled boulders. A small stream entering the abyss from the moor is often blown into a cloud of spray as the wind rushes up out of the depths.

High Cup is more commonly referred to as High Cup Nick, a name, however, strictly appropriate only to a cleft in the northern escarpment of the amphitheatre.

High Cup is a geological phenomenon, a natural wonder, and it is unique.

This slender pillar in the cliffs of High Cup is named after a Dufton cobbler who climbed it and, the story goes, soled and heeled a pair of boots while sitting on the top.

Nichol's Chair (or Last)

Caldron Snout

The Battle for the Gentians

The geology of the upper Tees, with bands of limestone and dolerite alternating, is a fascinating study, but it is the remarkable flora of the district that has established its place among the most important areas of natural interest in Britain and as one especially worthy of conservation: it has, indeed, an international reputation as a place of outstanding significance and is regularly visited by scientists and students, while a permanent resident team conduct a continuous research and voluntary wardens stand guard: "the Gentian Patrol."

This interest is shared by many who, seeking beauty rather than knowledge, simply love to wander in flowery pastures, finding their pleasure in a search for varieties of plants that are rarely seen — not with any thought of wanton pillage but for visual enjoyment.

It was against this background of amenity, scientific study, and conservation that a proposal to establish a reservoir at Cow Green excited and stimulated so much public opposition a few years ago. Objections failed, and Cow Green Reservoir came into being, but not before a rescue operation was manned to remove from the site to be flooded many rare plant specimens, these being given new locations above the water line. Sad to relate, it is mainly Westmorland water that is filling the new reservoir and destroying the habitats of those left to perish.

Moor House Field Station

Even more remotely situated than Birkdale, the Nature Conservancy's Field Station, Moor House, overlooks a feeder of the River Tees at an elevation of 1825'. The Reserve covers the vast moorland plateau of Milburn Forest and Dufton Fell on the Westmorland flank of the Tees, extending to the edge of the incline from the Eden Valley. Certain areas of study are fenced. Access to Moor House is by private road from Garrigill; permission is necessary.

Spring Gentian
(Gentiana Verna)

FAWCETT FOREST

Fawcett Forest is a parish with few habitations, few people, and thousands of sheep. It is mainly rough moorland rising to around 1800 feet between the valleys of Bannisdale and Borrowdale, including their headwaters: a barren and lonely wilderness of peat mosses, not regarded as Lake District country although almost wholly within the National Park. There are rolling fells but no exciting mountains, and yet the landscape, with a quieter beauty, is more typically Westmorland than the frequented Langdales and Grasmere. Both Bannisdale and Borrowdale are long valleys, one feeding the Kent and the other the Lune, descending from desolate uplands, a habitat of fell ponies, but assuming a softer character in the lower reaches, where the main streams, having gathered in their tributaries, flow sedately amongst trees. Bannisdale Head and Borrowdale Head are isolated sheep farms; Forest Hall, also a sheep farm, is situated on the A.6, the main road over Shap Fells until the opening of the M.6 motorway in 1970 and carrying before then a steady stream of traffic, and having, in the Jungle Café, a well-known halt for heavy transport. Today the road is quiet and the café has closed its doors. Another former landmark on the A.6, the Leyland Clock, has been removed to Kendal.

Recent activity has resulted in an improvement to a section of the old road to Shap used before the A6 but for the purpose only of facilitating the construction of a new aqueduct to convey supplies from Haweswater, and when this work is done, unless schemes for flooding the valleys for reservoirs are sanctioned, Fawcett Forest will revert to the pervading quiet of a vast sheep pasture.

FAWCETT is a version of the ancient manorial name, FAUSIDE.

FOREST is a common Westmorland place-name for an unenclosed moorland tract of ground, usually bare of trees.

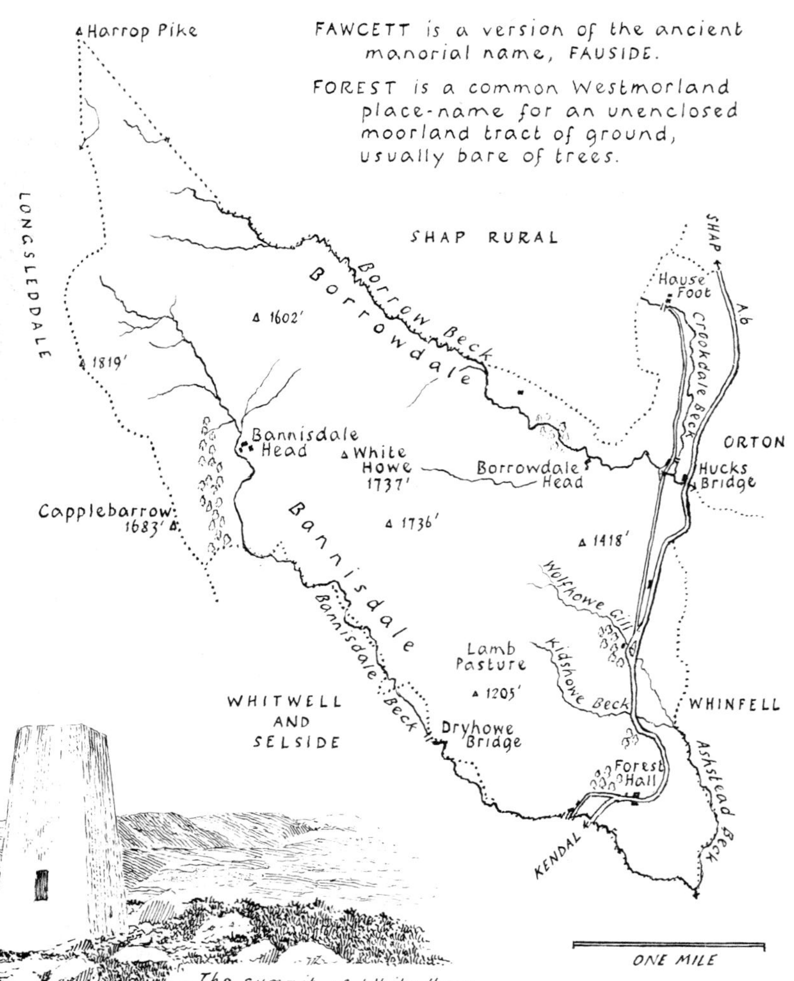

The summit of White Howe

Fawcett Forest

Dryhowe Bridge

Bannisdale, from Lamb Pasture

White Howe,
from Dryhowe Bridge

Fawcett Forest

Bannisdale Head

Bannisdale Beck, near Lowbridge House

Forest Hall, the most imposing house in the parish, stands on the site of an ancient hall, part of which is now used for farm purposes. This is one of the largest sheep farms in the county.

Forest Hall

Fawcett Forest

Borrowdale Head

White Howe, from Huck's Bridge

The old road to Shap

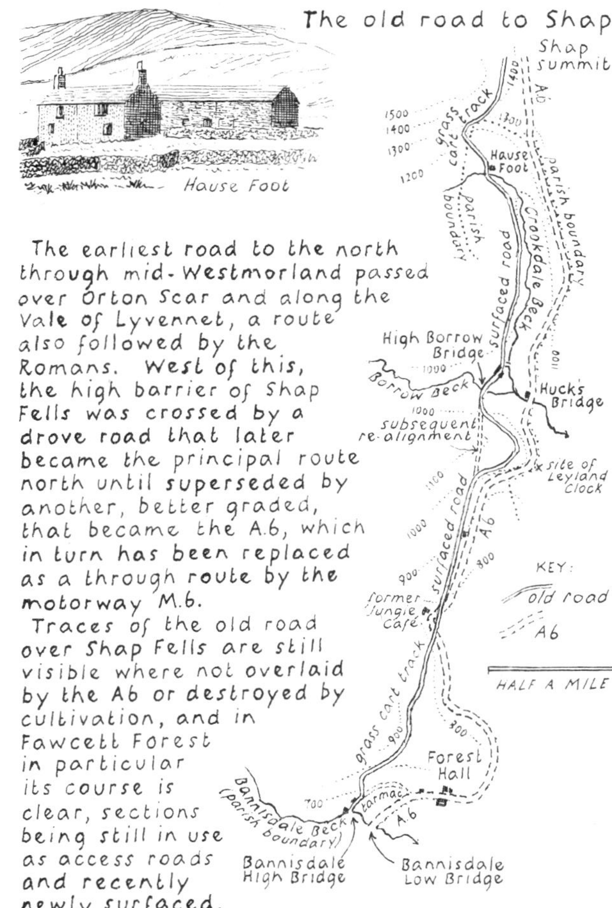

Hause Foot

The earliest road to the north through mid-Westmorland passed over Orton Scar and along the Vale of Lyvennet, a route also followed by the Romans. West of this, the high barrier of Shap Fells was crossed by a drove road that later became the principal route north until superseded by another, better graded, that became the A.6, which in turn has been replaced as a through route by the motorway M.6.

Traces of the old road over Shap Fells are still visible where not overlaid by the A6 or destroyed by cultivation, and in Fawcett Forest in particular its course is clear, sections being still in use as access roads and recently newly surfaced.

FIRBANK

Firbank might never have been written into the annals of the history of the county were it not for an event that happened on June 13th 1652. On this day George Fox, the founder of Quakerism, addressed a gathering of a thousand people from a rock on Firbank Fell and sowed the seeds of a religious movement represented by the Society of Friends. The name of George Fox is still associated with Firbank, and the rock, popularly known as Fox's Pulpit, has become a place of pilgrimage.

Much of the parish is moorland but to the east a pronounced slope descends to the fertile valley of the Lune, with the lofty Howgill Fells beyond — a beautiful picture. Running roughly parallel to the river (which forms the parish and county boundary) but at a higher level, is Firbank's main highway, the classified road B.6257, but nevertheless nothing more than a narrow country lane between flowery hedgerows. Along this are scattered farmhouses and cottages, few in number, and the little parish church of St John; other isolated farms occur on the fellsides. Accompanying the road is the track of a former railway that linked Clapham and Lowgill: it impinges on the scenery not at all except where it crosses the Lune on a spectacular viaduct. An active railway, the main line to Scotland from Euston, crosses the northern part of the parish and since 1970 has had a close companion in the motorway M6.

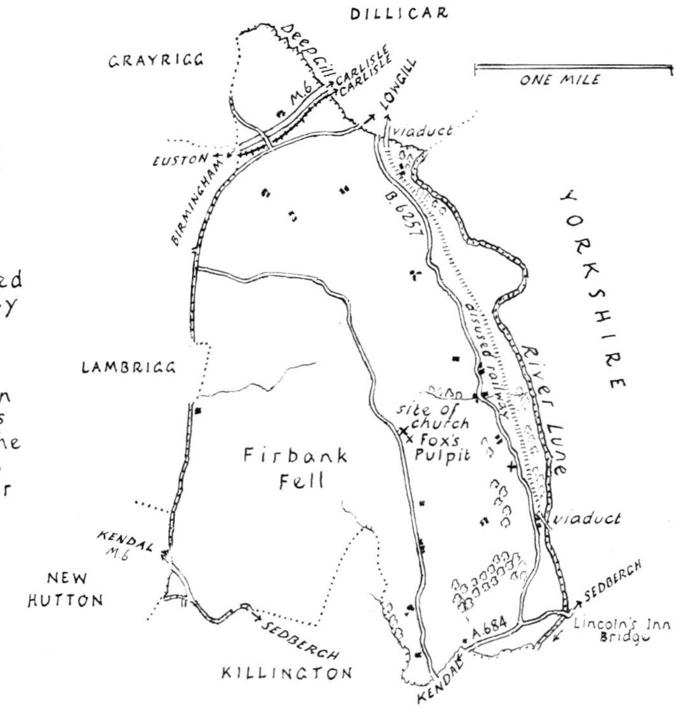

The southern Howgill Fells, from Fox's Pulpit

Firbank

Lincoln's Inn Bridge, a traffic hazard on the A.684, where Westmorland and Yorkshire meet, is named after the house adjoining, once an inn. The 17th bridge crosses a popular reach of the River Lune.

There is always sadness in things obsolete and discarded, and this is especially so when they still retain elegance and beauty. The only present function of the fine Lune railway viaduct is to serve as a monument to the proud men who fashioned it — and were spared by death from witnessing its fall from favour.

Firbank

The parish church of St John the Evangelist, built 1842

The site of the old church on the fell with Fox's Pulpit in the background.

Tablet affixed to the rock, Fox's Pulpit:

LET YOUR LIVES SPEAK

HERE OR NEAR THIS ROCK GEORGE FOX PREACHED TO ABOUT ONE THOUSAND SEEKERS FOR THREE HOURS ON SUNDAY JUNE 13, 1652. GREAT POWER INSPIRED HIS MESSAGE AND THE MEETING PROVED OF FIRST IMPORTANCE IN GATHERING THE SOCIETY OF FRIENDS KNOWN AS QUAKERS. MANY MEN AND WOMEN CONVINCED OF THE TRUTH ON THIS FELL AND IN OTHER PARTS OF THE NORTHERN COUNTIES WENT FORTH THROUGH THE LAND AND OVER THE SEAS WITH THE LIVING WORD OF THE LORD ENDURING GREAT HARDSHIPS AND WINNING MULTITUDES TO CHRIST.

Fox's Pulpit

Visitors refer to this familiar structure simply as Grasmere Church; strictly it is the parish church of St Oswald. Of uncertain origin but undoubtedly medieval, it is a building of unusual character, and the traditional venue of an annual Rushbearing Festival. In the churchyard a well-trodden path leads to the graves of William and Mary Wordsworth.

GRASMERE

Grasmere enjoys international fame as a place of pilgrimage, both for those who come from afar to see the environment in which the poet William Wordsworth lived, and for those who return year after year to renew acquaintance with the supremely lovely setting of village and lake and fell. There is beauty here, and romance. The scenery lacks the excitement of Langdale, being more restful and a welcome balm to visitors from urban areas. This green bowl in the hills has a peace all its own.

The village caters for tourists on a grand scale. There are hotels and boarding houses and shops sufficient to make it very nearly a self-contained community. No longer, however, is the village the haven of peace it once was for a discerning minority seeking quiet sanctuary. Crowds and cars throng it's streets in summertime, reaching a climax on the occasion of the famous annual Sports. It is an itinerary halt for coaches in profusion, a whistle-stop for travellers en masse, a spot to dismount not for a survey of the landscape but for ice cream. The discerning minority now come out of season.

The parish adjoins Cumberland to the north and the boundary follows a skyline of lovely fells; within its limits are many popular hill climbs, with the curious rocks of Helm Crag a prime objective. Romantic paths and byways abound, notably in the twin valleys of Easedale. Everywhere there is beauty — best appreciated, nowadays, from some quiet eminence distant from the motor roads.

Grasmere

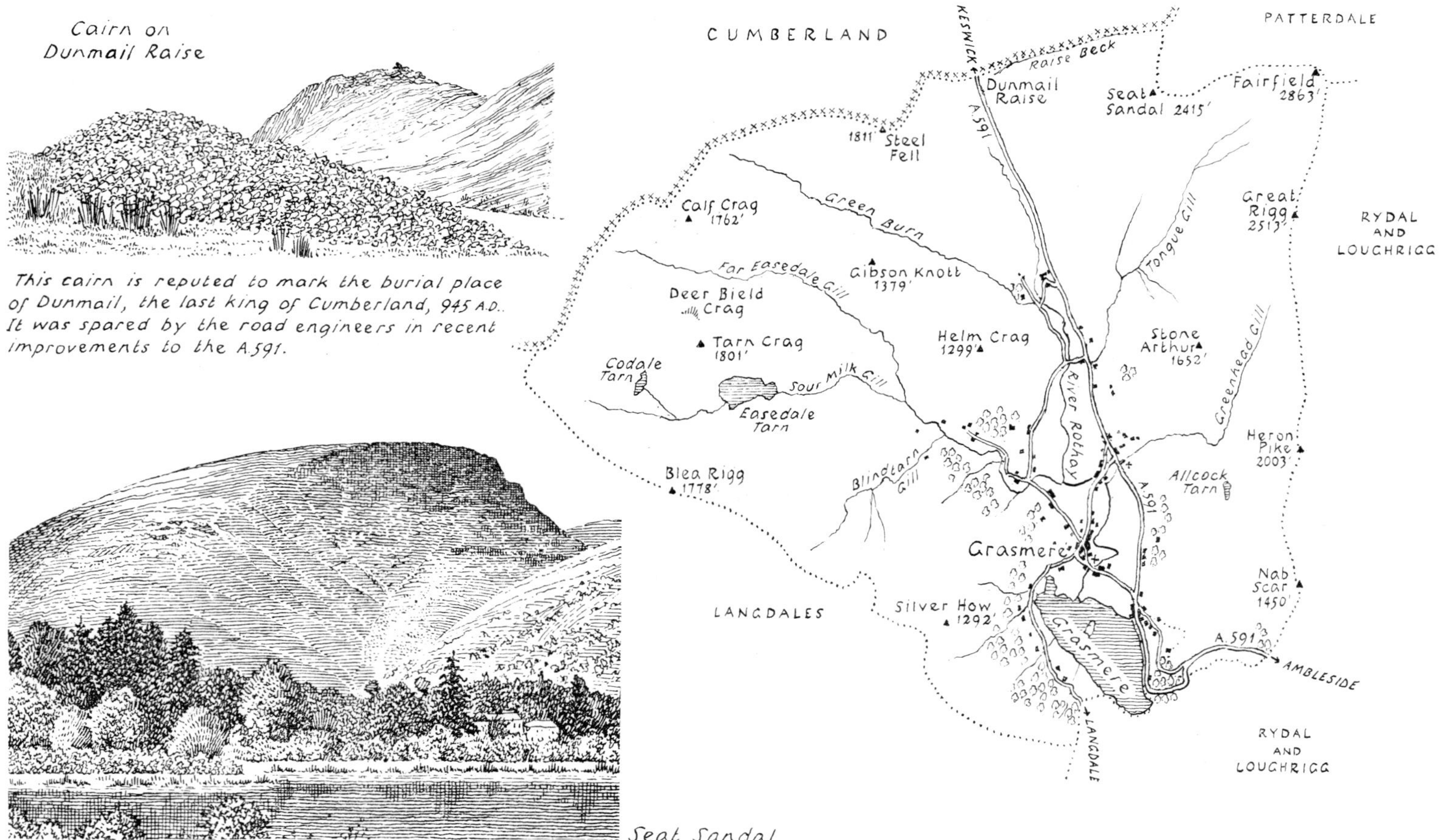

Cairn on Dunmail Raise

This cairn is reputed to mark the burial place of Dunmail, the last king of Cumberland, 945 A.D. It was spared by the road engineers in recent improvements to the A.591.

Seat Sandal

Grasmere

The Vale of Grasmere

Grasmere

modern Roman Catholic church

Allan Bank

Wordsworth lived at Allan Bank from 1808 to 1811. Later it was the home of Canon Rawnsley, a champion of conservation of the Lake District and a co-founder of the National Trust in 1895.

The Swan Hotel

"Who does not know the famous Swan?"

Grasmere

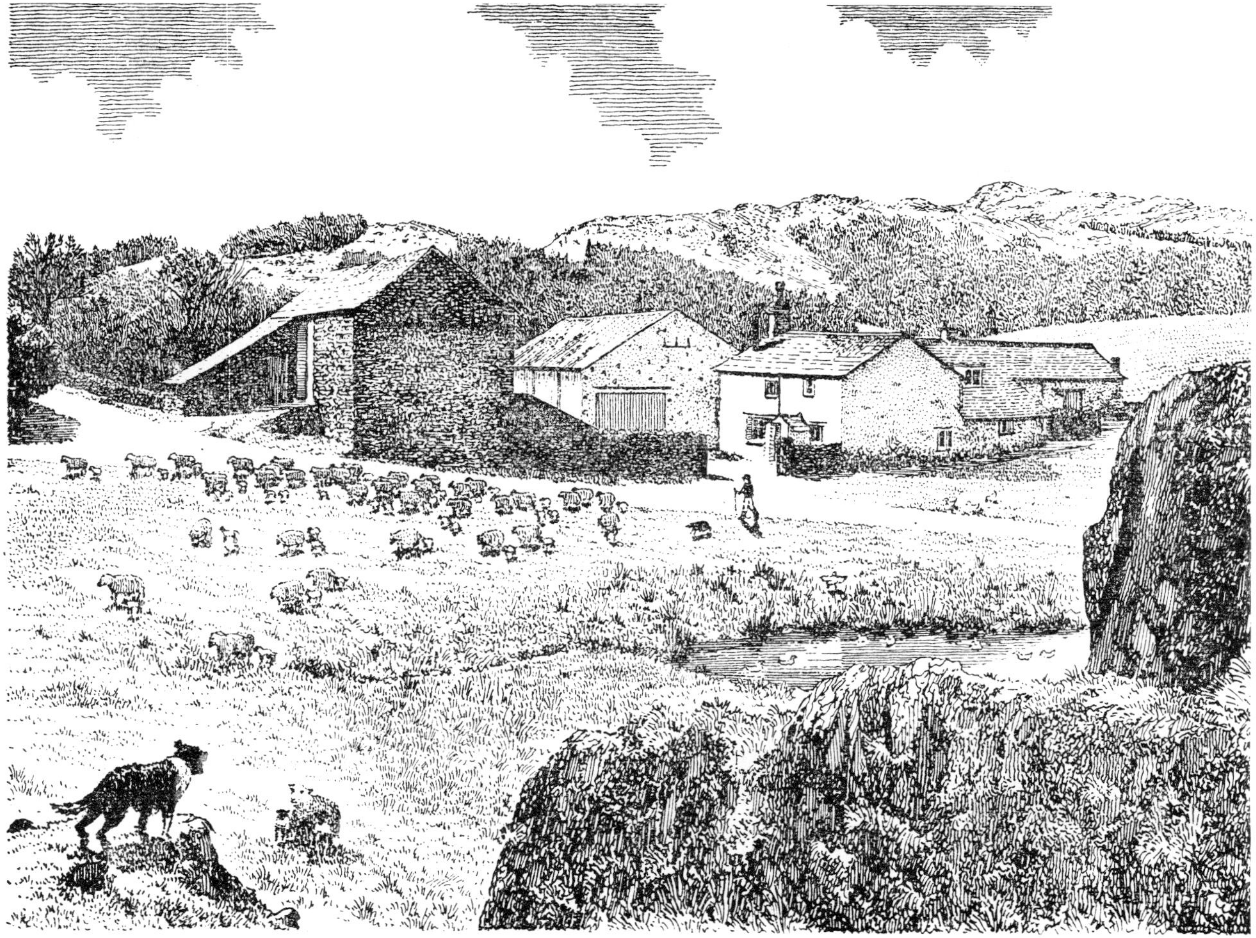

A Grasmere farm

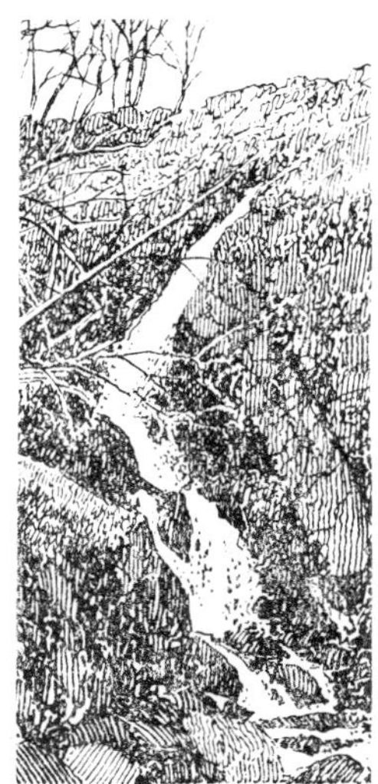

Waterfall, Green Burn

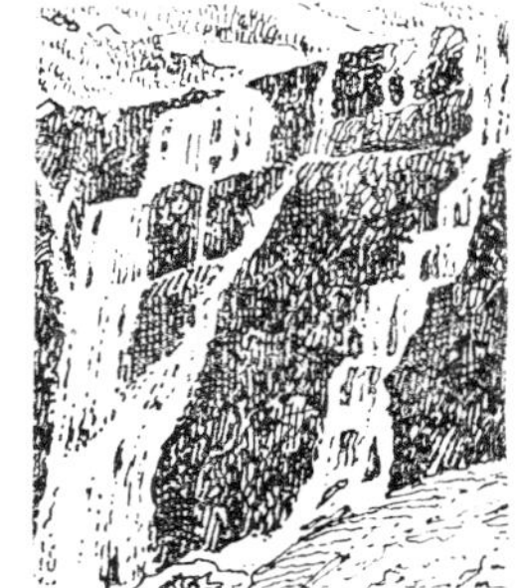

Cascade, Raise Beck

Grasmere

Visitors used to call at Dove Cottage in ones and twos to commune with Wordsworth. Today, 160 years after he left it, they come in coachloads to respect his memory. This modest dwelling, once an inn and now a museum of the poet's relics, has become the most-frequented building in the Lake District. It is a cottage turned shrine.

Deer Bield Crag,
Far Easedale

Grasmere

Of all Lakeland fells, Helm Crag is the most widely recognised on sight, but to almost all visitors it is known as "The Lion and the Lamb," a name derived from the silhouette of its summit rocks. The likeness to a lion and a lamb surprisingly occurs in different groups of rocks at either end of the summit ridge.

Grasmere

some Grasmere fells

Helm Crag

Tarn Crag

Silver How

Blea Rigg

some Grasmere fells

Great Rigg

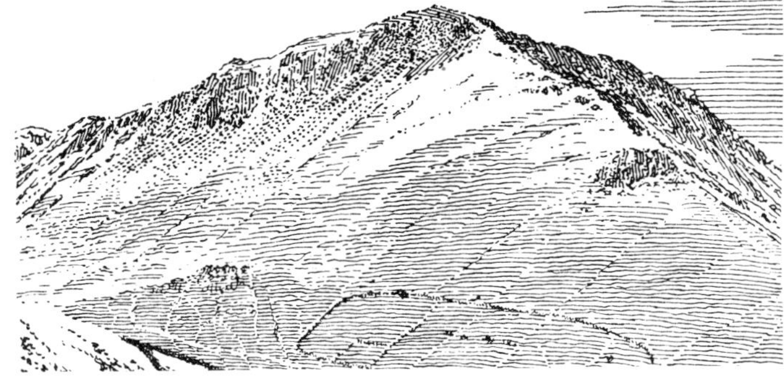

Steel Fell

Fairfield

Gibson Knott

Grasmere

In Easedale

left: Sour Milk Gill

right: Willy Goodwaller Bridge

below: Easedale Tarn

GRAYRIGG

Grayrigg is a moorland parish comprising the south-eastern end of the Whinfell ridge and extending to the River Lune at Low Borrow Bridge. For ecclesiastical purposes only, it includes the adjoining churchless parishes of Dillicar, Docker, Lambrigg and Whinfell.

The road A.685 out of Kendal skirts the wildest part of the area, crossing a bare watershed and passing below the two glacial combes that form such a spectacular background to the Lune Gorge when viewed from the north. The debouching valley of Borrowdale, here crossed by road, motorway and railway bridges in close company, joins the River Lune in scenery that is still, despite these defacing works of man, of considerable interest, enhanced by the near presence of a Roman Fort. Borrowdale in particular is a lovely valley, unspoilt as yet but living under a threat of flooding by the water authorities.

The parish, however, is best known on the western side, where rough pastures descending gradually from Grayrigg Common give way to green fields and scattered farmsteads, with a small population based mainly in the hamlet around the church. Here, although on elevated ground, the scenery is more sylvan: trees line the becks and quiet lanes; flowery hedgerows contrast with the stone walls of the moors. Grayrigg had a railway station (in the neighbouring parish of Lambrigg); since its closure the A.685 provides the main access to the parish.

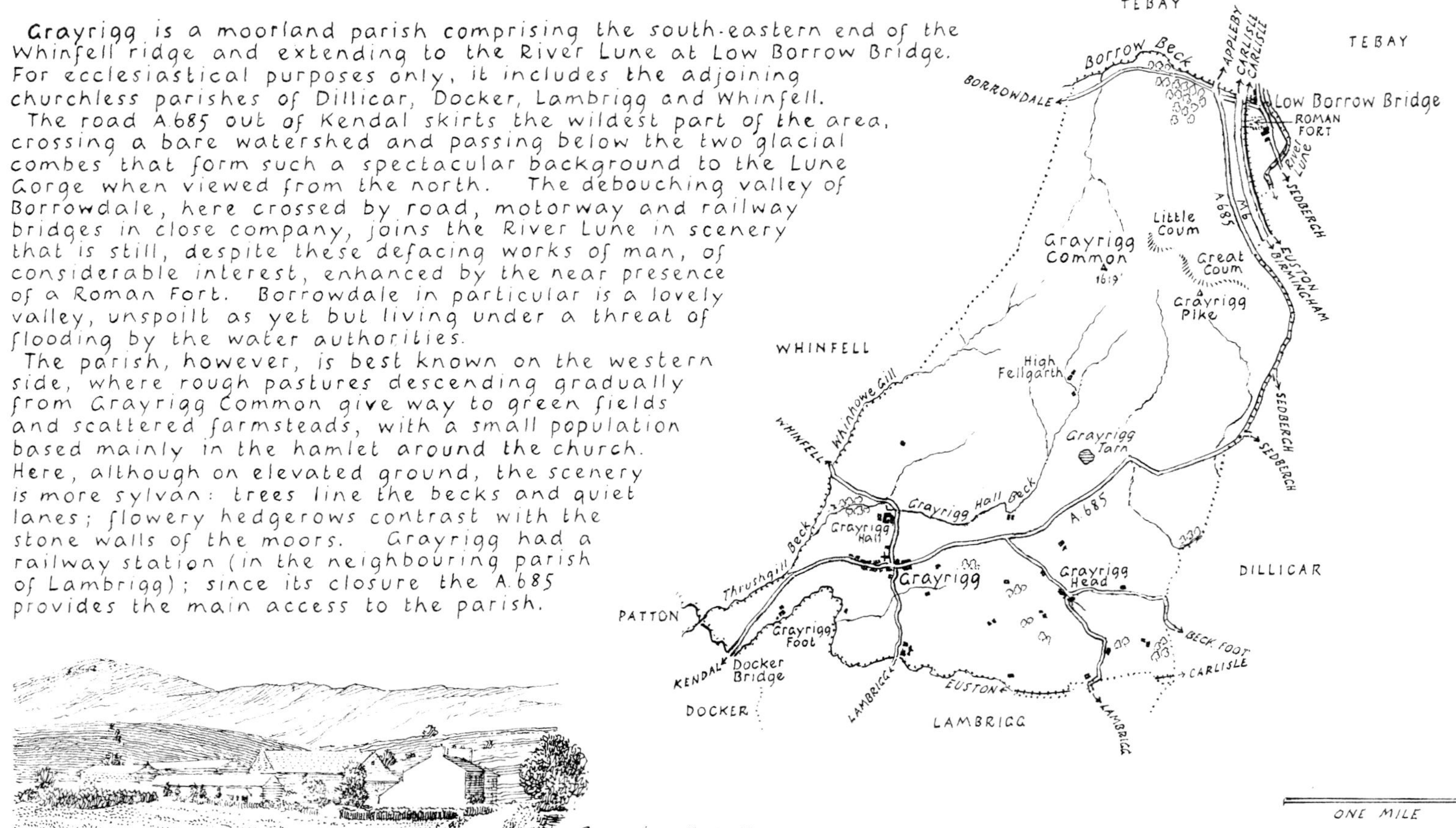

Grayrigg Hall Farm

Grayrigg

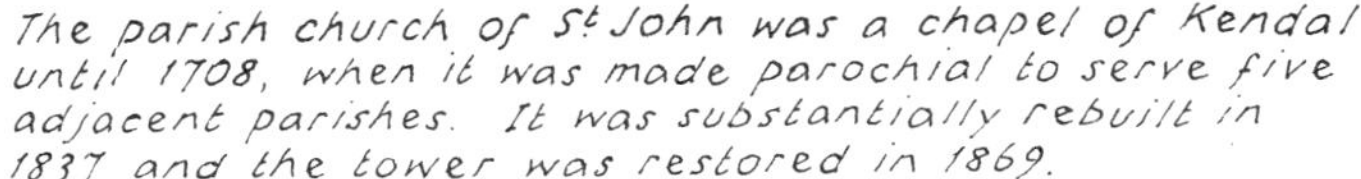

The parish church of St. John was a chapel of Kendal until 1708, when it was made parochial to serve five adjacent parishes. It was substantially rebuilt in 1837 and the tower was restored in 1869.

Grayrigg Tarn

The A.685 at Grayrigg

Grayrigg

The cairn above Great Coum

The summit of Grayrigg Common

Great Coum

The road in Borrowdale

Little Coum

Low Borrow Bridge

The Romans were the first to note the attractions of the little delta in the Lune Gorge where Borrow Beck joins the main river, and stationed a garrison here. Little is now to be seen of the earthworks of the fort but its existence has been confirmed by excavations, and discoveries on the site are displayed in Kendal Museum.

After the departure of the Romans the area reverted to its former wild inhospitability. A thousand years passed by with only the occasional nomadic visitor before the gradual cultivation of the valley floor by native settlers and the establishment of a few farms brought a change to the scene. A rough road linking Kendal and Appleby developed from the tracks of early travellers and threaded an uneasy course along the gorge between the hills, crossing Borrow Beck by a rubble span known as Low Borrow Bridge, which was restored in its present form late in the 17th century.

The construction of the main-line railway last century caused a major disturbance in the peaceful life of the valley but did not greatly alter its character. Recent changes in travelling habits, with emphasis on wider and faster carriageways for road traffic, have, however, brought a transformation. What was tranquil has become turbulent. What was rural has become urban. The sounds of the countryside are drowned by the noise of commerce.

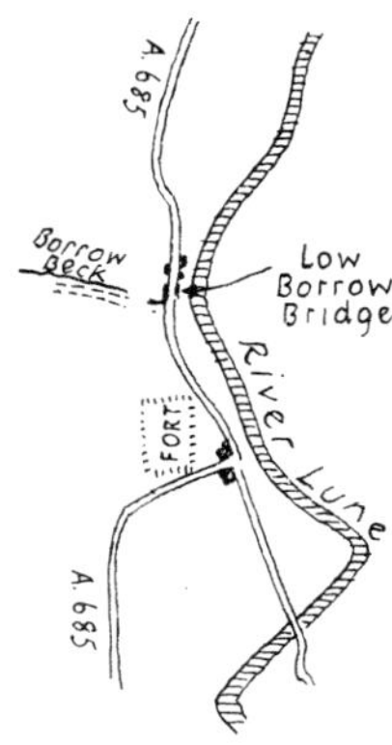

early 19th century

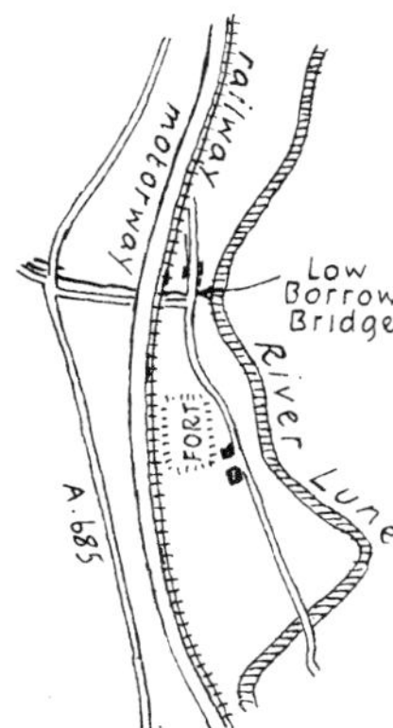

late 20th century

The Kendal-Appleby road, A.685, has been re-routed (as have the Borrowdale and Carlingill junctions) by massive removals of rock, leaving it flanked by an impressive cliff; hitherto a narrow, tortuous lane it has become a fast highway furnished with a carpark from which one may survey the wonders of nature or the wonders of man, according to choice. The new motorway, M6, where no man may halt, is laid near to this local road and alongside the railway.

Low Borrow Bridge will never be the same again. But it keeps its name, in the singular, although now there is a plurality of bridges crossing Borrow Beck: a new bridge for local traffic and a mammoth span for the motorway, both of concrete and contrasting sharply with the stone railway viaduct, a structure of Victorian solidity. The original bridge is quite insignificant in the new arrangement and virtually obsolete...... The hills look down inscrutably at the commotion below. They remember Low Borrow Bridge as it used to be. The scene was fairer then.

On this drawing of the Low Borrow Bridge area the site of the Roman fort is marked A-A

GREAT STRICKLAND

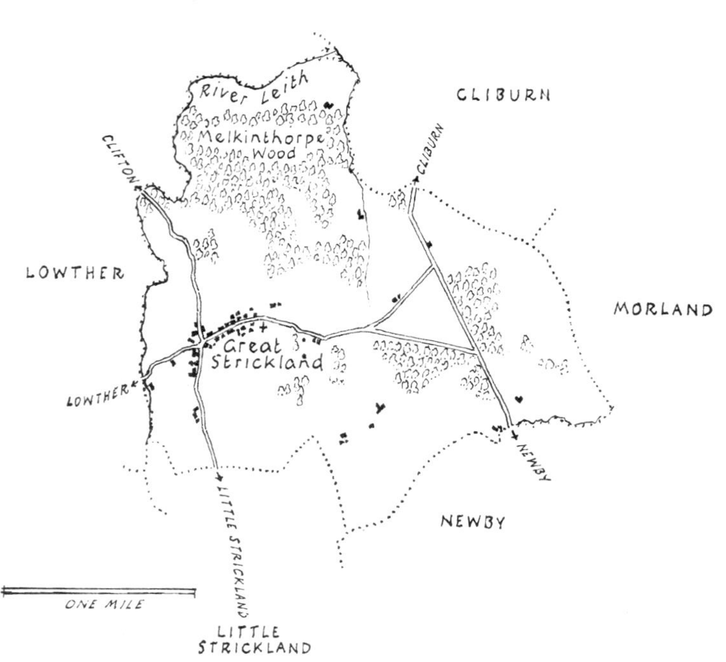

Mid-Westmorland, the area of undulating country between the A.6 and the River Eden, is the region most typical of the county and yet the least known. It is entirely agricultural, without a town in a hundred square miles and without a major road. Tourists pass it by. There is no guidebook for the area, no stately mansion to see, no grand hotel to stay at: no advertising is done for it, no publicity given. It has no mountain peak, no great waterfall, no outstanding natural wonder. No signposts point the way to places of special interest. The region is served by a network of country roads, along many of which a motorist is more likely to meet a farm tractor than another car. All is in low key. The scenery is extraordinarily pleasant, but unexciting. It is a green landscape.

Every few miles there is a village or hamlet: quiet places, all of them, usually straggling a road and embowered in trees. These rural communities go about their work uninterrupted by picnic parties and curious visitors. The environment is far removed from the turmoil of the towns. One feels that this is the way life should be lived.

Great Strickland is a village very much like its neighbours. Cottages line a country road, but singly, not in terraces. The few vehicles parked are farm tractors and waggons, delivery vans and travelling shops. There are no idle groups at street corners, no transistors disturb the peace, children behave with respect. Like most of the villages Great Strickland has both a parish church and a chapel, a post office, an open green and the luxury of an inn. Its river is the Leith, forming the boundary with Lowther.

Out of character, although secluded, is a caravan site: a sign of changing times, a herald of the coming of holiday-makers to this unassuming countryside, possibly the vanguard of a tourist invasion as the nearby Lake District gets more and more crowded. Not yet have the bed and breakfast notices gone up, nor the hotel advance signboards along the roads. These things may well happen. But better far Mid-Westmorland remain as it is.

Great Strickland

The church of St Barnabas was erected in 1872 (it cost £700!) as a chapel of ease to the parish church of St Mary at Little Strickland; at that time both Stricklands were part of the nearby parish of Thrimby.
An unusual feature is the wooden bell-turret.

The name of Strickland was originally *Stircaland*, according to the Domesday Book, and seems to have been adopted in medieval times by the Strickland family, in residence here before removal to Sizergh Castle near Kendal.

Great Strickland

The Vicarage

The Post Office

Waterfalls Bridge carries the Clifton road over the River Leith

HARTLEY

Hartley, half a mile east of Kirkby Stephen, has a deserved reputation as one of the prettiest villages in Westmorland. Well-spaced cottages line its street, along which flows the tree-shaded Hartley Beck on its way from the hills to join the River Eden, and a general air of quiet serenity is induced by the lovely surroundings. The village is a pleasant place indeed, and not without a page of history because here stood the medieval Harcla Castle, the ancient seat of the Musgraves: it is now but a fragmentary ruin with farm buildings superimposed on the site. The road through the village winds up an incline to an active quarry of immense proportions, served by a preserved section of the defunct Kirkby Stephen - Darlington railway. Above the quarry rises a wild Pennine moorland, culminating on the watershed in the remarkable aggregation of cairns known as Nine Standards, a prominent landmark and the subject of many legends.

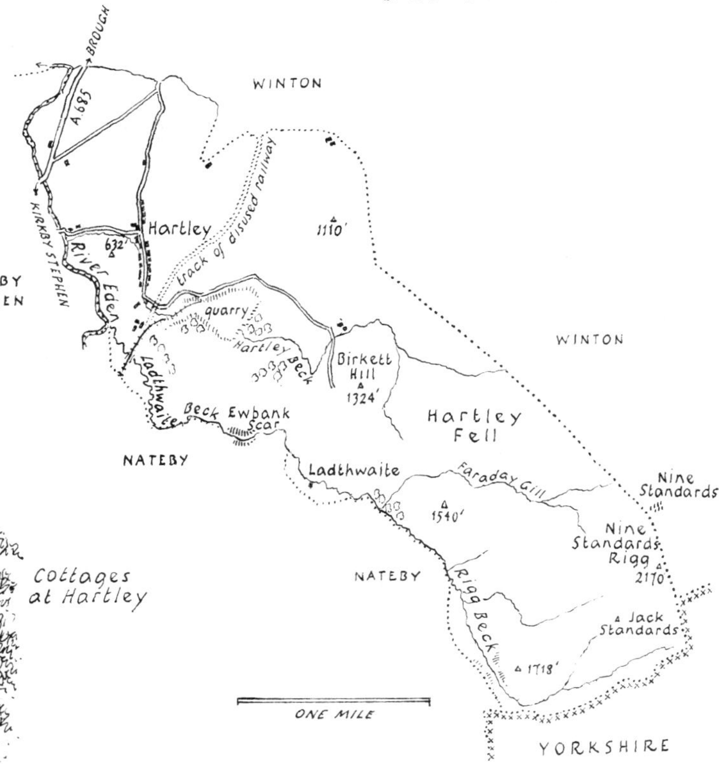

Cottages at Hartley

Ladthwaite Beck is a watercourse of unusual interest. In its upper reaches, as Rigg Beck, it is partly subterranean and flows in a canyon of limestone, a haunt of botanists; lower, at Ewbank Scar, it displays a waterfall, and near the railway viaduct at Podgill passes through an area of rocks noted for lichens and mosses.

Hartley

in Hartley village

Nine Standards

The Nine Standards are massive drystone cairns of uncertain age, built so well that they have withstood Pennine gales for centuries. Their remoteness, too, on the crest of a hill at 2150,' has been a factor in preserving them from wilful damage. They are conspicuously seen from afar and an impressive sight at close quarters.

There is no authentic documented explanation of the cause of their existence and, in the absence of fact, many legends are attributed to them, the most popular being that they were built to delude Scots invaders passing up the valley of the Eden, from where they are prominently in view, into the belief that an English army was encamped there. Less romantic is the theory that they mark the county boundary (actually they do not, standing well to the north of this as at present delineated; but they do indicate the boundary with the neighbouring parish of Winton).

That they are of considerable age is undoubted. They appear by name on 18th century maps and are mentioned in Sir Walter Scott's "Bridal of Triermain." The crest on which they are situated has also long been known as Nine Standards Rigg.

Ordnance column, Nine Standards Rigg

HELSINGTON

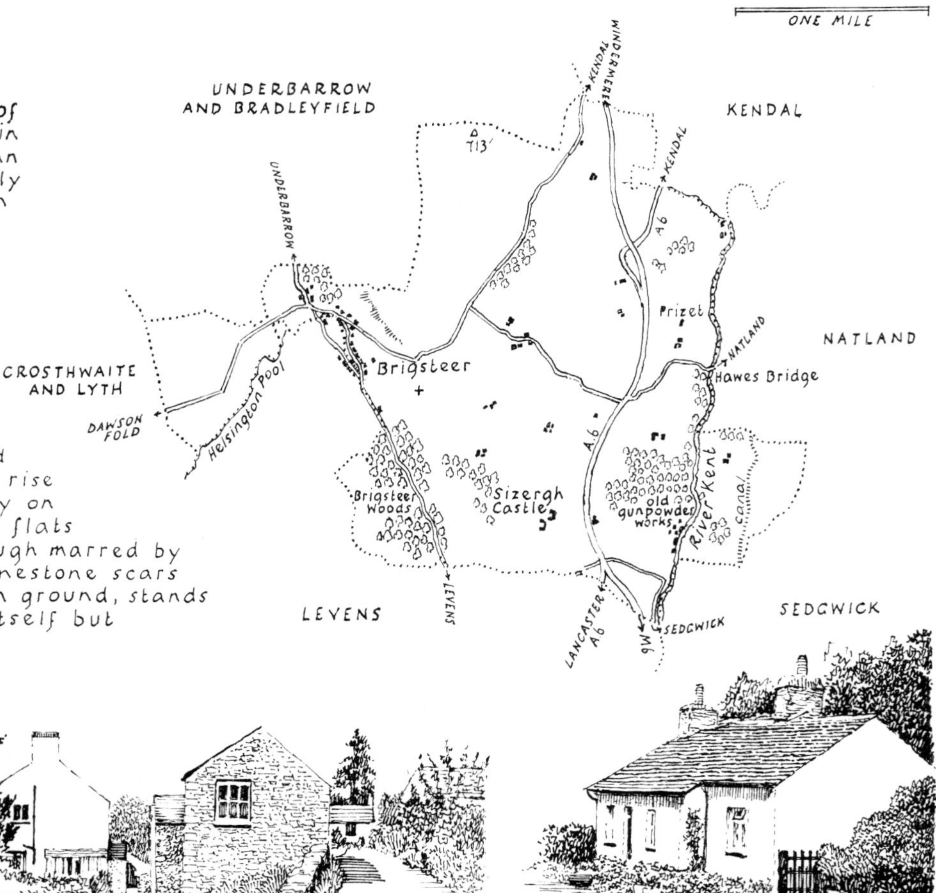

Helsington is a parish without a village of that name, although traces of earthworks in fields at Prizet, alongside the A.6, suggest an early settlement on this site. Today the only concentration of dwellings within the parish is at Brigsteer, a charming village shared with the adjoining parish of Levens on the edge of the Lyth Valley.

Helsington is entirely rural, rather surprisingly so since it is adjacent to the expanding town of Kendal, and, within small compass, exhibits a wide diversity of scenery. In the eastern sector the River Kent flows through woodlands that once housed a gunpowder works; across the busy A.6 and the new Kendal bypass, the A.591, pastures rise gently to limestone scars, which break away on the west to descend abruptly to the alluvial flats of Lyth. All this is pleasant country, although marred by traffic on the main roads, and along the limestone scars attains a spectacular beauty. Here, on high ground, stands the shy little church, not extraordinary in itself but commanding a view few others can match.

There are two popular tourist attractions, the most notable being the stately Sizergh Castle, owned by the National Trust and open to the public on certain days, and the other is the springtime display of wild daffodils amongst the trees of Brigsteer Woods.

Meeting of roads, Brigsteer

Cottage, Brigsteer Woods

Helsington

The parish church of St John, formerly a chapel of Kendal, was built in 1726. Restorations took place in 1857, 1898 and 1910.

Cottages at Brigsteer

Helsington

Sizergh Castle

Sizergh is splendid: a Westmorland treasure house. Although now the property of the National Trust it remains the ancestral home of the Stricklands, having been since 1239 in the continuous occupation of this family, many of whom have given distinguished service in various fields. The present head is High Sheriff of the county. Originally a border castle, built for defensive as well as residential purposes, it has had many additions and alterations during the centuries, but the fine pele tower remains substantially as built. The Great Hall and other rooms are especially notable for 16th century ornamental wood-carvings of rare excellence. Portraits by eminent painters, Elizabethan furniture, exceptional structural details and relics of the past make the castle a showplace of absorbing interest.

Certain of the rooms, and the gardens, are open to the public, admission being restricted to one day per week during the summer months.

The Courtyard and Main Entrance

Helsington

The delights of Sizergh Castle are not confined to the architecture of the building and the treasures within. The extensive parkland has many noble trees, and an area in the rear, below terraces, has a small lake remarkable for a profusion of aquatic plants. Nearby are rose and rock gardens and displays of conifers, shrubs and ferns, the whole linked by pleasant paths both formal and informal among flower beds and woodland groves.

The pele tower is the finest specimen of its kind in the county and the only one still preserved and furnished in its entirety. It was built around 1340, the walls at the base being nearly ten feet thick. There are three floors, linked by a spiral staircase, above a vaulted basement, the total height being sixty feet to the embattled parapet. An unusual feature of its construction is the attached turret rising twelve feet higher than the tower itself.

Helsington

The Snuff Mill

Once commonplace, now almost an anachronism, the waterwheel as a means of power for driving machinery has been superseded by other motive forces and it is rare indeed in these modern times to find one still in position; rarer still to find one in working order. Waterwheels have become tourist attractions.

Helsington Mill was built on the site of a medieval corn mill and used for marble polishing before being taken over for the preparation of snuff by the old-established Kendal firm of Gawith, Hoggarth and Co. Ltd over a century ago.

The waterwheel installed here was continued in use and ever since has performed its function, faithfully serving the 200-years-old grinding machinery inside. Paddles have been renewed but the spindle is original. It is the sole source of power, and the mill is thought to be the only water-powered snuff mill in England.

The water is supplied from the nearby River Kent by a system of races and sluice gates. The wheel never stops its rythmic movement as long as water is provided. It never complains. It is a most loyal servant. Helsington Mill has never suffered a power strike.

Looking at it, one really begins to doubt the efficacy of the manifold technicological inventions, the complex of complicated contraptions with which present-day civilisation is encumbered, that cause so much frustration when anything goes wrong. Here, at Helsington Snuff Mill, is a simple device that never fails, that uses only river water and returns it unpolluted, that costs next to nothing to operate, that produces no fumes or other noxious substance, that generates no heat that would impair the flavour of the finished product, that leaves no litter, makes no noise, and always works perfectly.

It could have a lesson for the 20th century.

Helsington

A surprising complex of ruined industrial buildings is screened by the trees of Low Park Wood on the west bank of the River Kent. These are the remains of the Sedgwick gunpowder works, so named although in the parish of Helsington. Still to be seen are the mill race, the deep pit for the waterwheel, the saltpetre house, the refining sheds, office and stores, all now overgrown with coppice, the site being carpeted with snowdrops and wild daffodils. Several dangerous open shafts call for extreme care in exploration of the site.

Gunpowder manufacture was an important local industry for more than a century and a half from 1764. Appropriately the main block of the Sedgwick works served as an ammunition store in the last war.

Sedgwick
Gunpowder Works

HEVERSHAM

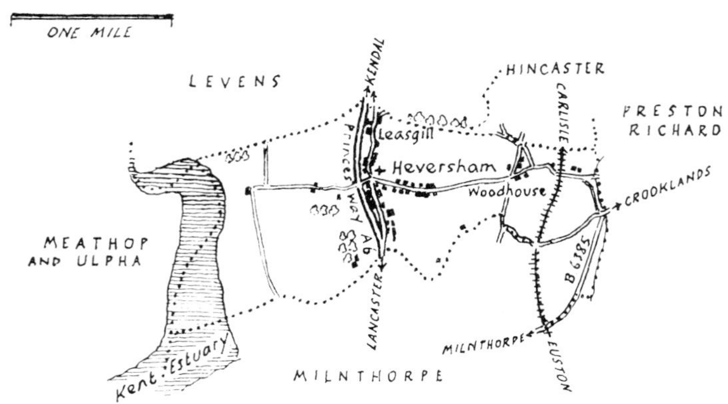

Heversham is a pleasant blend of old and new properties occupying a limestone hill with a commanding view of the estuary of the Kent. Once a busy village astride the main road to Scotland it was an early victim of traffic congestion and in 1927 the narrow village street was bypassed. The respite was short-lived, the village and precincts having become favoured as a residential area.

The Church of St. Peter was formerly the ecclesiastical centre serving the adjacent parishes of Levens and Milnthorpe also. It has 12th century features but has been much rebuilt and restored during its long history. The west tower is comparatively modern (1870).

Heversham

Heversham is best known for its Grammar School, which, being a boarding establishment with a good scholastic record, draws its pupils from a wide area It was founded in 1631 and moved to new premises in 1878, since when extensions have been necessary from time to time to meet the growing demand for places. Pictured above is the original school, still in use as a classroom, on the hillside above the church.

Westmerians of old did not all spend their leisure hours knitting or Bible reading: some found sadistic pleasure in cock-fighting, a 'sport' now outlawed. Heversham's outdoor cockpit is the best specimen of those still to be seen: circular, within a parapet, it is situated in the field above the old school.

Heversham once had the distinction of a railway station of its own. The main line (Carlisle-Euston) was linked with the West Cumberland line (Carnforth-Whitehaven) by a single-track branch between Hincaster and Arnside with stations at Heversham and Sandside, and provided a direct run from Kendal to Arnside. One of the engines, "Kendal Tommy" is still affectionately remembered.

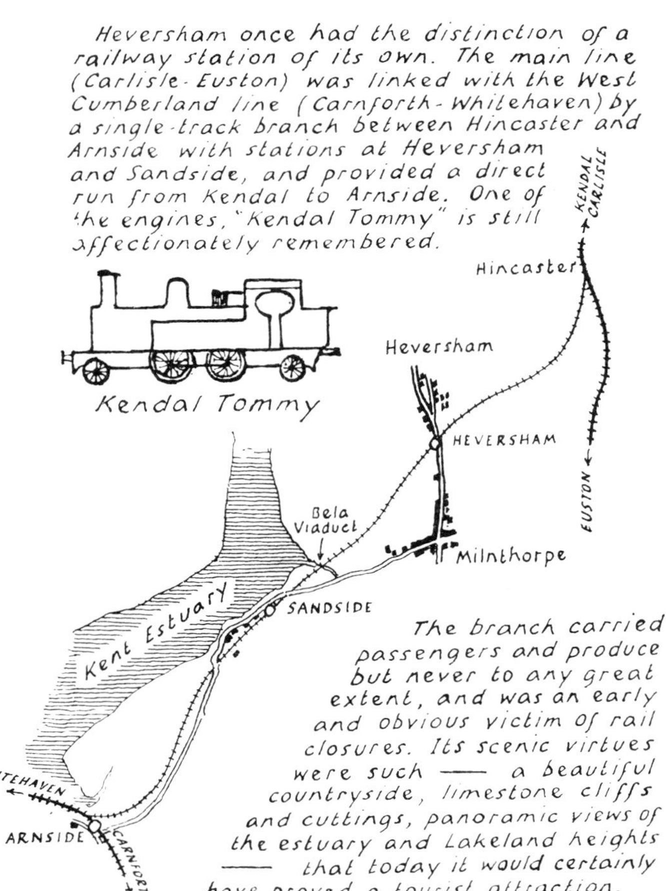

The branch carried passengers and produce but never to any great extent, and was an early and obvious victim of rail closures. Its scenic virtues were such — a beautiful countryside, limestone cliffs and cuttings, panoramic views of the estuary and Lakeland heights — that today it would certainly have proved a tourist attraction.

Heversham

9th century Anglian cross shaft in the church porch

Heversham Hall, now a farmhouse, has a long history. Parts of the fabric, including a ruined pele tower, are of the 14th century.

Deepthwaite Bridge is basically 17th century on its south side, here illustrated.

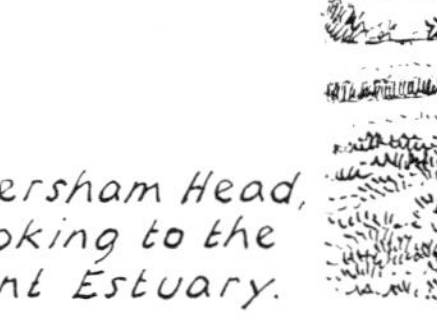

Heversham Head, looking to the Kent Estuary.

HILLBECK

The little-known parish of Hillbeck adjoins Brough to the north and is identifiable from afar by its terraces of limestone crags and a huge disused quarry. A side road leaves the A.66 to serve the small hamlet. The extensive woodlands of Hillbeck Hall, topped by the crags, present a lovely picture; in sharp contrast, to the east, the quarry has clawed a gaping scar in the fellside but the deep wooded ravine of Swindale Beck provides scenic compensation. Beyond the upper crags a moorland extends to the Yorkshire boundary.

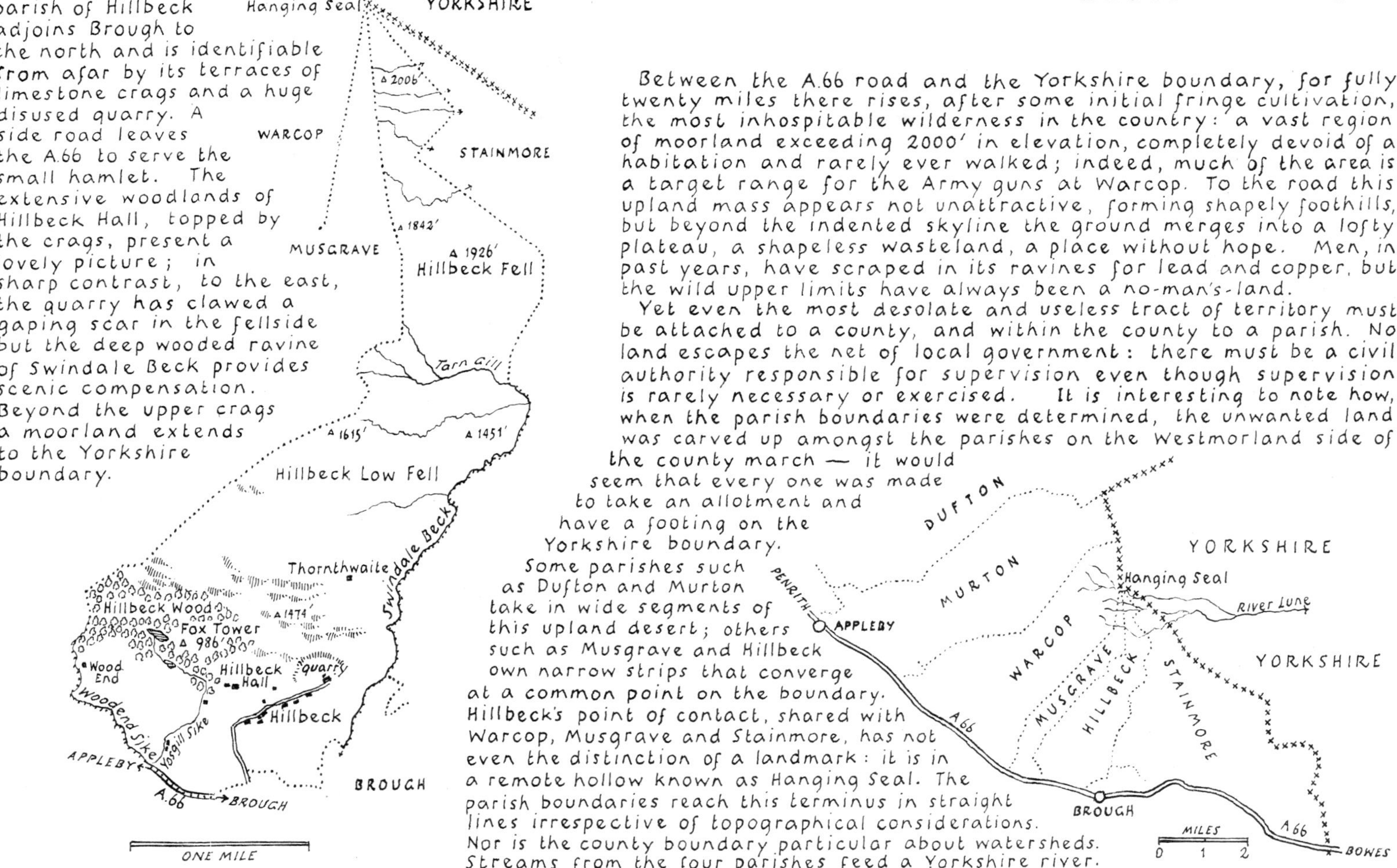

Between the A.66 road and the Yorkshire boundary, for fully twenty miles there rises, after some initial fringe cultivation, the most inhospitable wilderness in the country: a vast region of moorland exceeding 2000′ in elevation, completely devoid of a habitation and rarely ever walked; indeed, much of the area is a target range for the Army guns at Warcop. To the road this upland mass appears not unattractive, forming shapely foothills, but beyond the indented skyline the ground merges into a lofty plateau, a shapeless wasteland, a place without hope. Men, in past years, have scraped in its ravines for lead and copper, but the wild upper limits have always been a no-man's-land.

Yet even the most desolate and useless tract of territory must be attached to a county, and within the county to a parish. No land escapes the net of local government: there must be a civil authority responsible for supervision even though supervision is rarely necessary or exercised. It is interesting to note how, when the parish boundaries were determined, the unwanted land was carved up amongst the parishes on the Westmorland side of the county march — it would seem that every one was made to take an allotment and have a footing on the Yorkshire boundary.

Some parishes such as Dufton and Murton take in wide segments of this upland desert; others such as Musgrave and Hillbeck own narrow strips that converge at a common point on the boundary. Hillbeck's point of contact, shared with Warcop, Musgrave and Stainmore, has not even the distinction of a landmark: it is in a remote hollow known as Hanging Seal. The parish boundaries reach this terminus in straight lines irrespective of topographical considerations. Nor is the county boundary particular about watersheds. Streams from the four parishes feed a Yorkshire river.

Hillbeck

Helbeck Hall

Helbeck Hall retains the former name of the parish, derived from the early owners of the manor, the de Hellebecks. The present building is Georgian and occupies a magnificent site, with a parkland in front and a background of woods topped by limestone scars. Current maps prefer the name 'Hillbeck Hall.'

Fox Tower is a remarkable structure of limestone some fifty feet high, crowning an eminence in the midst of Hillbeck Wood. It was built by a former owner of the Hall for the purpose of observing the progress of fox-hunts in the district, over which it has a commanding outlook, and has a spiral staircase and a lunch room with a fireplace. It stands in private grounds and, being within the firing range of the army guns at Warcop, is subject to danger from this source.

Fox Tower

Hillbeck

A Hillbeck farmstead

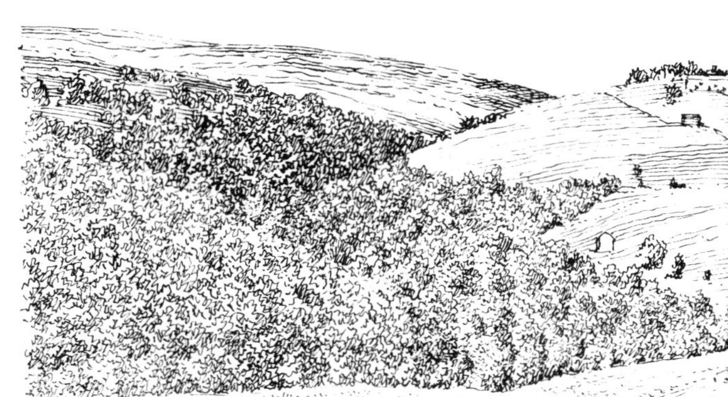

The wooded valley of Swindale Beck

Hillbeck Fell

Exotic weeds have taken over the task of refurbishing the landscape devastated by the now-disused Hillbeck Quarry, since man seems unwilling to do anything about it, and they have a thousand years of work ahead of them. The place is a shambles of collapsed buildings and spoil heaps, a sterile wilderness, a stony desert. In its heyday the quarry provided stone for the construction of the Warcop army establishment and was commercially prosperous.

HINCASTER

Although the small parish of Hincaster is crossed by two railways (one defunct), a canal (defunct) and a new link road connecting the A.6 and the M6 used by holiday traffic, the hamlet retains a quiet rural character quite undisturbed by these arteries of communication. As the name suggests there was a Roman station here, presumably on the route from Ribchester to Carlisle via Lancaster and Kendal. In the Domesday survey it is recorded as *Hennecastre*. This is a farming community, with some recent residential development. The most notable building is Hincaster Hall.

Hincaster is a parish without a church or a chapel or an inn or a shop. A small mission room administered from Heversham caters for the spiritual needs of the little community and a bus service on two days each week for the material.

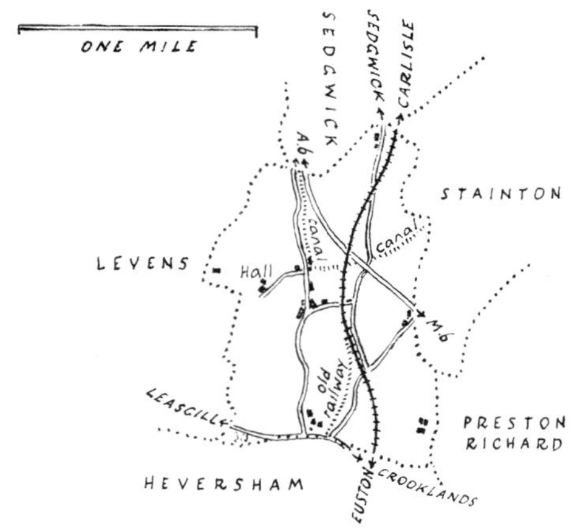

Hincaster Tunnel
above: *the overland horse path*
below: *the west entrance*

The location of the site of the Roman camp at Hincaster has long been a matter of much conjecture, there being no obvious traces on the ground either of a camp or access roads. The doubt may now have been resolved.

Early in 1974 an avid searcher after things Roman, a Mr. Billy Nicholson of Kendal, examined the spoil from the new link road then under construction, where it cuts through the canal basin and crosses the brow of Tunnel Hill, and discovered a large quantity of Roman relics, mainly pottery. Subsequent visits have yielded more. Subject to excavation, it now seems that the camp was on the crest of Tunnel Hill.

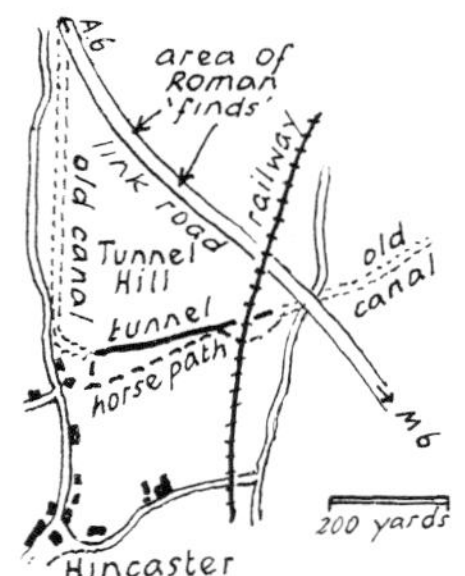

The Lancaster Canal, opened in 1819, follows an uneventful course through rural scenery south of Kendal, maintaining an even contour along the low hillsides of the valley of the Kent, but at Hincaster its one great excitement occurs where a straight tunnel of 377 yards carries it under a small hill to the Bela valley. Progress in the tunnel was by propulsion, manually, the horses being led by a path over the brow of the hill. This section of the canal is now dry and overgrown.

Hincaster

Hincaster Hall

Hincaster's proudest treasure is its 16th century Hall, a delightful house retaining many original features, notably the stone-mullioned windows and cylindrical chimney-stacks; internally, too, in spite of some alterations, the interesting design of the rooms has been largely preserved, one actually being constructed within the thick outer wall. An extension was added in the 18th century. There are farm buildings adjacent but the house is now occupied as a private residence. An intervening hill ensures its seclusion from the road through the hamlet and effectively conceals it.

above: the south aspect

right: the original building and 18th century extension.

Not the least of the many charms of the Hall is its wide panoramic view of the Lakeland and Howgill Fells.

HOFF

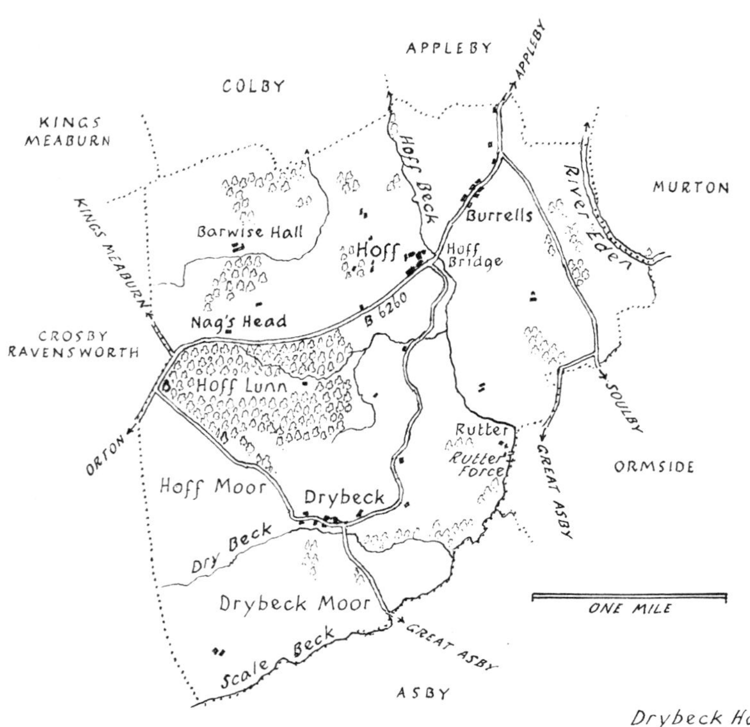

The countryside around Appleby is everywhere serene and pleasant, being entirely agricultural: a pattern of green fields and meadows decorated with mature trees. The parish of Hoff, adjoining the borough, is typical of the rural scene. Little clusters of cottages, well-spaced farmhouses and a few isolated barns are merely slight interruptions in the general picture of rich, undulating pastures and woodlands and grazing cattle and sheep.

Hoff is a civil, not an ecclesiastical, parish. There is no church, and a former chapel has been converted for residential use. Some of the material needs of the tiny population are provided by the New Inn, on the B.6260; two other hostelries on this road, the Nag's Head and the Crown and Falcon, have been adapted to other uses. There are three small communities: Hoff, the 'capital', Burrells, on the outskirts of Appleby (the name being a corruption of 'Borough Walls'), and Drybeck, on a stream of unreliable flow, where there are several picturesque cottages. Barwise Hall and Drybeck Hall are buildings of considerable interest.

A stretch of the River Eden forms a boundary but the relatively insignificant tributary of Hoff Beck, which is distinguished by a fine waterfall at Rutter, is a greater influence in the affairs of the parish.

Drybeck Hall 1679

Some of the minor place-names in the parish provide pleasurable exercise for the imagination: Lady's Walk, Cuddling Hole, Little Clinch, Big Clinch — but perhaps it is unfair to the good folk of Hoff to assume they are indicative of local pastimes.

Hoff

Barwise Hall 1579

two former inns

The Nag's Head

The Crown and Falcon

Hoff Bridge

Rutter Force

HOLME

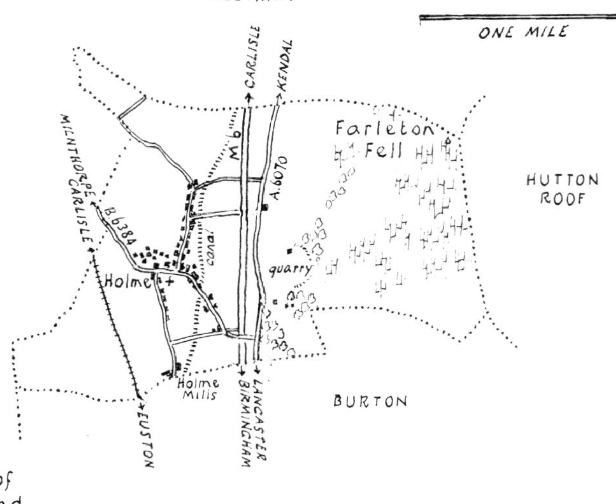

Holme, once a wayside village on the old north road, has developed greatly in the last two decades, and a spate of new dwellings, some sandwiched between old cottages, some laid out in estates, has radically changed its appearance to that of a sprawling suburb, and, sadly, its character. Nor has the motorway, constructed alongside, done anything to improve the amenities. Holme is no longer a welcome halt for travellers. It quite lacks the dignity of nearby Burton.

Holme is an ecclesiastical parish, formerly part of Burton until its own church was built and established in 1843.

The most interesting part of the village is Holme Mills, with a long history of coconut matting manufacture. Within this old industrial complex the terraced mill cottages retain a rather grim exterior, and the mill ponds, becoming reedy after years of neglect, provide sanctuary for swans, mallard and coot.

Holme's other main industry is quarrying, limestone being taken from a growing cavity at the foot of Farleton Fell, which is thereby disfigured. But the upper slopes and top of this imposing fell are an undisturbed and lonely wilderness of unusual beauty, a place of spectacular rock formations, and its soaring outline, familiar to all who live in its morning shadow, gives the landscape of Holme its greatest claim to distinction.

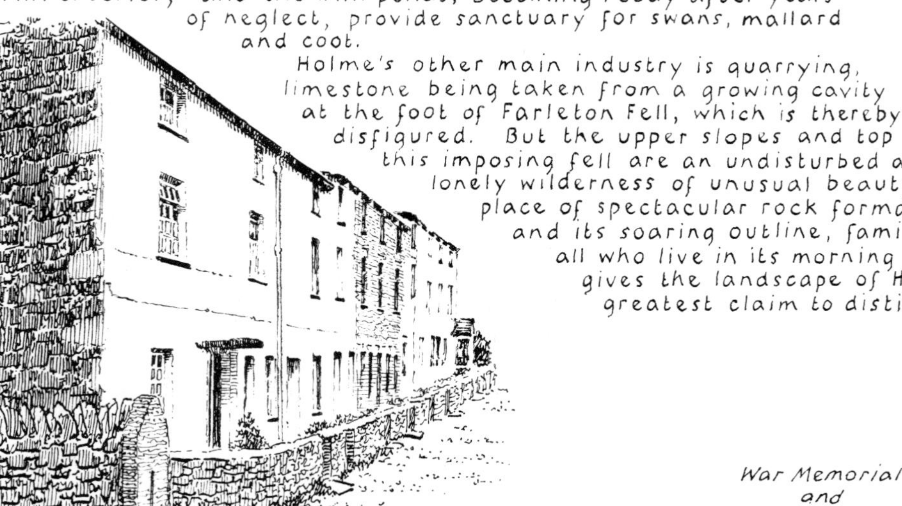

Cottages, Holme Mills

War Memorial and main street, Holme

Holme

The parish church of the Holy Trinity

The days of the Lancaster Canal, here pictured at Holme, may not yet be numbered. After being closed as obsolete and suffering a worse indignity by its use as a refuse tip on the section between Kendal and Stainton, a newly-formed Canal Trust is seeking to give it a fresh lease of life, not for commercial but for recreational purposes.

Houses at Holme

Holme

Farleton Fell

The one great dominating feature in the landscape of Holme is the massive limestone hill that rises steeply to the east of the village and is so pronounced in every view in this part of south Westmorland that all who live within sight of it know it as Farleton Fell (or Farleton Knott, a name strictly applying only to the summit). The fell makes a splendid backcloth to the scene; even better is the extensive panorama revealed from the top, where surface limestone in the form of cliffs and pavements makes a fascinating foreground. Man, with his usual penchant for destroying natural beauty wherever he finds it is, alas, eroding his heritage here by quarrying operations on a big scale at the base of the fell.

Farleton Knott

The highest point is the crest of an immense sloping slab of fissured limestone, indicated by a cairn.

HUGILL

Hugill is a name not well known outside the parish and even some inhabitants might find it difficult to define its boundaries. Much more familiar is the little community of Ings, which is within the parish on the busy main road A.591, used by traffic bound to and from Windermere. Indeed, alternative names of *Ings* and *Hugill and Ings* are occasionally applied to the parish, but administratively it is *Hugill*.

The pleasant environs of Ings, where two sites for caravans are concealed by woodlands, are not at all typical of the Hugill landscape. Rising from the shallow valley of the River Gowan are pastures that soon reach a wild moorland expanse of moss and heather: unfrequented territory culminating at 1400′ on the northern boundary. The southern terminus of this upland is the abrupt Reston Scar, overlooking the main road almost threateningly, the high ground continuing over Hugill Fell to a conspicuous cairn, Williamson's Monument. This section falls steeply eastwards to the deep wooded valley of the River Kent.

That the remote fastnesses of Hugill were once populated is evidenced by an ancient settlement, a site of archaeological importance.

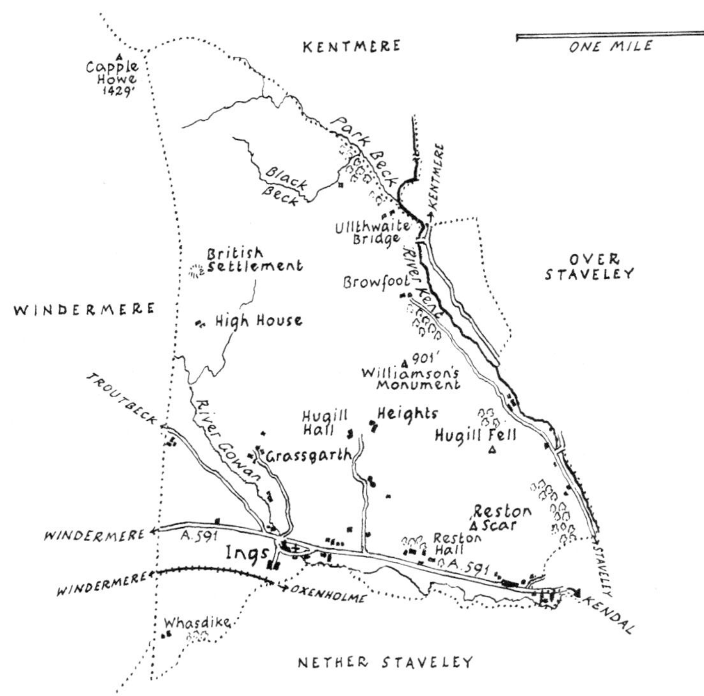

The parish church of St Anne, at Ings

The church, built in 1743, was the munificent gift of a local man, Robert Bateman. A floor of Italian marble is an unusual feature. An earlier chapel was situated at Grassgarth, a farmhouse later occupying the site and retaining the name of St Anne.

Hugill

Cairn on Hugill Fell

Williamson's Monument, High Knott

This fine cairn, restored in 1962, has a tablet with the following inscription:

In Memory of
THOMAS WILLIAMSON
of Height, in Hugil, Gent.
who died Feb. 13th 1797
Aged 66 years.
Erected 1803

Reston Hall was built in 1743 by Robert Bateman, the local benefactor who provided Ings Church.

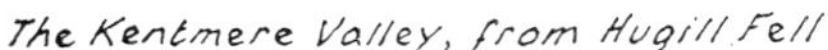

The Kentmere Valley, from Hugill Fell

Hugill

Ullthwaite Bridge (17th century)

High House

The British Settlement

The earliest British settlers in the district lived communally in hut villages on the fellsides above the then-swampy valleys. The Hugill village is a good example, being, as most were, enclosed by a walled embankment intended more to define the camp than to defend it, the area within forming an irregular pattern of hutments. The drystone buildings have not survived the weather of many centuries, but the sites, the footways between and the entrances to the village may still be discerned. The ancient boundary wall, for most of its length, has been used as the foundation of the present stone farm wall.

The site is in fields a quarter of a mile north of High House.

PLAN OF THE VILLAGE

modern sheepfold

Details from the Report of the Royal Commission on Historical Monuments (Westmorland) 1936

YARDS

0 20 40

A massive cylindrical chimney shaft and walls nine feet in thickness make High House the most interesting building in the parish. Dating probably from the late 16th century, it was originally the family home of the Braithwaites.

HUTTON ROOF

All roads to Hutton Roof lead uphill, and the village is well named, lying along an elevated slope with far-reaching panoramas across the valley of the Lune. The name is even more appropriate to the parish as a whole, much of it being a limestone plateau rising to the west of the village. This plateau exhibits remarkable rock formations of a purity of whiteness that, in sunlight, produces very beautiful effects while the summit provides an outstanding distant prospect of range after range of mountain and fell to every point of the compass: a superb viewpoint. Without this splendid natural belvedere the parish would call for little comment, being mainly agricultural and having few points of historical interest, although it is believed that the Romans had a road through the district and there is an ancient settlement near the boundary with Kirkby Lonsdale.

The small village has some pleasant cottages, many being occupied as holiday homes, and there is a caravan site for visitors: a rather surprising development because Hutton Roof is remote from the usual routes of tourists and served by narrow and tortuous country lanes. There are scattered farms, and, at Newbiggin, a long-established hamlet, this too being sited in the lee of spectacular limestone crags.

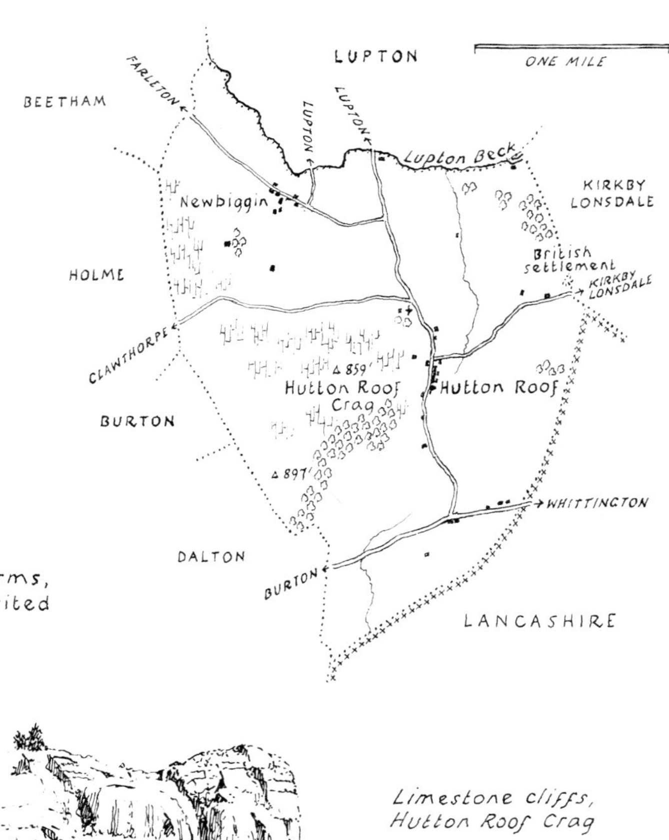

Limestone cliffs, Hutton Roof Crag

Hutton Roof

Almost hidden amongst mature trees, the parish church of St John was once a chapel of Kirkby Lonsdale. The present structure dates from 1881 and retains a few features from earlier churches on the same site, one preserved stone bearing the date 1601.

The war memorial, in the churchyard, is an uncut block of local limestone.

The village street, Hutton Roof

Hutton Roof

View from Hutton Roof Crag,
looking north-east to Middleton Fell,
Barbondale and Crag Hill
across the Lune Valley

on Hutton Roof Crag

This massive block of limestone, 15 feet in height, is a prominent landmark near the path on the lower slopes of the Crag. It is not a natural outcrop but a fallen boulder come to rest on embedded rocks that form a plinth, protected from weather erosion by the overhangs of the block.

This is a splendid example of a 'perched' limestone boulder and is the biggest of its kind in the county.

Limestone pavement and summit cairn, looking to Ingleborough

KABER

For a hundred years the parish had a railway (but no station), this being the branch line linking Kirkby Stephen and Darlington; a scenic joy, providing magnificent views across the valley of the River Eden and being itself an engineering triumph needing several viaducts to bridge the deep gills and side valleys, the Belah Viaduct in particular being a wonderful structure 1000 feet long and 200 feet high, built in 43 days in the summer of 1859. A document deposited in the fabric contained the following verse:

"To future ages these lines will tell
Who built this structure o'er the dell —
Gilkes Wilson with these eighty men
Raised Beelah's Viaduct o'er the glen"

The railway has been totally dismantled. The poem has become a lament, shared by all who knew this romantic line.

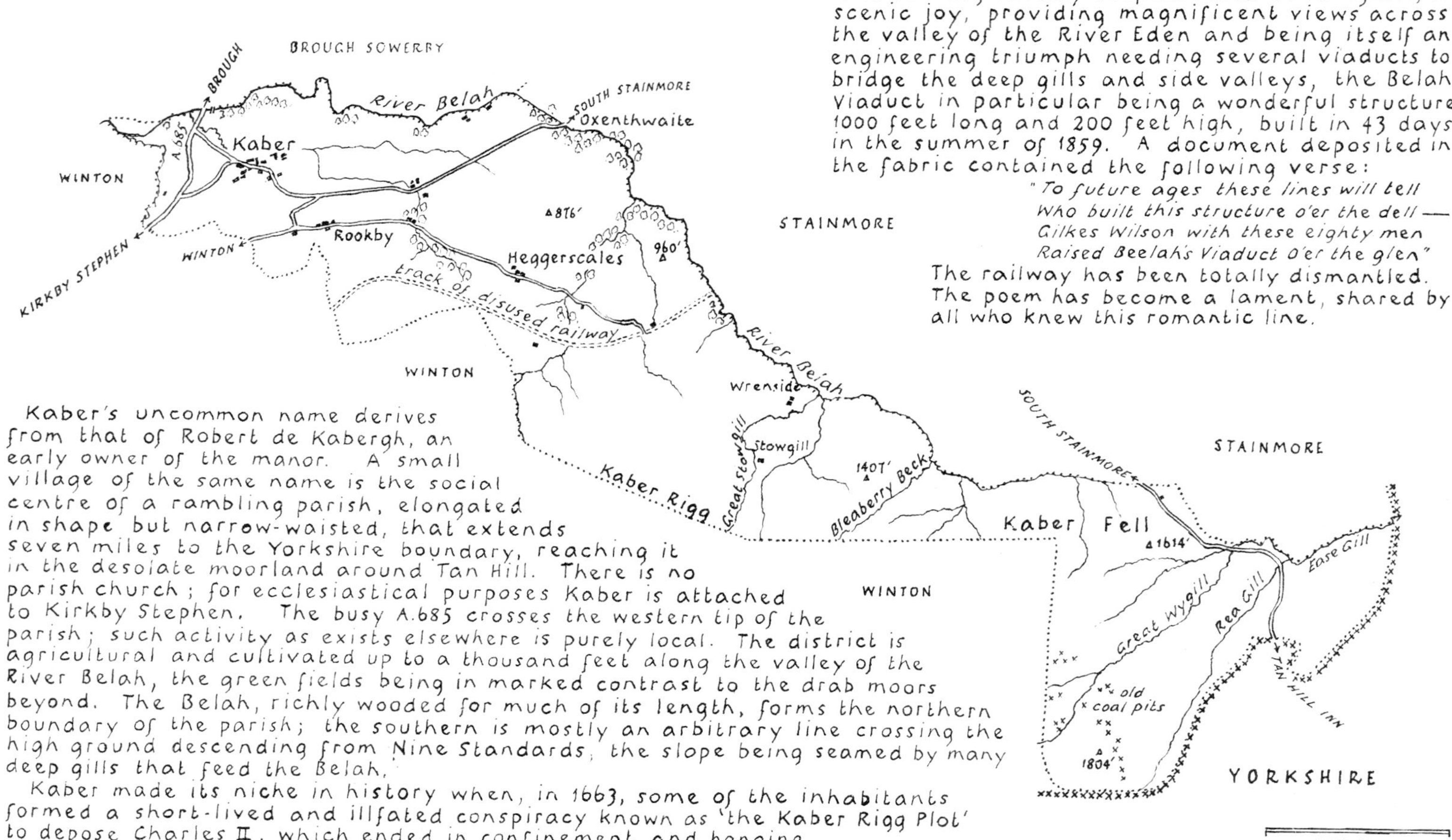

Kaber's uncommon name derives from that of Robert de Kabergh, an early owner of the manor. A small village of the same name is the social centre of a rambling parish, elongated in shape but narrow-waisted, that extends seven miles to the Yorkshire boundary, reaching it in the desolate moorland around Tan Hill. There is no parish church; for ecclesiastical purposes Kaber is attached to Kirkby Stephen. The busy A.685 crosses the western tip of the parish; such activity as exists elsewhere is purely local. The district is agricultural and cultivated up to a thousand feet along the valley of the River Belah, the green fields being in marked contrast to the drab moors beyond. The Belah, richly wooded for much of its length, forms the northern boundary of the parish; the southern is mostly an arbitrary line crossing the high ground descending from Nine Standards, the slope being seamed by many deep gills that feed the Belah.

Kaber made its niche in history when, in 1663, some of the inhabitants formed a short-lived and illfated conspiracy known as 'the Kaber Rigg Plot' to depose Charles II, which ended in confinement and hanging.

Kaber

Village street, Kaber

Rookby

Heggerscales

Oxenthwaite Bridge

Coal pits on Kaber Fell

In the remote fastnesses of Kaber Fell near the ravine of Great Wygill, the moorland is scarred by a profusion of coal pits, long abandoned and since filled in and naturally grassed. Output was for local needs only, none of the pits being sufficiently productive for commercial use.

A flooded pit shaft

Great Wygill

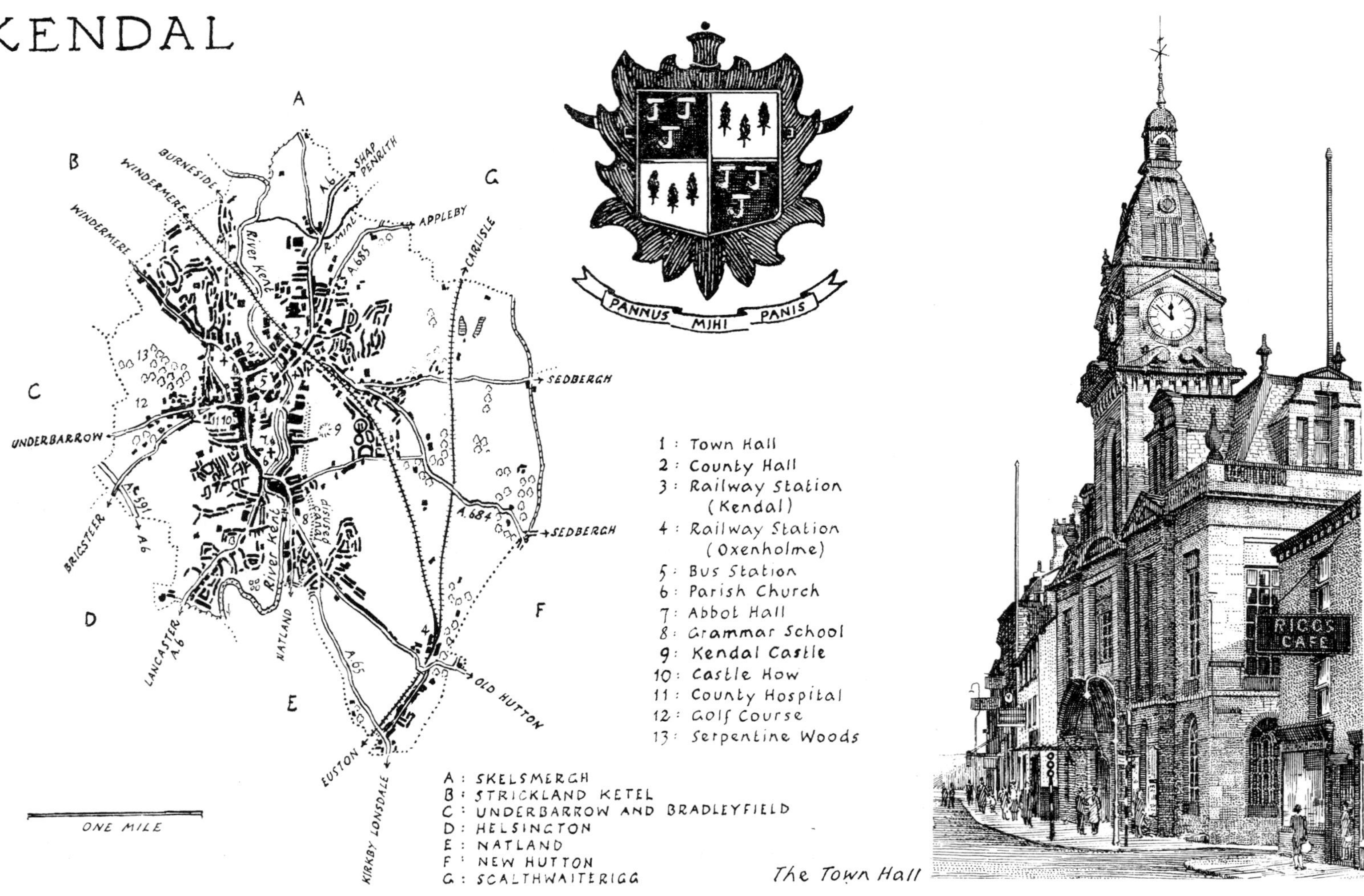

The Town Hall

Kendal

Kendal is a municipal borough, and an ancient one, having received its first charter of incorporation in 1575 during the reign of Queen Elizabeth. It is the largest town in Westmorland and the administrative centre of the county: three local authorities have their headquarters here, as have the electricity and water undertakers for the area. The town is the focus of commercial and industrial interests: there are large factories manufacturing a diversity of goods — mainly shoes and carpets and engineering equipment — and a miscellany of smaller businesses producing a wide range of distinctive commodities such as snuff, mintcake and horn; much of Kendal's output is of international repute. An insurance company has its head office in the town; a number of commercial firms are represented by branches. Kendal is an important shopping centre, with a market dating from 1189, but despite a resident population now exceeding 20,000, it is not the county town, a distinction held always by Appleby.

Kendal has a long history. There are traces of an early British settlement on Castle How; the Romans built a fort in a curve of the River Kent at Watercrook; a Saxon occupation is indicated by fragmentary remains. Not until the time of the Normans is there documented evidence of events. The Castle, of uncertain date, and the Church, built in 1232 on Saxon foundations, then became the focal points of an embryo town known as Kirkby Kendall that survived raids by Scottish invaders and plagues, and in due course pioneered a woollen industry of some renown, to which both Shakespeare and Scott contributed not a little by their references to Kendal Green. The trade prospered and the growing town adopted as its motto: *Pannus Mihi Panus* (Wool is my Bread).

The arrangement of the old town, with houses huddled in yards leading off the main streets, to which they had narrow barricaded access, is a unique feature adding a picturesque interest still although many quaint corners have been sacrificed to modern development. All the buildings were constructed in local limestone: hence Kendal became known as 'The Auld Grey Town.' Many of the older buildings have survived among new properties: if incongruity there be ascribe it to the new, not the old.

Collin Croft — one of the few old Kendal yards unscathed by 20th century development

Kendal

The Kent, one of the fastest-flowing rivers in the country, has always played an important part in the life of the town. It has powered waterwheels, caused devastation in times of flood, washed wool and for leisure hours provided a variety of delights. It nourishes the fertile dale in which the town nestles.

Kendal occupies a strategic position at a meeting of three valleys and is sheltered by limestone heights to the west and heathery moors to the east. It stands astride an ancient and historic trade route, the last outpost before the rigours of Shap Fell, and, in days gone by, was a welcome staging post for packhorses, passenger coaches and the mail. With the coming of the motorcar the town acquired a wide reputation as a holiday centre, its location, giving easy access to the Lake District, the Yorkshire Dales and Morecambe Bay, being unrivalled. The rapid development of road travel, however, proved a burden for Kendal's ancient thoroughfares and the town soon became a notorious traffic bottleneck, the congestion in the streets and especially on the main trunk road being only partly relieved by the recent construction of the motorway and a bypass. The branch railway to Windermere from the main line at Oxenholme passes through the town on a single track and under a threat of closure. The Lancaster Canal, now defunct, had its north terminus in Kendal.

In the midst of modern shopfronts and garish signs the old Fleece Inn (1656) stands defiant and unaltered, its upper storeys projecting and supported by pillars, almost the last survivor of many such buildings that fronted the main streets in days gone by. Internally, too, an old-world atmosphere is preserved. Now in picturesque isolation the Fleece Inn has what its modern counterparts have not: dignity.

Kendal

Many Kendalians have achieved distinction. Henry VIII's sixth wife, who survived him, was Katherine Parr, born in Kendal Castle. The portrait painter, George Romney, served his apprenticeship in the town, which has produced also eminent men of science, Everest climbers, a famous architect, and others who have given distinguished service in various fields. Mary Wakefield's name is perpetuated by a popular bi-annual Music Festival. The Lord Lieutenant of Westmorland, Paul N. Wilson, is a local man. Nor has the town lacked generous benefactors, their munificent gifts contributing greatly to the welfare of the inhabitants.

In the last few decades, the once-notorious insularity of 'the locals' has broken down to admit 'offcomers', and the infusion of new outlooks and ideas and attitudes has widened horizons and proved an advantage to all.

Cultural, social, charitable and leisure interests are well represented by an art gallery, two museums and a wide miscellany of societies and associations; religious interests are served by churches of all denominations.

Kendal's great attraction is that it caters for almost all tastes: it is small enough to retain its character as a country town yet large enough to provide for activities and pursuits of every sort. Few people who make it their home ever willingly leave.

It is a proud town. And not without cause.

Oddities in the streets

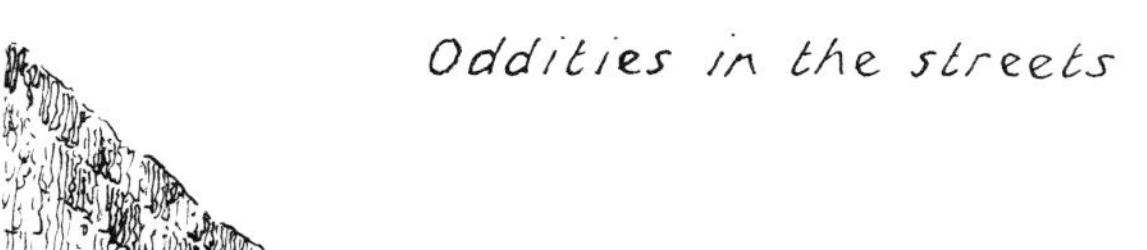

Steps leading down to platforms at the side of the river were provided for the washing of wool

Sign outside a former brush factory

Sign outside a chemist's shop

Sign outside a hotel

A panel over the entrance to Sandes Hospital incorporates the arms of the Shearman Dyers Co. and the date 1659.

Milestones outside the Highgate Hotel

The Ca' Stone is believed to be the base of an ancient market cross that formerly stood in Stricklandgate. From it royal proclamations are traditionally announced

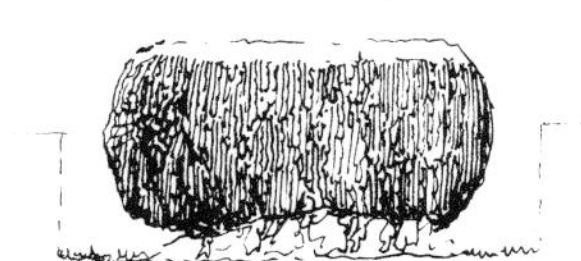

The Ca' Stone (Call Stone) outside the Town Hall

Kendal

Parish Churches

The parish church of the Holy Trinity is of Saxon foundation, but no part of the present structure is earlier than the 13th century and there have been many later additions and restorations. It has the distinction of being the largest church in the Carlisle Diocese, and is of unusual width, having five aisles. In medieval times it served as mother church to a very extensive parish and had several dependant chapelries. The interior contains many historical monuments and a collection of military colours.

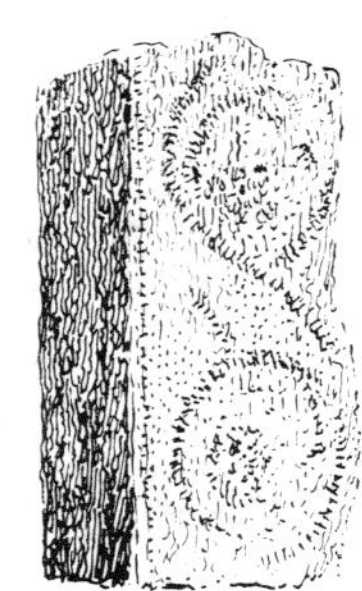

On a window sill of the south aisle is this fragment, 18 inches high, of a ninth century Saxon cross

The Parish Church of St George

St George's, built in 1839-41 and given the status of parish church in 1848, replaced an earlier chapel. The chancel is a later addition (1911). Originally the twin towers supported low spires, which became defective and were dismantled and removed in 1927.

St Thomas's was erected in 1837 to serve the growing needs of the north end of the town.

Both churches were built to the designs of a local architect, George Webster.

The Parish Church of St Thomas

Kendal

Historical Monuments

The origins of **Kendal Castle** are uncertain, and although substantially of Norman period, probably 12th century, it is thought to be a replacement of a Saxon fortress. It was the birthplace of Katherine Parr, the sixth, and last, of the wives of Henry VIII. Since the 16th century it has been in an advanced state of decay and is today merely a fragmentary and neglected ruin.

Castle How was an ancient fort of the motte-and-bailey type, probably early British. The obelisk superimposed on the mound is a memorial to the Revolution of 1688.

Castle Dairy, in Wildman Street, is regarded as the oldest house in the town, the present Tudor structure, dating from 1564, being adapted from a 14th century house on the site. It has retained its external appearance with very little change and the interior has also been largely preserved in its original state with dated items of furniture and fittings. When the Castle was in occupation, the house served as its dairy, and according to an unconfirmed and improbable legend, the two were connected by an underground passage. Castle Dairy has since been in continual use as a residence, and by arrangement with the Corporation, as owners, the tenants are required on request, but at certain times only, to allow visitors to inspect the premises.

Kendal

Cultural Centres

Abbot Hall, *a mansion built in 1759, reputedly to a design of John Carr, was after years of neglect fully restored and opened as a public Art Gallery in 1962, and nine years later a similar rescue operation provided a Museum of Lakeland Life and Industry in the adjoining derelict stable block. Both projects were financed privately, with generous help from the Francis C. Scott Charitable Trust, and are administered by Governors.*

Behind the rather grim facade of a former wool warehouse, the Borough Museum has a display of natural history specimens and exhibits unrivalled in the provinces, the collections of birds and animals being unusually complete and attributable to the gifts of two dedicated benefactors, Colonel E. G. Harrison and Dr. W. R. Parker. Additionally the Museum houses a wide miscellany of interesting objects, also donated, comprising archaeological and Roman relics, Lakeland geology, and items relating to the social history of Kendal.

It was an inspired idea, a few years ago, to convert the disused Highgate Brewery into a Community Centre for the Arts and Sciences, an object since achieved, mainly by private subscriptions.

Kendal

The Grammar School

The Grammar School was founded in 1525 by Adam Pennyngton, then living at Boston, Lincolnshire, and until 1888 occupied a building near the Parish Church; this became inadequate and the present more commodious premises were built in 1888-93 upon a site given by W. H. Wakefield, several extensions and spacious sports fields being added later. The School has been richly endowed with legacies over the years of its existence, these providing many scholarships. Several pupils have achieved later fame in various professions.

The old Grammar School, erected in 1588 to replace an earlier building on the site, was closed in 1888 upon the transfer of the school to its new site and since then has been used as a residence. Recently it was acquired, with the object of adapting it as a children's museum, by the Museum of Lakeland Life and Industry adjoining. It has served the town well.

Kendal

Streets

Captain French Lane

Low Fellside

Finkle Street

New Shambles, *opened in 1804 primarily for the use of butchers is a narrow arcade of small shops, out of character but with the virtue of providing the only pedestrian shopping precinct in the town.*

Up to a decade ago **Fellside** *had retained the appearance and unique atmosphere of the old town, being a picturesque disarray of cottages and steps and alleys, a limestone jungle, on the steep hillside overlooking the main streets. Now, new Council houses have risen on the foundations of the old. Little has been left unchanged — except the contours.*

Although defaced by too many and too large road and shop signs (omitted from the drawing) **Branthwaite Brow** *has kept its architectural quaintness and its cobbles.*

Kendal

Bridges

There are four road bridges across the River Kent in Kendal — three stone arched structures of pleasing design and architectural merit, and an iron one; Victoria Bridge, erected to commemorate the Queen's Jubilee in 1887, the only redeeming feature of which is safety. The stone bridges belong to an age, long past, when men allied beauty with craftsmanship, the iron one to an age, continuing into the present, when the only consideration seems to be utility. Victoria Bridge does not deserve an illustration.

Nether Bridge *is the most attractive of the bridges and is listed as a monument of special interest. It dates from the 17th century and was originally quite narrow, having been twice widened. A ford alongside was also in use until rendered obsolete.*

Kendal

Miller Bridge, *formerly named Mill Bridge, was erected in 1818 to the design of John Rennie; it was a replacement of earlier bridges, one of which was destroyed by a flood.*

Stramongate Bridge, *as seen today, dates from 1794, but parts of a 17th century structure are embodied. There has been a bridge here since time immemorial and it is mentioned in records as early as 1379, when it was known as "De ponte de Strowmondgate."*

Stramongate Bridge

Kendal

Farmhouses

Collin Field is a 16th century manor house, built in Elizabethan style and designed for defence. It was occupied for many years by a Secretary of Lady Anne Clifford, who was a frequent visitor. It has interior fittings of unusual interest.

Wattsfield is 17th century. Temporarily unused, it is the subject of current proposals to convert it into an agricultural museum.

Helsington Laithes is a 16th century house of imposing proportions and many distinctive interior fittings and plasterwork.

In Serpentine Woods

KENTMERE

Thanks to a single narrow access lane that the highways authority has never sought to improve, and the dead-end terminus that gives motorists no alternative exit, Kentmere remains virtually unspoilt and free from commercial exploitation. It is the loveliest of the few Lakeland valleys that have not yet succumbed to tourism. It is still a place for the discerning lover of beauty and solitude. Ways out of it are reserved for walkers.

The parish boundary is uncomplicated. It follows the skyline of fells around the valley, which is logical. It is a watershed boundary. Standing in mid-valley, everything in sight is Kentmere. Standing beyond the confines of the valley, nothing of Kentmere is seen..... The parish is a bowl, the rim of which forms its limits.

Approaching from the south, the only road access, the parish is entered where the valley of the Kent widens after a two-mile leafy avenue hemmed in by low fells and gives an unrestricted view ahead to the church, prominent on a hillock and backed by a mountain skyline. Beyond the church is a rocky maze of outcrops and, further, there is revealed the splendid amphitheatre of the head of the valley: a wild and compelling scene shadowed by lofty mountains, the birthplace of the Kent.

There is much of interest in Kentmere, best seen by those who travel on foot. This is walkers' territory.

Upper Kentmere, from Hartrigg

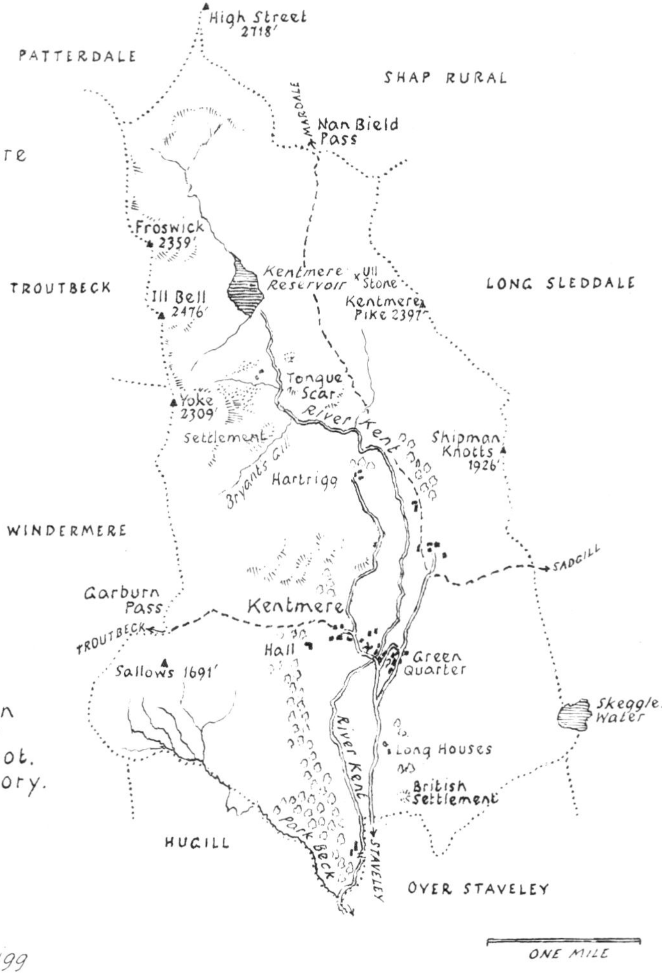

Kentmere

The Parish Church of St Cuthbert

The origin of the church is obscure, the early records having been lost, but although much of the masonry and rooftimbers are 16th century it is thought that a much earlier structure of the Saxon or Norman period occupied the site. In 1866 a major restoration was undertaken. It stands in a splendid position on an eminence in the middle of the valley, but its appearance at close quarters is marred by a patchy and stained roughcast, which, if removed to expose the rubble stonework, may enhance the visual effect. A memorial to Bernard Gilpin is inside.

Long Houses

Two Kentmere farmhouses

Scales

Kentmere

Kentmere Hall, the most interesting house in the parish, has a ruinous 14th century pele tower of four storeys with a vaulted cellar and a staircase; the adjoining manor house is of rather later date. It was originally the seat of the Gilpin family, a notable member of which was Bernard Gilpin, born here in 1517, who had a distinguished career in the Church and became known as 'The Apostle of the North.' It is now occupied as a farmhouse.

Mr. Paul N. Wilson has recounted the fascinating story of the events and proposals resulting in the construction of the reservoir, in an article 'Kendal Reservoirs' (Transactions of the local Archaeological Society, 1973).

Kentmere Reservoir

In the mid-19th century no fewer than fifteen mills on the banks of the Kent were drawing water from the river for driving their machinery, this being the only source of power, and often in times of drought production was halted or restricted. To avert this occasional failure of supplies an Act of Parliament in 1845 authorised the construction of reservoirs, in the valleys of the Kent and its tributaries, the Mint and the Sprint, to be administered by Commissioners (the mill owners) for the purpose of impounding water that could be released when needed to maintain an adequate flow in the rivers. Five reservoirs were proposed but only one was made — Kentmere Head Reservoir, as it was then named, completed in 1848. The others were never proceeded with because the cost was greatly in excess of the estimate and an alternative source of power, coal, became readily available as means of transport improved. The industrial use of the reservoir has almost ceased, but, surprisingly, it has never been adapted to serve domestic needs.

The River Kent has its source on High Street, oozing from the peat mosses into Hall Cove and there forming a definable stream engulfed by the reservoir after a rapid fall of one mile

Waterfall, Hall Cove

Kent Mere

Kentmere gets its name from a shallow lake that occupied the flat strath of the valley south of the church until 1840, when it was drained to provide more land for cultivation — a purpose not entirely achieved, much of the reclaimed ground remaining too marshy for the plough or even for grazing. Analysis of the former bed of the lake in the present century revealed the presence of diatomaceous earth, which when extracted and processed proved a valuable insulation material and led to the establishment of a works on the site. The draining of the lake was probably a factor in the erratic flow of the Kent, causing the promotion of the Act to ensure storage of water.

Ancient Kentmere

British Settlement, Millrigg:

The existence of an early village settlement in Kentmere has long been known, and the site, near the present farm buildings at Millrigg, has been examined in detail, partially excavated, and mapped, the plan revealing an arrangement of hut circles within a rampart enclosing an area of three-quarters of an acre, and four entrances.

British Settlement, Bryant's Gill:

The discovery of another ancient settlement in the valley was made as recently as 1974, when investigation of a site near Bryant's Gill, south of the plantation at the foot of Rainsborrow Crag, disclosed an extensive system of earthworks, not clear on the ground but revealed distinctly by the aerial photographs taken by the Ordnance Survey. The site has been authenticated, and a detailed examination is proceeding.

Nearby, at the ruins of Tongue House, other earthworks are being investigated.

The Kent Mere boats:

Excavation of the drained bed of the former Kent Mere by the Cape Asbestos Co. Ltd. in their extraction of diatomaceous earth has brought to light two boats in the form of dug-out canoes, believed to be of the Viking period. The better specimen is now in the National Maritime Museum; the other, fragmentary only, is on display at the Borough Museum in Kendal.

The site of the Bryant's Gill settlement

Kentmere

Rainsborrow Crag

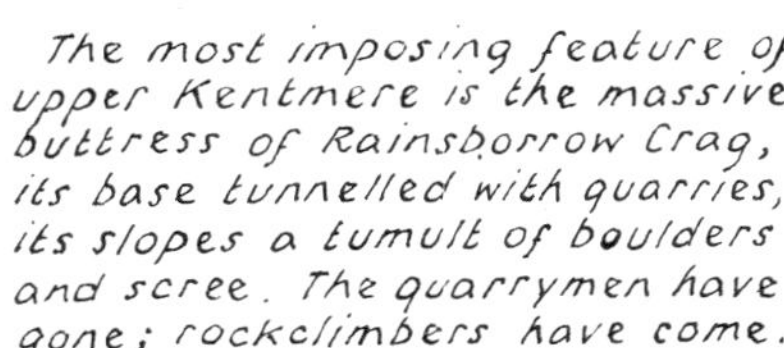

The most imposing feature of upper Kentmere is the massive buttress of Rainsborrow Crag, its base tunnelled with quarries, its slopes a tumult of boulders and scree. The quarrymen have gone; rockclimbers have come.

The fellsides of upper Kentmere are pitted with huge slate quarries, all now disused and sinister traps for unwary walkers.

Tongue Scar

Tongue Scar may be classed as another of the ancient settlements of Kentmere, for its rocks have housed a colony of badgers, generation after generation, probably for centuries.

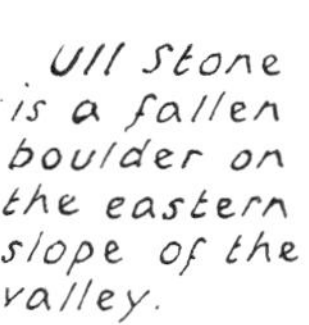

Ull Stone is a fallen boulder on the eastern slope of the valley.

Kentmere

The head of Kentmere

Kentmere

right:
the summit of Ill Bell

below:
the Ill Bell range, from the north

View north from Ill Bell

KILLINGTON

Present-day Westmerians tend to associate the name of Killington with a reservoir constructed last century as a feeder for the Kendal-Lancaster canal, and, recently, with a service station alongside the new motorway, both having adopted the name, but to Westmerians of earlier vintage Killington was an old-established parish of local significance and the home of some distinguished families. Having no part to play in modern commerce and communications it has declined in importance, and the five inns that once catered for the inhabitants and occasional passing travellers have ceased to function as such. Its story lies in the past and is found in legends of Cromwell's military occupation of the area and more tangibly in the romantic and picturesque buildings of Killington Hall, the old church and farmhouses and the remnants of mills.

There is no village. A cluster of cottages in a sequestered hollow near the church is the social centre of the parish and there are hamlets at Hallbeck and Beckside. The district is entirely rural, rising to low moors west of the River Lune, which forms a boundary of the parish. Two large tracts of upland have recently been tight-planted with conifers. In the north the Kendal-Sedbergh road, the A.684, and a link with the A.683 are the only traffic-routes of note; elsewhere the parish is served by narrow winding lanes, many merely of car-width, between fragrant hedges, and these tortuous avenues are sufficient to cope with the sparse local traffic and to deter the inquisitive tourist on wheels.

Killington (anciently known as Chillington), having contributed much to the history of the county, has gone to sleep. The world passes it by. It is ignored by outsiders — and nobody in Killington sheds tears because of this neglect.

Killington Reservoir, constructed in 1820, is not wholly within the parish of Killington, the western half being in Old Hutton, as is Killington Service Station also.

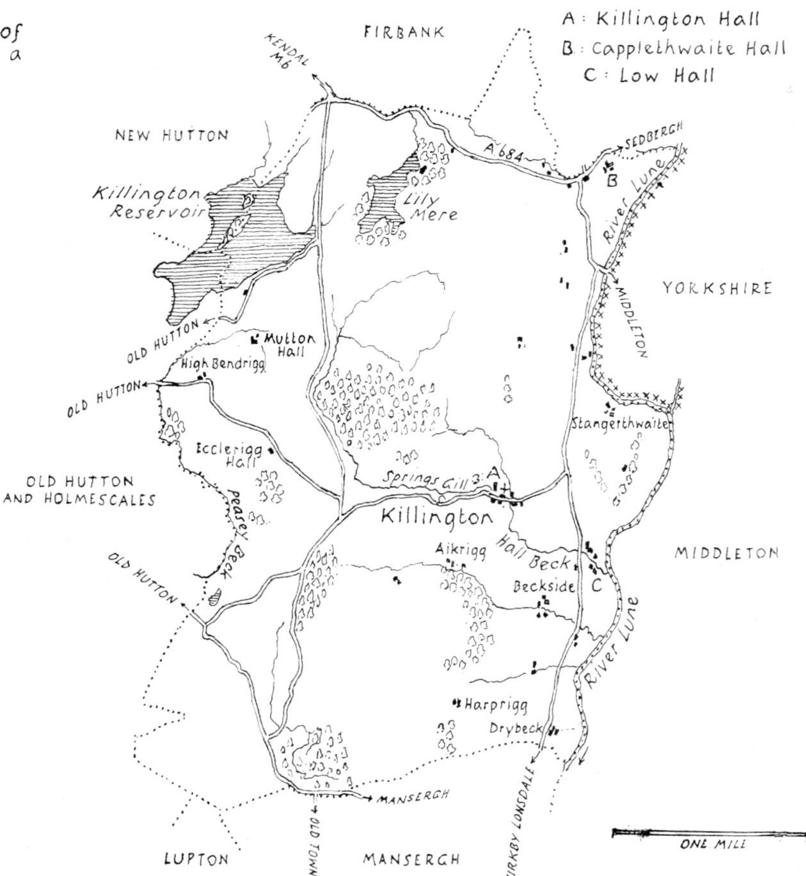

Killington

The parish church of All Saints was built in the 14th century, originally for the use of the Hall, and later adopted as a chapel of Kirkby Lonsdale. There have been major restorations, principally in 1868 and 1895.

Lily Mere

Killington

above : *Low Hall, known also as Low Hallbeck, has an interesting porch with inscriptions and a panel dated 1684.*

top right : *Capplethwaite Hall*

bottom right : *A cottage at Killington*

Killington

Killington Hall

Killington Hall was built as a fortified residence for the Pickering family in the 15th century, the Pickerings being of more than local distinction: they held office in the household of the King, Henry III. Subsequently the Hall had other distinguished occupants, notably a Thomas Kitson, Speaker of the House of Commons. It is believed also to have been used as a monastery at one stage in its history, there being a secret passage formerly leading into the adjacent Church of All Saints.

The main building, now a farmhouse, shows later extensions inscribed with the dates 1640 (attics) and 1803 (doorway). The front of the house is attractive, with panelled initials and heraldic symbols. Several alterations have been made in the interior of the house. The south wing, which rises directly from the little ravine of Springs Gill alongside, was a battlemented tower of two storeys. It is completely ruinous but retains two handsome trefoiled windows, seen on the left in the drawing.

KINGS MEABURN

Kings Meaburn gets its royal name from an early ownership of the manor by the Crown, taken as a forfeit from Sir Hugh Morville, the previous owner, for his part in the assassination of Thomas à Becket. The village, although pleasantly situated on an eminence on the east bank of the River Lyvennet, does not quite measure up to expectations induced by its proud name and lacks the charm of the neighbouring township of Maulds Meaburn (which Sir Hugh was permitted to retain as a settlement on his sister Maud).

But the Lyvennet hereabouts is seen at its best, winding along a wooded valley rimmed by a vertical cliff where since time immemorial jackdaws have found sanctuary. Here the scenery is sylvan.

Away from the village street, a few farmhouses are the only habitations in a rural landscape. There is a Wesleyan chapel, built 1866, but no parish church: for ecclesiastical purposes Kings Meaburn is served by Morland.

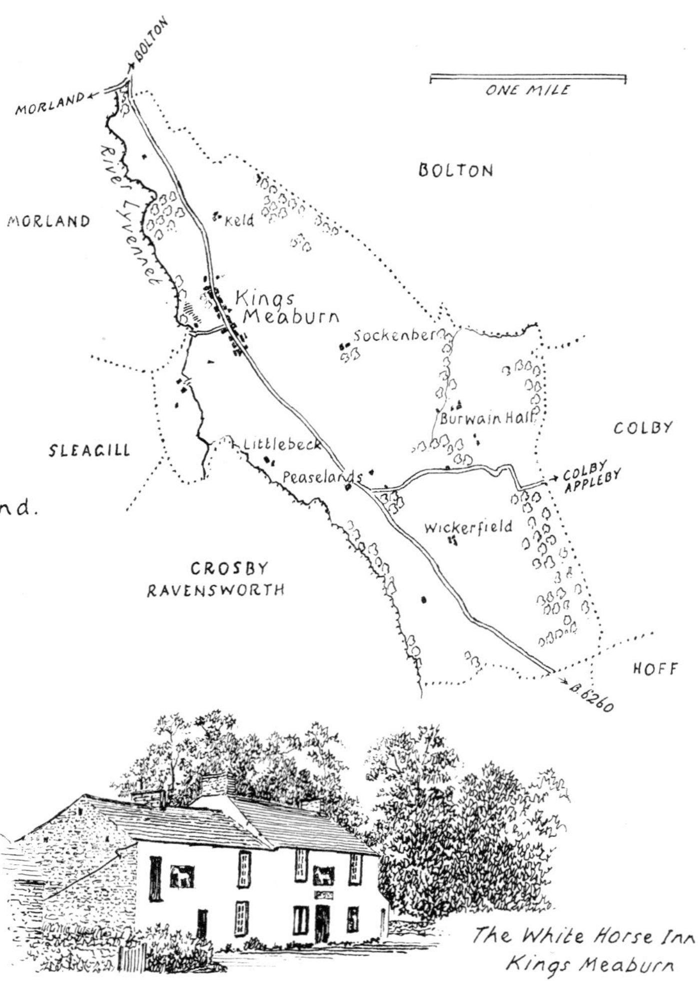

The White Horse Inn
Kings Meaburn

Peaselands: a farmhouse (built 1707) with a topiary garden

The decline of rural industries

The most significant change in the countryside over the past century has been the sad decline of rural crafts and industries. Gone are the village blacksmiths, the cobblers, the workers in iron, the wheelwrights. Gone are the hundred little Westmorland mills that stood at the side of streams and, each with its waterwheel, made goods and produce to meet the material needs of the surrounding district. Power was supplied by the wheel, and a handful of workers milled corn or made bobbins or woollens for local use. Almost all of the rural mills have ceased to operate: some have been converted to other purposes, mainly residential; some stand as gaunt memorials of days gone by, deserted, derelict, ivy-covered, with the wheel rotting; some are reduced to a heap of stones amongst rampant weeds. Not one has been saved as a working museum..... *Pictured above is an old mill by the River Lyvennet at Kings Meaburn.*

Kings Meaburn

KIRKBY LONSDALE

Kirkby Lonsdale is a small market town in the southeast corner of Westmorland: the 'capital' of the mid-Lune valley. Its status as a town derives more from its appearance than its population or size, the cluster of tall buildings and hotels and shops, crowded in small compass, fostering the impression of an active and independent urban community. A town in miniature perhaps... but still a town.

Happily the planners have been content merely to bypass the through traffic, and the dignified antiquity of its streets and alleys has suffered little: the centre and older parts of the town retain their original aspect and are a joy to look upon. Few towns like Kirkby remain. Few towns have kept their romance.

Neolithic man, the Celts, Romans, Saxons, Vikings, Danes and Normans have all left evidences of settlement in the district long before the town took shape. Kirkby's buildings are old but its history is very much older.

The war memorial

The Parish Church of St. Mary the Virgin has a Saxon foundation but the present building is mainly 12th century and has retained, in spite of renewals and extensions, splendid fragments of Norman architecture.

A screen of buildings hides the church from the main street, but its position on a high bank of the Lune affords a fine prospect over the valley to the fells.

Kirkby Lonsdale

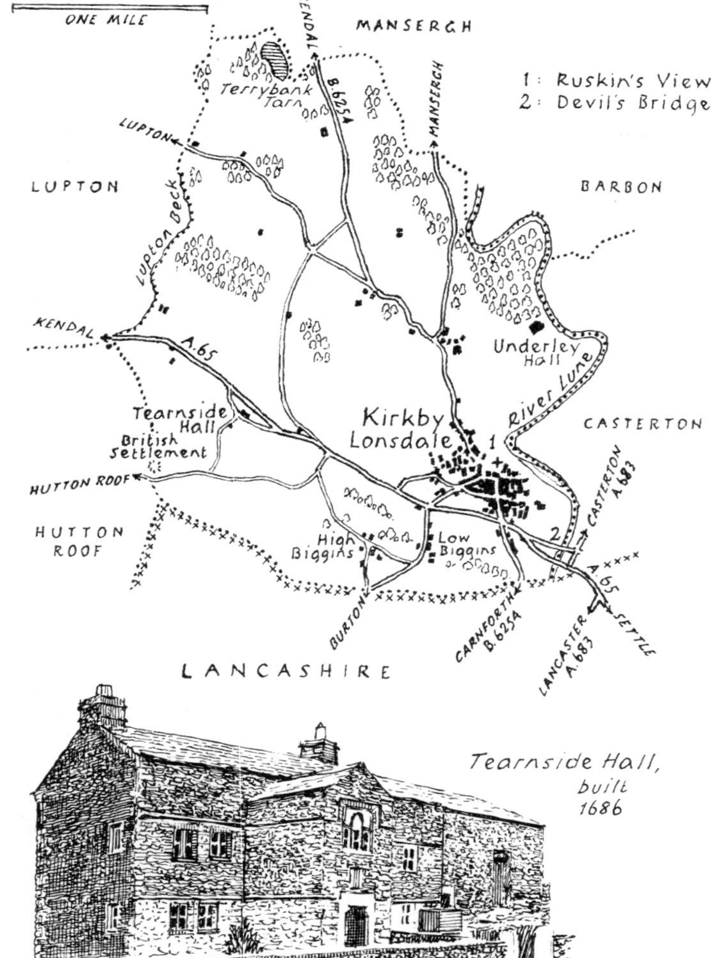

Tearnside Hall, built 1686

Along a terrace north of the church is a celebrated view of the Lune, painted by Turner and described by Ruskin as one of the loveliest scenes in England — after which eulogy the Kirkby folk were proud to name it as 'Ruskin's View'. One can understand Ruskin's enthusiasm for this beautiful prospect without sharing his opinion.

In a field on the west boundary of the parish, adjoining the by-road to Hutton Roof, are the remains of an ancient settlement. The parapets are distinct but only a few stones of the rampart wall have survived. Excavations have proved inconclusive.

The rampart

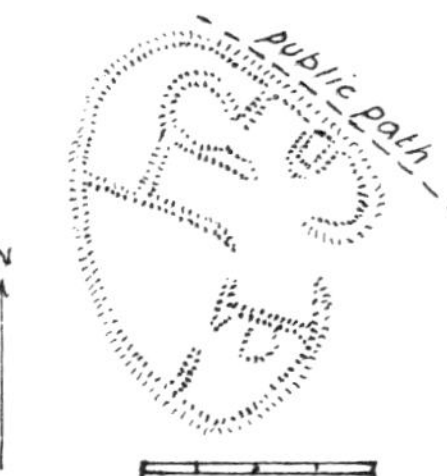

PLAN OF SETTLEMENT

Kirkby Lonsdale

right: *The Horsemarket*

below: *The Manor House, Mill Brow*

bottom right: *Market Street*

Kirkby Lonsdale

Situated in a spacious parkland north of the town, Underley Hall was built as a mansion in 1825-31 to the design of George Webster, a Kendal architect. It became the home of the Earl of Bective, and later of Lord and Lady Henry Cavendish-Bentinck. Its present use is that of a Roman Catholic diocesan college and seminary, St. Michael's.

The mediaeval Devil's Bridge over the Lune, a graceful structure of three ribbed arches, is a renowned attraction and a familiar sight to travellers on the nearby A.65, many of whom halt awhile at this lovely stretch of the river, which is also a favourite haunt of photographers and artists and anglers. Thought to be late 15th century, the present bridge replaced an earlier one a legend attributes to the Devil. In 1932 the bridge, hitherto carrying the highway, was bypassed and now has pedestrian access only.

KIRKBY STEPHEN

Kirkby Stephen is an ancient market town of pre-Norman origin and the commercial centre of the north-eastern part of the county. A perambulation of the main thoroughfare gives the impression that the town is larger than it really is, being tightly built up, but it has little width, the River Eden forming a close boundary on the east side and hill pastures flanking it on the west. Interest is centred mainly around the market place, which has a picturesque grouping of buildings in many individual styles and is overlooked by the venerable old church. The market has had a charter since 1351, but the greatest volume of business is conducted in the auction marts. There is a grammar school, in new premises but founded in 1556, several institutions for social, educational and recreational pursuits, places of worship for religious denominations in variety, and a public hall. Not long ago the town enjoyed the luxury of two railway stations, both inconveniently sited at high levels; one, on the now-disused Tebay to Darlington branch line, is closed as such, and the other caters for the still active Settle-Carlisle railway. The main road through the town is the A.685, carrying traffic between Kendal and Brough.

The parish exhibits markedly the same topographical characteristics as the town, being seven miles from end to end but of no great width and indeed culminating in the south in a very narrow tract of bleak moorland extending almost to Wild Boar Fell, this section being completely without habitations and rising to over 1700'. It is common land, open to all, but only sheep frequent it.

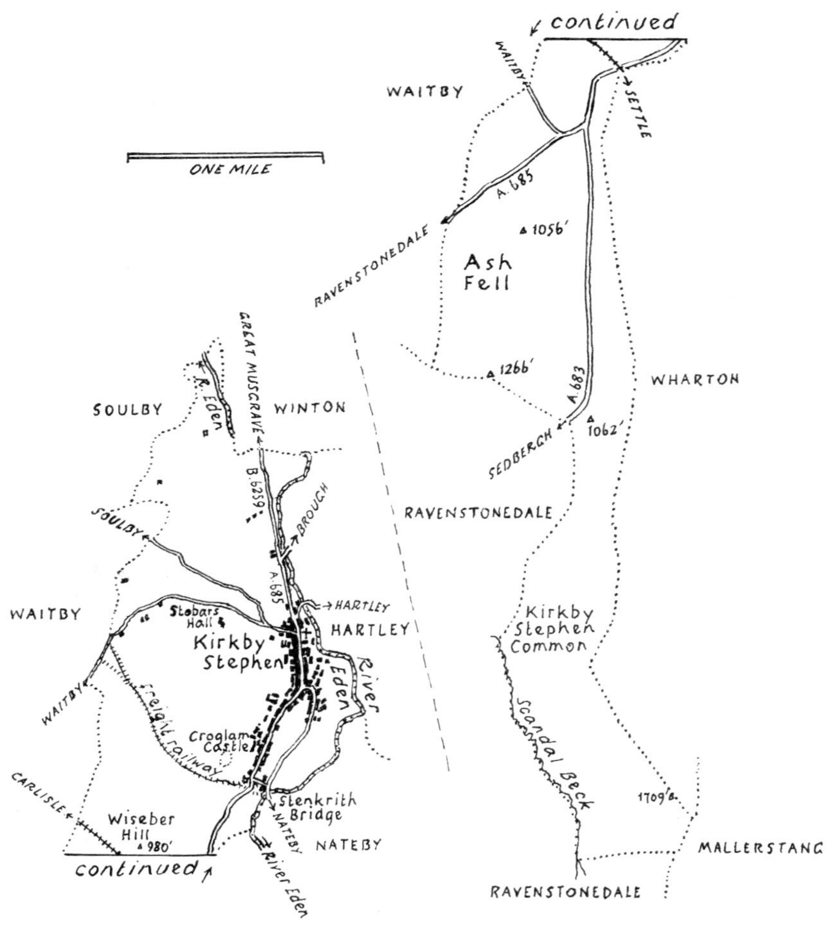

Kirkby Stephen

For the information of visitors to the parish church of St Stephen, a notice inside tells the story of the three churches that have stood on this site: first a Saxon church, probably of timber, followed in 1170 by a Norman church, which in turn was replaced in 1240 by the present structure, itself altered and enlarged subsequently. The chancel and porch are relatively modern.

This is a large church, second only to that at Kendal in size, the internal proportions being impressive. Many Saxon stones are on view in the nave and the 13th century arcades and the elaborate pulpit of polished granite and marble (a gift in 1873) are items of special interest.

The entrance to the churchyard, a pillared shelter known locally as the Cloister, was provided in 1810 out of the estate of a Navy officer named Waller, a native of the town, at his direction. On the inner wall is an interesting record of the early market tolls.

Adjacent to the church are the former parsonage house, with a stone inscribed 1677, and the old grammar school, a 1566 foundation, now replaced by a modern building on a more commodious site.

Kirkby Stephen

Street scenes

Stobars Hall has the appearance of a castle, but its crenellations were added for ornament, not for defence, when it was built in 1829. Situated on an eminence, this is the most imposing residence in the parish.

Croglam Castle

Croglam has the name of Castle but not the appearance of one, being merely a ditch and rampart around the top of a small hill. Nevertheless it was a primitive fort, probably pallisaded, and, although never excavated for confirmation, is thought to be one of the many hill forts used by tribes of Brigantes prior to the coming of the Romans. They chose the site well: it is a fine point of vantage.

Ditch and rampart

Frank's Bridge — a 17th century footbridge over the River Eden

KIRKBY THORE

Kirkby Thore was a place of importance during the Roman occupation, lying astride the road from York to Carlisle; a fort, Bravoniacvm, was established here. Today it is one of the few villages growing in size and population, a development due to a large gypsum (plaster) works in the parish, this being of long standing with a labour force drawn mainly from the village; agriculture is the only other industry. Both the A.66 road and an active railway pass through the parish, which lacks outstanding natural landmarks, but has, in the church and the hall, buildings of considerable charm and antiquity.

Kirkby Thore Hall, a 14th century manor house, is reputed to have been built from the stones of Whelp Castle, of which no traces remain, and was for many generations the home of the Wharton family.

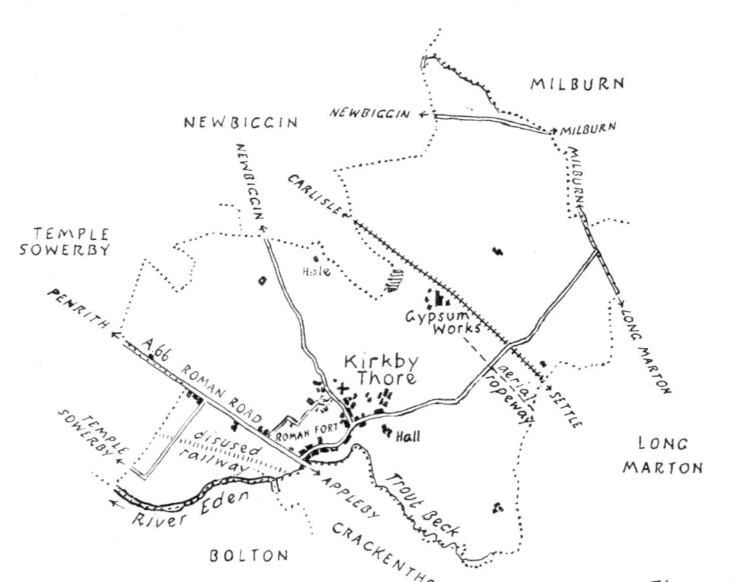

BRAVONIACVM

There is little left to see of the Roman fort, almost all traces having been obliterated by cultivation although a rampart still exists alongside the A.66. The site has, however, contributed greatly in relics of the occupation, producing coins, pottery and other artifacts in quantity, the finds being dispersed to various museums.

Parts of the fabric of the parish church of St Michael are 12th century, notably the base of the tower. The bell-cote, with a single bell (thought to have come from Shap Abbey) is unusual and was added later. Inside are many antique items; the outer walls and the gravestones also merit a detailed inspection.

Kirkby Thore

The parish church of St Michael

LAMBRIGG

Lambrigg is a civil parish, dependant on Grayrigg in ecclesiastical matters, having no church, no school, no village, no hamlet, no shop. Three large houses, a dozen farms and a few cottages accommodate the sparse population. The parish is completely rural but rises to bare moorland in the south. The eastern fringe has been cut into by the motorway and some country lanes have been closed or re-routed. For a hundred years Lambrigg had a railway station just within its boundaries, although this was Grayrigg's; it still has a manned level crossing, one of the few remaining. It is a commentary on the quietness of the Lambrigg countryside that the crossing has more trains than cars.

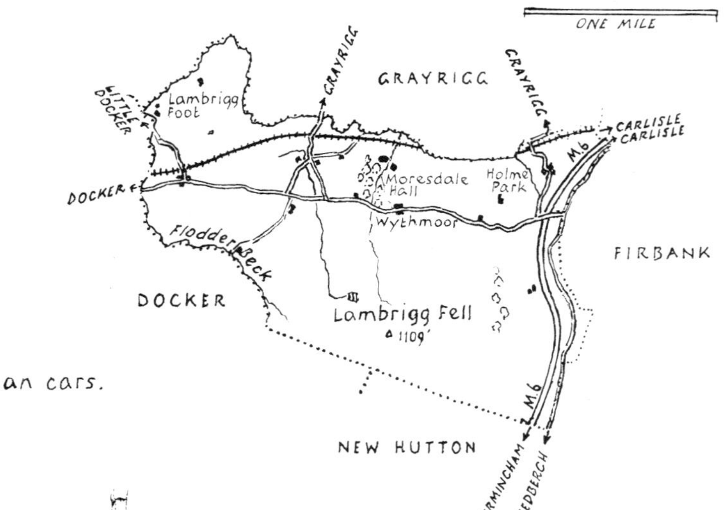

Lambrigg, essentially a farming community, is not the sort of place where one expects to find a mansion of the dimensions of Moresdale Hall, and it is a surprise, approaching by the rhododendron-fringed drive, to come suddenly upon it in a surround of noble trees. The Hall was the seat of William Thompson, D.L., J.P., but latterly has had periods of non-occupation. During the making of the motorway it housed some of the construction engineers.

Holme Park, formerly a farmhouse, was used as a preparatory school for boys for many years but reverted to private occupation upon removal of the school to premises nearer Kendal.

Lambrigg Foot, in a sylvan setting at Little Docker, was until recently the home of the Farrer family.

LANGDALES

Langdales is a parish comprising the whole of the valley of Great Langdale and the north side of Little Langdale. It is the most westerly parish, abutting on Cumberland and Lancashire, three quarters of its boundary being the county march also.

The area thus enclosed is a mountainous district extremely popular with visitors; indeed, although it sees fewer tourists than the neighbouring Rothay valley, which is a through route for road traffic, Great Langdale's dramatic dead-end attracts a legion of devotees who return often to admire again the magnificent scenery, surpassed in Westmorland only by that of Patterdale parish. At the head of Great Langdale, in the heart of the Lake District, the compelling attractions are the towering skyline all around and the craggy declivities falling therefrom to the flat green strath of the valley — an impressive contrast of colour and contour. There is no lake, nor would the scene be enhanced by one: here is a primeval rocky landscape, complete as it is and needing no embellishment. It is walkers' terrain *par excellence*, offering a wide choice of mountain ascents, the arresting and almost bizarre pinnacles of the Langdale Pikes and the challenging skyline of Bowfell and Crinkle Crags making them favourite objectives. Great Langdale is also a Mecca for rock-climbers, second only to Wasdale Head in this respect, and, being more conveniently situated in relation to motorways and public transport, crags here are the subject of activity throughout the year. Little Langdale, too, has a mountainous surround but is of gentler aspect and has an exciting through route for cars.

Langdale Pikes

Great Langdale Beck drains the main valley, which has consistently the county's greatest rainfall, and in Elterwater is joined by the River Brathay issuing from Little Langdale, where it forms the county boundary.

There are small villages at Chapel Stile and Elterwater and hamlets at Little Langdale and Dungeon Ghyll. Tourist accommodation, taxed to capacity in summer, is provided by hotels, many farmhouses and cottages, and camping sites.

So great has become the pressure of tourist traffic that the problem of catering for cars and caravans and coaches is acute, the congestion being accentuated by the tortuous and hazardous valley roads. The closing of the upper reaches to other than local traffic has been proposed: a drastic remedy, but better this than that a radical 'improvement' of the existing roads — delightful country lanes between lichened walls — should be made. The Langdales are magnificent because they still enjoy the romantic atmosphere of a century ago. Destroy part and the whole is destroyed.

Langdales

CUMBERLAND
BORROWDALE
Stake Pass
Martcrag Moor
Sergeant Man 2414'
GRASMERE
Pavey Ark
Blea Rigg 1776'
WASDALE
Rossett Pass
Rossett Pike 2106'
Stake Gill
Pike o' Stickle 2323'
Harrison Stickle 2403'
Stickle Tarn
Mill Gill
Rossett Gill
Gimmer Crag
Dungeon Gill
Great Langdale
Mickleden
Mickleden Beck
Bowfell 2960'
B.5343
Great Langdale Beck
The Band
Chapel Stile
Hell Gill
Oxendale
Oxendale Beck
Side Pike
Lingmoor Tarn
Crinkle Gill
Kettle Crag
2816'
Crinkle Crags
Elterwater
quarry
Lingmoor Fell 1530'
Pike o' Blisco 2304'
Blea Tarn
Blake Rigg
Red Tarn
Little Langdale
River Brathay
Little Langdale Tarn
Wrynose Pass
DUDDON VALLEY
ESKDALE
CONISTON
LANCASHIRE
GRASMERE
RYDAL AND LOUGHRIGG
AMBLESIDE
Langdale Pikes
ONE MILE

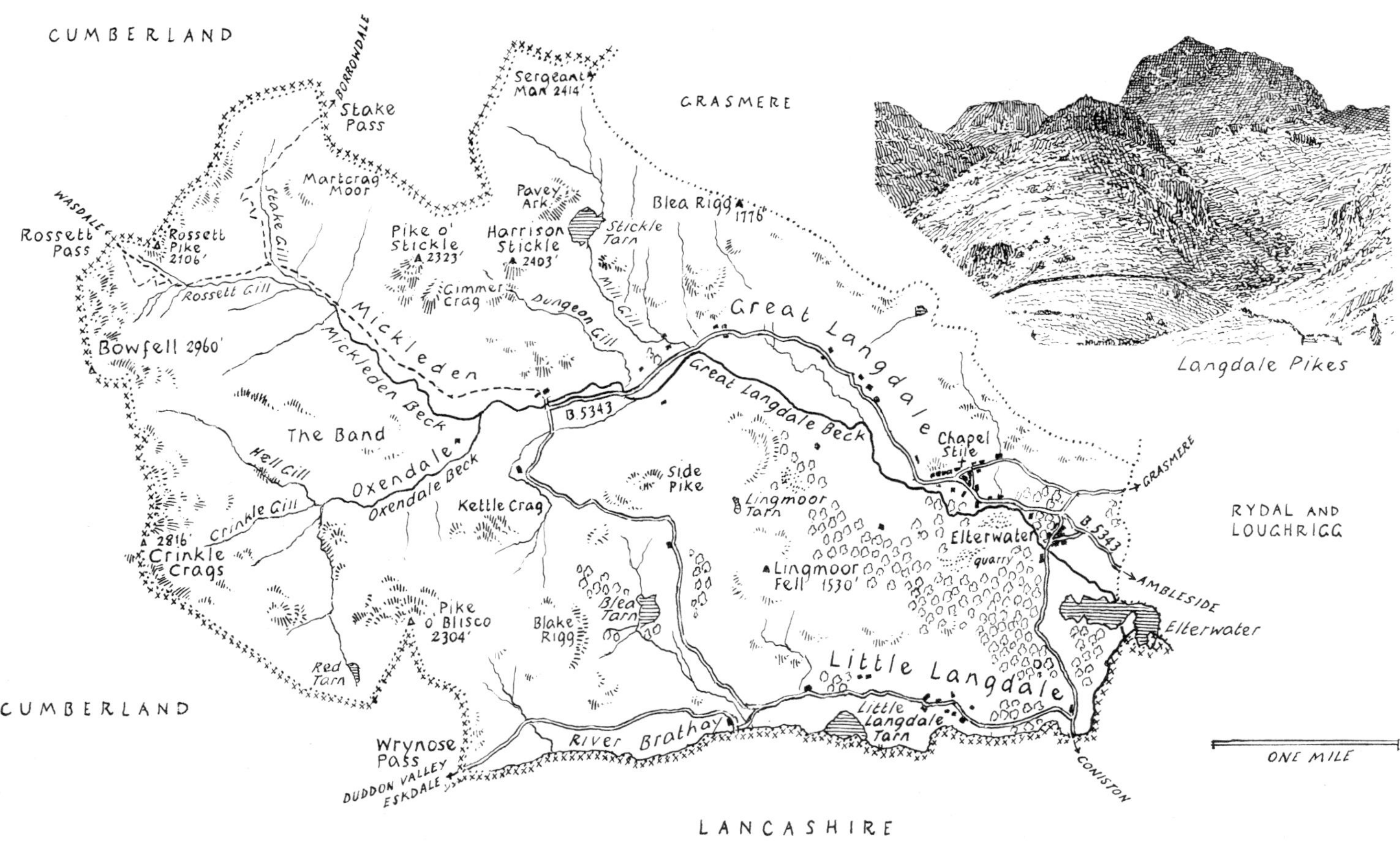

Langdales

The parish church of the Holy Trinity, built in 1857 to replace an earlier chapel

Climbing huts, adapted from farmhouses and barns, are a feature of Great Langdale. Pictured above is Raw Head, occupied by the Fell and Rock Climbing Club.

Cottages at Chapel Stile

Chapel Stile

Chapel Stile is, or was, a quarry village in a landscape of rock and hewn stone. The spoil of the immense Thrang Quarry spills over to the valley road; the village is alongside, as though it has grown naturally out of the stone won there, and one could imagine that the church was quarried on the site, so perfectly does it merge into the surroundings of rock and crag. Since the closing of the quarry and the advent of tourists in quantity the village has become a supply base and holiday centre, even the quarry floor having been requisitioned for accommodation.

The head of Great Langdale, from Rossett Gill

Langdales

Elterwater

Elterwater is the name of a tarn and a village, side by side in a lovely setting. Nothing in the scene suggests industry, but hidden amid rich woodlands there flourished a gunpowder works for a hundred years until it closed in 1930, and there flourishes still, and to a much greater extent, the quarrying, cutting and polishing of the stone to which Westmorland has given its name and thereby acquired a world-wide reputation: a close-grained blue-green slate that has won international acclaim as building material for its durability and not less for its handsome appearance.

If stone has beauty, here it is.

Elterwater Quarry

Elterwater

Blea Tarn

Blea Tarn

'One bare dwelling, one abode, no more'

Immortalised by Wordsworth, Blea Tarn House is still solitary but no longer lonely, the congestion of cars on the narrow road alongside being acute every summer weekend, and to such an extent that closure of the road, which has superlative views, has been seriously suggested. The peace that once made the tarn a lovely sanctuary has been destroyed and its charm is today more elusive. Its romantic beauty, as a foreground for Langdale Pikes, is undiminished — this is one of the classic Lakeland scenes.

Langdales

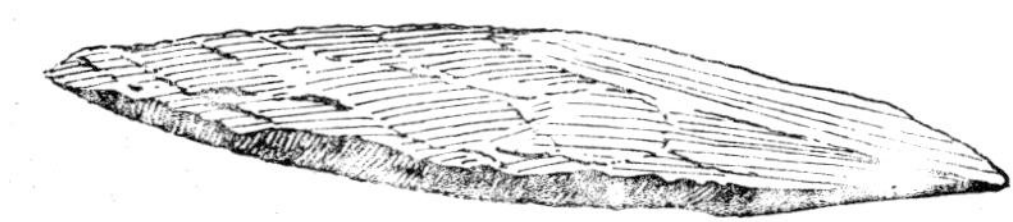

The Stone Axe Factory

Great Langdale's best-kept secret, undisclosed for upwards of 3000 years, was first revealed, by chance, in 1921, when a walker on Martcrag Moor found a "chipping site" evidently used for the making of stone axes of neolithic type. Since then, at diminishing intervals, a number of similar sites, yielding more prolific discoveries, have been located in the area by avid searchers, notably in the south screes of Pike o' Stickle.

The material used was a very hard fine-grained stone from a narrow strata extending around the head of the valley about the 2000' contour, insignificant amongst the dominant volcanic rocks, and it is remarkable that the primitive inhabitants of Lakeland located the stone and realised its value for the making of weapons and implements. This was the valley's first industry, and it had an export trade, axes of Langdale stone having been found in distant parts of the country.

Pike o' Stickle

Summit cairns

Sergeant Man

Pike o' Stickle

Langdales

Bowfell

the highest and grandest of the Langdale fells

the summit cairn

Bowfell Links

Bowfell, from Lingmoor Fell

Bowfell, from Pike o' Blisco

The Great Slab, Bowfell

Crinkle Crags, from Pike o' Blisco

Langdales

Crinkle Crags

Gladstone's Finger

from Pike O' Blisco

Bowfell, from Long Top

Rock scenery on the main ridge

Crinkle Crags and Bowfell, from Red Tarn

Crinkle Crags, from Oxendale

Langdales

Rock for climbing

below and right:
Gimmer Crag

opposite page:
left: *Bowfell Buttress*
right: *Pavey Ark*

Langdales

In Little Langdale

Wilson's Place

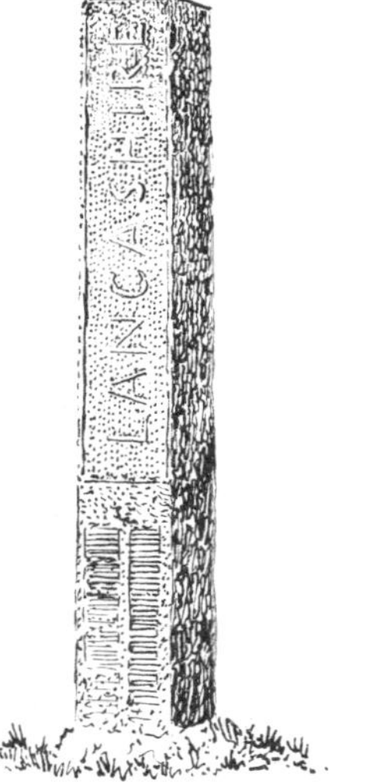

The Three Shire Stone on Wrynose Pass was erected to mark the meeting of three counties, although naming only one. Its purpose became suddenly obsolete at midnight on March 31st 1974.

The most picturesque bridge in the Lake District is the 17th century Slater's Bridge over the River Brathay, with a flagged causeway on each side. It gives access to the slate quarries on the Lancashire bank.

Langdales

Little Langdale

Langdales

Great Langdale

Langdale Pikes, from Lingmoor Fell

LEVENS

Levens is best known to people outside the county for Levens Bridge, an important junction of roads, and Levens Hall, an Elizabethan mansion open to the public and of national renown. The village of this name, earlier known as Beathwaite Green, lies off busy traffic routes, on a west-facing eminence overlooking an alluvial flat and the estuary of the Kent, and enjoys a mild climate, being, it is said, 'a topcoat warmer than Kendal'. Considerable housing development has taken place here recently and the old parts of the village are being dwarfed by a surrounding suburbia: testimony to the pleasant environment.

Levens Hall, with its park and estates, is the dominant influence in the parish, contributing much to the visual amenities, but everywhere within the parochial boundaries, which enclose the final reaches of the River Kent, the limestone scenery is gentle, unassuming, and greatly favoured by its location. Archaeological remains suggest that early man also found it a good place to live.

On Sizergh Fell are the remains of an ancient settlement, the ramparts of which can still be traced. Illustrated is a burial cairn on this site.

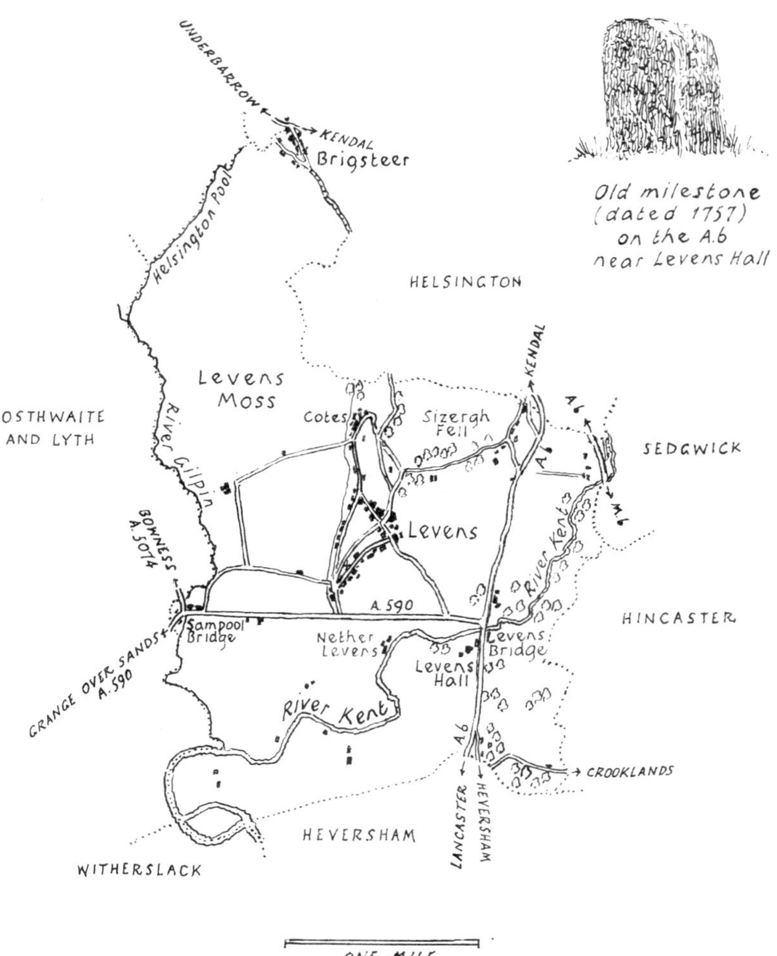

Old milestone (dated 1757) on the A.6 near Levens Hall

Levens

The parish church of St John the Evangelist, built in 1828

Village street

Three bells are preserved under cover in the rear of the churchyard. They have no clappers, but can be rung by striking them with a mallet. This is done on occasions of festivity.

There are hundreds of limekilns in the limestone districts of the county, unused since last century and derelict, but a few remain in good condition, among them this one at Levens.

Levens

Levens Hall

Levens Hall, the home of the Bagots, is an attractive Elizabethan house of unique character in a lovely setting of garden and parkland. Its founding is a long way back in history but the present building is mainly attributed to the late 16th century although parts are much older. It is a house of fascinating detail with distinctive architectural features, and its interior fittings are no less delightful, there being a wealth of carved oak chimney-pieces and panelling and elaborate plasterwork. The house is open to the public in the summer months, when a collection of steam engines is an added attraction.

Levens Hall

The Howard Tower, overlooking the gardens, is an early 19th century addition to the Hall, named after the then owner of the estate. The cylindrical shafts are those of the chimneys of the older east wing.

The spectacular topiary gardens are famous, and unexcelled. They were laid out around 1700 to the design of a Monsieur Beaumont, a gardener of James II, and have been scrupulously maintained.

Levens

Chimney shaft detail

Nether Levens

The farmhouse of Nether Levens stands on the western bank of the Kent, across the river from Levens Hall and half a mile distant. It is a structure of exceptional interest and has a long history, mainly connected with the early occupiers, the Prestons. In period it is a contemporary of Levens Hall and was formerly named Low Levens Hall. The main body of the house is early 16th century, but parts of it are much older and a ruined crosswing may have contained a pele tower. The cylindrical chimney shafts, works of art, are an impressive feature.

Levens

Levens Park

In a wood on the Levens estate there is a good example of a type of ice-house in common use by many large houses for preserving food before the introduction of more sophisticated refrigeration methods. A flagged tunnel entered by slate doors leads to a pit surrounded by a gallery, the whole being enclosed by masonry and surmounted by an artificial circular mound pierced by a vent pipe. A low temperature within was thus ensured.

Measurements: Mound — height 15'; diameter 45'.
Tunnel — height 6'6"; length 13'; 3 slate doors.
Pit — width (at top) 12'9"; depth 15' approx.

The centuries-old, mile-long avenue of oaks in Levens Park received national publicity in 1972, when strong opposition was made to a proposal to construct a road, a link with the motorway, that would have caused the destruction of many of the trees. Evidence was also submitted that an ancient village settlement in the Park would be sacrificed too. Following a public enquiry, the proposal was rejected and the road re-routed to bypass the Park. The avenue was saved and with it the site of the settlement, the rights of way enjoyed by walkers and the grazing grounds of the deer and the handsome 'Bagot' goats introduced to this country from mid-Europe at the time of the Crusades. Levens Park will continue to give delight.

LITTLE STRICKLAND

Both Little Strickland and Great Strickland were formerly grouped with Thrimby as a single parish under the latter's name, the parish church being situated in the hamlet of Little Strickland, a small community tidily arranged along a country road within the sound of busy through traffic but hidden from it, an out-of-the-way place that rarely sees a stranger. It has a few old farmhouses of character, and formerly an inn, the business of which has not survived. In a field west of the church is an earthwork suggesting an ancient settlement. The western boundary of the parish, following the course of the River Leith, here in its infancy, is impinged upon by the main railway line, and the motorway skirts the southern edge; otherwise Little Strickland is entirely rural.

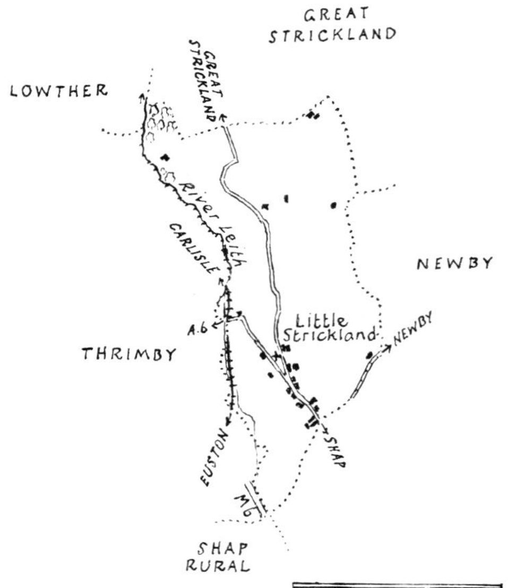

The plain exterior of the parish church belies its interesting contents, some of them preserved from an earlier church on the same site, notably a stone tablet known as The Thrimby Inscription, 1695, and several pews with 17th century date carvings. The present building dates from 1814 and retains its association with Thrimby, being still named the Parish Church of St Mary, Thrimby.

Buildings in the main street

Little Strickland

Low Hall,
previously known as
Little Strickland Hall

Low Hall, late 16th century, retains its original external appearance but is most notable for its interior decorations and fittings, in particular elaborately designed plaster ceilings and some panelled walls and partitions.

High Hall has a wide arched fireplace with the arms of Crackenthorpe on adjoining panels, and the date 1600, the probable year of building. The stone mullioned windows are original.

Long House, embowered in trees, has a doorway with the initials and date R.B.M. 1687 inscribed thereon.

High Hall

Long House

LONG MARTON

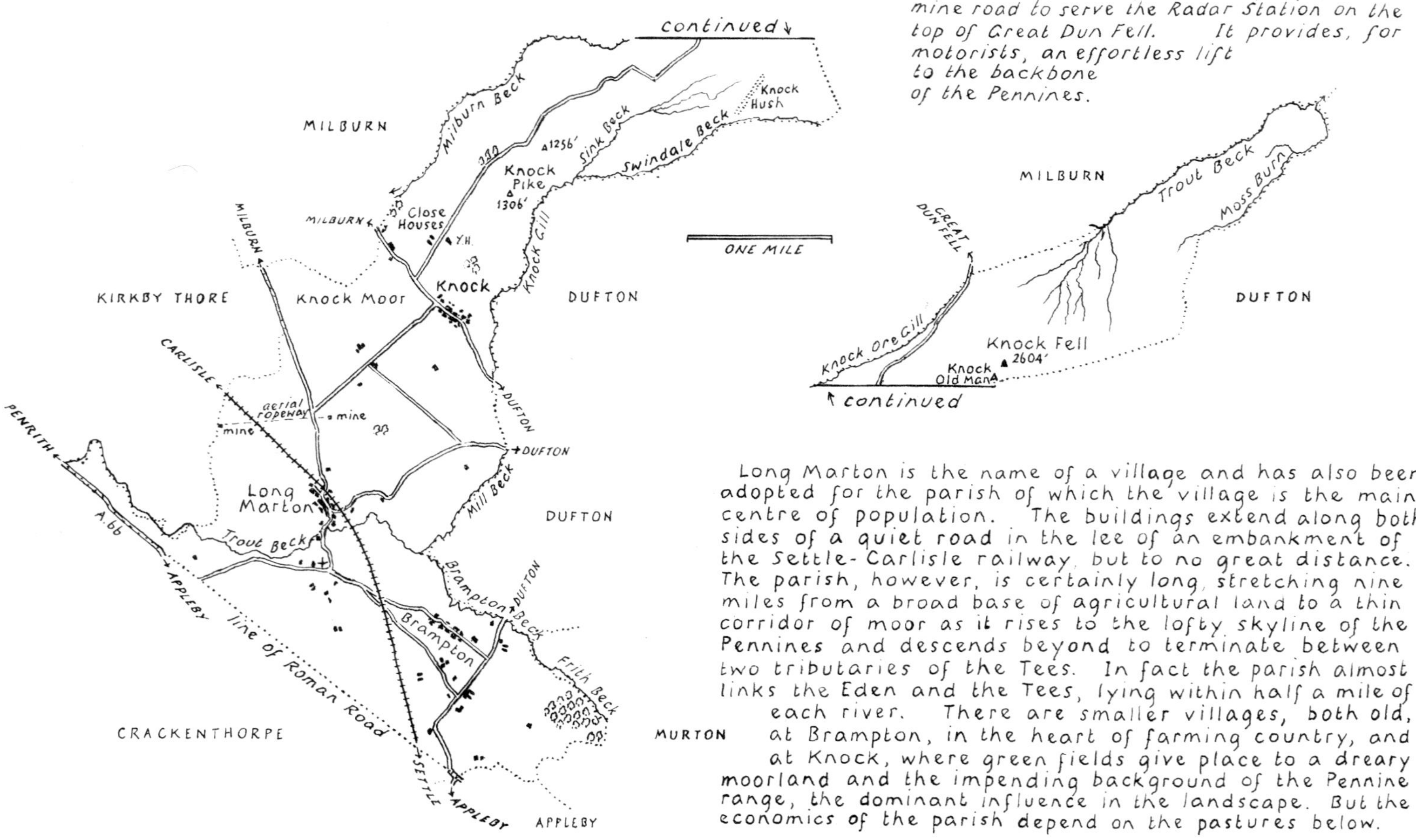

The mountain road climbing up from Knock via Close Houses is the highest tarmac strip in the country, having been adopted from a mine road to serve the Radar Station on the top of Great Dun Fell. It provides, for motorists, an effortless lift to the backbone of the Pennines.

Long Marton is the name of a village and has also been adopted for the parish of which the village is the main centre of population. The buildings extend along both sides of a quiet road in the lee of an embankment of the Settle-Carlisle railway, but to no great distance. The parish, however, is certainly long, stretching nine miles from a broad base of agricultural land to a thin corridor of moor as it rises to the lofty skyline of the Pennines and descends beyond to terminate between two tributaries of the Tees. In fact the parish almost links the Eden and the Tees, lying within half a mile of each river. There are smaller villages, both old, at Brampton, in the heart of farming country, and at Knock, where green fields give place to a dreary moorland and the impending background of the Pennine range, the dominant influence in the landscape. But the economics of the parish depend on the pastures below.

Long Marton

Most of the churches of north Westmorland are built of the local red sandstone, the colour, warmth and beauty of which is well displayed in the lovely old church of Long Marton. It is the 12th century tower that arrests attention: the structure is plain but gains in strength and impressiveness by its simple lines, unbuttressed and unbroken by ornamentation. Inside the church, much of the original masonry can be seen in the nave and chancel and there are fittings of great antiquity.

The parish church of St Margaret and St James

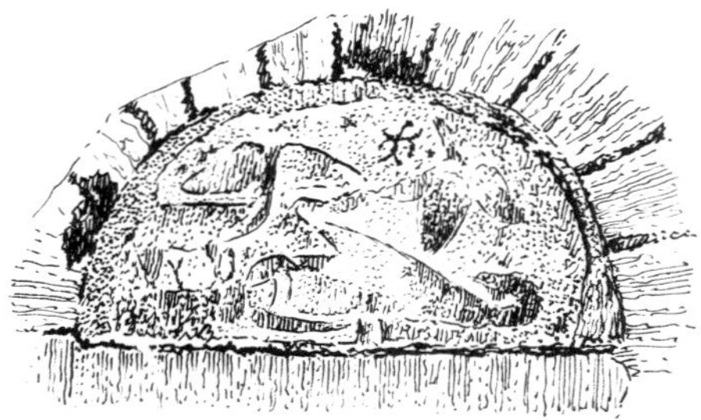

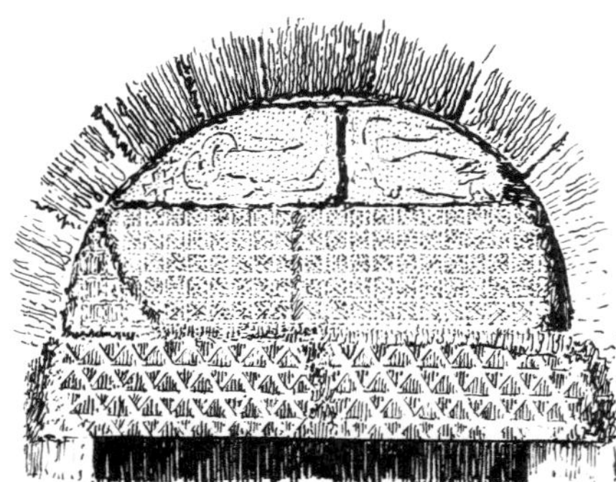

Among the many treasures of the interior are ancient carved stones set beneath two doorway arches (11th or 12th century), inscribed with grotesque monsters and a variety of devices, and also neat decorative patterns.

Long Marton

Knock Pike

Brampton Hall (17th century)

An old mill by Brampton Beck has been converted into a residence but retains its waterwheel.

Close Houses, Knock (1695)

Knock Fell

Knock Fell is the highest ground in the parish, exceeding 2600 feet in altitude. It is a broad, indefinite watershed, the western slopes draining into feeders of the River Eden and the eastern gently descending to the infant Tees. This is a wild landscape, utterly desolate, and until the coming of (a) the Pennine Way, which traverses the summit, and (b) the Moor House Field Station of the Nature Conservancy, which has fenced a few patches of land for research, infrequently visited, although, in days long past, men scratched the ground for lead and other minerals — an activity that may account for the many cairns on this fell, possibly serving as guides for miners and shepherds in bad weather. A few relics of mining operations have survived, among them Knock Hush, an excellent example of the many of this type in the north Pennines. Hushes are ravines on fellsides, artificially contrived by damming streams to impound water, then releasing it in sufficient volume to scour the surface of the ground, with the aim of revealing any mineral content that might indicate the presence of a vein.

Knock Hush

The summit of Knock Fell looking to Cross Fell and Great Dun Fell

Knock Old Man

LONGSLEDDALE

The parish boundary coincides with the watershed around the valley

Longsleddale is the most easterly of the valleys that have the characteristics and atmosphere of true Lakeland scenery, the last oasis of beauty before the landscape merges into the bleak Pennine moors. For motorists it is a *cul de sac*, and the one narrow road is a deterrent to those tourists on wheels who like to travel quickly, nor are there any parking and picnic places: hence the valley is happily spared the weekend crowds that invade the more accessible parts of the Lake District. The whole of the valley is within the National Park but is not sullied by commercialism.

There is no village or hamlet, merely a spacing of farmsteads along both sides of the valley's river, the Sprint, and a church. At the highest farm, Sadgill, cultivation ends and a stony quarry track leads up amongst wild fells, with walkers' paths branching to Mardale and Wet Sleddale over high passes.

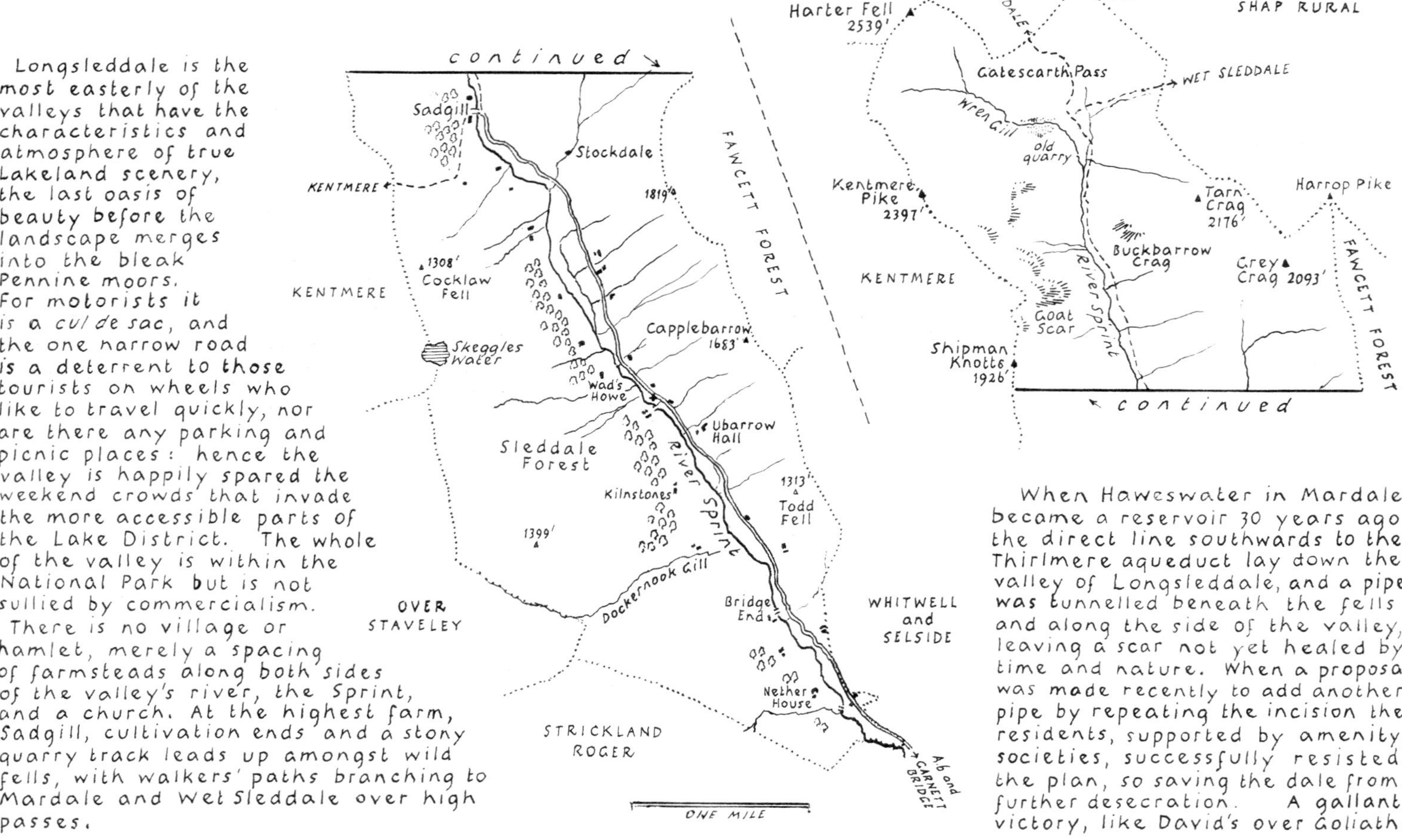

When Haweswater in Mardale became a reservoir 30 years ago the direct line southwards to the Thirlmere aqueduct lay down the valley of Longsleddale, and a pipe was tunnelled beneath the fells and along the side of the valley, leaving a scar not yet healed by time and nature. When a proposal was made recently to add another pipe by repeating the incision the residents, supported by amenity societies, successfully resisted the plan, so saving the dale from further desecration. A gallant victory, like David's over Goliath!

Longsleddale

The foot of Longsleddale, as seen from the A.6 at Watchgate

The parish church of St Mary is situated on a knoll midway along the valley in isolation from other buildings. It was a chapel of Kendal until rebuilt in 1712 and then given parochial status. The present structure is the result of a further rebuilding in 1863. Some fittings are retained from the older church, notably a carved oak door dated 1662 and a silver chalice dated 1571.

Longsleddale

17th century packhorse bridge over the River Sprint at Nether House — later widened to admit vehicles

Ubarrow Hall (alternatively spelt Yewbarrow, or Yewborrow) is the oldest property in the parish. The pele tower is late medieval but has been reduced in height and gabled; its walls are six feet thick and contain a splendid vaulted basement (now used as a dairy) and a staircase. The adjoining house is 17th century.

Bridge End

Longsleddale

Sadgill Bridge

The proposed Sadgill Reservoir

Above Sadgill there is a hiatus in the swift movement of the Sprint where the river meanders along a flat section of the valley, and it was here that a reservoir was planned in 1845, in pursuance of an Act of Parliament, to regulate the flow of water to the wheel-powered mills lower down the valley and on the banks of the Kent. The scheme was never proceeded with and not even Manchester has dared to revive it.

Sadgill

Sadgill is the last inhabited outpost in Longsleddale, and the first refuge for distressed walkers coming down from the lonely hills around the head of the valley. The farm here is a Mountain Rescue Post.

Low Sadgill

Longsleddale

The eastern face, with Harter Fell beyond, from Goat Scar

on Kentmere Pike

looking down a scree gully, eastern flank

Buckbarrow Crag

Steel Pike

Longsleddale

The head of Longsleddale

Longsleddale

When Manchester's engineers had constructed the Haweswater aqueduct they left, to rot, their survey posts on Tarn Crag (above) and Grey Crag.

A castellated garage, built in 1921, on the roadside at Nether Bower has a wealth of carved inscriptions including the mileages to Edinburgh (138), Yarmouth (267) and London (261); the latitude (54 24 N), longitude (245 W) and altitude (520 feet) of the site; panels of Greek lettering that would puzzle even an expert in the language; and a cheerful greeting that makes the rest forgivable:

HAIL! BELOVED ONES

Waterfall on the River Sprint

LOWTHER

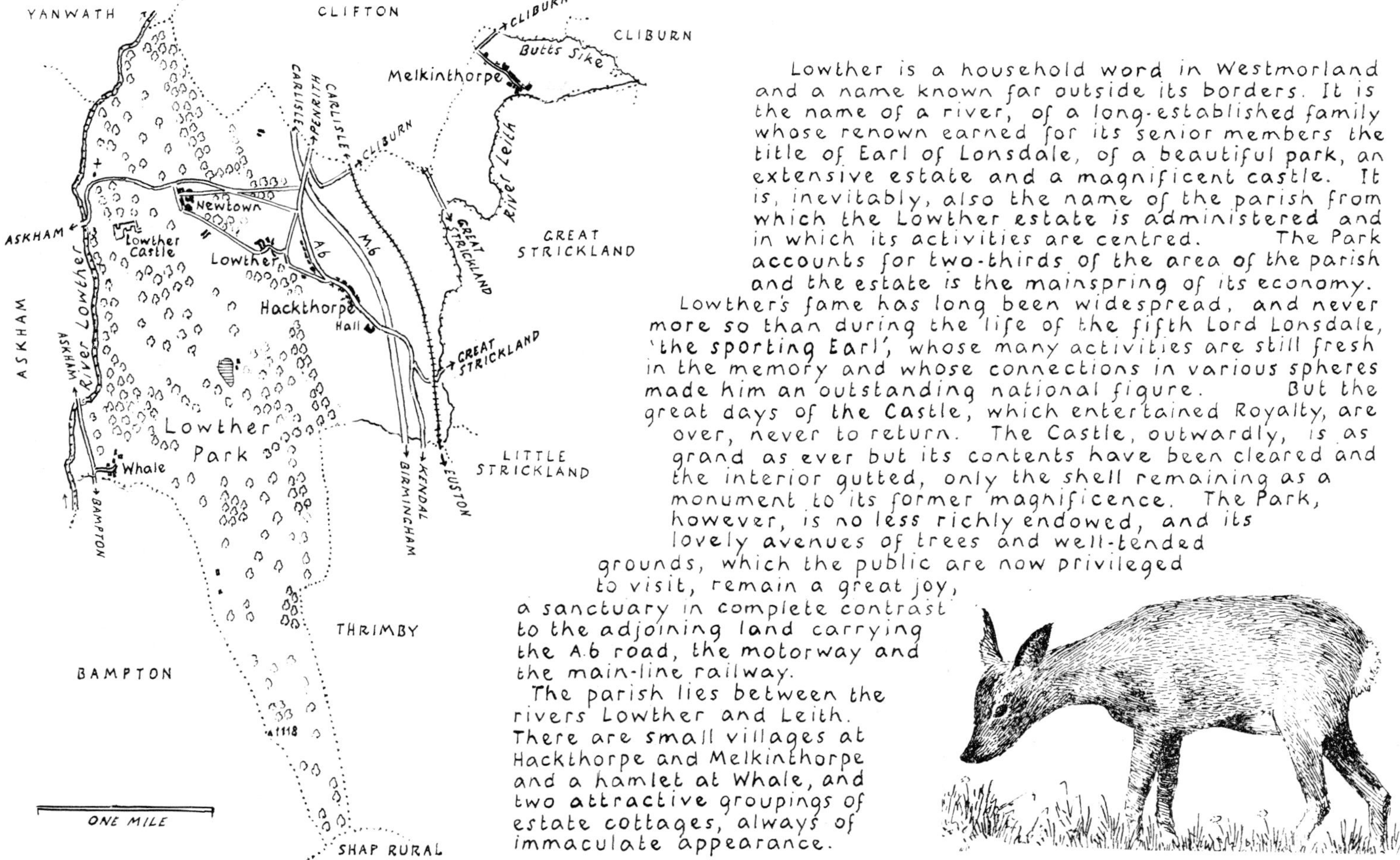

Lowther is a household word in Westmorland and a name known far outside its borders. It is the name of a river, of a long-established family whose renown earned for its senior members the title of Earl of Lonsdale, of a beautiful park, an extensive estate and a magnificent castle. It is, inevitably, also the name of the parish from which the Lowther estate is administered and in which its activities are centred. The Park accounts for two-thirds of the area of the parish and the estate is the mainspring of its economy.

Lowther's fame has long been widespread, and never more so than during the life of the fifth Lord Lonsdale, 'the sporting Earl', whose many activities are still fresh in the memory and whose connections in various spheres made him an outstanding national figure. But the great days of the Castle, which entertained Royalty, are over, never to return. The Castle, outwardly, is as grand as ever but its contents have been cleared and the interior gutted, only the shell remaining as a monument to its former magnificence. The Park, however, is no less richly endowed, and its lovely avenues of trees and well-tended grounds, which the public are now privileged to visit, remain a great joy, a sanctuary in complete contrast to the adjoining land carrying the A.6 road, the motorway and the main-line railway.

The parish lies between the rivers Lowther and Leith. There are small villages at Hackthorpe and Melkinthorpe and a hamlet at Whale, and two attractive groupings of estate cottages, always of immaculate appearance.

Lowther

The parish church of St Michael

The Mausoleum

The parish church is situated, appropriately, within Lowther Park, near the public road crossing it to Askham. This is an old church, still preserving a 12th century arcade, but greatly altered to unusual proportions, especially in 1696 and 1856.
Inside are many tombs, effigies and monuments of members of the Lowther family, and a remarkable collection of pre-Conquest stones, others of which are in the churchyard.

The Mausoleum, in the churchyard, was built in 1857, and contains a fine marble statue and sarcophagus of William, second Earl of Lonsdale, who died in 1852.

Lowther

A formal village: Lowther

An informal village: Melkinthorpe

Hackthorpe Hall, a fine range of buildings alongside the A.6, was built early in the 17th century. An ancient barrow nearby, containing many burial remains, was opened in 1866 and, unfortunately, completely removed.

Lowther

Lowther Castle occupies the site of earlier mansions dating back to the reign of Edward I but of these few traces remain, a disastrous fire in 1726 laying the place in ruins until the present impressive structure was commenced in 1802 by the second Earl of Lonsdale from designs by Sir Robert Smirke. The architecture has variety of styles, which combine well to give a grand effect of elegance and massive strength.

Wordsworth wrote of it: "Lowther! in thy majestic pile are seen
Cathedral pomp and grace, in apt accord
With the baronial castle's sterner mein; ...."

Sadly, the interior has now been abandoned; but the shell is to remain as a spectacular memorial to past glories.

Lowther Wildlife Country Park

In 1969 an area in Lowther Park was opened to the public as a wildlife reserve and has proved a very popular innovation. Here may be seen many species of deer, cattle and sheep, a variety of exotic birds, wild animals in enclosures and, on a small lake, colonies of waterfowl. There is a café, a shop, play and picnic areas and a garden centre.
All the birds and animals are well cared for, and those with freedom to graze, whether native or foreign, live together happily in lovely environs.
Visitors are appreciative, but not all enthuse about the caging of wild animals. To these creatures liberty is life, and the instinct for freedom is not curbed by regular feeding. Cages are robbers of dignity.

LUPTON

Lupton parish is a tract of undulating farmland, crossed by a few narrow surfaced lanes provided for local use only, and containing three sheets of water, two of which are reservoirs supplying the southern parts of the county. It is a parish that, despite proximity to Kendal and Kirkby Lonsdale, induces a feeling of remoteness, for there are few habitations away from the main road and not many on it, and the rolling hills, although small, are sufficiently elevated to hide one part of the parish from the next. There is little traffic on the lanes but both the new Kendal-Kirkby Lonsdale road, the A.65, and the old one, the B.6254, cut through the parish and the former is a ribbon of pulsating life and constant movement through a countryside that is elsewhere entirely at peace.

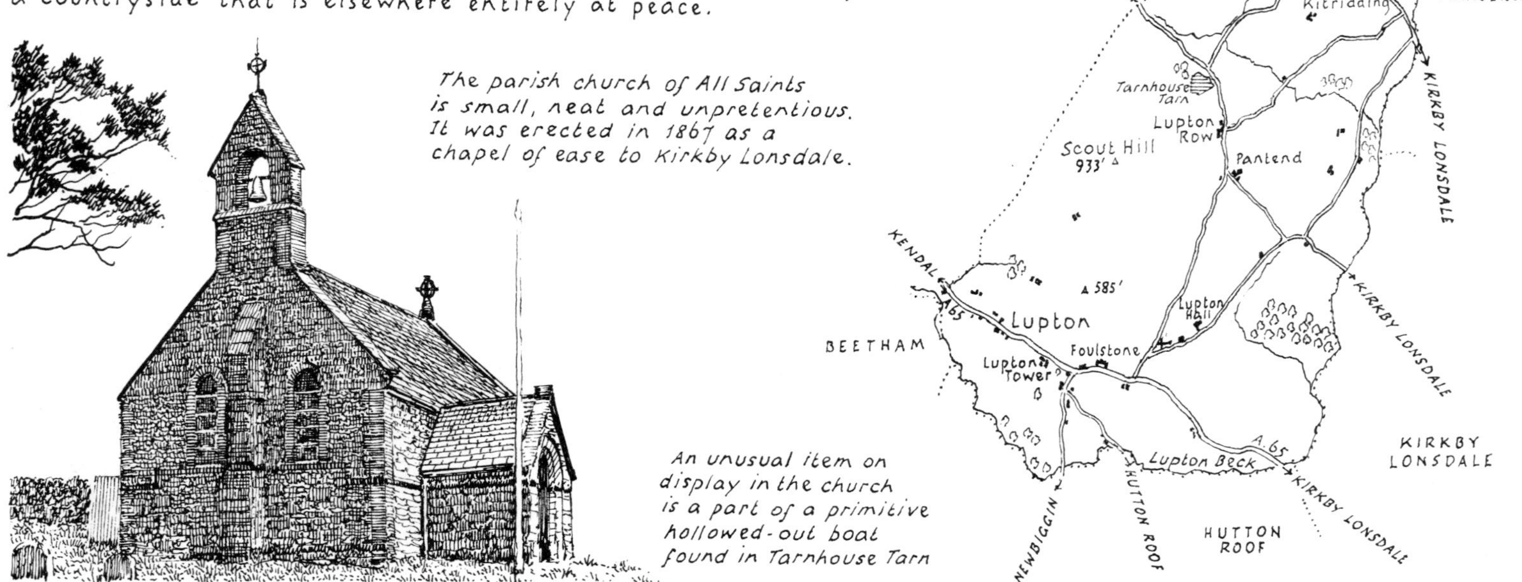

The parish church of All Saints is small, neat and unpretentious. It was erected in 1867 as a chapel of ease to Kirkby Lonsdale.

An unusual item on display in the church is a part of a primitive hollowed-out boat found in Tarnhouse Tarn

Lupton

Three farmhouses.....

Foulstone, 1655

..... and three tarns

Wyndhammere

Tarnhouse Tarn

Tarnhouse Tarn and Lupton Reservoir impound water for the Lakes and Lune Water Board

Lupton Hall, 1721

Lupton Tower

Lupton Reservoir

MALLERSTANG

Mallerstang's name is thought to be derived from "mallards' stank": the pool of the mallards. It is a valley not well known, its one road not being used overmuch by tourists and lying away from the more popular through routes, a circumstance considered greatly in its favour by the relatively few who love the quietness of the dale and the striking scenery of the craggy escarpments enclosing it. Here is the birthplace of the River Eden, which drains the fells and brings fertility to the lower pastures, flowing closely in company with the road; parallel but at a higher level runs the Settle-Carlisle railway, which is, at the head of the valley, the highest line in the country (1169'). On both sides, the skyline is etched by rocks: those of Wild Boar Fell on the west, those of Mallerstang Edge on the east, the parish boundaries following the watershed and for several miles being coincident with the county march.

Mallerstang is lonely, and there are tales of theft and assault by roving bands of highwaymen and of a herd of deer that once roamed the valley, the latter story being the better authenticated; and, of course, there is Pendragon, a castle fortress that for many centuries stood guard against intruders. Today the robbers and the deer and the wild boars are seen no more and Pendragon is a sad ruin. The new 'capital' of the valley is the small concentration of buildings at Outhgill, which, despite its church and chapel, is merely a hamlet. Other properties in the valley are mainly farms, and they are widely scattered within the zone of cultivation below the rocks and scree.

A few years ago a singularly insensitive proposal to open up Mallerstang for tourist entertainment, in disregard of the character of the dale and the dalesfolk, was seriously put forward, and rightly given short shrift. Those who know Mallerstang want it as it is.

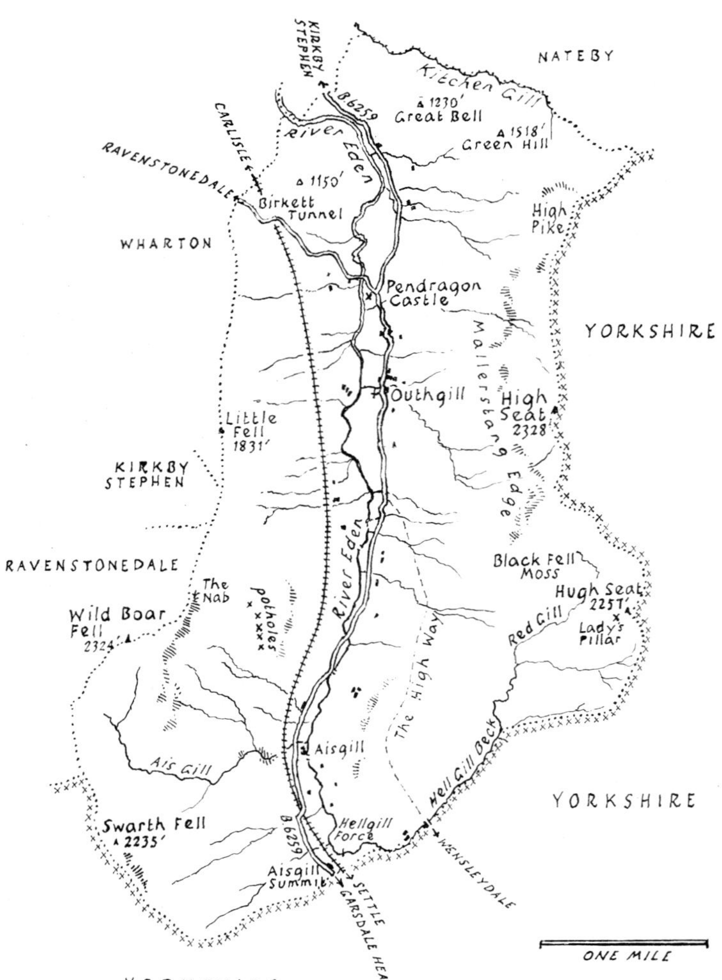

Castle Bridge was provided by Lady Anne but has since been widened.

Pendragon

The origins of Pendragon Castle are lost in antiquity. Legend ascribes a 5th. century fortress here to Uther Pendragon, a man of great influence and the supposed father of King Arthur, and is supported by a couplet that still survives:

"Let Uther Pendragon do what he can,
Eden will run where Eden ran"

referring to his abortive attempt to divert the course of the river to surround the fortress. Since those early times the castle has been rebuilt and laid waste many times. It was in a ruinous condition when Lady Anne Clifford inherited and restored it in 1660, but the next owner dismantled the structure, which has stood in decay since 1685. At the present time repairs to the crumbling walls are being made.

The castle and ditch

The ruined interior

Mallerstang

Aisgill Farm

The little parish church of St Mary, at Outhgill, is of obscure foundation. A panel over the porch records that it was found in a ruinous condition by Lady Anne Clifford and restored by her in 1663.

Cairn on Swarth Fell

So-called "giants' graves" are clearly seen on the slopes of Birkett Common above the Eden. The origin and purpose of these elongated pillow-mounds, obviously man-made, which occur also elsewhere, have not been determined, the only certain fact about them being that they are not graves of giants.

The Settle-Carlisle railway runs for several miles along the base of Wild Boar Fell.

Wild Boar Fell, 2324'

Wild Boar Fell is Westmorland's finest mountain outside the Lake District and conspicuously in view from northern parts of the county, a distinctive outline making it easily recognisable. The fell has the reputation of being the last place in England where a wild boar was killed, an incident giving the fell its name and so adding substance to the story.

The Nab

The small mound on the top of the Nab, occupied by a cairn, is a tumulus. The altitude here is 2296'.

The highest point of the flat summit is indicated by a triangulation pillar of the Ordnance Survey set within a stone wind-shelter.

The gritstone escarpment

Mallerstang

The limestone areas

The gritstone summits around Mallerstang are based on a thick bed of limestone, which outcrops on both sides of the valley and is most evident in the spectacular ravines of Hell Gill and Ais Gill, the latter especially providing splendid scenery and a noteworthy variety of mosses and plants.

Angerholme Pots

The limestone shelf below the escarpment of Wild Boar Fell is surfaced by large expanses of naked rock, or 'pavements', amongst which about twenty potholes penetrate the moor to a maximum depth of 65 feet. These holes are known to cavers as Angerholme Pots.

Ais Gill : White Kirk

Ais Gill : Low White Kirk

The source of the River Eden

Mallerstang

The Eden must be regarded as Westmorland's principal river. It is the longest, flowing across the county from one boundary to another, growing in beauty as well as width as it makes its way north through a fertile valley, and passing into Cumberland *en route* for the Solway Firth as a watercourse of great dignity.

Its beginnings, however, are in a landscape very different from that of the mature river, in the desolate moors of Mallerstang, where its waters ooze from the peat of Black Fell Moss and take shape as Red Gill, becoming Hell Gill Beck on the descent to the valley in a limestone gorge and, after tumbling over Hellgill Force, reach gentler gradients and assume the name Eden.

Hellgill Force is the highest, yet the least known, of the waterfalls in the county, the stream plunging 60' over a fault in the limestone strata.

Hellgill Bridge carries the old road from Hawes to Kirkby Stephen, now merely a grass track (the High Way), over the spectacular rift of Hell Gill.

Lady's Pillar is a column of cut stones erected on instructions of Lady Anne Clifford in memory of Sir Hugh Morville (of Pendragon) in a conspicuous position on the top of the fell named after him: Hugh (or Hugh's) Seat, 2257'. One of the stones is inscribed A.P. 1664, the year of erection; another has the initials and date F.H.L. 1890, this relating to a rebuilding of the pillar following its collapse.

An unlikely legend relates that Dick Turpin, the highwayman, on Black Bess, leapt across Hell Gill at a spot still known as his 'Leap'.

MANSERGH

Mansergh, pronounced Manser, is a quiet parish in a favoured position on the west bank of the River Lune, which forms a four-mile boundary. The only concentration of dwellings is at the hamlet of Old Town; elsewhere the small population, mainly engaged in agriculture, is based in the few farmhouses near the river. Much of the northern part of the parish is the beautiful parkland and rich pastures of the Rigmaden Estate, long owned by the Wilson family, but the fine mansion here is unoccupied and abandoned. Up to a century ago annual horse races were held on land near the tarn of Kitmere, but no such excitements today disturb the peaceful environment of Mansergh.

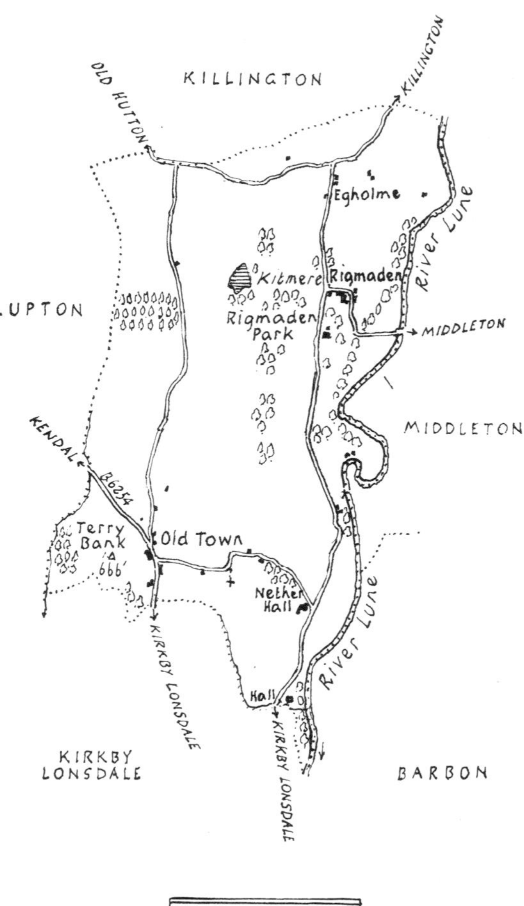

The parish church of St Peter was erected in 1880. A tablet on the outer wall records that the present building replaced an earlier one, the date panel of which (1726) is affixed: this was situated at Nether Hall.

The stone for St Peter's was quarried at Hutton Roof.

Mansergh

Rigmaden Park, built in 1825, was the seat of the Wilson family for over a century but is today unoccupied and falling into decay. This once-handsome mansion is on a splendid site with a superb outlook over the valley and fells of mid-Lunesdale.

Cottages at Old Town

Terry Bank — for many centuries the home of the Conder family

Mansergh Hall

MARTINDALE

Westmorland has several deer parks but only one deer forest where the herd roams freely, unconfined by fencing, and this is in Martindale, one of the loneliest and loveliest of Lakeland valleys, its beauty unimpaired as yet by tourism and commercial activities. The parish is extensive, and lies between Ullswater and a lofty ridge carrying the Roman road, High Street, on its declining northerly course over the mountains; it covers three valley systems that drain into the lake. The enclosing and intermediate fells are rough, somewhat confusing in arrangement, diverse in character, and excellent territory for walkers with a liking for solitude. More conveniently reached is Hallin Fell, a superb viewpoint from which the whole area may be appraised; near here are the old and the new churches and most of the buildings. Howtown, with a pier on the lakeside and an hotel, and Sandwick are the only hamlets; farmhouses line the narrow roads to the limits of cultivation, but, beyond, the parish boundary crosses unfrequented fells, following the watershed at a high elevation.

This is wild country, but all of it is beautiful. Its isolated position relative to the usual routes of Lakeland tourists, the absence of through roads and the exclusion of visitors from the deer forest have all contributed to the preservation of the character of the parish, and the long years since men first settled in this rural backwater have brought but little change — except, sadly, in the name of the Parish Church: St Martin's for 800 years, but superseded by a modern St Peter's.

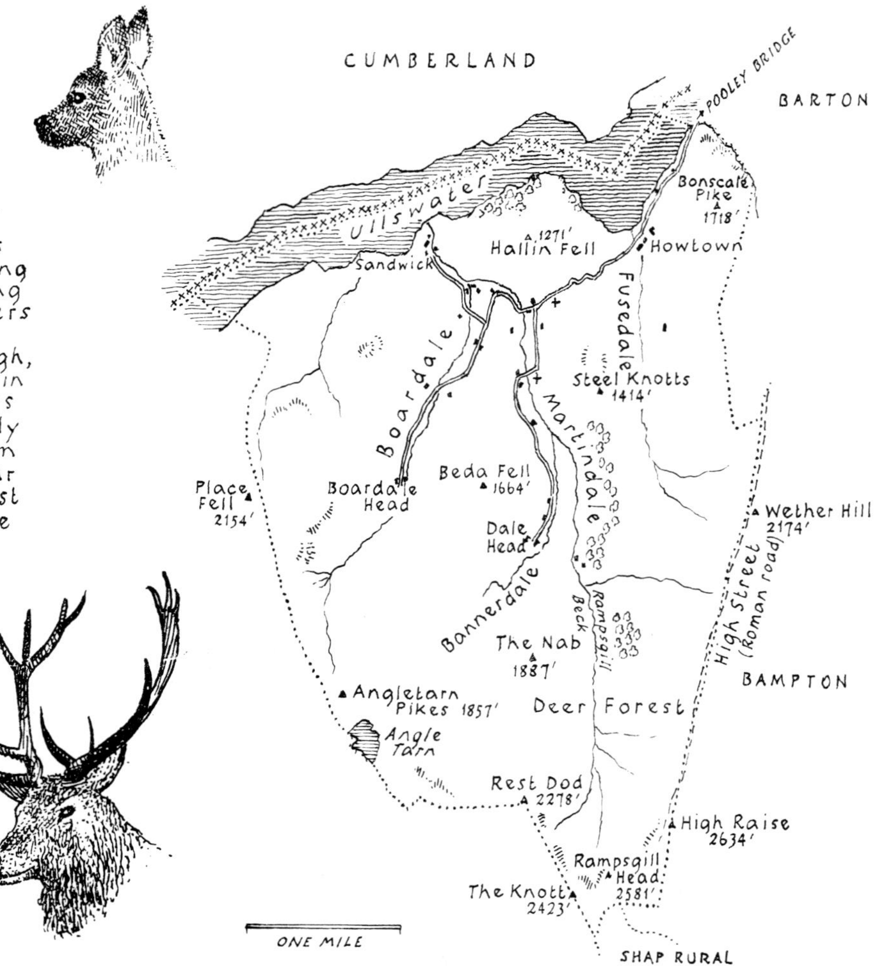

Road bridge,
Howe Grain.

Martindale

The parish church of St Peter, splendidly sited on Martindale Hause above the serpentine loops of the road from Howtown, dates from 1882, when it replaced the old church of St Martin — just in time, for on the day of its consecration a storm tore the roof off the old church, leaving it ruinous.

Martindale

The old church of St Martin, rebuilt in 1633 on the site of an ancient chapel, fell into decay and was closed in 1881. It has recently been restored, and a few summer services are held.

St Martin's

Sandwick

Martindale

Some Martindale Fells and landmarks

The Nab

Bonscale Tower

Bonscale Pike

Hallin Fell

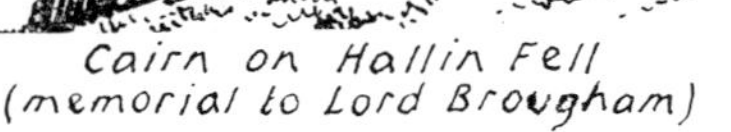

Cairn on Hallin Fell (memorial to Lord Brougham)

Beda Fell

Dale Head, the last farmhouse in the valley, has massive buttresses: these originally supported a gallery. A dated stone, 1666, probably gives the year of building. Further up the valley are the remains of an ancient village settlement.

Christy Bridge

In deer country—
on the left the Fleshing House where deer are skinned; in the background the Nab, a deer preserve.

MEATHOP AND ULPHA

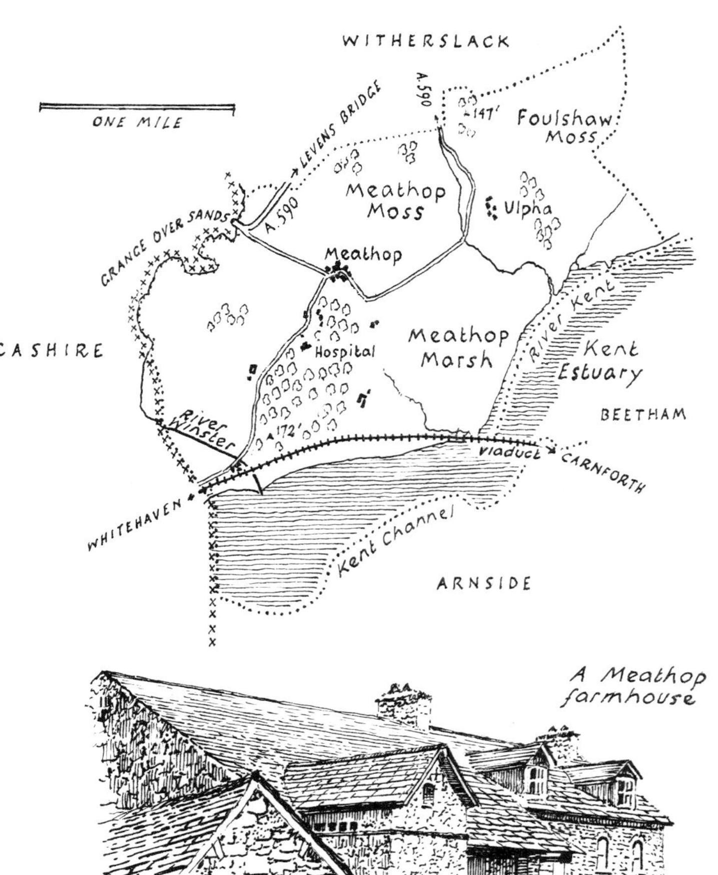

Meathop, to most Westmorland people, is the name of a hospital; to those more intimately concerned with its affairs it is the name of a maritime parish lying between the main road to West Cumberland and the northern shore of the Kent Estuary facing Arnside. The land, being mainly alluvial salt marshes and extensive mosses, is flat, lacking in interest except to birdwatchers and wildfowlers, and without scenic quality apart from a few limestone knolls, once islands, that rise abruptly from the plain and have attracted tree growth. Examples of the general low level of the surface are seen in the elevations recorded on Ordnance maps — at one point, over a mile inland, the height above sea level is two **feet**! This is a landscape totally uncharacteristic of the county. Meathop Moss is a nature reserve.

The hospital, formerly a tuberculosis sanatorium, is the principal building in the parish, which has no church, but the most notable is Meathop Hall, in the complex of farm buildings and cottages forming the small village of Meathop. Ulpha, distinguished by inclusion in the parish name, is a farming hamlet a mile distant.

A corner of Meathop village

A Meathop farmhouse

Meathop and Ulpha

Below a steep cliff of tiered limestone the River Winster passes through a culvert under the railway to reach the sea beyond.

Meathop Hall looks Elizabethan, but was built around 1700. The distinctive facade retains its original mullioned windows, and the cylindrical shimney shafts are also of interest.

Meathop Hall

MIDDLETON

The parish of Middleton covers a considerable area between the River Lune and the Yorkshire boundary, mostly fell country rising to 2,000 feet but having a strip of valley land along which lies the main road linking Sedbergh and Kirkby Lonsdale, following approximately the line of the Roman road heading north to Low Borrow Bridge and another abandoned artery of communication: the track of the branch line from Clapham to Lowgill. There is no village; a few scattered homesteads and farms occupy the lower pastures on the east bank of the river.

Middleton is well known in archaeological circles for its medieval Hall, which still retains much of its early appearance, and for a Roman milestone in almost pristine condition, having been protected from damage during the passage of time by being buried in the ground until unearthed last century.

Beckside Hall
1616

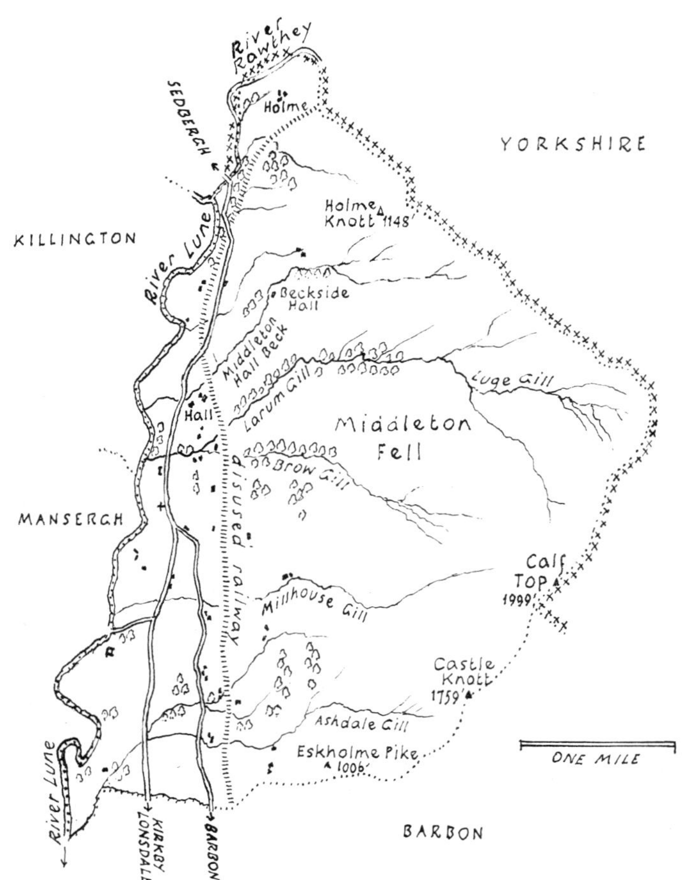

Middleton

Middleton Hall

Middleton Hall, a medieval manor house, is one of the best remaining examples of 14th and 15th century domestic architecture in the county. The present house is 15th century; a range of earlier buildings adjoining is more interesting, a feature being an arched screen passage. But the most exciting relic of the past is the high curtain wall with a gateway admitting to the hall and enclosed courtyards and which had a gatehouse, the two windows over the arch being all that survives of it: a most impressive defence. The Middleton family occupied the hall for ten generations and had a deer park adjacent. More recently a room in the hall was used as a chapel. A former north wing is in ruins, the habitable part of the hall today being a farmhouse.

The curtain wall is a monument of unique archaeological importance and access to it by the public is permitted.

The gateway in the curtain wall

On the approach to the Hall, the buildings are concealed by the massive curtain wall

Middleton

The parish church of the Holy Ghost, referred to in church notices simply as Middleton Church, was built in 1879, and is of plain appearance, but the neat and pleasing interior is distinguished by a fine memorial window. Set in the churchyard wall are **two dated stones**, 1634 and 1813, these being the years of erection of the original and a subsequent chapel on this site.

Summit cairn, Eskholme Pike

This Roman milestone, excellently preserved, was re-erected at the place of its discovery in 1836. It bears an original inscription: M.P.L.III (53 miles).

The following was added upon re-erection

SOLO ERVTVM RESTITVIT
GVL MOORE
MDCCCXXXVI

The stone, a cylindrical shaft, is 5½ feet high, and stands in a field 300 yards south of the church.

Middleton Bridge

Middleton

Middleton Fell is an extensive moorland rising to 2000 feet on the eastern side of the Lune Valley in slopes of gentle gradient although deeply cleft by gullies, but beyond the long summit, the highest point of which is Calf Top, there is a steep and uniform declivity into Barbondale, most of this side of the fell being Yorkshire territory. The area is wild and little visited, but affords excellent walking on unenclosed sheep pastures.
The viewpoint of the drawing is Egholme Gate, Mansergh, looking east over and across the valley.

MILBURN

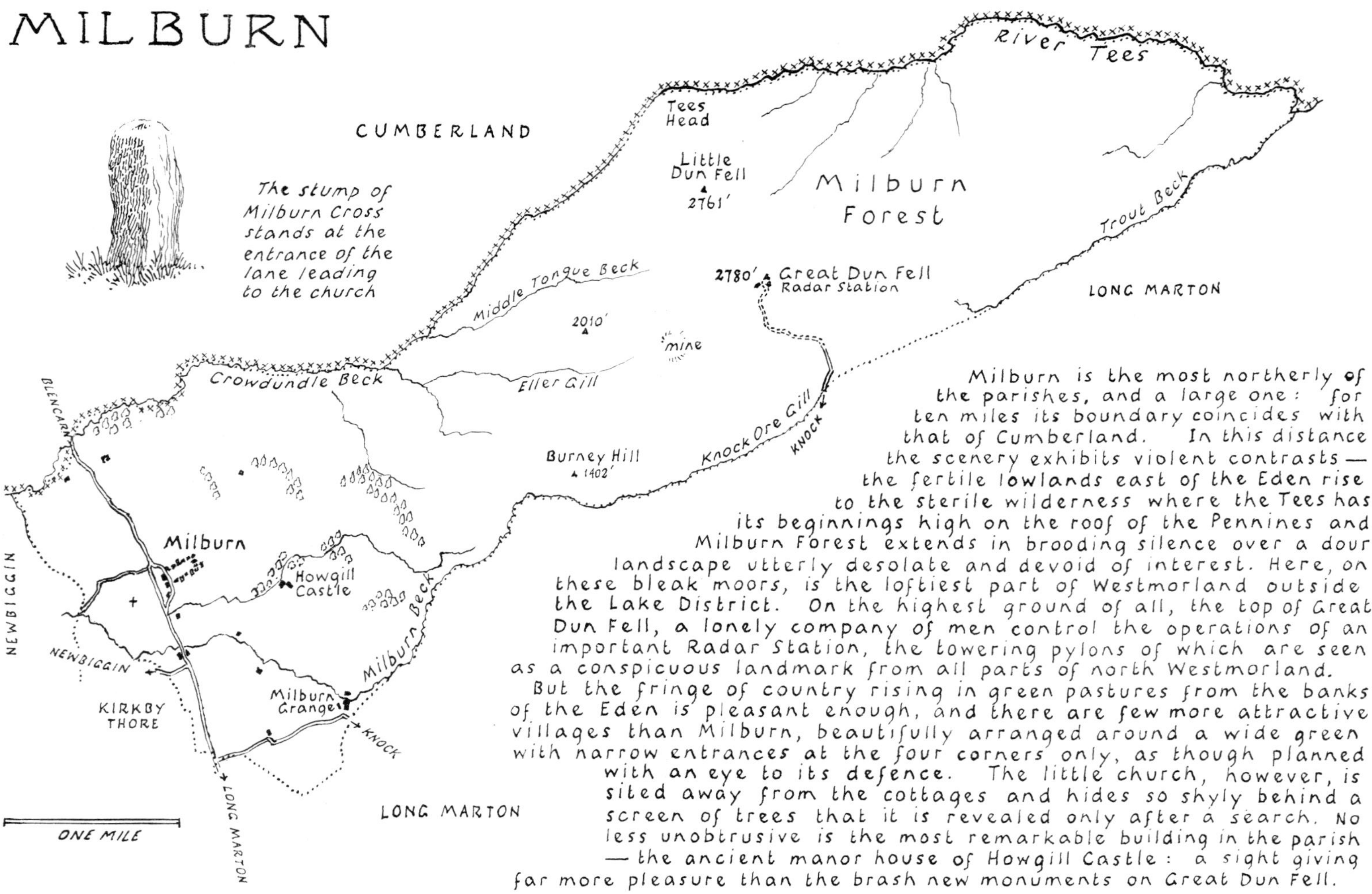

Milburn is the most northerly of the parishes, and a large one: for ten miles its boundary coincides with that of Cumberland. In this distance the scenery exhibits violent contrasts — the fertile lowlands east of the Eden rise to the sterile wilderness where the Tees has its beginnings high on the roof of the Pennines and Milburn Forest extends in brooding silence over a dour landscape utterly desolate and devoid of interest. Here, on these bleak moors, is the loftiest part of Westmorland outside the Lake District. On the highest ground of all, the top of Great Dun Fell, a lonely company of men control the operations of an important Radar Station, the towering pylons of which are seen as a conspicuous landmark from all parts of north Westmorland.

But the fringe of country rising in green pastures from the banks of the Eden is pleasant enough, and there are few more attractive villages than Milburn, beautifully arranged around a wide green with narrow entrances at the four corners only, as though planned with an eye to its defence. The little church, however, is sited away from the cottages and hides so shyly behind a screen of trees that it is revealed only after a search. No less unobtrusive is the most remarkable building in the parish — the ancient manor house of Howgill Castle: a sight giving far more pleasure than the brash new monuments on Great Dun Fell.

Milburn

The shyness and seclusion of the little parish church of St Cuthbert seem, to a visitor, to stem from an awareness that it has not the size nor the grandeur of the neighbouring churches, Long Marton and Kirkby Thore, but it has a peculiar quaintness and charm the others lack, and is greatly esteemed by the people of Milburn. The date of building is not certain, but there is Norman stonework, notably the south doorway, although the interior is mainly of a later period, and the bellcote was rebuilt in 1894 during an overall restoration.

It is thought that the church may have been founded by the monks of Shap Abbey.

Milburn village

Very few village greens today retain a maypole, but Milburn's has one: a replacement, erected in Coronation Year, 1953.

Milburn

Howgill Castle

Milburn Forest

Milburn Forest is without trees. No vegetation other than mosses and moor grasses can survive the conditions prevailing in the wild fastnesses of the Forest, which is elevated above 2000 feet. Part of the area is now a Nature Reserve, a section is crossed by the Pennine Way, and the Radar Station has a permanent staff, yet despite these recent infusions of life the Forest remains an inhospitable desert — as the men who once laboured in scattered lead mines here would have readily testified: all these workings are abandoned but the artificially-contrived ravines, or hushes, are still a conspicuous feature of the barren landscape.

First appearances are often deceptive, and the facade of Howgill Castle suggests a large Georgian residence built in formal style, with only a single mullioned window to hint at an earlier origin. The front of the house, however, is a 1733 reconstruction, and conceals the true character of a quite remarkable building, which was a massive stronghold in its day, with walls ten feet thick, vaulted basements, and a defensive moat. The rear of the building, much of it 14th century masonry, gives the best indication of its strength. As the manor house of Milburn, some notable families have lived here. Today it is occupied as a farmhouse and is supplemented by a fine range of stables, the whole in so clean and tidy a condition, with wellkept gardens, that it ranks amongst the most handsome of farms.

Radar Station, Great Dun Fell

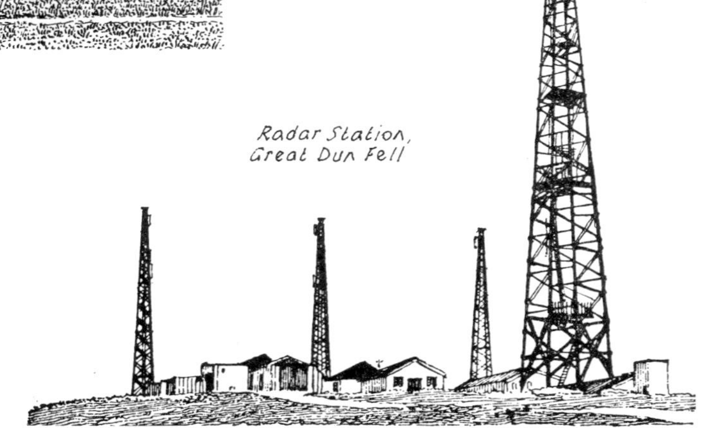

MILNTHORPE

Milnthorpe was, in days gone by, the port of Westmorland, although no harbour nor even a jetty is to be seen today and navigable sea waters are too distant for exploitation as a maritime artery of supply. Before the erection of the railway viaduct at Arnside, however, there were channels by which ships could reach wharves at Sandside for the discharge of their cargoes of grain and other produce and take aboard goods manufactured locally; smaller boats could continue along the River Bela almost to the outskirts of the village, which served also as a centre of distribution for the fisheries in the northerly waters of Morecambe Bay. This trade started to decline early last century when the Lancaster Canal was opened to traffic and the railway later effectively sealed its doom.

Milnthorpe survived this blow to its economy, developing into a large and active village and becoming involved in another form of transport. It stands astride an ancient turnpike road that has become a major highway, the A6, and is especially busy when the weekend crowds throng to the Lake District in cars and cause severe congestion along the main street — a position soon to be relieved by a bypass link from the motorway.

The parish is small, being detached from the neighbouring parish of Heversham and given a separate status as recently as 1896. The church also dates only from last century, the former dependence on Heversham in all ecclesiastical matters being illustrated by the retained name of Church Street, which leads not to Milnthorpe's new church but to Heversham's old one.

The village is favourably situated with easy access to both seaside and open country. A pleasant boundary is formed by the River Bela, flowing alongside the attractive deer park of Dallam Tower, and the head of the estuary has good seascapes; otherwise the scenery of the parish, although predominantly rural, is becoming increasingly subject to influences of an urban nature, a large factory having contributed to the spread of houses outside the confines of the old village, and the busy railway and main road creating noise alien to the countryside.

The River Bela at the pedestrian entrance to Dallam Park

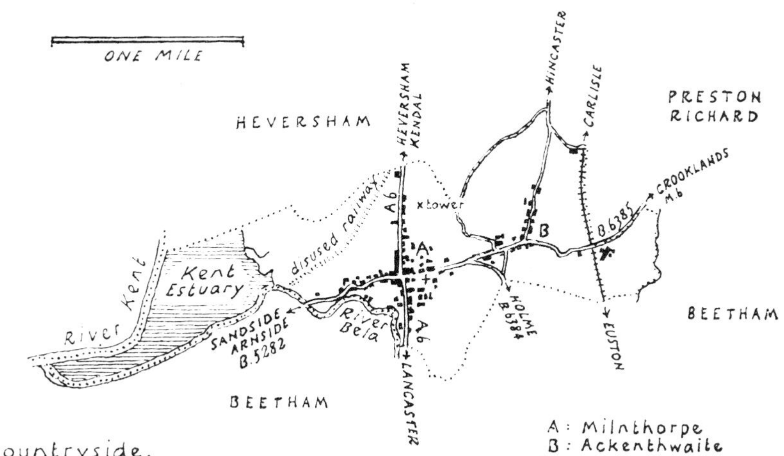

Milnthorpe

The church of St Thomas, splendidly situated at the top of the village, was erected in 1837 and assigned full parochial rights in 1838. It was substantially re-designed in 1883, when the chancel was added and other alterations made.

The parish church and war memorial

Iron ankle shackles from the old market cross (now replaced) are on display in Kendal Borough Museum

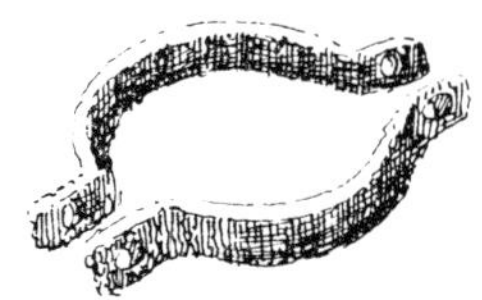

The market place

Milnthorpe

Owlet Ash was the home of the authoress Constance Holme, who was born in Milnthorpe and wrote about the district in many novels.

St Anthony's Tower, the most prominent landmark in the parish, crowns a green hill north of the village and enjoys a commanding view of the surrounding countryside and the Kent Estuary. It was built in early Victorian times as a summerhouse for St Anthony's House on the main road nearby, and served as an observation post for the Home Guard during the last war. Since neglected, the tower could, if kept in repair and provided with a simple approach path, be a fine viewpoint amenity for the village.

Bela Mill commenced operation as a rope and canvas factory in the early years of the 19th century, but since 1886 has been, and still is, engaged in comb manufacture.

A splendid iron waterwheel of 14' diameter, silent now but remaining in situ, formerly provided power for the mill and nearby properties on the banks of the Bela.

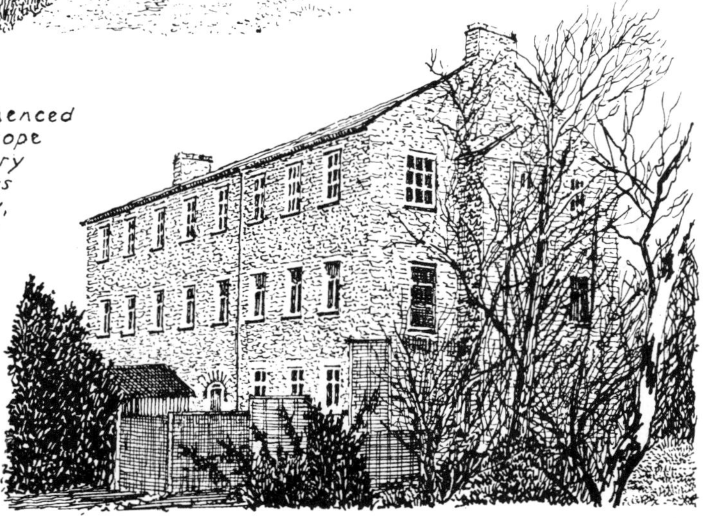

MORLAND

The parish church of St Laurence

CLIBURN
ONE MILE
CLIBURN
River Leith
BOLTON
Morland Beck
503'
BOLTON
KINGS MEABURN
GREAT
STRICKLAND
Morland
River Lyvennet
KINGS
MEABURN
568'
NEWBY
NEWBY
KINGS
MEABURN
ford
SLEAGILL

Morland Church is one of the loveliest in the county and parts of its fabric may well be the oldest masonry in any. The unbuttressed tower of mellow red sandstone, a joy to behold, has stood since the 11th century, before Norman builders brought their own styles of architecture; the nave and chancel are 13th. The interior too has many noteworthy features and fittings.
This is a church of which Morland's parishioners may rightly feel very proud. As doubtless they do.

Morland

The Vale of Lyvennet has many charming villages and none is more delightful than Morland, happily remote from railway and motorway, privileged in its setting, and enjoying the enviable tranquillity of an undisturbed countryside. The scenery everywhere is lovely, green fields being sheltered by woodlands and watered by pleasant streams, and the village street, through which flows Morland Beck, remains picturesque and unspoiled.

But the greatest of Morland's treasures is the Saxon church of St Laurence, serving as mother church to several adjoining townships formerly within the old parish when its boundaries extended to the Eden; for civil purposes they are confined by the lesser rivers of Leith and Lyvennet.

Cottage by the ford, Morland Beck

Morland Bridge

Morland

Rural limekilns are usually built singly, but at the farm of Byesteads they are built with double hearths.

A village street in Morland

Flowers still bloom in the grounds of Morland Hall but the once-elegant house with distinctive brick chimneys, which did service as a war-time hospital, stands abandoned and ruinous with rampant ivy clothing the skeleton.

MURTON

Murton is a large parish and its scenery ranges between extremes, one boundary being the River Eden in surroundings sylvan, while another, eight miles away, crosses the slopes of Mickle Fell at a height of 2550 feet in surroundings not at all sylvan. Rising gently from the valley of the Eden the western part of the parish is under cultivation and has two neighbouring villages, Murton (a name derived from Moor-town) and Hilton, but beyond these last outposts of civilisation the gradients steepen into an escarpment cleft by deep gullies that pierce the moor to a plateau above, but the parish extends even further, covering an upland wilderness of fifteen square miles and including the basin of Swarth Beck, which feeds the River Tees and is therefore over the Pennine watershed, before rising finally to the county boundary near the remote top of Yorkshire's highest mountain: Mickle Fell, 2591'. In the gullies above the villages are the ruins of lead and barytes mines, and an isolated shooting box on the plateau is a reminder of the days when these moors provided extensive grouse shoots. The water issuing from the gullies as becks has the reputation of being the purest in the country. A hamlet, Flakebridge, emerged from obscurity to win a short-lived fame a few years ago when a syndicate proposed to develop the locality as a tourist centre with all manner of 'attractions'. Friends of Murton voiced their opposition at a public enquiry, and the decision that such a scheme should not proceed met with general acclaim: an injection of fun-fairs would be fatal to the wellbeing of the parish and alien to the attractions provided by nature; even the Appleby golf course on Brackenber Moor seems an anachronism in a setting so rural.

The parish is crossed in the south by a mile of the busy A.66 road and a mile of active railway, otherwise a few minor roads and farm tracks form a threadbare network of communications sufficient only for local needs.

As in the neighbouring parish of Dufton the church serves two villages and for the convenience of both is sited in isolation midway between the two communities, in this case Murton and Hilton. The cemetery, detached from the church, is similarly placed.

The parish church of St John the Baptist, built in 1855, looks older than its age, standing in a position exposed to the weather and unprotected by trees. A feature is a three-decker pulpit.

Murton

Cottages at Coupland (on the A.66)

Mill Bridge, Hilton

Murton

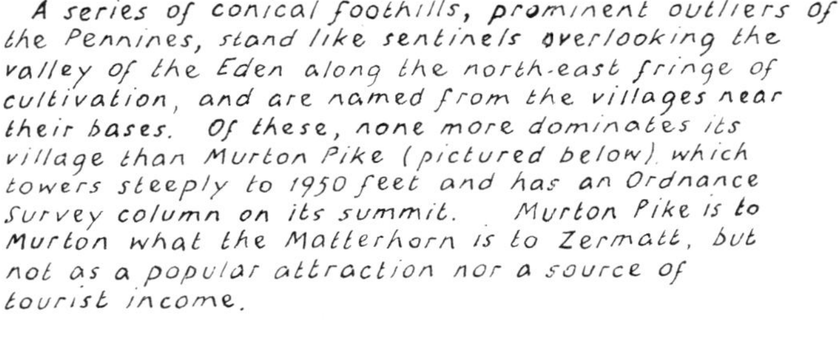

A series of conical foothills, prominent outliers of the Pennines, stand like sentinels overlooking the valley of the Eden along the north-east fringe of cultivation, and are named from the villages near their bases. Of these, none more dominates its village than Murton Pike (pictured below) which towers steeply to 1950 feet and has an Ordnance Survey column on its summit. Murton Pike is to Murton what the Matterhorn is to Zermatt, but not as a popular attraction nor a source of tourist income.

Village scenes at Murton

Murton

Murton Hall, an ancient manor house, cannot fail to appeal to anyone having an antiquarian interest. It is a splendid example of a late medieval residence, the older parts being of the 14th century and remaining little changed. The transomed windows are a special feature, and the interior retains many original fittings. It is now a farmhouse.

Murton

Brackenber Hall, built in the 17th century, retains its original picturesque appearance.

On Brackenber Moor is an ancient earthwork, known as the Druidical Judgment Seat, in the form of an enclosure of ¾ acre, oval in plan, on the top of a flat mound.

Roman Fell, from Hilton.

Roman Fell is within firing range of the army guns at Warcop and all paths thereto have warning notices forecasting sudden death to those who venture beyond when the red flag is flying (e.g. DO NOT TOUCH ANYTHING. IT MAY EXPLODE AND KILL YOU).

Sandstone cliffs and caves on Brackenber Moor

Murton

Village scenes at Hilton

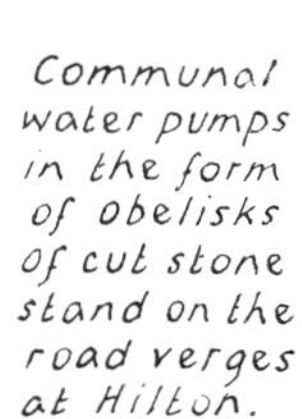

Communal water pumps in the form of obelisks of cut stone stand on the road verges at Hilton.

MUSGRAVE

As with the neighbouring parishes, the boundaries of Musgrave have been extended in the present century to include a strip of uninhabited Pennine moorland terminating on the Yorkshire county march at an arbitrary spot known as Hanging Seal without regard to topographical considerations: all the streams of Musgrave Fell flow eastwards across the parish boundaries and enter Yorkshire. In former years the parish occupied only the valley lands of the Eden and was compact; the extension has given it a most irregular and elongated shape.

The centre of social activity is the village of Great Musgrave, on a pleasant eminence overlooking the River Eden. The railway and station here are post-war casualties but the western extremity of the parish is crossed by the still-active Settle-Carlisle line. It is the A.66 road, however, ceaselessly carrying through traffic, that is the parish's most effective lifeline.

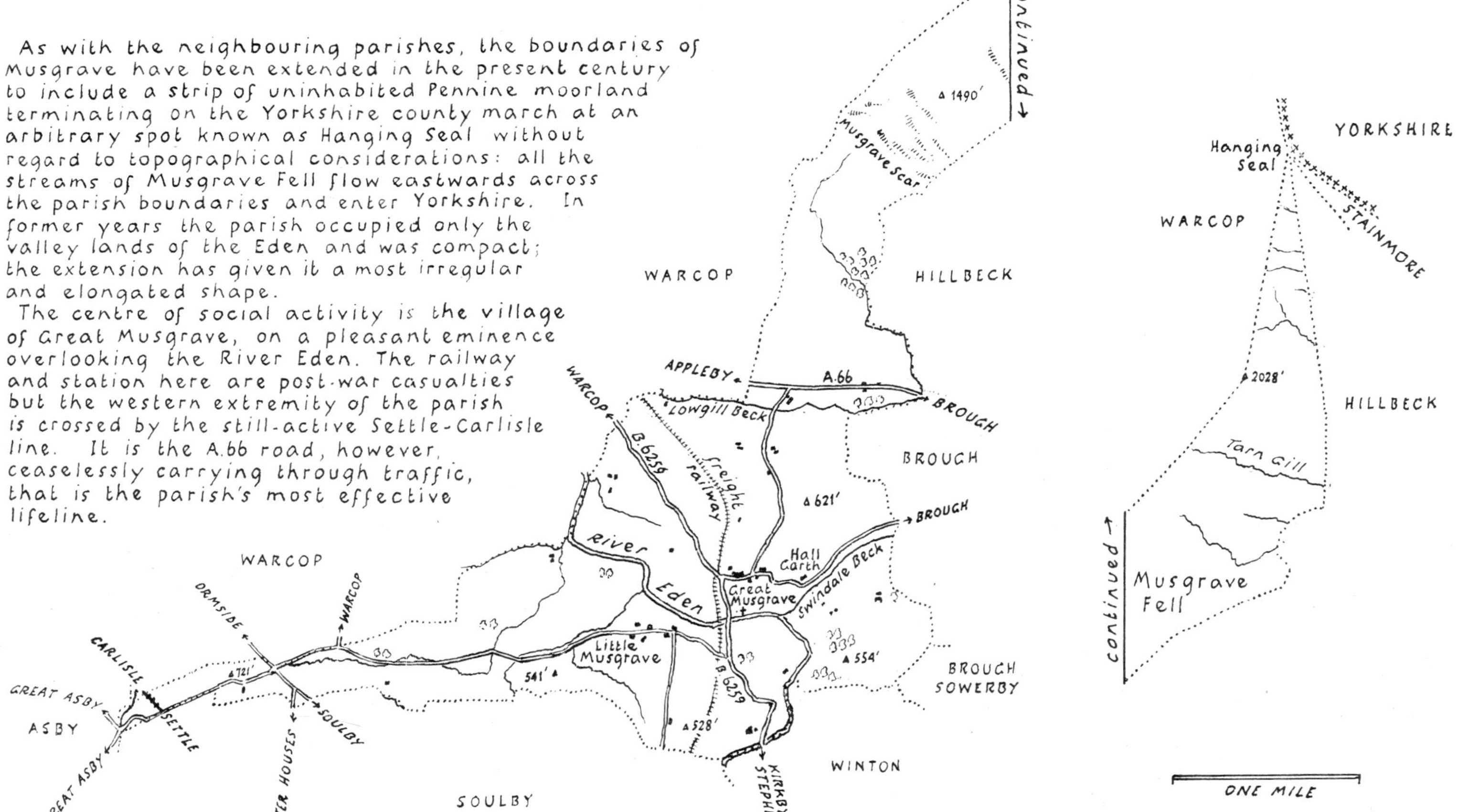

The hamlet of Little Musgrave was, until 1894, within the parish of Crosby Garrett.

Musgrave

Musgrave Bridge

The parish church of St Theobald stands on the north bank of the River Eden. It is the third on this site, being rebuilt in 1845 at a higher level than its predecessor, which suffered greatly from inundation when the river was in spate; even so, the present church has not proved immune and in 1883 flood-water entered to a depth of over 4 feet. Fittings from the former church have been incorporated, the two bells being 15th century. Rushbearing services are a traditional annual event here.

Musgrave

The manor house, ancestral home of the Musgrave family after the Norman Conquest, has long been demolished but traces of the estate remain. At Hall Garth a drive leads over a quaint turreted bridge across Swindale Beck. Nearby are lynchets.

Farmhouse at Little Musgrave

Cottages at Great Musgrave

NATEBY

Nateby is a dependency of Kirkby Stephen, having no parish church and sharing a common boundary. The small village of that name stands at a junction of the Mallerstang and Swaledale roads, the latter climbing high over the Pennines and providing a scenic route of absorbing interest and sustained beauty. The River Eden flows near the village and at Stenkrith Bridge enters a deep limestone gorge, here attaining, in a romantic setting, the highlight of its long journey to the sea. There are other natural features of merit, notably Ewbank Scar, but in general the greatest appeal of the landscape lies in the open sweep of fell rising over Nateby Common to the Pennines beyond.

Nateby is a place of considerable antiquity. As the name testifies, the first settlers here were Danish invaders.

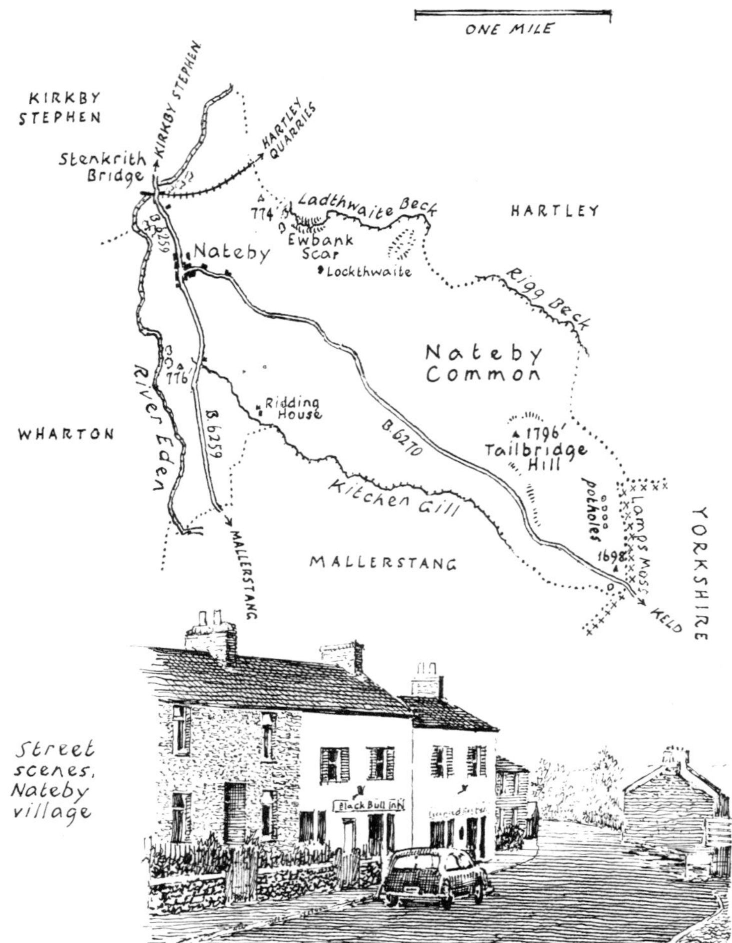

Street scenes, Nateby village

Nateby

Stenkrith Bridge. *Stenkrith Bridge carries the Kirkby Stephen - Nateby road over the Eden, which here courses through a deep tree-lined gorge. In the vicinity of the bridge the river bed is formed of great slabs of limestone, the water pouring through fractures, often out of sight, and swirling in confined channels and whirlpools. With the passing of time the agitated waters have worn circular pits and hollows in the bedrock, assisted in the scouring action by pebbles carried along by the river when in flood. At one point, where a subterranean channel has been carved out, the noise is like that of machinery in motion and has earned for the spot the name of 'The Devil's Mustard Mill.' The results of this natural erosion by the force of water are spectacular.*

Tailbrigg Pots

Tailbrigg (or Tailbridge) Pots are a sequence of potholes in the limestone of Lamps Moss, north of the summit of the Keld road, and penetrate the moor to a known depth of 75 feet. South of the road summit is another cavity, Jingling Pot.

NATLAND

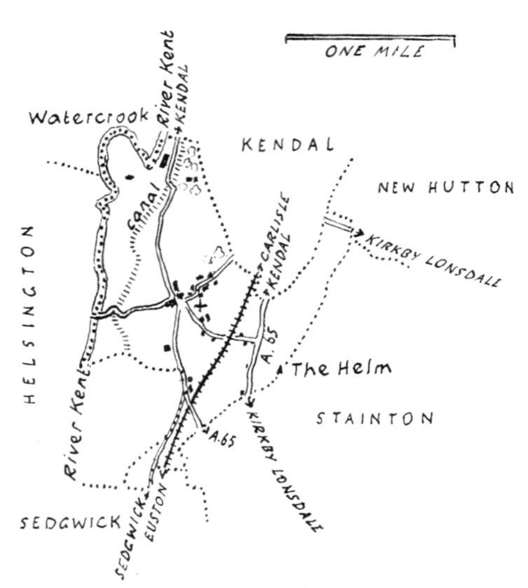

The parish of Natland has shown little change since its land was first husbanded, remaining predominantly agricultural despite the cutting of a canal and the laying of a railway track across its green fields, disturbances met with resilience and not too much sacrifice of amenity. It is, as always, a desirable rural location.

But the village of Natland has altered radically in recent decades, the older buildings, once an isolated group around the village green, being now the centre of a sprawl of residential development. Not long ago it was a village without suburbs; now, but for a green belt not yet profaned, it would be a fringe of Kendal, for which indeed it has become a dormitory. One built-up area, Oxenholme, has been annexed by the borough within easy memory.

The River Kent forms a pleasant boundary to the parish, having a spectacular limestone bed at Hawes Bridge, but the finest natural asset is the open common of the Helm, a hill of modest proportions but with a commanding outlook: a magnificent vantage point.

History is long at Natland, the settlement forming as a feudal manor in pre-Conquest times and being mentioned in the Domesday Book; much earlier, the Romans had an important establishment near the river. There was an association in medieval days with St Mary's Abbey of York, owners of the tithes, and this is perpetuated in many local place-names. The handsome edifice of St Mark's Church is new but its foundation is old, dating from the 12th or 13th century, and being first represented by small chapels. The villagers created historical facets to their existence by instituting an annual Palm Fair and leaving behind them a cockpit to illustrate a bygone pastime. Life was not easy in old Natland but it has never lacked interest.

Hawes Bridge

Natland

The parish church of St Mark, erected in 1910, is the successor to other churches and chapels on or near the present site since the 12th century.

Natland

right:
Old mill buildings, Natland Mill Beck

bottom right:
Natland Hall

below:
Natland Abbey

Ancient Natland

Legends ascribed to Natland need to be sifted to ascertain truth and fiction. There are no evidences, for instance, of the treacle mines associated with the place.

But there is no doubt that long before the Norse invaders settled here and named it *Naetlund* other communities lived or sojourned in these parts. On the summit of the Helm are the remains of an ancient hill-fort, although today only the grassgrown ramparts can be distinguished. This is thought to have been a camp of the Brigantes, a native tribe, and earlier in time than the Roman occupation. It is known as Castlesteads.

Much better recorded, and more obvious to the eye, is the Roman fort of Concangium in a loop of the River Kent at Watercrook, the importance of which is only now being brought to light by excavation of the four-acre site. Many finds, ranging from coins to altars, have been discovered here in past years and are distributed in various museums, and outline plans prepared from surveys on the ground, but not until 1974, when a working party sponsored by Lancaster University made a systematic dig, were the foundations laid open and a wealth of Roman artifacts unearthed. This work is to continue in future years, and it is hoped that sufficient material may be produced to justify the establishment of a site museum.

The summit of the Helm

Earthworks, Castlesteads

Excavations, Watercrook, 1974

NETHER STAVELEY

Staveley is a large village on the road and railway to Windermere from the south and a familiar name to many travellers for whom the primary objective of their journey is not Staveley but Lakeland. For them, it is a place to get through quickly, an unavoidable stepping stone. Visitors to Lakeland see Staveley and its environs but do not linger. The district would lose some of its modest charm if they did.

For administrative purposes Staveley is divided into two parishes, Over Staveley and Nether Staveley, the boundary between them following the low straths of the rivers Gowan and Kent traversed by the main road A.591 and the railway. Nether Staveley lies to the south, being a tract of undulating country rising from green fields to rough slopes of bracken interspersed with coppice woods: not an exciting landscape but pleasant and colourful, attractive not merely because it is on the fringe of Lakeland and has high mountains within view but in its own right.

The railway station and a small part of the village are in the parish of Nether Staveley but there are no other centres of population. The lower ground is cultivated or dairy pasture in the care of a dozen farms; of these the one most worthy of mention is Hollin Hall, which retains, in altered form, a medieval pele tower.

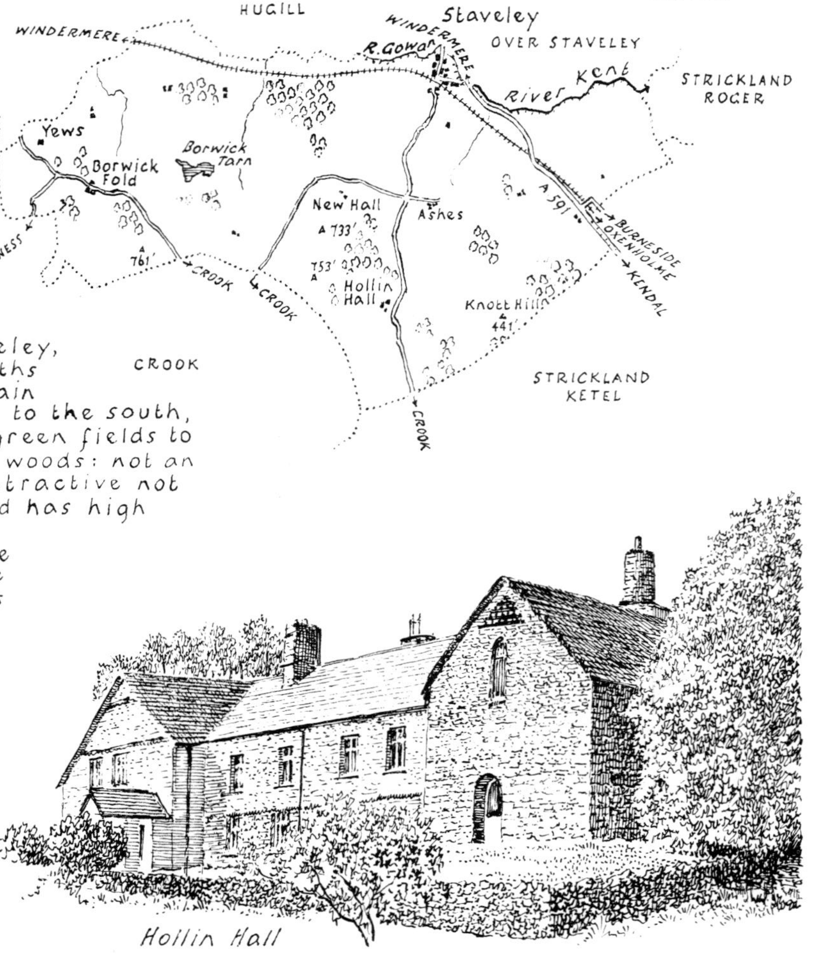

Hollin Hall

Hollin Hall (sometimes referred to as Hollin How) is the oldest and most interesting house in the parish, the year 1450 being recorded as the date of erection although this can refer only to the medieval pele tower, since gabled and incorporated with adjoining buildings added in the 16th or 17th century.

Nether Staveley

17th century farmhouses

Ashes is of different periods and the layout suggests that access to the older parts was originally through an arch in the outbuildings dated 1737 and now walled up. Ashes has a long history; in earlier days a chapel was established here.

Yews, recently improved and converted, enjoys an open situation secured from disturbance by tourists on the A.591 nearby by numerous gates. Cattle grids have disadvantages!

Borwick Fold (below) occupies a delightful hidden position amongst rocky foothills; it is served by narrow much-gated roads that effectively defend the farm from intrusion by exploring motorists. Nearby is a pleasant tarn.

NEWBIGGIN

Newbiggin enjoys a sequestered woodland setting in the valley of Crowdundle Beck, which forms the county boundary with Cumberland. The village, lying well away from main roads, is quiet and pleasant and endowed with some fine buildings, notably the large turretted hall and the quaint old parish church. The parish is small, and of neat and sylvan appearance. Occasionally the peace is disturbed by the noise of trains on the Settle-Carlisle railway, which bisects the parish; otherwise Newbiggin hears only the sounds of the rural countryside.

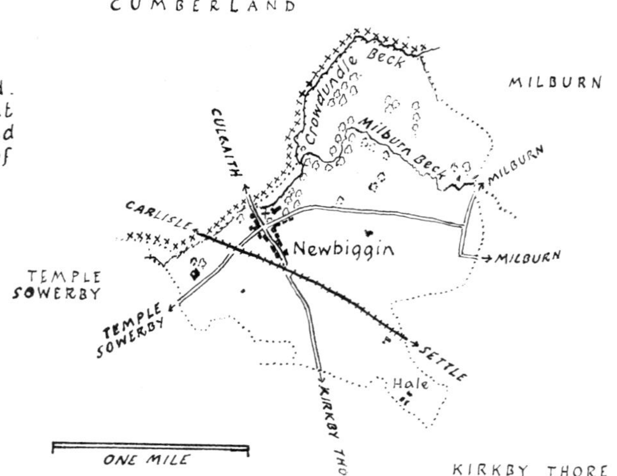

The modest parish church of St Edmund, with only 150 sittings, is a very ancient foundation, and although the registers date only from 1572, the earliest building was probably 12th century, as evidences of Norman masonry suggest, but rebuilt in the 14th century; it was again rebuilt in part in 1853-4. The exterior of the church is unassuming but inside are a number of items of special interest: a 12th century piscina, several fittings of the 14th century, and the emblazoned arms of the Crackanthorpe family are displayed in the east window. In the churchyard are to be seen a medieval sundial and the shaft and base of an ancient cross.

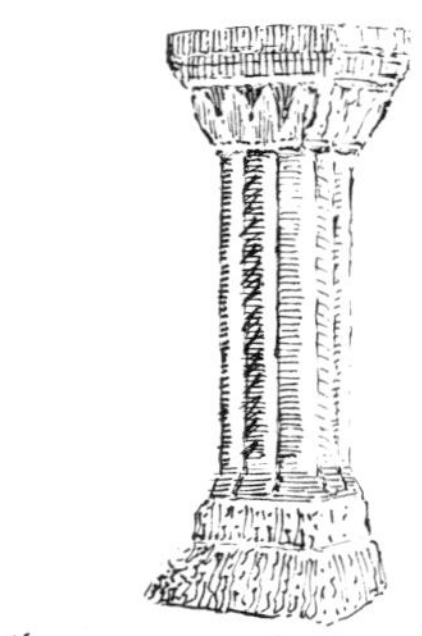

12th century piscina (communion basin)

Newbiggin

Home Farm, 1695

This derelict water-powered corn mill at Newbiggin still retains its wheel-shaft.

Newbiggin Hall

Newbiggin Hall is a very imposing castellated mansion, built in 1533 on a site formerly occupied by a 13th century manor house, but much of the present building is the result of Georgian and Victorian alterations and extensions, bearing the dates 1759 and 1844. It was the home of a well-known family, the Crackanthorpes, for no fewer than fifteen generations, and some of the members of it represented the county in Parliament.

A stone tablet set in the west wall has the following carved inscription:

'Cristofer Crakanthorp thus ya me calle,
Wiche in my tym dyde bylde this halle,
The yer of owr lorde who lyst to se,
a M fyve hundreth thyrty and thre'

NEWBY

Newby, formerly known as Newby Stones, is typical of the parishes situated between the A.6 and the A.66 — pleasant and unexciting of landscape, entirely agricultural, little known and rarely in the news, content in its seclusion.

There is no Anglican church, St Laurence's at Morland being the mother church for this and neighbouring civil parishes.

Cottages at Newby

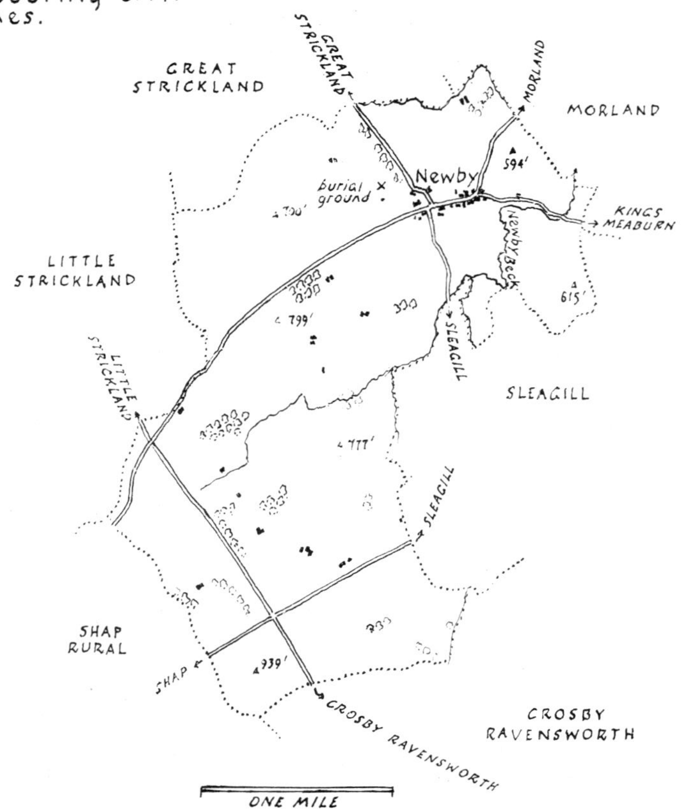

Newby

Newby is a village with several interesting buildings, mainly 17th century, individually sited along both sides of a country road, but quite outstanding is Newby Hall, of charming appearance and little changed. One door has a panel dated 1685; above the front entrance is a tablet displaying the arms of the Nevinson family, owners of the manor for many generations.

Newby Hall

In addition to the Hall and the cottages, there is interest both for the antiquarian and Quaker visitors in an old burial ground of the Society of Friends. This, enclosed by a wall and planted with trees, stands in isolation from the village. In it is an inscribed vault and a few gravestones of the 17th century.

NEW HUTTON

New Hutton, despite its name, is an old township, being a part originally of an extensive district known generally as Hutton, anciently named *Hotun*, which also included much of the present parish of Scalthwaiterigg and the adjoining areas of Old Hutton and Holmescales. Since medieval times there have been changes in township and parish boundaries, the present parish of New Hutton being constituted in 1897.

The landscape is undulating, consisting mainly of farmland patterned by green fields but rising to 1000' on the rough pastures of Docker Fell and Roan Edge, from which several streams flow south, destined for the Kent Estuary *via* the River Bela. The small village of New Hutton, formerly Raw Green, clusters by the church and there is a hamlet at Millholme, but elsewhere the population is widely distributed, mainly at farms. In the parish, at Fisher Tarn, is the impounding reservoir for Kendal.

The uninhabited eastern part of the parish, disturbed by the creation of a reservoir to supply the Lancaster Canal last century, has recently been transformed by the construction of the motorway M.6 but apart from the re-routing of minor roads in the vicinity this has had little impact on the life of the parish.

Crake Hall, which had a cockpit, has been unoccupied for 20 years following a disastrous fire.

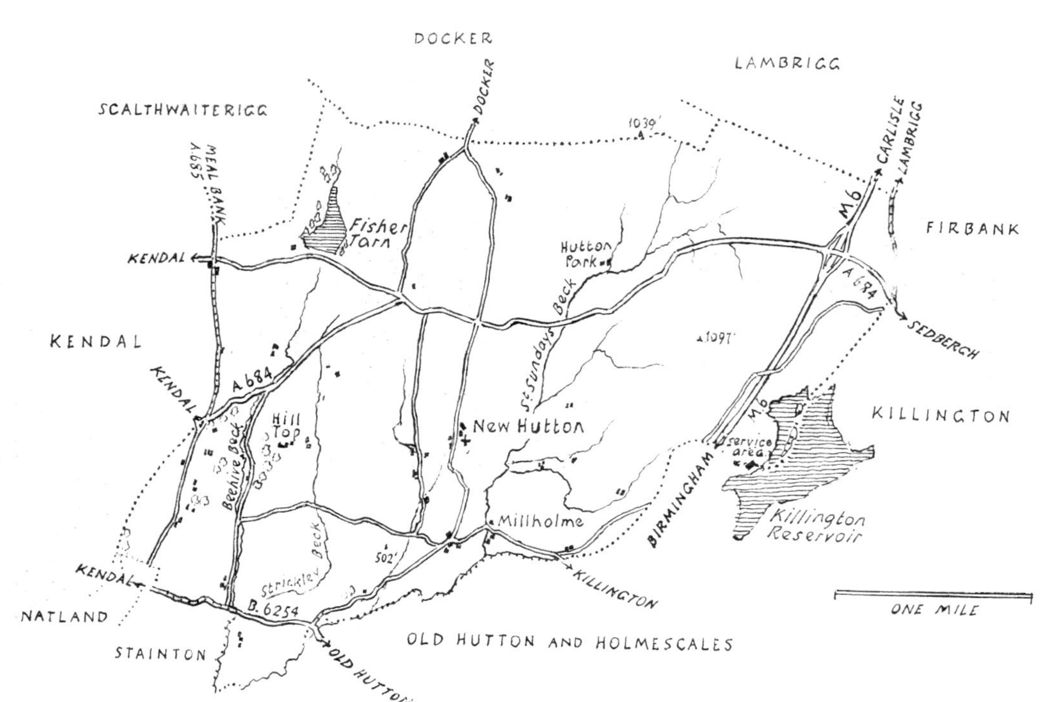

New Hutton

This monument, in the grounds of Hill Top, is a memorial to a mare named Midge, which was reputed never to have lost a race. It was built in 1766.

The church of St Stephen was rebuilt in 1828, replacing a chapel of 1739. The embattled tower is decorated with the arms of prominent families, and the pillars of the churchyard entrance have the most unusual adornment of two stone greyhounds, removed from the now-demolished Sleddall Hall, the family home of the Sleddalls, whose many benefactions included a school and almshouses in Kendal.

Hayclose

Hill Top, an elegant late-18th century mansion formerly owned by the Bentincks of Underley is now occupied as a preparatory school under the name of Holme Park.

OLD HUTTON AND HOLMESCALES

Old Hutton and Holmescales is the considerable remnant of the once-large and ancient district of Hutton, the present parish boundaries dating only from 1897.

The village of Old Hutton stands on the old road from Kendal to Kirkby Lonsdale and has lost some of its importance since the A.65 was routed further south. Unusually, the buildings are grouped along the roadside in three sections, each concealed from the others by low hills and all having distinctive names: Middleshaw, Chapel Houses (where the church is situated), and Old Hutton proper. Holmescales is a farming complex a mile south; Beckside and Eskrigg End are small communities reached by narrow lanes. A pleasant stream, Peasey Beck, flows through the parish, and forms a lovely waterfall at Beckside.

The landscape is undulating farmland rising to hillier pastures in the east, and recently suffered a radical change due to the construction of the motorway M6 and a service area at Killington Reservoir. The M6 has sliced through the heart of the parish and brought the noise of traffic to a district that had hitherto known only the sweeter music of a contented countryside.

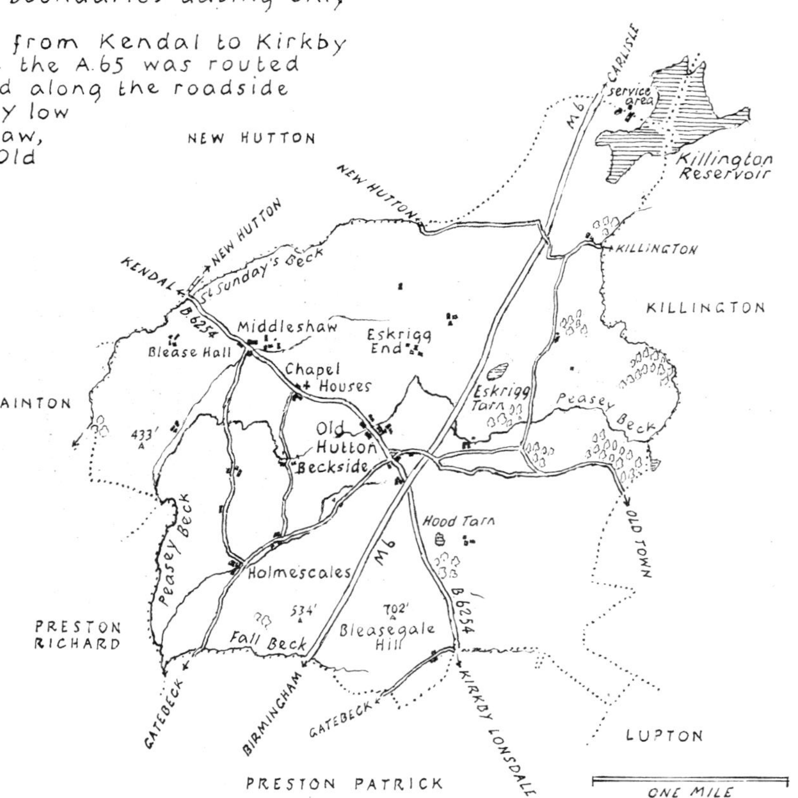

Middleshaw Hall

Old Hutton and Holmescales

The parish church of St. John the Baptist has twice been rebuilt, in 1699 and 1873, but retains a 14th century window from an earlier structure of unknown date. A particular treasure is a medieval chalice, possibly of 1459 and the oldest in the county, but this has recently been removed for safe custody.

A tablet over the doorway of a cottage opposite the church proclaims that John Wesley lodged there on a night in 1740 during a journey on horseback from Whitehaven to Leeds.

Cottages at Old Hutton

Old Hutton and Holmescales

Holmescales

Peasey Beck at Beckside

Old Hutton and Holmescales

Bleaze (or Blease) Hall

Rural Industries, R.I.P.

In the years before the opening up of communications Old Hutton had attained, in economic affairs, an insular independence with a variety of small industries supplying community needs. In mills and workshops there were joiners, sawyers, leather tanners, wheelwrights, blacksmiths, builders, shoe makers and corn-millers, and the farms and a store provided food. It is a commentary on changing times that many occupations within the parish have become moribund.

Built into the side of the lane leading to Bleaze Hall is a relic of another former rural industry. This is a lye-kiln, used for the burning of bracken, the ashes of which, mixed with fat, produced a soft soap.

Bleaze Hall has not been improved in appearance by many alterations to the fabric since its erection around 1600: a number of stone mullioned windows and the entrance gates have been walled up and the south wing demolished, but it remains nevertheless a picturesque house of considerable interest. The interior has fittings of the Jacobean period, although many of its old treasures have been removed, in particular a massive oak table; today it is best known for the elaborate plasterwork of a first-floor ceiling.

The house was originally the seat of the Batemans, who, among other interests, maintained a train of packhorses operating regular services from the extensive stables.

Associated with Bleaze Hall is the superstition of a ghost, kept at bay by a "dobbie stone", a magic charm, in the attic.

Its great days over, the Hall is now a farmhouse.

Lye-kiln, Bleaze Hall

ORMSIDE

A quiet road leaves the Kendal highway south of Appleby and cuts across pleasant pastureland, with isolated farmsteads appearing only rarely, to reach Soulby after several lonely miles. From it there branches an even quieter road signposted Ormside, but, because maps show this to be a *cul de sac*, few turn aside. Ormside remains the most peaceful of backwaters, the stillness disturbed only by trains racing along the railway bisecting the parish and on which there was once a station. In this tranquil countryside are the small communities of Great and Little Ormside, the former being Great merely because it houses a few more people, but not enough to raise its status above that of a hamlet. Yet, unexpectedly, where the road comes to an end in farm precincts, there is to be seen the most remarkable of Westmorland's churches, a gem, a living relic of the middle ages. The River Eden, the parish boundary, flows alongside.

MURTON
CARLISLE
HOFF
Great Ormside
APPLEBY
River Eden
Little Ormside
Hoff Beck
Asby Beck
Helm Beck
Heights
tunnel
SOULBY
GREAT ASBY
WARCOP
Breaks Hall
ASBY
Helm Beck
ONE MILE
SETTLE

Ormside was formerly Ormeshead

The west tower of the church

Ormside Hall, set with farm buildings in a quadrangle and shadowed by the church, has a three-storied tower wing of the 15th century and substantial walls suggesting that the mansion, like the church, was built for protection. It is believed locally that a secret passage communicated with the church.

Little Ormside also has a surprise for visitors, this being a magnificent cedar, reported to have been brought as a seedling from Lebanon and nurtured on the journey with rationed water. Nearby is a cottage, sadly ruinous but still bearing an inscribed stone with the date 1686.

Ormside

Ormside's great treasure is the medieval church of St James, the second oldest in the Carlisle Diocese: a church remarkable not for its beauty but for the grim austerity of its design, the rugged stone walls of massive strength; a church built not only for worship but as a bastion of defence, a barn-like structure with Saxon and Norman characteristics and many internal features of exceptional interest, documented for visitors. Much of the fabric dates from the 11th century, and subsequent extensions have conformed to the original style of building. The beginnings of the foundation may be earlier still, for a famous bowl of gold and silver (the Ormside Cup, now in York Museum), ascribed to the 7th century, was found here in 1823, and remains of Viking burials have been unearthed in the graveyard. The site of the church is also out of the ordinary: it crowns an abrupt knoll, part of which is artificial, overlooking a wide sweep of the Eden valley. Ormside Church is unique.

ORTON

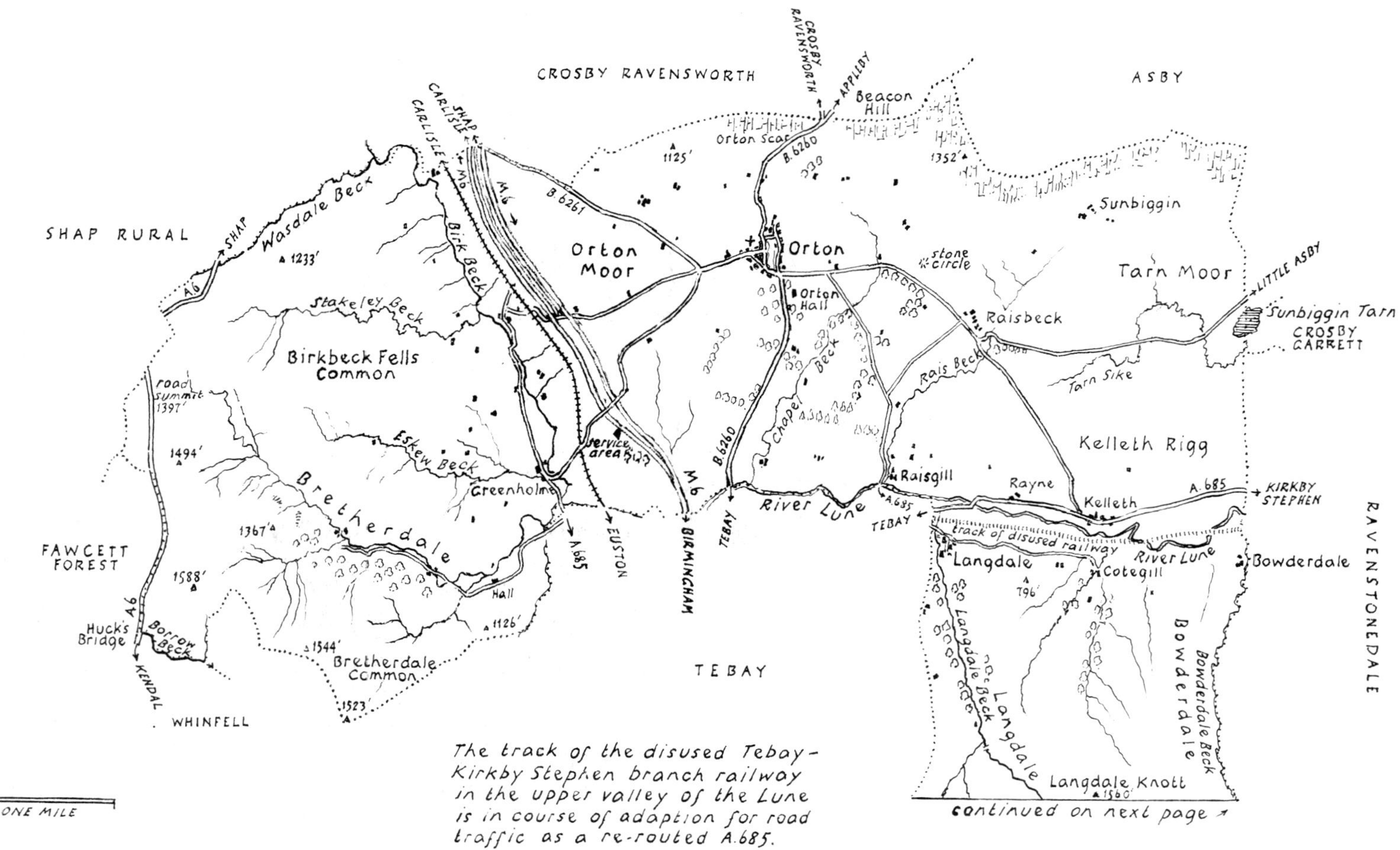

The track of the disused Tebay-Kirkby Stephen branch railway in the upper valley of the Lune is in course of adaption for road traffic as a re-routed A.685.

continued on next page

Orton

Orton is a large parish occupying the southern slope of the lofty limestone plateau that effectively divides the waters of the rivers Eden and Lune and extending west and south to include substantial areas of moorland, the whole forming a diversified landscape of considerable scenic appeal, more particularly in the limestone regions and along the valley of the Lune. The western sector, consisting of peaty uplands, and devoted more to sheep than dairy farming, is deeply cleft by the unfrequented valley of Bretherdale, served only by a narrow access road, beyond the terminus of which is a tangle of wild fell reaching to a notorious highway: the A.6 over Shap Fells. The parish extends southwards, across the Lune, to take in a slice of the Howgill Fells — rather surprisingly, because the terrain here is much more akin to that of Tebay and Ravenstonedale, the flanking parishes; not only does Orton penetrate this lonely wilderness but it perseveres into the heart of the *massif* and culminates in the highest point: the Calf at 2,220 feet. The eastern sector, on attractive limestone, includes the Sunbiggin region, a favourite haunt of birdwatchers and botanists. Orton Scar, despite its elevation, yields marine shells that confirm the natural convulsions that occurred before the land settled in its present configuration.

There are several archaeological sites of importance, and a Roman road intersected the area on its way north from Low Borrow Bridge. The latter can now be traced only in parts; it has been replaced by a modern motorway, which has defied the rising contours to Shap by forming two separate lanes at different levels with a strip of moorland between. Nearby is the main-line railway on the long gradient to Shap Summit.

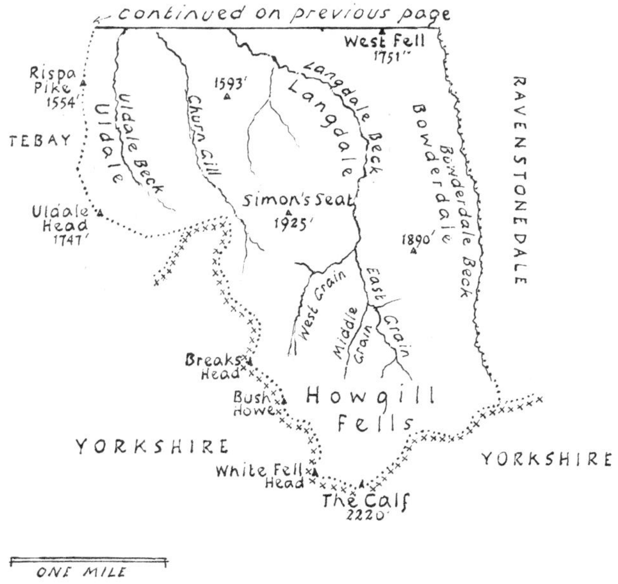

The village of Orton, known in earlier times as Scar Overton, is a place of great antiquity, holding a market charter granted by Edward I; and annual fairs and rushbearing festivals were important occasions in the village calendar. Its significance diminished as a centre of events, Orton today enjoys a quiet rural life in a setting of unique charm and ranks amongst the loveliest villages in the county.

← continued on previous page

West Fell 1751′
Rispa Pike 1554′
TEBAY
Uldale
Uldale Beck
Churn Gill
1593′
Langdale
Langdale Beck
Bowderdale
Bowderdale Beck
RAVENSTONEDALE
Simon's Seat 1925′
Uldale Head 1747′
1890′
West Grain
Middle Grain
East Grain
Breaks Head
Bush Howe
Howgill Fells
YORKSHIRE
YORKSHIRE
White Fell Head
The Calf 2220′
ONE MILE

A bridge in Orton

Orton

A street in Orton

The parish church of All Saints

The church stands on a knoll overlooking the village. Most of the fabric, including the massive west tower, dates from a rebuilding in the 15th - 16th centuries but retains some masonry from an earlier Norman church of the 12th or 13th centuries. Inside, three 'captive' bells form an uncommon decoration. The very extensive churchyard features the stump of a medieval cross.

Orton

Twin becks coming down from Orton Scar bisect the village, and, crossed by a dozen small bridges, form a distinctive and pleasant amenity.

Orton Old Hall was the manor house. It was built in 1604 by the Birkbecks, who were succeeded as owners by the Petty family, since when it has had the alternative name of Petty Hall. It is now occupied as a farmhouse.

Orton Old Hall

Orton Hall

In Bretherdale

Bretherdale Hall

Footbridge, Bretherdale Head

Midwath Stead

The end of the road, Bretherdale Head

Orton

Birk Beck is a considerable tributary of the Lune, draining from Shap Fells along a shallow valley in which are the hamlets of Scoutgreen and Greenholme — a valley unspoilt and unfrequented until the M6 motorway carved a double passage in the adjoining fellside and caused necessary re-alignments of some of the rural roads.

Scoutgreen

Yew Tree Farm

Greenholme

Orton

The stone circle

In a field known as Gamelands is a circle of 36 stones about 50 yards in diameter, locally known as the Druidical Temple. Although many of the stones have fallen it is still an impressive monument. A curious feature is the selection exclusively of erratic boulders of Shap granite, the natural bedrock of limestone being ignored.

Raisgill Hall

Raisgill Hall is dated 1707.
Here manor courts were formerly held
(and cockfights arranged in a cockpit behind the house).

The end of the road, Langdale

The Howgill Fells and the upper Lune valley, from Orton Scar

In the heart of the Howgill Fells: looking up West Grain to Bush Howe, with the Calf on the far left, from Simon's Seat

Orton

A footbridge in Langdale

Fell ponies roam freely on the northern slopes of the Howgill Fells

Orton in the Howgills

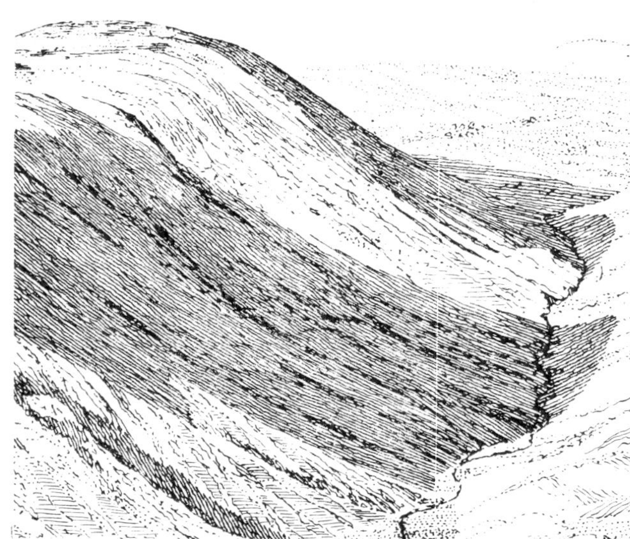

The summit of the Calf, 2220'

left: The middle reaches of Bowderdale

Bowderdale Foot

OVER STAVELEY

Over Staveley, as the name implies, is that part of Staveley highest in the valley (of the Kent), and it contains the highest ground: a lonely upland reaching 1400 feet in altitude, much of it an unfrequented wilderness of heather and bracken and marsh, suitable only for sheep grazing.

Compensation for this lack of scenic attractiveness is, however, amply provided by the River Kent on its way down from the lofty surround of fells at the head of Kentmere, and forming the western and southern boundaries of the parish. It pursues a delightful course hereabouts between wooded banks that, in springtime, produce a lovely display of wild daffodils and bluebells.

The church and most of the village of Staveley are in this parish. Here are factories engaged in wood-turning and the manufacture of cardboard boxes and photographic papers, replacing the old mills that stood on the riverside and of which the weirs and races can still be seen. The village generally is a place of much activity, both social and commercial. Traffic on the main street, the A.591, is an increasing problem, soon to be remedied, in part, by a bypass of the village.

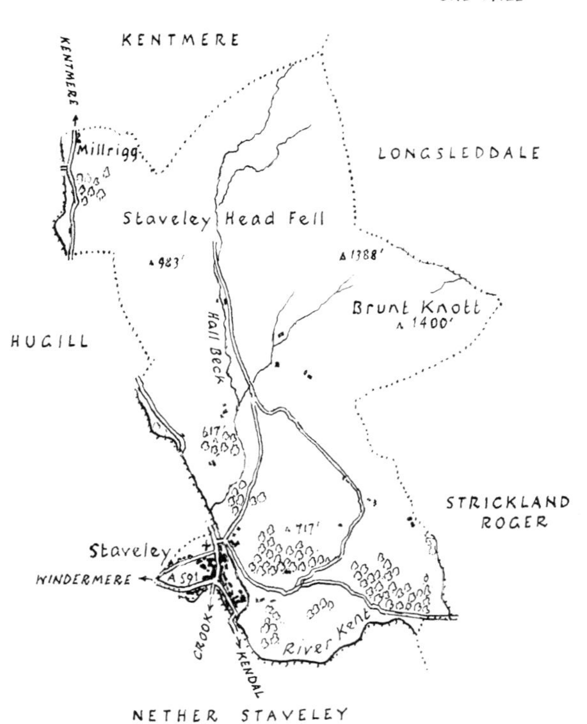

High Scroggs — a 17th century farmhouse

Over Staveley

The parish church of S[t] James was built in 1863-5 to replace the church of S[t] Margaret.

Of S[t] Margaret's Church, only the 14th century tower survived demolition in 1865; the decision to preserve it was a happy one, for although it has suffered alteration from time to time it remains an attractive monument. Closure of the church after nearly five centuries was due to a decay of the fabric, to which both time and weather had contributed, and after rain the site was often waterlogged. The church was the venue of a notable event in 1620 when a successful protest meeting of northcountry farmers resisted a threat to invalidate their title to certain lands by James I. A plaque on the wall commemorates this meeting.

Over Staveley

The summit of Brunt Knott, at 1400,' is the highest point in the parish.

Abbey Home was built in 1844 as a residence for private occupation and was later acquired and administered as a Poor Law Institution by the Kendal Board of Guardians for use as a home for boys. Subsequently the Abbey (so named by the original owner) was taken over by the County Council and adapted for its present use as an Old People's Home.

Main Street, Staveley

The Abbey

Over Staveley

Scroggs Bridge

The River Kent at Staveley

The river above Scroggs Bridge

The weir near Barley Bridge

PATTERDALE

Westmorland is uniformly lovely in all its parts, and the loveliness is represented by widely diverse landscapes ranging from seashore and estuary to wild moorland and exciting mountains, and influenced by a variable bedrock of limestone and red sandstone and green slate; and the choice of a most-favoured area must always be a personal one. But, put to a vote, the Patterdale region would probably find most support. There may be no mountain outline here as dramatic as Langdale Pikes, no stretch of water as large as Windermere, nor is the scenery interwoven with literary associations as at Grasmere, but for panoramic views of mountain and lake and valley, enchanting in their colourful beauty, the countryside enclosed by the boundaries of the parish of Patterdale is a perfection of natural sculpture, boldly executed yet of exquisite detail. Within wide extremes of landscape there is nothing that is not in harmony.

The parish includes the whole of the gathering grounds feeding into the head of Ullswater, which is a prosaic way of saying that the rim of the surrounding mountains is coincident with the boundary. It is, however, the intervening ground that builds up in ascending ridges and buttresses from the valley that endows Patterdale with great charm: the soaring fellsides, the deep defiles and rocky combes, the tarns, the tumbling becks, the sombre crags, the labyrinth of tracks. This is sublime territory for those who come to walk, sublime territory also for those who come only to look.

Fairfield

On the western edge of the parish is Westmorland's loftiest mountain, the mighty Helvellyn; in the heart of the parish is the head of Ullswater, the fairest jewel of all. Glenridding is the largest community, Patterdale village the only other; Low Hartsop is a hamlet of unique character. The A.592 road (Penrith-Windermere) runs through the parish and is the artery of communication, climbing to an exit at the famous Kirkstone Pass, where visitors sensitive to beauty stop for a last lingering look back.

Helvellyn

Ullswater

Patterdale

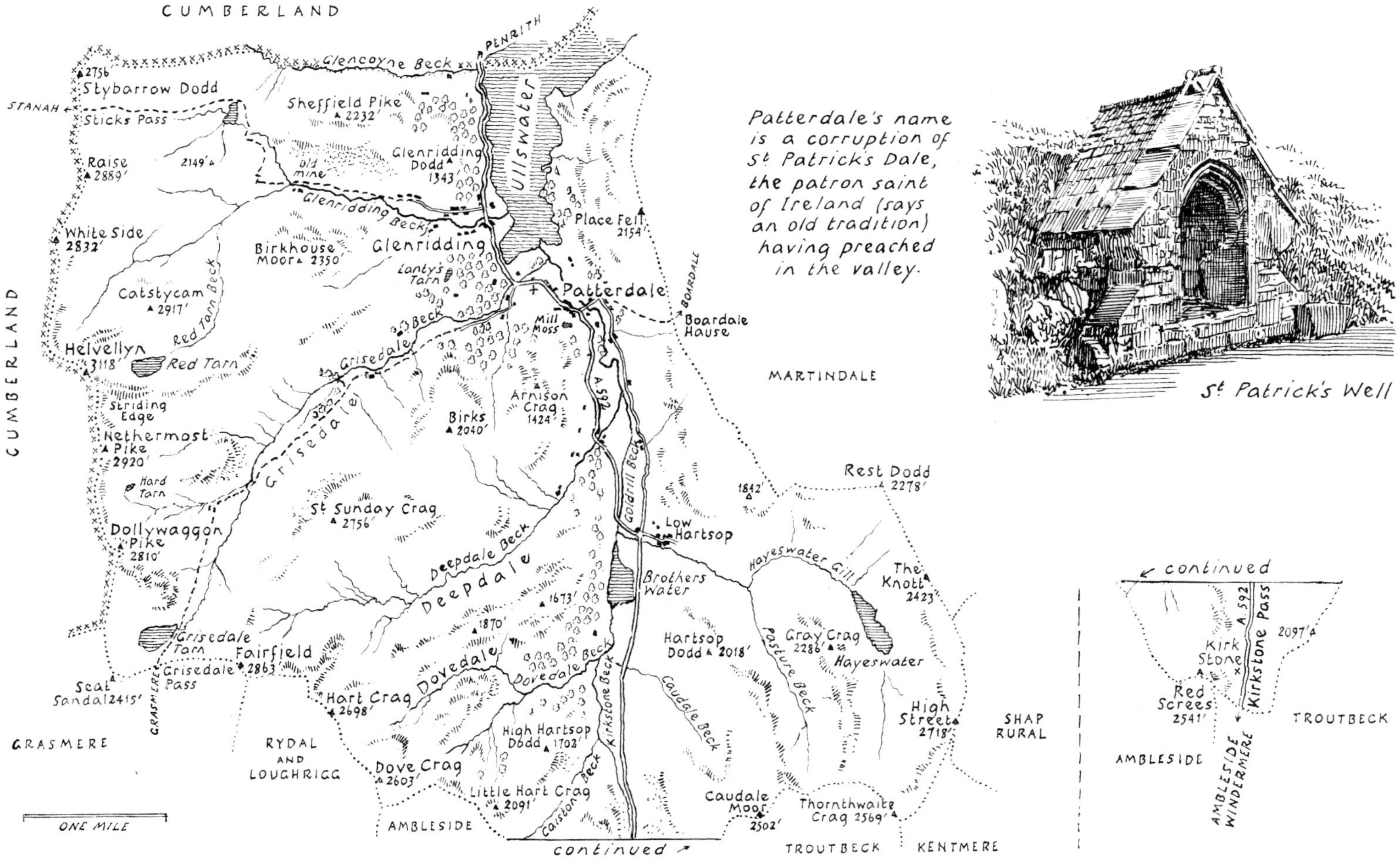

Patterdale's name is a corruption of St Patrick's Dale, the patron saint of Ireland (says an old tradition) having preached in the valley.

St Patrick's Well

Patterdale

There is a distinctive Alpine atmosphere about the little huddle of buildings forming the village of Patterdale, and here as much as anywhere a visitor experiences the indefinable "feeling" of Lakeland. Encompassed by delectable mountain scenery, it is an excellent centre for fellwalking expeditions.

Patterdale

The church of St Patrick was erected in 1853 and given parochial status in 1866. It adjoins the site of a former chapel from which several fittings have been preserved. The useful but oddly-placed clock is a recent addition.

Helvellyn, from Fairfield

Patterdale

Striding Edge

Helvellyn

Helvellyn is ascended more often than any other mountain in Lakeland: it is a magnet to those who climb and to many who normally do not. Its great popularity is not earned merely by its altitude, although only two other summits in the district are higher, nor by superior topographical merit, for several lesser fells offer more rewarding ascents, but by the aura of romance, prompted by legend and poetry, which is associated with its lovely name. The top, at 3118', is the highest ground in Westmorland and forms a boundary with Cumberland: it is a magnificent viewpoint, and, having an easterly position in the district, is a well-favoured place for witnessing the sunrise, for which purpose the mountain is often climbed during the hours of darkness, as it may be by the easy western approaches without hazard. In complete contrast, the Patterdale side is rugged and dramatic: here is the rocky crest of the exciting Striding Edge, beloved of walkers, and Swirral Edge, a near twin, with Red Tarn deep between them; and a landscape strongly carved.
Helvellyn is shared, but Westmorland has the best of it.

The monuments of Helvellyn

The Gough Memorial, erected in 1890, to commemorate a death in 1805, the subject of poems by Scott and Wordsworth.

This tablet, near the summit, records the landing of an aeroplane in 1926.

The Dixon Memorial, erected on Striding Edge in 1858, marks the scene of another fatality, occurring during a fox hunt.

Satellites of Helvellyn

White Side

Nethermost Pike

Catstycam

Raise

Dollywaggon Pike

The Patterdale valley

Patterdale

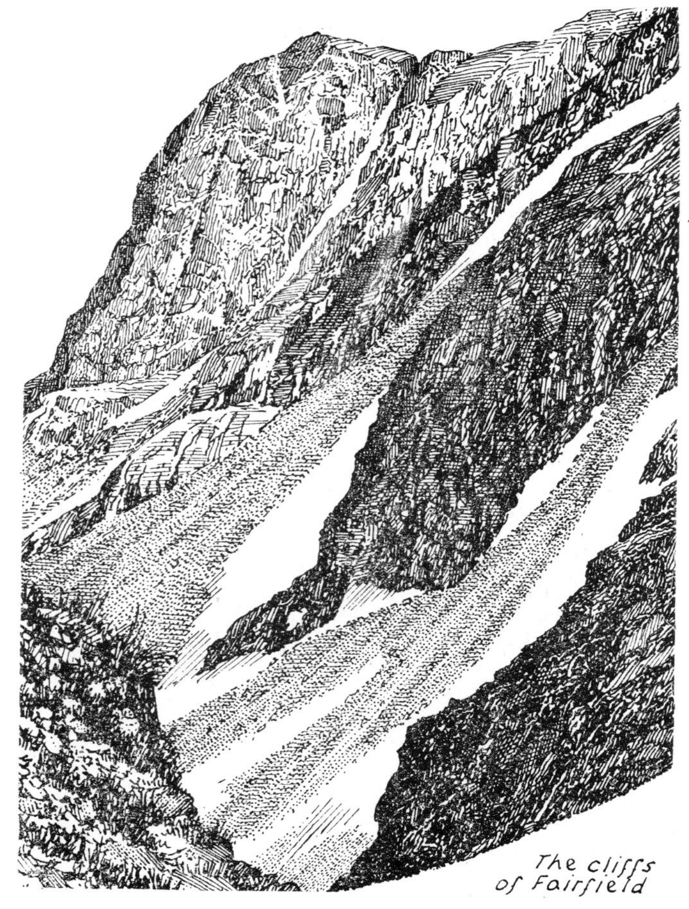

The cliffs of Fairfield

Thornthwaite Crag, from Caudale Moor

Patterdale

Hart Crag

Dove Crag

Patterdale

Patterdale Fells, west of the A.592 road

Birks

Birkhouse Moor

Arnison Crag

St Sunday Crag

Caudale Moor

Patterdale

Patterdale Fells,
east of the A.592 road

Rest Dodd

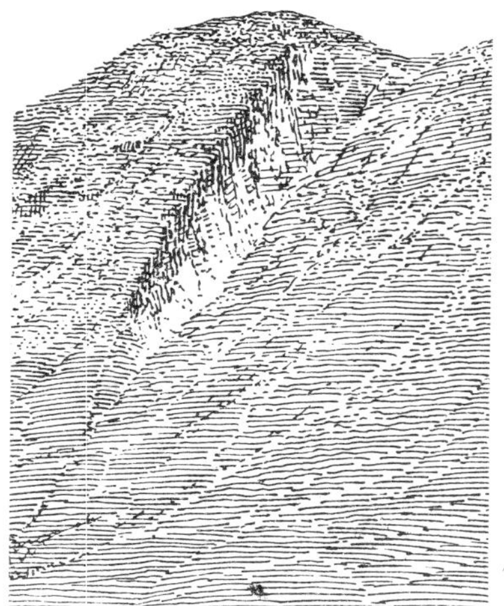

The Knott

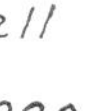

Place Fell

Low Hartsop

The 17th-century hamlet of Low Hartsop, mercifully situated off the main road, preserves its old-world atmosphere remarkably, the only deference to modern pressures being in the provision of a public car-park at the terminus of the narrow lane leading between picturesque cottages, some of which retain outside spinning galleries. Lead mines and slate quarries in the vicinity are closed and ruinous but the glories of the scenery are undiminished and unspoilt.

This unassuming fell had a brief period of fame in 1948 when it won headlines in the press as rescuers toiled for a fortnight to release two terriers trapped in a foxhole on the Caiston side.

High Hartsop Dodd

Thorn House

Brothers Water, reputedly so named following the drowning here of two brothers while skating.

Hartsop Dodd

Hayeswater Gill

Walker Bridge

Wath Bridge

Bridges at Hartsop

Conspicuous on the long climb to the pass from the Patterdale side and resembling a ridged church tower in appearance is the Kirk Stone, a fallen boulder that gave the name to the pass.

Kirkstone Pass

Road (and vehicle) improvements have robbed Kirkstone Pass of its former terrors for motorists and its crossing today causes no apprehension, yet this well-known highway has lost nothing of its visual appeal and the rock-strewn slopes and lofty ramparts have still a thrilling impact on travellers. On the Patterdale side the approach to the summit of the pass, at 1489', is especially exciting, the scenery being wild in the extreme with the craggy declivities of Red Screes dominant.

Kirkstone Pass and Red Screes, from Caudale Moor

This memorial cairn on Caudale Moor is inscribed:

HIC JACET
MARK ATKINSON
OF
KIRKSTONE PASS INN
DIED 14 JUNE 1930
AGED 69 YEARS

Dovedale

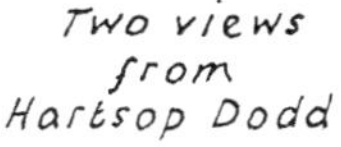

Two views
from
Hartsop Dodd

Patterdale

Patterdale

Glenridding

Glenridding village, once primarily a mining community, has developed into a busy tourist resort, due mainly to its footing on Ullswater and a pier from which passenger boats sail on the lake. Here are large hotels and shops, sites for caravans and boarding houses. The hinterland is splendid fell country and culminates in the Helvellyn range, but it is Ullswater that draws the crowds to Glenridding.

Glenridding Beck

The Greenside Mine

Sheep-farming and tourism are the main industries of the parish today but until its closure in 1962 a large and long-established mine producing galena operated at Greenside, a mile up the Glenridding valley, and was a contributor of much importance to the employment of local labour, the metal extracted from rich veins being high in quality and output. This mine was a pioneer in introducing an electrified system of underground haulage.

Since closure an attempt has been made to efface unsightly spoil-heaps by grassing, but the ramifications of the mine are extensive and the ruins of old workings are in evidence over a wide area, the most notable being a smelt-mill chimney on Raise with a connecting stone-lined flue crossing the fellside, water cuts and breached dams. The main levels and shafts, now blocked, are deep below Sheffield Pike.

Sheffield Pike

the chimney

the flue

a breached reservoir dam

The head of
Ullswater

Ullswater, from St Sunday Crag

Ullswater, from Watermillock Common

PATTON

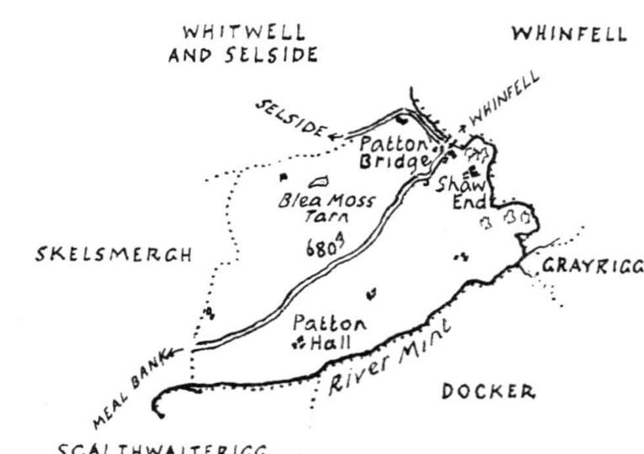

Patton, one of the smallest of Westmorland's parishes both in population and acreage, occupies rising ground in the angle formed by a sharp change of course by the River Mint, which serves as the eastern and southern boundaries. The only road is elevated above the river and has good views of the Whinfell range and the Howgill Fells, the foreground being entirely agricultural except for the elegant mansion and park of Shaw End, without which Patton would be even less 'on the map'. There is no church of any denomination, nor enough parishioners to support one, Patton in ecclesiastical matters being since 1871 under the jurisdiction of Skelsmergh. The parish derives its name from the de Pattons, early owners of the Manor.

Patton Hall

Patton Bridge

Patton

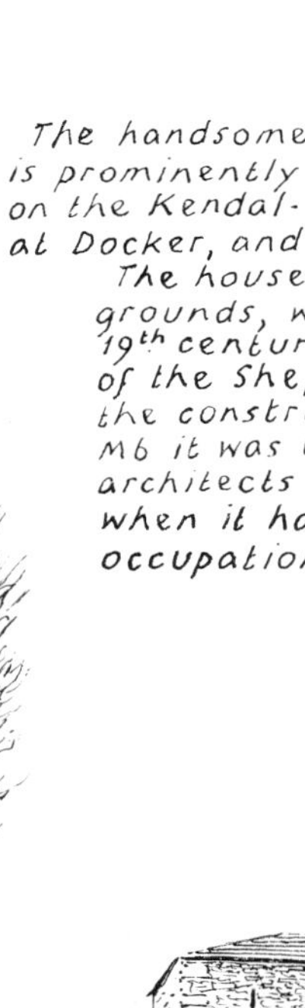

Shaw End

The handsome facade of Shaw End is prominently in view of travellers on the Kendal-Grayrigg road, A.685, at Docker, and excites admiration.

The house, standing in lovely grounds, was built in the early 19th century and was the home of the Shepherd family. During the construction of the motorway M6 it was used as offices by the architects of the scheme, since when it has reverted to private occupation.

The stable block

PRESTON PATRICK

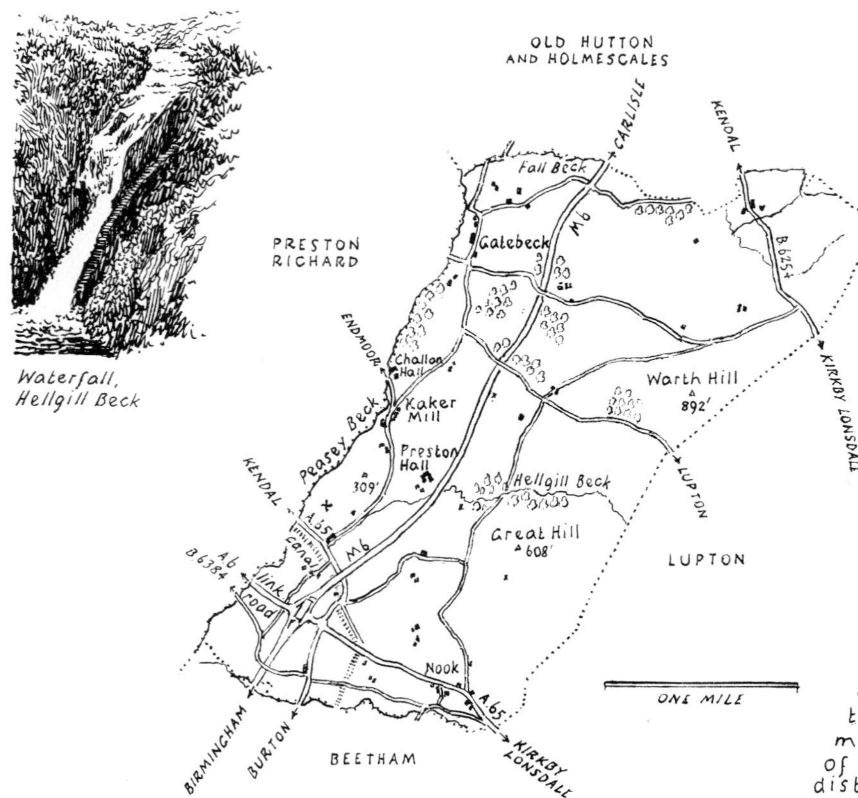

Waterfall, Hellgill Beck

Early records show that Preston had its origins in Saxon times, the name (= Priests' Town) being suggestive of some connection with the Church; later it was adopted as the name of a family of great distinction in the locality. The addition of Patrick about the time of the Conquest is thought to derive from a Patrick de Culwen and it was a descendant of his who, as owner of the manor, founded an Abbey here in 1119, this moving to Shap subsequently. In ecclesiastical affairs Preston Patrick was attached to Burton in Kendal until 1873, when parochial status was granted.

The parish is entirely agricultural but formerly had a gunpowder industry near Gatebeck and mills at Kaker and Millness. A major disturbance of farm holdings was caused recently during the construction of the motorway, which cut through the heart of the parish from one end to the other on the long climb to Killington, and although the scars have healed the tranquillity of the country scene has gone. Preston Hall, for six centuries a haven of rural peace, is now in the shadow of a massive embankment and doomed to suffer the constant noise of traffic; other farms, too, have undergone transformation. At the south end of the parish a motorway access is being joined by a controversial link road to the A.6.

There is no village. Gatebeck, Millness and Nook are hamlets where most of the population is centred. The handsome church, crowning an eminence near the A.65, stands in spacious ground that was once a deer park; notable, too, is a small meeting-house and burial ground of the Society of Friends, founded in 1652 following a visit to the district by George Fox.

Away from the trunk road and the motorway, remote from habitations, the land rises gradually, with many undulations, to the northeast, and here at least Preston Patrick remains quiet and unchanged.

Preston Patrick

The oldest house in the parish, and the most interesting both architecturally and historically, is Preston Hall (locally, Preston Patrick Hall), for centuries the seat of the Preston family but now occupied as a farmhouse. In the absence of dated stones in the structure it is generally assumed that the older parts of the building are of the 14th century. The recessed middle section was originally one large hall open to the ceiling. The first floor of the east wing (on the right in the drawing) was the Court Room, from which the Lord of the Manor conducted his business and dispensed justice. The Court Room has very thick walls and is further supported by barrel-vaulting beneath.

window detail
14th century

Preston Patrick

The parish church of St Gregory

Meeting House of the Society of Friends

In the neat burial ground the graves are indicated by small inscribed slabs of stone set flat in the turf. There are no headstones nor any other ornament.

Few are the travellers along the main road at Crooklands who do not glance admiringly at the handsome parish church of St Gregory, rebuilt in 1852 and conspicuously set in isolation on a green hill, formerly the deer park of Preston Hall. In the churchyard is an ancient yew, many centuries older than the present church.

Preston Patrick

House at Kaker Mill

Old corn mill, Millness

Black Yeats

The site of the once-important gunpowder works on the east bank of Peasey Beck near Gatebeck, operated by W. H. Wakefield and Co since 1852, is today occupied by holiday caravans and only a derelict building remains as a reminder of the industry. The works were closed in 1937.

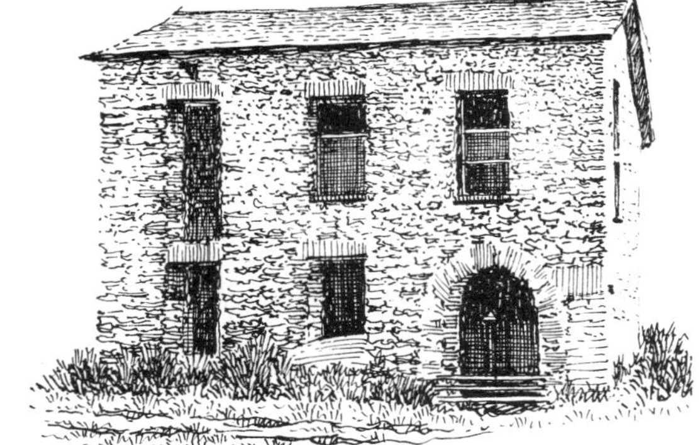

PRESTON RICHARD

A worthy native of Preston Richard was Ephraim Chambers, still famous for his encyclopaediac literature. He was born at Milton in 1680 and buried in the cloisters of Westminster Abbey in 1740.

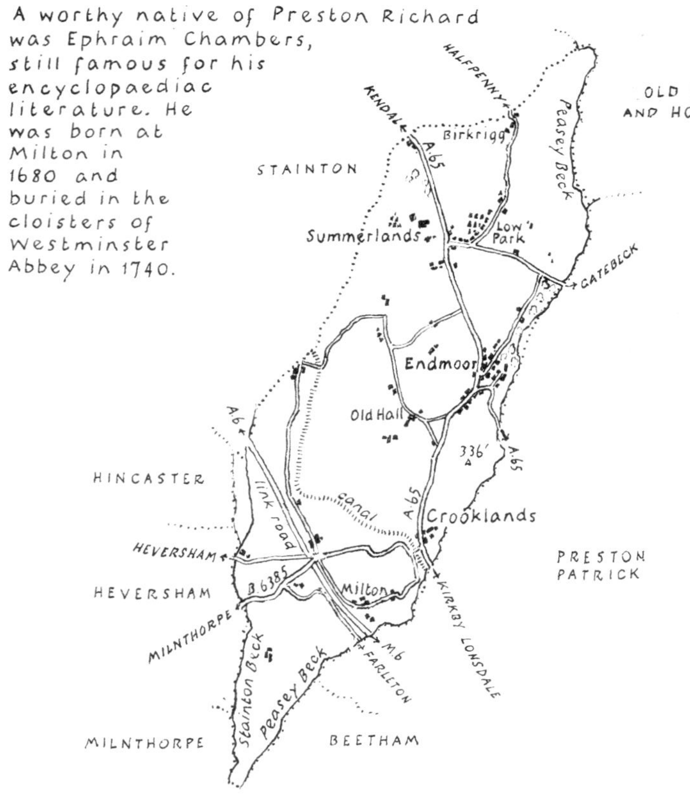

Preston Richard was originally, in Saxon times, known as Preston Ucthred, the name Richard being substituted later, following the Norman Conquest, when a succession of Richard de Prestons were the owners of the manor. There is an obvious affinity with the neighbouring Preston Patrick, but not until comparatively recently did they become an ecclesiastical unit, Patrick being attached to Burton in Kendal before 1873 and Richard, which has no church, being administered by Heversham.

The parish is intersected by the A.65 road, Kendal-Kirkby Lonsdale, and influenced by it. Bordering this busy highway is the village of Endmoor: here, and at Low Park a mile away, new residential estates have been developed. At Summerlands is a furniture industry and at Crooklands catering for road travellers. The Lancaster Canal, which formerly had wharves and coke ovens at Crooklands, is obsolete but may be brought back into non-commercial use. At Milton there is a mill, no longer operational but a notable industrial relic; another mill at Crooklands has been converted to a garage.

Away from the main road the scene is that of a quiet undulating countryside, with many farms and a network of narrow lanes, and has changed little, but deer have long ceased to graze in the pleasant surroundings of the Old Hall.

Loop Cottage, near the Old Hall

Preston Richard

The mansion of Summerlands was built and occupied as a private residence until 1944, when it was acquired by the Merchant Navy for use as a Rest and Rehabilitation Centre, large workshops being provided within the grounds for the making of furniture.

Summerlands

Preston Richard

The Old Hall

An old burial ground of the Society of Friends, known locally as the Sepulchre, is enclosed by walls at the end of a lane (Sepulchre Lane) off the A.65 opposite Summerlands. Neglected and densely overgrown, only one gravestone (1702) is visible. No burials have taken place for about 200 years.

Storth End

Preston Richard

A corner of Milton

Two cylinder retorts, of the type used to produce charcoal in the manufacture of gunpowder, now, painted white, serve as gateposts at the entrance to the old works at Gatebeck.

Few of the county's small rural mills are still operating; almost all have become derelict since closure or been converted to other use. Milton Mill, however, remains as a splendid example of mill architecture, the buildings being intact and the waterwheel in position, this being unusually sited inside the mill and fed by a water race passing under the walls.

Two aspects of Milton Corn Mill

RAVENSTONEDALE

Ravenstonedale is many times blessed. It has a lovely name (although cut down to *Rassendl* by prosaic locals); a venerable church with a monastic foundation and a charming village in pleasant environs; an array of ancient and medieval earthworks; a history rich in legend and interesting fact; and a wealth of splendid landscape pictures in variety, both sylvan and austere and greatly influenced by geological factors, green lowland pastures converging on wild and sombre fells that form a shadowy backcloth to the scene. It is one of the fairest of Westmorland parishes, always a joy to visit and doubtless a good place to live. There is a certain proud dignity in Ravenstonedale. It is better endowed than most. And knows it.

This is a large parish and for convenience is divided into four districts uniquely known as Angles. The hub of activity is Ravenstonedale village, which once held a weekly market; Newbiggin on Lune is also a village, having its own small Anglican church (St Aidan's) and formerly a railway station; Bowderdale, Stennerskeugh and Weasdale are out-of-the-way farming hamlets, the last-named having a tree nursery.

Although lying in a green bowl, within the parish boundaries is an important and unsuspected watershed — the Lune rises here, and, not far away, so does Scandal Beck, a principal feeder of the Eden and of greater significance in local affairs. The bedrock is limestone up to 1600 feet and is plainly manifest on the slopes of Wild Boar Fell, where high terraces have earned the name of Clouds.

The Fothergill family is intimately associated with the district, enjoying an unbroken residence of over four centuries and having produced several members who achieved distinction, and, as landowners, given many benefactions for the welfare of the community.

The disused track of the railway west of Newbiggin is in course of adaption as a re-routed A.685.

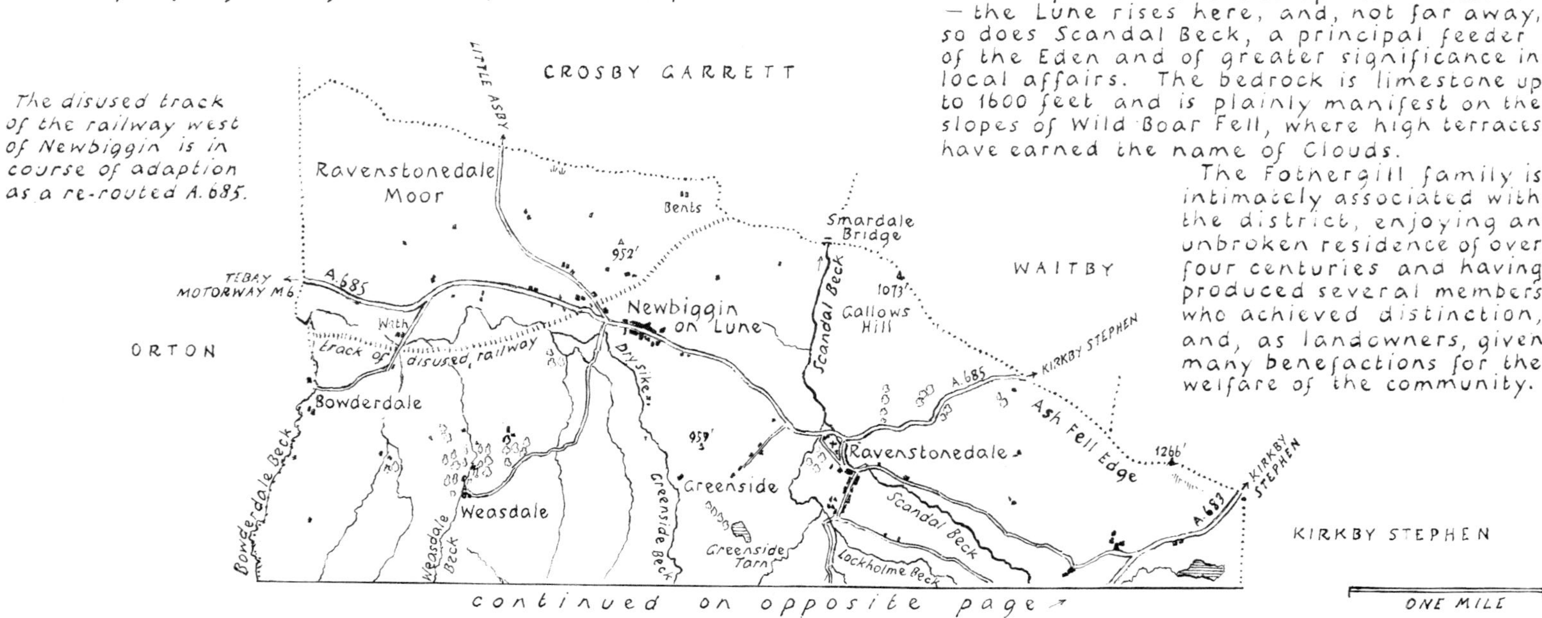

continued on opposite page →

Ravenstonedale

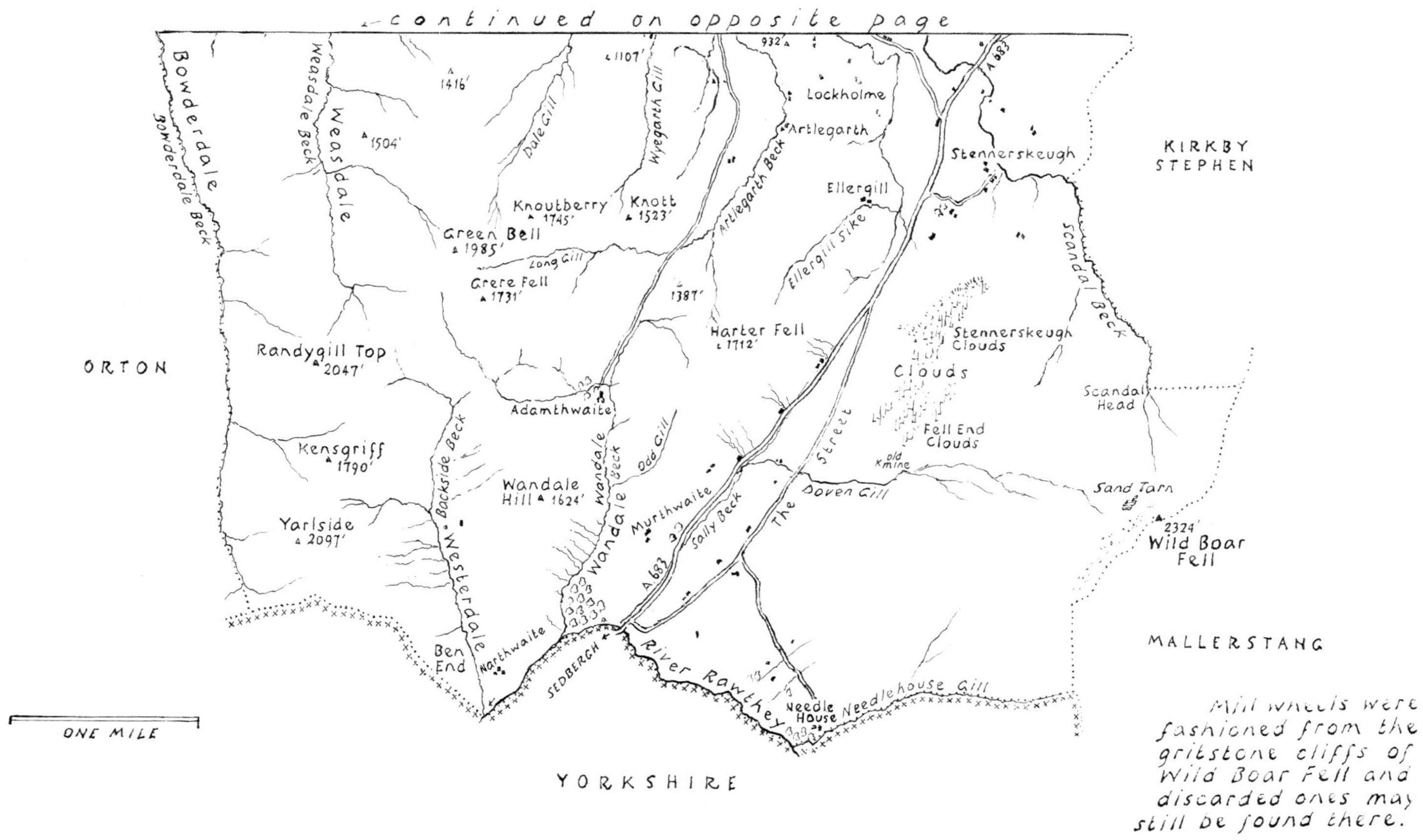

Mill wheels were fashioned from the gritstone cliffs of Wild Boar Fell and discarded ones may still be found there.

Ravenstonedale

The parish church of St Oswald

Until the reign of James I Ravenstonedale had the privilege of sanctuary for criminals who gained immunity from pursuit by ringing a refuge bell hanging in the church tower.

The ruined foundations of the Gilbertine cell.

The parish church of St Oswald was erected in 1744 adjacent to the site of an earlier structure of which parts of the fabric are incorporated, notably the chancel arch and the rebuilt south porch. An unusual arrangement of the pews and a three-deck pulpit are features of the interior. A medieval cross surmounted by a sundial stands in the churchyard, where, on the north side, can be seen the ruinous foundations of a cell of the Gilbertine Canons of Watton (12th century).

in Ravenstonedale Park

In 1560 the first Lord Wharton, having become possessed of the manor, cleared the tenants from an area extending north from the village to Smardale Bridge and made a deer park enclosed by an earthen rampart or dyke, which can still be easily followed on both sides of Scandal Beck. The confines of the area of the entire Park were indicated by a stone wall nine feet high, much of which remains intact.

The south-east terminus of the dyke

The dyke (foreground) passes over Breakyneck Scar

Ravenstonedale

An ancient pillow mound ('giant's grave') — one of several within the Park boundary.

A small eminence within the Park, still known as Gallows Hill, was the scene of executions authorised by the Lord of the Manor and a jury of twentyfour. In days gone by, of course. (*Practice discontinued*).

Lynchets near Smardale Bridge

Ravenstonedale

Tower House, Brownber

Church and green

at Newbiggin

Betsy Croft retains its spinning gallery

Main street

Ravenstonedale

Main street,
Ravenstonedale

This remarkable 'field house', carved out of a crag on Ashfell Edge (probably as a shelter for cattle) bears inside an inscribed shield with names and the date 1720.

Tarn House, on the A.683, was built in 1664 by George Fothergill

Tarn House

Of Hwith House at Stennerskeugh, built in 1869 and then described as a large handsome mansion, nothing remains except a driveway and the battlemented walls of the garden. The curious name was compounded of the Christian initials of five brothers, and is preserved by a new house on the site.

Ravenstonedale

The Clouds

Of the many varied landscapes in the parish, the most interesting is the tiered and terraced escarpment on the lower western slopes of Wild Boar Fell, well seen from the A.683 road. Along here is a belt of limestone, sandwiched between the Howgill sandstone and the Pennine gritstone, and, after the manner of limestone, it makes its presence known by appearing as a surface rock, and, on closer acquaintance, delights the eye with its strange and beautiful formations. An abandoned mine suggests a source of underground minerals, and a number of lime-kilns, all in good condition, are reminders of the days when limeburning was a local industry and widely practised.

A conduit at the old mine workings

looking to Stennerskeugh Clouds from Fell End Clouds

A lime kiln

Uldale Force

The River Rawthey

Ravenstonedale has the birthplace of the Lune within its boundaries and is watered also by Scandal Beck and several tributaries of both, but for beauty of river scenery pride of place belongs to the Rawthey in Uldale, on the Yorkshire boundary, which flows in a series of waterfalls along limestone ravines.

Ravenstonedale

Ravenstonedale in the Howgills

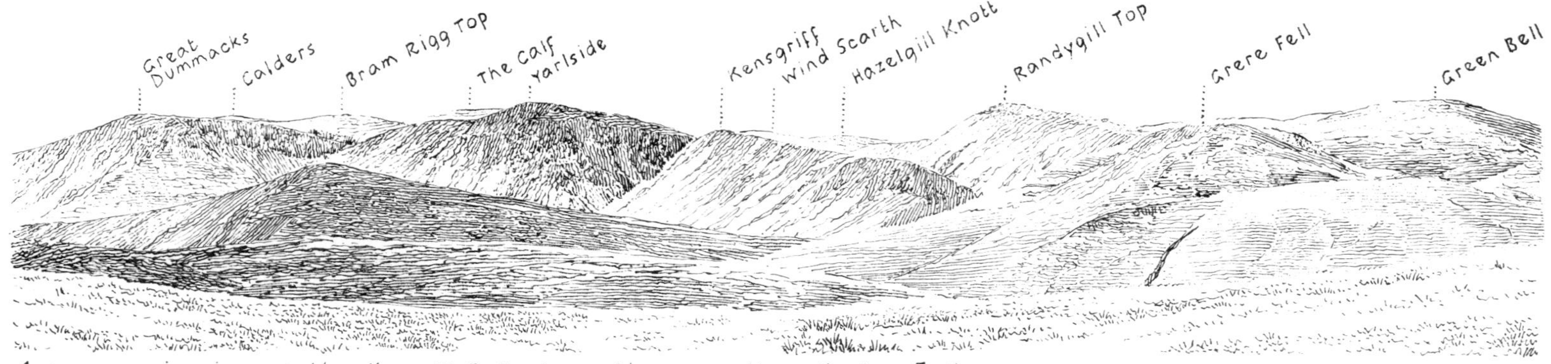

A panoramic view of the Howgill Fells from the summit of Harter Fell

Kensgriff

Narthwaite

Murthwaite

The head of Westerdale

The source of the Lune

The River Lune rises high on the eastern slope of Green Bell, where several springs join issue to form Dale Gill, the stream thereafter taking the names of Greenside Beck and Dry Sike before being known as the Lune at valley level. The place of its birth is desolate, remote and unfrequented — no footpath leads to it, no sign marks the spot and there is no evidence that it is ever visited except by sheep.

above:
The summit of Green Bell

right:
Weasdale, looking down the valley from its head

Ravenstonedale

Ravenstonedale in the Howgills

The isolated but beautifully situated farm of Adamthwaite, looking west up Adamthwaite Sike to Randygill Top.

RYDAL AND LOUGHRIGG

The parish of Rydal and Loughrigg may be fairly described as an epitome of Lakeland. Here, in smaller compass, are all the delights that attract visitors to the Lake District — tarns and rivers and waterfalls, low fells, high mountains, woodland and copse; and there is Rydal Water, a jewel in a setting of emerald and, in winter, gold. Without going outside the boundaries of the parish, a sojourner here may enjoy a feast of loveliness, a refreshment of mind and body. For fellwalkers there are high-level expeditions, for ramblers simple strolls, for photographers and artists scenes of rare beauty, for poets and writers a romantic environment.

There are three communities, at Rydal, Clappersgate and Skelwith Bridge, none of them large enough to be termed a village, and many private houses and hotels in idyllic isolation elsewhere. The main Kendal-Keswick road, the A.591, intersects the parish: north of it is the high skyline known to walkers as the Fairfield Horseshoe, enclosing the deep valley of Rydal Beck; south is Loughrigg Fell, everybody's favourite. Nothing mars. All is fair to look upon in the parish of Rydal and Loughrigg.

Wordsworth's Seat, Rydal Water

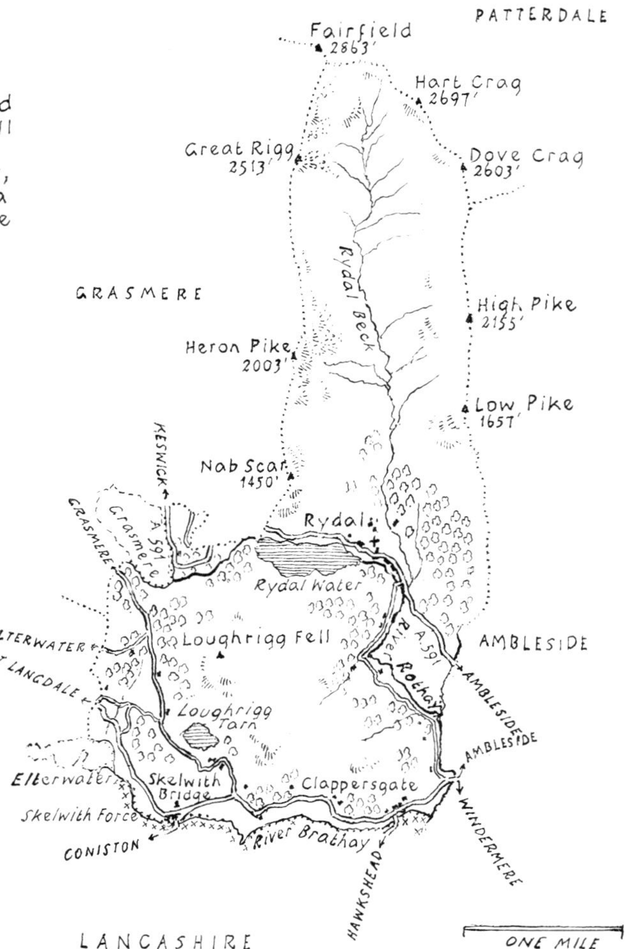

The parish church of St Mary, erected in 1824.

The viewpoint is Rash Field, popularly known as Dora's Field from its association with the daughter of Wordsworth, and now owned by the National Trust. In springtime it is a carpet of wild daffodils, a sight so lovely that for many admirers the field is a place of pilgrimage to be visited annually.

Rydal and Loughrigg

Literary associations

Rydal is particularly rich in its connections with literary celebrities whose names are still revered long after death and whose works are undiminished by the passing of time.
Nab Cottage had de Quincey and Hartley Coleridge as tenants; Rydal Mount was Wordsworth's last home; at Rydal Cottage lived the two Miss Armitts, well remembered locally for their researches into the history of the district and as founders of a library in Ambleside; Fox How was built as a residence by the renowned Dr. Thomas Arnold, headmaster of Rugby School, 1827-42, his occupation then being succeeded by that of his son Matthew, the poet and critic; Harriet Martineau had a house in the vicinity and Keats and Southey were among Rydal's many distinguished visitors.
The scenery was their inspiration. As it has been for a host of lesser mortals.

Nab Cottage, built 1702

Rydal Mount was the home of Wordsworth from 1813 until his death in 1850.

In 1970, following an appeal for funds, the house was acquired as a memorial and opened to the public, some of the rooms having displays of the poet's furniture and effects.

Rydal and Loughrigg

Rydal Beck

left: *The head of the valley*

bottom left: *Buckstones Jump*

Waterfalls in Rydal Park

Rydal and Loughrigg

Rydal Hall

Rydal Hall is a Rest and Conference House of the Diocese of Carlisle. It was built in the 16th century as a residence for the le Fleming family, owners of the manor, and subsequently much altered, the imposing south range being a 19th century addition. There are many fine specimen trees in the extensive parkland surrounding the Hall.

Rydal and Loughrigg

Church Cottage, Rydal

Pelter Bridge, Rydal

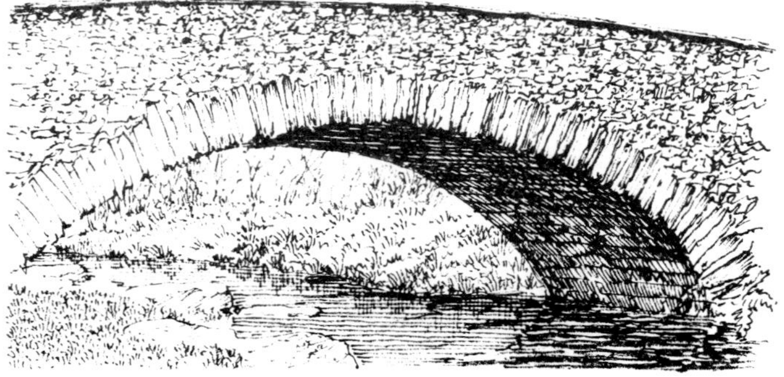

Nab Scar

Rydal Water

Rydal and Loughrigg

Loughrigg Fell

Of the lesser heights of Lakeland, Loughrigg Fell is pre-eminent. It has no pretensions to mountain status, being a sprawling and shapeless wedge of rough ground rising between the parklike valleys of Brathay and Rothay, and having a bulk out of all proportion to its modest altitude; yet no ascent is more rewarding, for Loughrigg has pleasant paths linking its many summits, charming vistas and superb views, fine contrasts of velvety turf, rich bracken and grey rock, a string of tarnlets like pearls in a necklace, and a wealth of stately trees interspersed with juniper and holly and yew on its flanks. It is well endowed with lakes, four sheets of water, all lovely, touching its lower slopes. And there is Loughrigg Terrace, too!

Loughrigg has many surprises for those who explore, amongst these being a tremendous cave on the slopes overlooking Rydal Water. This is a disused slate quarry, the rock being extracted not on the surface but out of the interior of the cave, a common practice in slate quarries in Lakeland.

White Craggs
— a house in a
famous garden

Clappersgate

Skelwith Force

SCALTHWAITERIGG

Bordering Kendal in the north-east, the small parish of Scalthwaiterigg rises sharply from the valley of the River Mint, which forms its boundary, to the elevated expanse of Hay Fell, over a thousand feet high and having from its summit at Benson Knott a superb view of the Lakeland mountains — a prospect also enjoyed by travellers on the main-line railway traversing the fellside and by motorists and walkers on Paddy Lane.

There is no church, Skelsmergh being the ecclesiastical centre, and the only concentration of dwellings is at Meal Bank, formerly a weaving village with a large woollen mill, the works premises now harbouring a variety of trades; the village occupies a secluded hollow off the A.685 in a curve of the river, which is delightfully wooded hereabouts, and, were it not for the scars of industry, would be a pleasant backwater indeed.

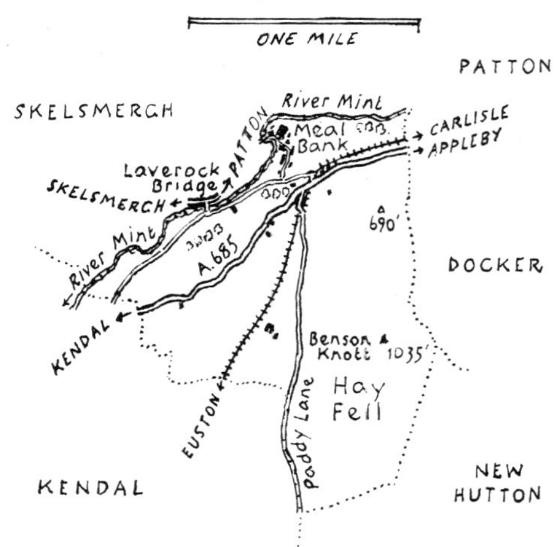

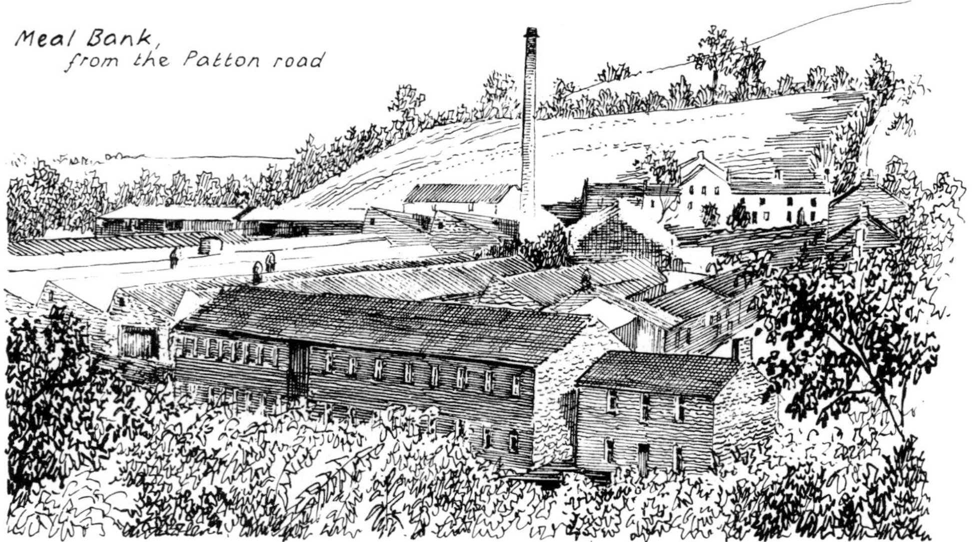

Meal Bank, from the Patton road

The summit of Benson Knott

Scalthwaiterigg

The River Mint
at Beck Mills

The double summit of Benson Knott
as seen on the northern approach

Laverock Bridge

SEDGWICK

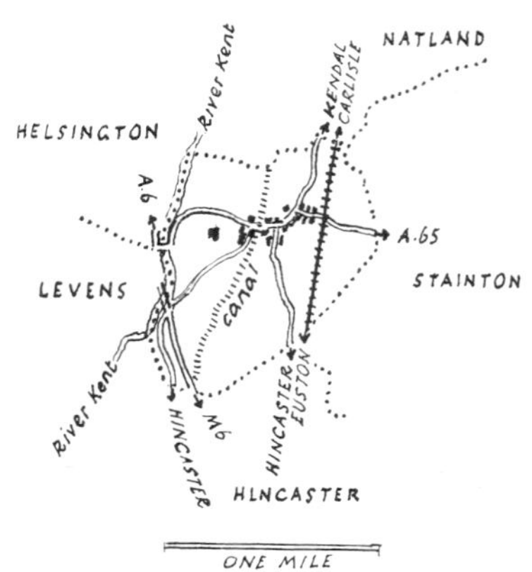

Sedgwick is a meeting place of five country lanes; it has an air of quiet wellbeing that can be attributed to the pleasant appearance of its neat terraced cottages, now outnumbered by modern bungalows, and especially of the handsome mansion, Sedgwick House, standing in spacious parkland to the west of the village: an imposing structure that was the home of Jacob Wakefield, a Mayor of Kendal and one of a notable local family that besides pioneering the gunpowder industry in the 18th century contributed much and in many ways to the administrative and commercial life of the district. Sedgwick House is today a school of the Lancashire Education Authority.

The village is away from the usual routes of tourists and is less generally known now than in its hey-day as an industrial centre over a century ago; then, too, the Lancaster Canal, which crosses the street by an aqueduct, was active in the transport of coal, slate, lime and other Kendal imports and exports.

Sedgwick is the smallest parish in the county. The River Kent forms the western boundary and is well-wooded and very pleasant hereabouts, Force Falls being a popular attraction.

Force Falls

Some issues of the Ordnance maps spell Sedgwick *Sedgewick*

left:

These ruins of gunpowder works are seen on the Sedgwick (east) bank of the Kent. Larger works were established later on the west bank and known as New Sedgwick, but are within the parish of Helsington (and are described in the chapter on that parish).

Sedgwick

Sedgwick House, built 1868-9

SHAP

The parish of Shap is the largest in the county and for administrative convenience is divided into two areas, an urban (the village of Shap and its immediate environs) and a rural (the surrounding district), the latter forming a separate civil parish known as Shap Rural.

Shap has been a byword amongst road travellers since coaching days. For many the very name invokes vivid memories of hazardous journeys in snow and storm and mist along the A6, the highest main road in the country, with a notorious history of accidents. But its importance as a main traffic artery to Scotland greatly diminished overnight when the motorway M6 was opened on a day in October 1970. This was a red-letter day for some Shap folk, a black-letter day for others. Commerce suffered, but the village became a better place in which to live. It was a change amounting to a metamorphosis.

Quiet now, Shap village has regained some of its lost charm. But industry, mainly quarrying, remains a paramount influence in the urban community. In addition to the long-established granite works, large limestone quarries are being increasingly developed in the rural outskirts of the village, which provides the labour force.

One unchanging feature of the landscape enjoyed by the urban parishioners is the panoramic view of the High Street range of fells. Shap village, 850 feet up, is a grandstand for this.

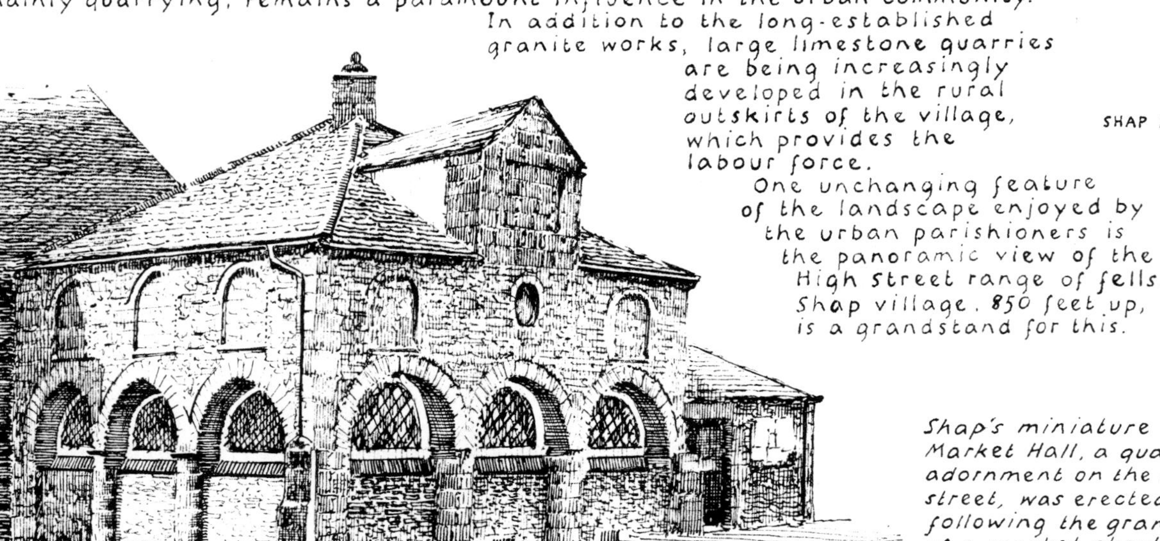

Shap's miniature Market Hall, a quaint adornment on the main street, was erected following the granting of a market charter in 1687.

Shap

Dating from the 13th century, the parish church of St Michael, although extensively restored in 1898-9, preserves some of the ancient fabric, notably the Norman arches of the nave, and two carved 12th century stones are reset in the outer wall. There is a tombstone memorial, dated 1846, for the men who lost their lives during the construction of the railway.

The humble 16th century Keld Chapel is in the care of the National Trust and used for occasional services.

In early medieval times, Shap's name was *Heppe* (recorded also as *Hep* or *Hepp*)

The parish church of St Michael

Shap

The Hermitage has an original doorway dated 1691

The Greyhound, a coaching hostelry, dates from 1680

Keld

Keld is a hamlet on the east bank of the Lowther, its Norse name, meaning "a place by a river", indicating the antiquity of the settlement.

Thornship is a nearby farming community.

Thornship

Of the stone circle, only six of the boulders remain in view, the others being covered by the embankment of the railway.

Shap Stones

Urban and industrial development at Shap has destroyed a megalithic monument that, according to early historians, was of great significance. They record the existence of an avenue formed by two parallel rows of huge unhewn granite stones, 25 yards apart and extending for nearly a mile northwest from a stone circle. The site of this circle is still distinct, in part, between the A6 and the railway at the south end of the village, but traces of the avenue have almost gone, although five large boulders, roughly in line, and thought to have been part, can still be seen in the fields.

The five stones

The Thunder Stone, 31 feet in girth, is in a field at High Barn.

This stone has been built into the wall of a narrow lane to Keld.

This stone, in a field, is distinctly inscribed with two ring marks.

The Goggleby Stone until recently stood erect on its narrow end.

Most accessible is this stone in a field near the village on the west side.

SHAP RURAL

Shap Rural has primary importance as the largest parish in Westmorland and an added distinction amongst ornithologists as the home selected by the golden eagle on its return to Lakeland a few years ago after an absence of a century and a half. The location of its eyries, three in number, is a closely-guarded secret.

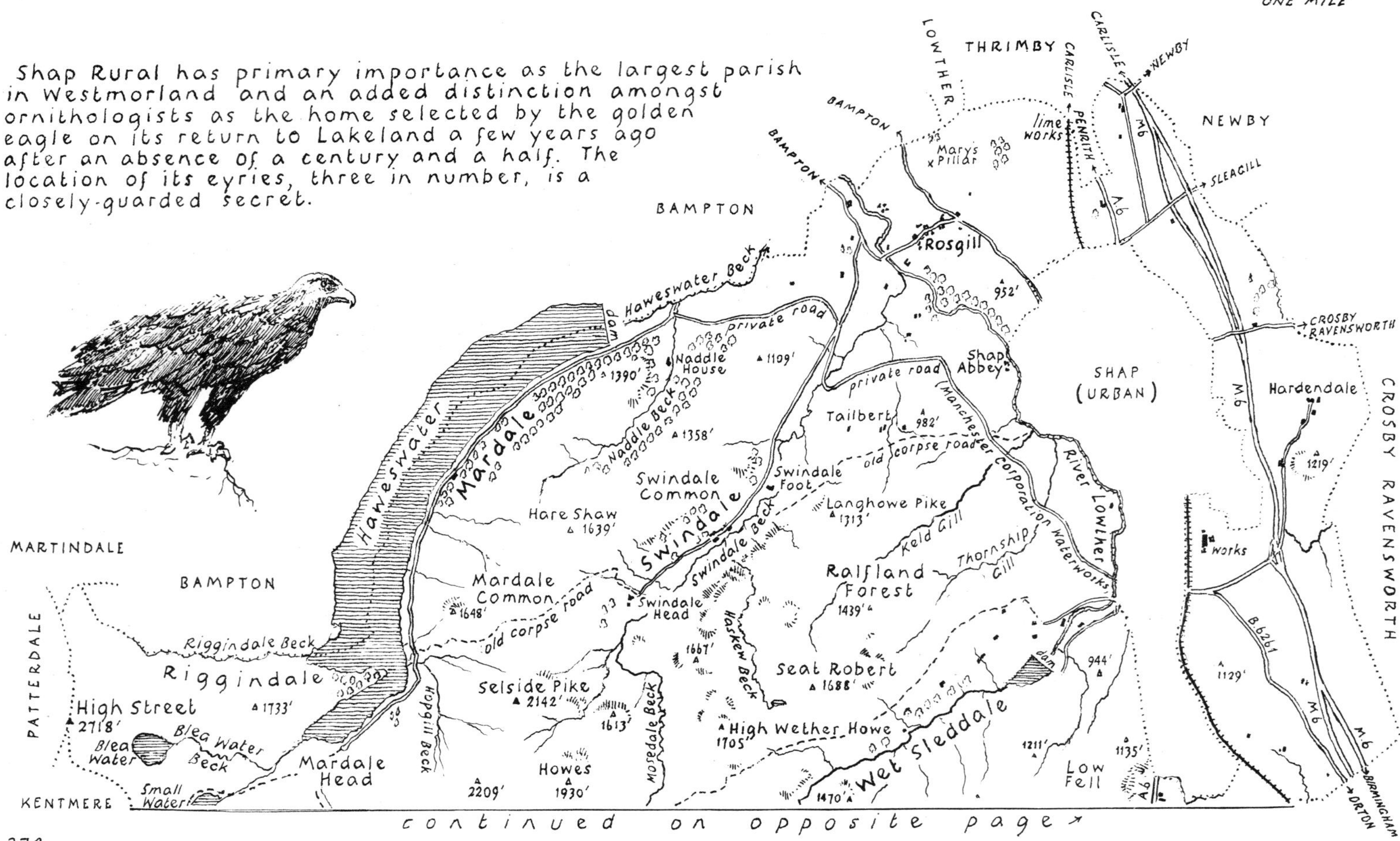

continued on opposite page →

Shap Rural

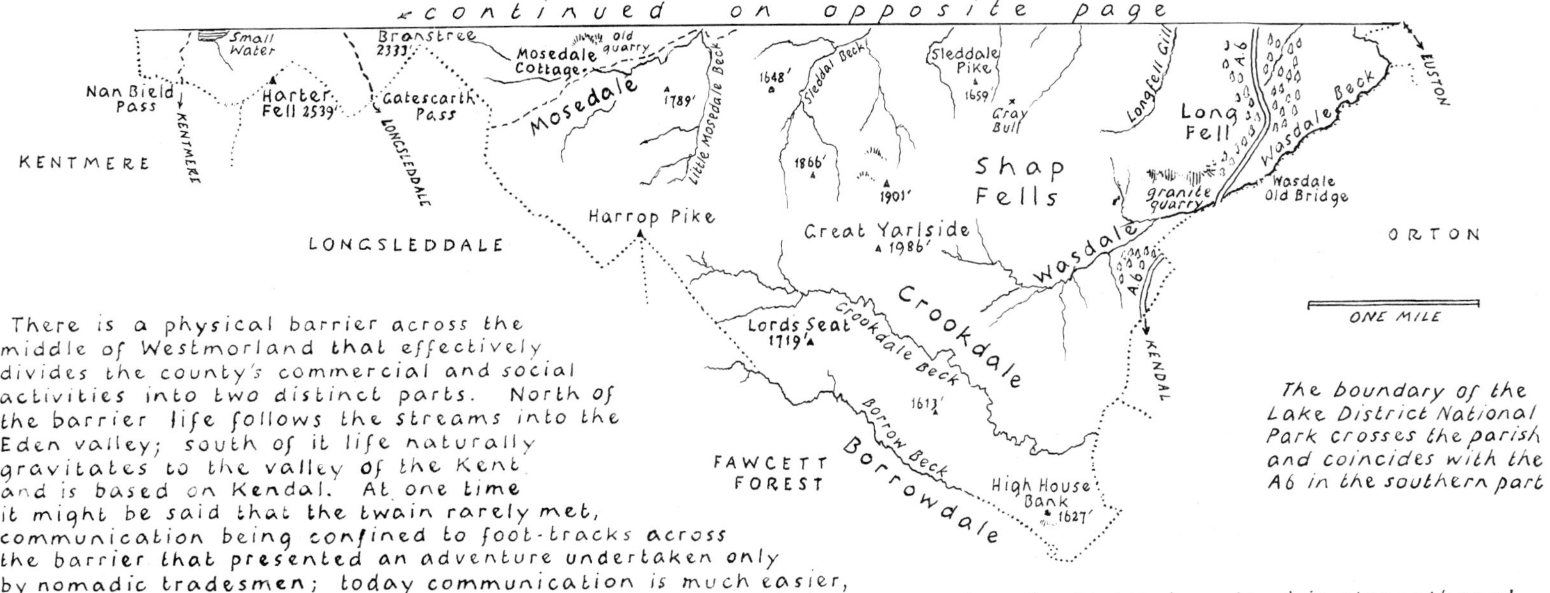

There is a physical barrier across the middle of Westmorland that effectively divides the county's commercial and social activities into two distinct parts. North of the barrier life follows the streams into the Eden valley; south of it life naturally gravitates to the valley of the Kent and is based on Kendal. At one time it might be said that the twain rarely met, communication being confined to foot-tracks across the barrier that presented an adventure undertaken only by nomadic tradesmen; today communication is much easier, there is a closer affinity between north and south, and the common loyalty to Westmorland is strengthened.

But the physical barrier remains. It is the upland region known by the general name of Shap Fells, a tract of moorland lofty in height and immense in girth, a natural obstacle the hurdling of which continues to this day to be occasionally fraught with discomfort and danger by its ally, bad weather. Much of it is a vast sheep pasture linked in the west to the mountains of Lakeland and in the east to the Pennines, a raised plateau deeply riven by a web of valleys.

Administration of this area is undertaken from the north, the greater part of it forming the civil parish of Shap Rural, completely surrounding the urban community of Shap village; through it, in a narrow corridor, are three major arteries of communication: the A.6 trunk road, the M.6 motorway and the main line railway. But elsewhere there is a diversity of non-industrial landscapes with many scenes of intimate beauty.

Yet the over-riding impression of the traveller (on wheels) is one of empty desolation.

It will always be so. Man cannot change Shap Fells.

Shap Rural

Shap Abbey

The history of Shap Abbey began in 1191 with the foundation at Preston Patrick of a convent for Premonstratensian Canons, this establishment being moved to Shap in 1199, when construction of the Abbey commenced, work continuing on various additions into the 16th century. In 1540 it was surrendered to Henry VIII and then fell into disrepair and ruin, many of the carved stones being removed to Lowther Castle. Early this century the structure was in a sad state but happily was taken over by the Ministry of Works in 1948 and further decay has been arrested by an excavation and consolidation of all the remaining fabric, of which only the west tower retains its original height. It is preserved as an Ancient Monument and access by the public is permitted for a small admission charge. A captive sheep is given the duty of keeping the grass short, a task it performs nobly and with evident pleasure.

Shap Rural

at Rosgill

Mary's Pillar, a conspicuous obelisk in a field east of the Shap-Bampton road at Rosgill, was erected in 1854 by Thomas Castley of The Thorn, Rosgill, as a memorial to his daughter Mary, who died at the age of 24.

Parish Crag Bridge
(an old packhorse bridge over Swindale Beck)

a lime kiln

Rosgill Bridge carries the village road over the River Lowther

Shap Rural

High Street

from Branstree

The western boundary of the parish runs along the spine of a mountain known today as High Street, being so named from a Roman road that crosses the summit and links Ambleside and Brougham – the highest Roman road in the country.

The summit, 2718'

Last century the mountain was more often referred to locally as Racecourse Hill, the broad top being the venue of annual horse races and shepherds' meets.

This is the highest ground in the parish.

from Mardale Ill Bell

Mardale

HAWESWATER
BEFORE
AND
AFTER

Measand
Hall
Whelter
corpse road to Shap
Mardale Green
Dun Bull
Mardale Head

Haweswater Hotel
corpse road to Shap
car
Mardale Head

Now, in 1974, there is talk of raising the water level, thus increasing the area of storage.

Before the consecration of the now-submerged church the dead were taken from Mardale Green to Shap for burial, using a direct path over the fells, climbing to 1600 feet and crossing Swindale on the way. This path was known as the Corpse Road and is still quite distinct.

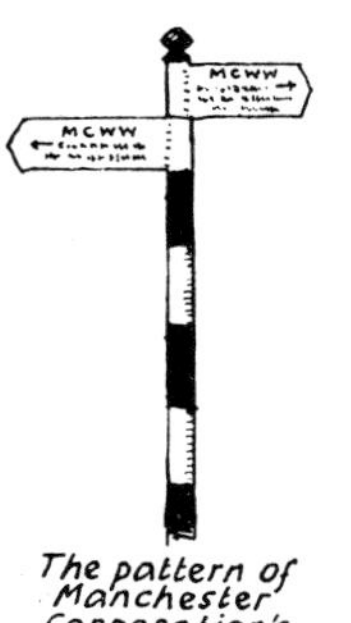

The pattern of Manchester Corporation's Haweswater signposts

The greatest transformation that Westmorland's scenery has suffered by the hand of man took place at Mardale in the 1930s, when this sweet valley was sacrificed to outside pressures. Its lovely natural lake, Haweswater, was converted to an unlovely reservoir, its church and village submerged, and the dalesfolk evacuated. This was not an act of vandalism because it was within the law; it was not confiscation either because cash changed hands. A part of Westmorland became Manchester.

But for those who loved Mardale as it was before, there is no compensation — nor could there be. Only memories.

The new Haweswater, from Harter Fell

Harter Fell and Mardale Head

Shap Rural

some Mardale fells

left: Mardale Ill Bell, 2496′

bottom left: Selside Pike, 2142′

below: Branstree, 2333′

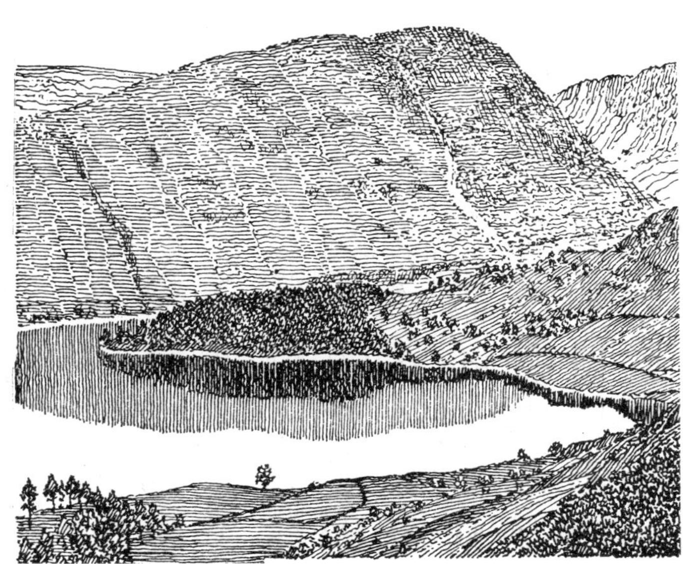

Swindale

Swindale is the last valley, coming eastwards from Lakeland, to exhibit scenery thoroughly characteristic of that district, forming a deep trench between steep fells rimmed with crags and clothed with bracken and heather and a scattering of coppice, a sanctuary of secluded farms and quiet pastures threaded by a sparkling beck that descends from the heights in cascades and waterfalls; and it is all the more charming for being little known and rarely visited. Its one solitary road has no signpost.

Manchester Corporation have acquired proprietary rights here too, but, being latterly more sensitive to the opposition of many amenity interests, have gone about the work of extracting water from the dale with commendable care, leaving no scars and taking the water away through a tunnel to Haweswater. They deserve full marks for Swindale.

Mosedale Cottage, the loneliest in the parish, is used as an occasional overnight refuge by shepherds.

some Swindale summits

Hare Shaw

Great Ladstones

Rowantree Crag

Gambling Crag

Langhowe Pike

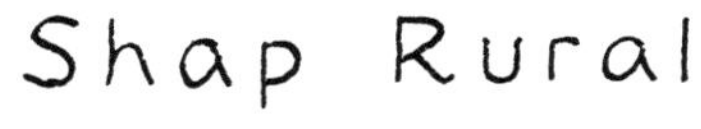

Shap Rural

left : Gouther and Outlaw Crags, Swindale

below : Swindale Head

Shap Rural

Swindale Beck starts its career as Mosedale Beck, pursuing a placid course along the dreary upland valley of that name but when it comes within sight of Swindale changes both name and character, descending into it through a spectacular ravine in a series of cascades and falls of great scenic appeal known as The Forces.

Shap Rural

A new bridge
in
Wet Sleddale

This is the only packhorse bridge built in Lakeland within the last two centuries.
It was erected a few years ago by Manchester Corporation as a replacement of a genuine antique due to be engulfed by the reservoir then in course of construction and since completed in Wet Sleddale.

Shap Rural

Wet Sleddale

Wet Sleddale is a long valley descending eastwards from a hub of Lakeland mountains but soon assuming the much less exciting characteristics of the Shap fells. The lower reaches of the valley, where it debouches into an open moorland, have been taken over by Manchester and a reservoir constructed there: a small reservoir, but, because of the widening contours, it is contained by a disproportionately long dam.

The inevitable consequences of abandoned buildings, broken walls and land turned sour, are all too obvious. Wet Sleddale is a valley less happy than it was.

The new reservoir

The ruins of Sleddale Grange

The pleasant middle reaches of the valley, where there are scattered woodlands and the River Lowther has its beginnings, have a unique feature: a pattern of walls still standing twelve feet high.

This is a medieval deer enclosure of archaeological importance known as Buck Park.

Shap Rural

Shap Granite Quarries

Shap granite has earned an international reputation. It is a beautiful stone distinguished by crystals of red felspar and speckled with mica and quartz; it has durable building properties and is much used also for decorative effect and architectural ornamentation. The quarries, which have been worked for more than a hundred years, are situated on Wasdale Crag, in full view from the A.6 road, and were formerly linked with the works, two miles nearer Shap village, by a light railway.

Boulders of Shap granite occur profusely in mid-Westmorland, often far from their place of origin and even across the Pennines, as a result of glacial movement at the end of the Ice Age.

To commemorate the accession of Queen Victoria, this tall column, surmounted by a figure of Britannia, was erected in 1842 at Shap Wells. The sculpturing was done by Thomas Bland of Reagill.

Shap Wells

(which, strictly, is in a corner of Crosby Ravensworth parish)

The discovery of a saline spa at Shap Wells in the eighteenth century, the waters of which had curative properties for many diseases, led to the later erection of a large hotel in spacious grounds. The waters were held in high esteem by medical men, being considered as effective as those of Leamington Spa, although described locally as tasting like "train smoke mixed with bad eggs".

Sufferers from rheumatism and gout and other like complaints do not now come here in numbers but the hotel remains a fashionable resort.

Wasdale Old Bridge

Before the road over Shap Fells adopted the line now followed, an ancient highway took a different route, descending north from the summit to cross Wasdale Beck by this bridge. It was repaired in 1974.

Afforestation

Recent large-scale plantings on both sides of the A6 between its summit and the granite works will soon transform the road journey into a forest ride.

Shap Rural

Wasdale and Crookdale

Shap Fells bear sad witness to the 20th century decline of small independent farmers. Many buildings are rotting skeletons, once-green intakes are overgrown with rank grass and rushes, walls are crumbling. Both Wasdale and Crookdale are formerly inhabited valleys that are abandoned and reverting to primitive marsh.

The summit of Wasdale Pike

Beacon on Robin Hood

Ruins of Wasdale Head farmhouse

Hause Foot, Crookdale

Hause Foot, on the old road to Shap from the south, is currently the scene of pipe-laying activities by Manchester Corporation (aqueduct from Haweswater).

Almost all the triangulation stations of the Ordnance Survey are indicated by columns of concrete or rough stone and it is unusual to find one marked only by a circular metal plate sunk into concrete at ground level. Such a one occurs on Great Yarlside (above); another is located on the summit of Seat Robert (below).

Shap Rural

On Shap Fells

Gray Bull

Of the many huge boulders of granite scattered on the fells, the greatest is Gray Bull, on the slope of Wasdale Pike overlooking Wet Sleddale.

Near Wasdale Head Farm an embedded boulder forms a massive plinth on which another rests.

Shap Rural

That the Britons of old had a liking for the district now known as Shap is evident from the many traces left of their occupation. Within the present rural parish, village settlements have been located in Mardale, near Shap Wells and at Naddle, burial cairns occur in Ralfland Forest and high on Selside Pike, and there are remains of stone circles on Wilson Scar at Rosgill and at Gunnerkeld Bottom.

The latter, pictured here, is formed of 48 granite boulders, arranged in an inner ring and an outer ring, most of which have fallen. Incongruously, this ancient monument finds itself today alongside a modern monument — the motorway.

Hardendale

Hall Farm

Hardendale Nab

Shap Thorn is a clump of trees conspicuous on a felltop overlooking the approaches to Shap from the south. Originally it was planted as an aid to direction for travellers.

Hardendale is a remote hamlet in a hollow of the limestone uplands east of Shap village. It was the birthplace of Dr. John Mill (1645-1707), an eminent Biblical scholar who devoted 30 years of his life to an edition of the New Testament in Greek.

Shap Rural

SKELSMERGH

The parish church, dedicated to St John the Baptist, was erected in 1871, the ecclesiastical parish also being formed in that year.

Skelsmergh is pronounced Skelsmer

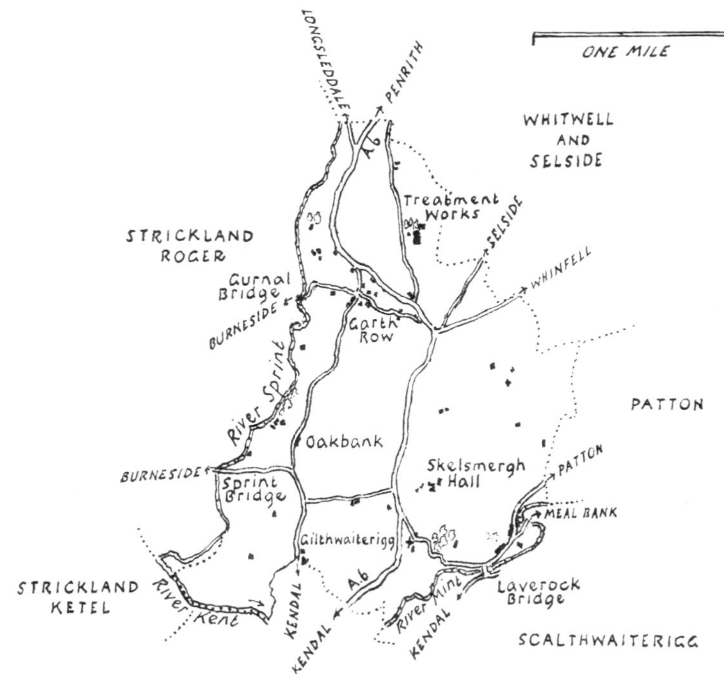

The A.6 north out of Kendal starts its long climb over Shap Fells gradually, and for the first three miles passes through a pleasant undulating countryside with panoramic views of an array of Lakeland peaks to the west. This is Skelsmergh, its church conspicuous on a knoll. The road bisects the parish and gives a good general impression of its pastoral character: a patchwork of fields and dispersed dwellings. With the closing of a bobbin and corn mills, agriculture is the only industry, but in recent years activity on a grand scale has produced a large complex of water works and plant. The parish occupies a triangle formed by the Kent and two main tributaries and these rivers help to define its limits.

Skelsmergh

Skelsmergh Hall

The pele tower of Skelsmergh Hall was built in the late 14th century as a residence of the Leyburne family, the house adjoining being added some 200 years later. The tower, which is barrel-vaulted and has a spiral staircase, has suffered by the passing of time, having lost its parapets and the top storey floor, and quite recently much of the outer stone has peeled off and two fine trefoiled windows have been sacrificed. Nevertheless enough remains to indicate the massive strength of the original structure and make the Hall, now a farmhouse, a still-impressive monument.

Skelsmergh

Laverock House (below), at Meal Bank, hitherto a private residence, is in course of conversion to use as a hotel.

Gilthwaiterigg, on the boundary with Kendal, is of 15th century origin.

Cottages at Garth Row

Skelsmergh

Dodding Green, a house in a sequestered corner of the parish, was left to the Roman Catholic Church for use as a presbytery by Robert Stephenson in 1723, a chapel (left) being added later. Alongside the entrance drive are the gravestones of some of the earlier priests in charge.

A contrast in Industrial Architecture

Oakbank Bobbin Mill (disused as such; now a depot for waste paper)

Watchgate Treatment Works (Manchester Corporation Waterworks)

Skelsmergh

Gurnal Bridge

Burton House

Beck Mills

Since closure both mills have been converted to residential use.

SLEAGILL

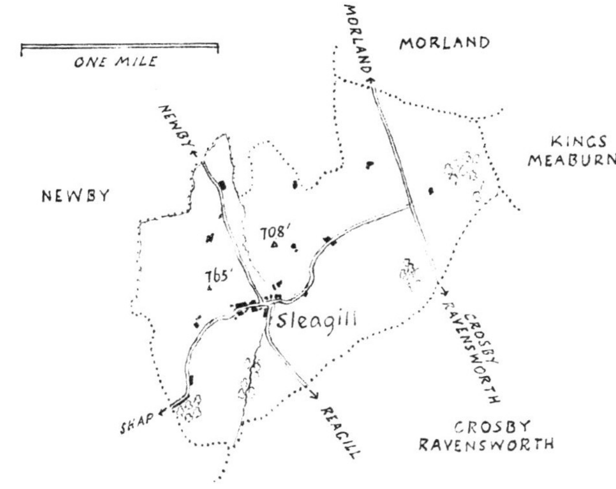

village street

New Mill Flat (rear)

footbridge over the beck

Mill Flat (built c.1600; original windows (stone mullions) recently replaced

Sleagill is important to Sleagill's inhabitants, but many people elsewhere in the county would be at a loss if asked to state its location, for like many of the parishes in the narrowing triangle between the A.6 and the A.66 it is a place rarely in the news, quite untroubled by tourists and well content with a peaceful rural life.

It is a green parish, all fields and trees, and, being slightly elevated to the west of the Lyvennet valley, has extensive views, but the small village that gives its name to the parish lies in a hollow watered by a tributary and sees nothing of the distant scene. There is no Anglican church, and the school has closed. The Royal Oak has ceased to function as an inn.

Sleagill today is quieter than ever.

SOCKBRIDGE AND TIRRIL

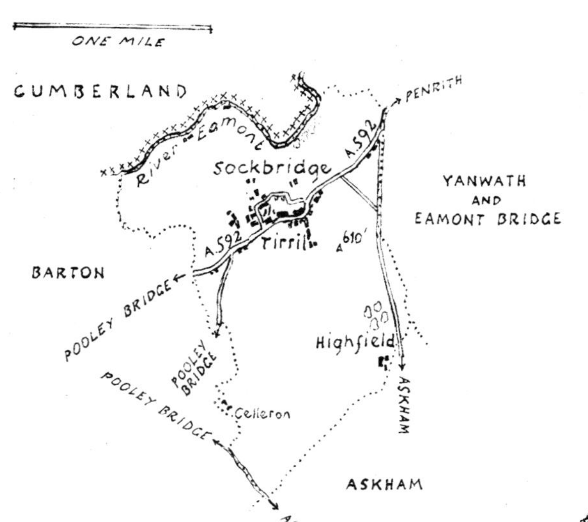

The parish of Sockbridge and Tirril adjoins Cumberland; the River Eamont issuing from Ullswater forms the county boundary. The small village of Sockbridge stands off the tourist road to Ullswater and remains quiet despite a large modern (and uncharacteristic) housing development. Here is a building of outstanding distinction: the 15th century Sockbridge Hall, now a farmstead but originally the manor house. Tirril, nearby, lines the A592 road to Ullswater, the heavy summer traffic detracting from its picturesque appearance. There is no Anglican church, Barton's serving as the ecclesiastical centre for the district.

Sockbridge Hall, still with an air of the middle ages about it, had a pele tower until 1830, when it was dismantled. The structure on the right of the drawing is thought to have been an old banqueting hall and appears to have been used later as a chapel. The Hall stands in a complex of farm buildings, of which a massive barn with slit windows is an impressive object.

Sockbridge Hall

Sockbridge and Tirril

Wordsworth House, Sockbridge, is so named because the poet's grandfather resided here when he settled in Westmorland. Built in 1699, it was earlier known as Sockbridge House. For a period, last century, it was used as a private Boarding School.

Sockbridge Mill

The former Friends Meeting House at Tirril, built in 1733. In the small burial ground was interred the body of Charles Gough who, in 1805, perished on Helvellyn; his faithful dog was the subject of poems by Wordsworth and Scott.

The arch of this semi-derelict 17th century outbuilding at Croftfoot is supported by a curved timber beam.

SOULBY

In the heart of the extensive rural 'backwater' west of Kirkby Stephen, and spared the traffic of main roads, of which it has none, is the village of Soulby, the centre of an agricultural parish watered by Scandal Beck, here a considerable stream in its last stages before joining the Eden. The village is spaciously arranged around a meeting of country lanes, with an open green. There is a church, a chapel and a shop, but the Black Bull is no more. The surroundings are pleasant without being exciting.

Soulby suffered an inadvertent bombing on one occasion during the last war. Nothing less like a military objective can be imagined. This is a place of peaceful pursuits, of serenity, of cows wending their way home over the fields, of farmers leaning on gates, of birdsong. Its only history is a catalogue of local affairs. Soulby lives a life to be envied and is content with it.

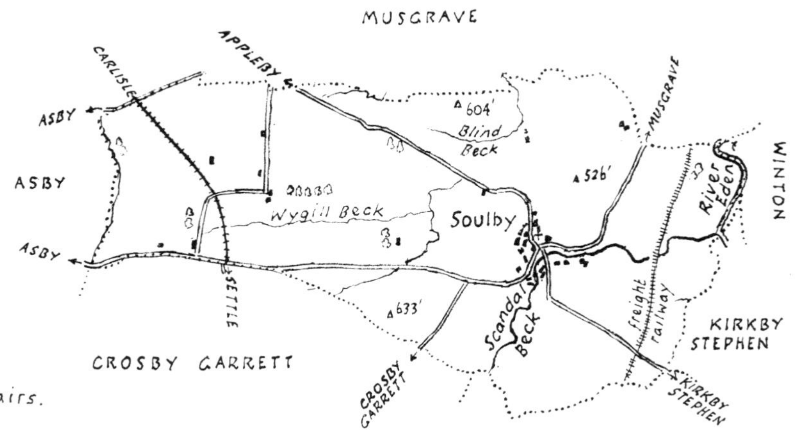

Soulby Bridge

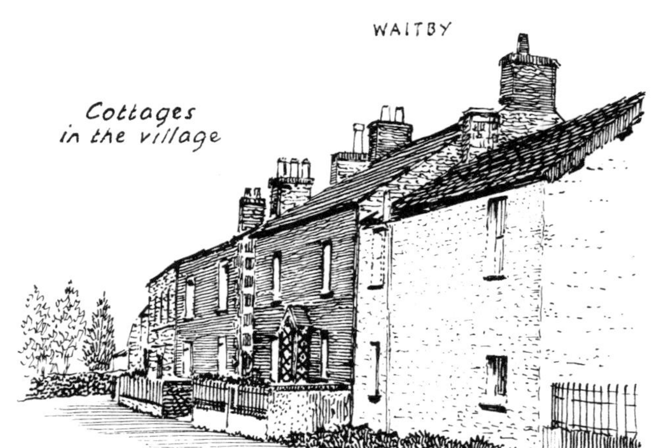
Cottages in the village

Soulby

Soulby Hall, 1682

This pump was erected on the village green in 1887 to commemorate Queen Victoria's Golden Jubilee.

The parish church of St Luke, a chapel of Kirkby Stephen until 1874, was erected in 1662-3 at the expense of Sir Philip Musgrave, lord of the manor, and restored and extended in 1774 and 1873. Over the porch is a tablet bearing the Musgrave arms and the date 1663. The 17th century bell turret is remarkable.

Bell turret detail

STAINMORE

Stainmore ("stony moor"), from which the parish is named, is a shallow depression in the Pennines accommodating a historic trade route between east and west, one of the few crossings in the range easily accessible to traffic. It has been used since time immemorial by all manner of men and at all ages of civilisation: on foot, on horseback, in coaches, in railway trains (for a relatively brief period) and today is a great highway, the A.66. During all this time it has had a bad reputation for hazards and dangers, being exposed and windswept, and despite modern improvements traffic is still on occasion brought to a halt by gales and blizzards. The surroundings are inhospitable and the picture is one of sombre desolation, with obvious signs of glacial movement and even of earth tremors. It is thought likely, so well known has Stainmore been throughout history, that Westmorland was given its name by travellers coming over the pass from the east, the county boundary being near the summit.

The parish of Stainmore is unusually large, taking in substantial areas of desert and moorland and extending from the mountain mass around Mickle Fell in the north almost to Tan Hill Inn in the south, its twelve-mile boundary co-terminous with Yorkshire nowhere falling below 1300 feet and generally being nearer 2000. Apart from the two roads that cross the boundary this is a trackless and lonely region, arduous to traverse and likely to attract only a few visitors pursuing special studies. But gradually the contours fall away to the west, the marshy plateaux break into deep gills and the first trees find shelter, and the unenclosed heath gives place to a pattern of fields and a wide scattering of farmsteads. Nowhere, however, is there a concentration of population sufficient to form a defined community, the two churches being sited for convenience in the two separate areas of North Stainmore and South Stainmore.

Stainmore has provided a harvest for the archaeologist, the district having produced both Bronze Age and Iron Age finds, but it was the Roman occupation that left for us the indelible ground traces of a road, a fort and a signal station.

Industry, represented by quarrying, mining and the railway, has ceased to play a part in the economy of the parish, agriculture being the mainstay with traditional sheepfarming. Forestry is a recent innovation along the road to Tan Hill.

The parish boundary

That section of the parish boundary coincident with the county boundary is extraordinary. It is obviously arbitrary, disregarding the Pennine watershed entirely and being fixed by straight lines a mile or so east of it, so that rain falling on a wide corridor of the parish flows not into Westmorland but across the boundary into Yorkshire. Even more surprising in this wasteland to which nobody could conceivably have any territorial aspirations is the marking of the 12-mile boundary with over a hundred boundary stones, as though one party or the other was jealous of its rights. In fact the boundary was fixed in 1847 by the Tithe Commissioners following a dispute (which a cynic with knowledge of the terrain might suppose to be concerned with a common disclaimer of ownership).

Stainmore

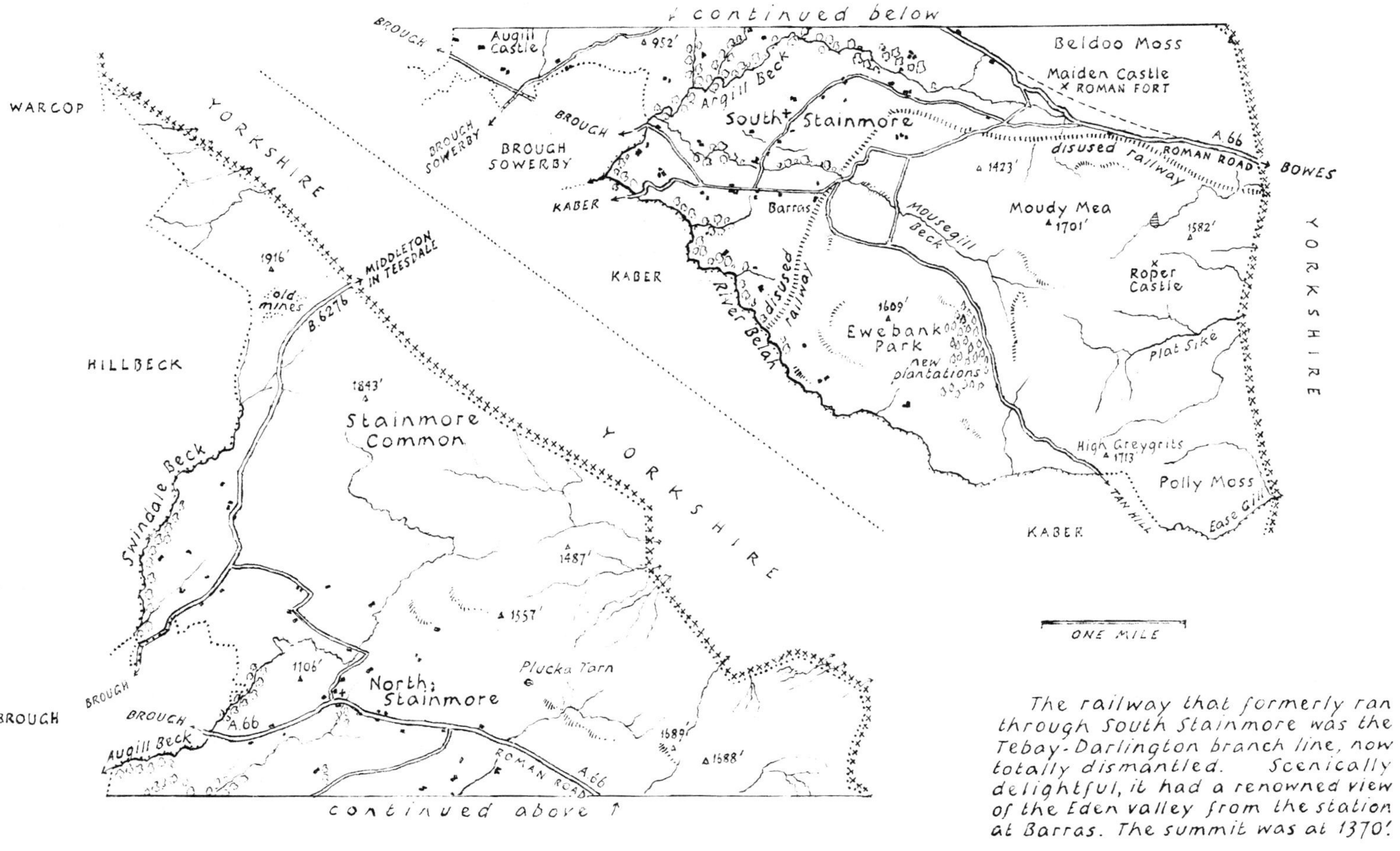

The railway that formerly ran through South Stainmore was the Tebay-Darlington branch line, now totally dismantled. Scenically delightful, it had a renowned view of the Eden valley from the station at Barras. The summit was at 1370'.

Stainmore

Two Stainmore churches

St Mary's, North Stainmore

St Mary's was erected in 1861 as a chapel-of-ease for Brough. Recently its doors were closed for public worship and the building is in course of conversion to other use.

St Stephen's, South Stainmore

St Stephen's is the parish church. It was rebuilt in 1842, replacing a chapel consecrated in 1608.

— and a most surprising Stainmore castle

In a district so influenced by its impending moorlands and extreme weather, where life tends to rawness, the sophisticated residence of Augill Castle is unexpected. This is a most imposing mansion, built in the grand style, with castellated parapets, towers, turrets, buttresses and an impressive facade looking over private grounds. Despite its appearance as a defensive stronghold the castle is early Victorian, being erected (for £10,000) in 1842.

Stainmore

Waterfall, Borrowdale Beck

Argill Bridge

Skirrygill Farm

Gritstone boulders by the quarry track

High Greygrits

Overlooking the road to Tan Hill and within sight of the inn is the bouldery outcrop of High Greygrits, with a track leading up to a disused quarry where there is a spectacular display of gritstone.

Nearby is the summit of the fell, at 1713 feet, a triangulation point of the Ordnance Survey, with a windshelter of rough stones.

The Ordnance column and windshelter on the summit

Stainmore

The pass of Stainmore was a great Roman highway leading across the Pennines to link York and Carlisle, its importance emphasised by a series of forts and signal stations along the route, the sites of which are still clearly visible.

On the Westmorland side of the pass, at an elevation of 1400 feet and commanding an extensive outlook to the west, is the site of a camp known as Maiden Castle. It is indicated by a notice of the Department of the Environment (formerly the Ministry of Public Buildings and Works), which describes it as a Roman fortlet. The earthworks take the form of a rectangle about half an acre in extent and surrounded by a rampart interrupted by two gateways. The Roman road runs alongside and the fort is also served by sunken trackways.

The present motor road, A.66, deviates hereabouts to follow an easier gradient around the hillside, and Maiden Castle thus stands in isolation undisturbed by traffic.

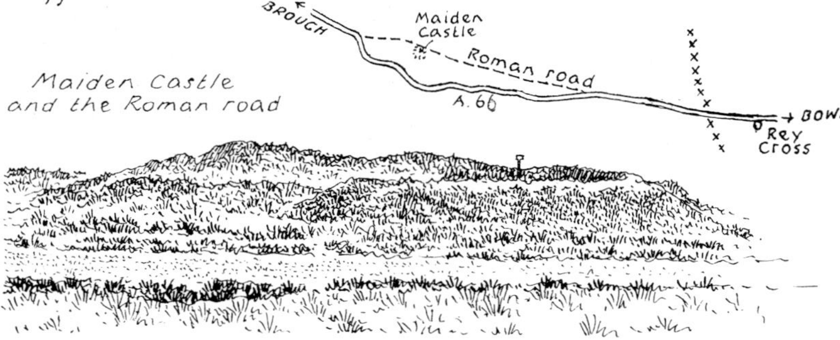

Maiden Castle and the Roman road

The antiquities of Stainmore

Roper Castle, looking south

Roper Castle, also known as Round Table, was used by the Romans as a signal station. It is a raised platform, almost circular in plan, situated on the brow of a lonely hill south of the Roman road and a mile distant from it, with a view of the eastern approaches to the pass and placed so that it had visual contact with both Maiden Castle and the next fort to the east, near Rey Cross.

Although a quarter-mile beyond the county boundary and therefore outside Westmorland, the thousand-year-old roadside monument of Rey Cross is of significance because it is thought to be a boundary stone erected by Edmund, King of Northumbria, to mark the division between his English kingdom (east) and the then-Scottish Cumberland out of which Westmorland was later formed.

It is a 'protected' monument, and enclosed by a low railing.

Rey Cross

Stainmore's abandoned industries

Stainmore men are today mainly engaged in farming but in the past they have turned their hands also to digging for coal, mining for lead, quarrying for stone, burning lime and maintaining a railway — operations that have all been abandoned. Pits and mines and quarries and kilns remain as scars on the landscape and the railway line has been dismantled, leaving a graceful but purposeless curve along the hillside. All these activities have had their day. Stainmore men have gone back to the land.

Particularly forlorn is the track of the railway, an especially sad sight because it is remembered as providing a train journey famed for its high scenic qualities and for its distinction as the loftiest railway in England. Its one defect was that it did not pay its way. The rails have been lifted and removed and some of the bridges and viaducts destroyed. In a fold of the hills near the summit, a small reservoir, used as a water supply for the steam engines, is reverting to nature.

Smelt mill, Augill Beck

Summit Reservoir

A ruinous railway footbridge
(A rusted iron notice on the gate says PENALTY FOR NEGLECT £2)

STAINTON

Stainton, "the stone-built town," is a place of great antiquity although evidences of its existence in the middle ages are now confined to some place-names and a few old records. Later it became a centre of industrial activity, with five mills operating along the beckside, all now closed. Today, its importance diminished, it is entirely agricultural. A 17th century packhorse bridge remains as a tangible link with the past.
At Stainton the Lancaster Canal, filled in from Kendal, is still a pleasant tree-lined waterway, frequented by swans, but modern commercial transport favours the busy A.65, which bisects the parish, and the new link road crossing the southern extremity; a furlong of the railway is also in the parish. There are hamlets at Barrows Green, Halfpenny and Crosscrake, in addition to Stainton, all overlooked by the eminence of the Helm.

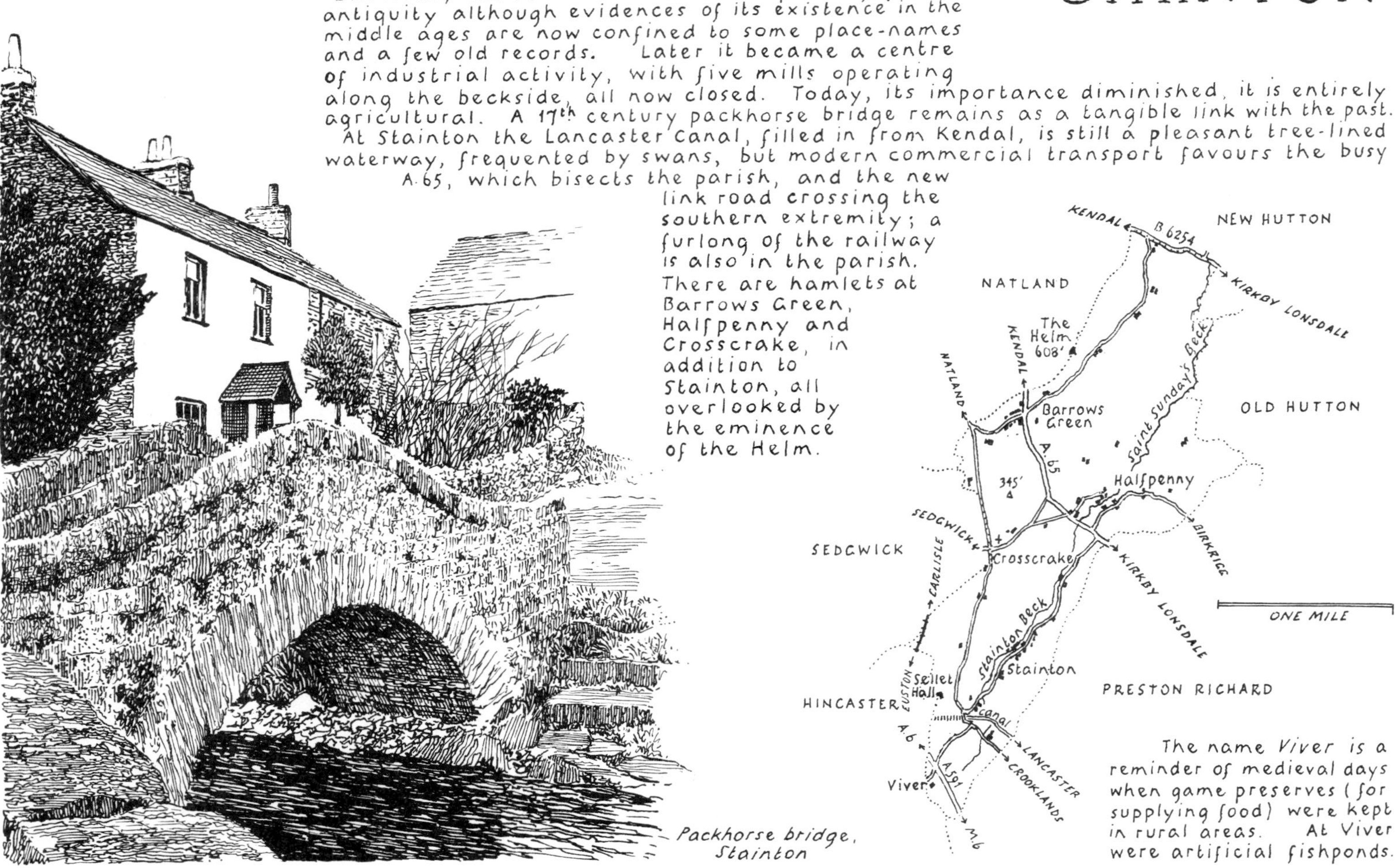

Packhorse bridge, Stainton

The name *Viver* is a reminder of medieval days when game preserves (for supplying food) were kept in rural areas. At Viver were artificial fishponds.

Stainton

Bridge End, Stainton

A plaque on the house proclaims it as the birthplace, on November 1st 1808, of John Taylor, Third President of the Church of Jesus Christ of Latter-Day Saints (Mormon) and World Leader of the Church 1877-87.

An old corn mill on the A.65 has been most attractively converted to residential use and the mill race made into a pleasant amenity.

Sellet Hall, of the late 16th century, retains its stone-mullioned windows; the interior is notable for a fine staircase and many other original fittings.

Stainton

The parish church of St Thomas is situated in the hamlet of Crosscrake, and is always referred to as Crosscrake Church, never as Stainton Church. The present building was erected in 1875 but other places of worship preceded it, there being a chapel as early as 1190.

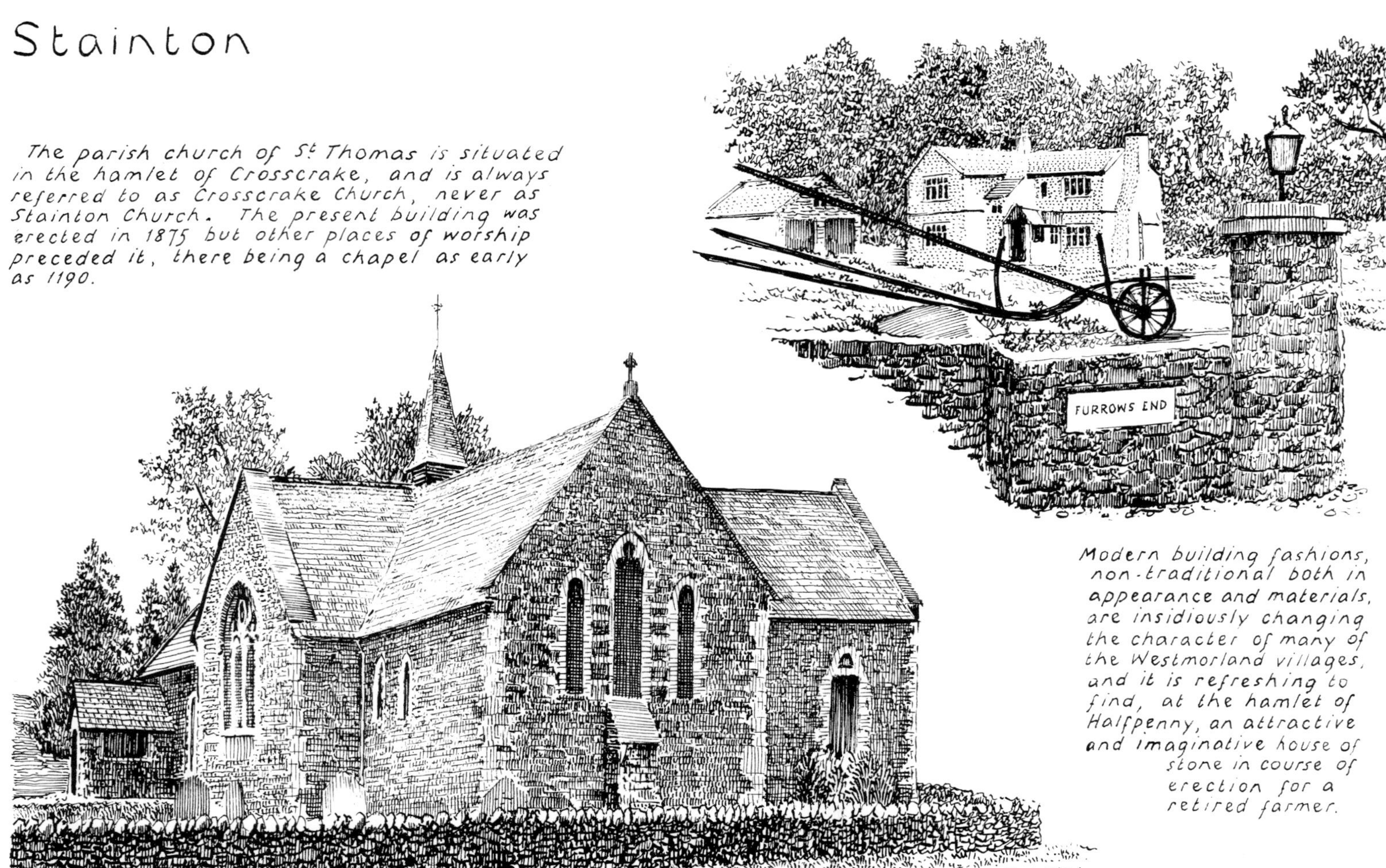

Modern building fashions, non-traditional both in appearance and materials, are insidiously changing the character of many of the Westmorland villages, and it is refreshing to find, at the hamlet of Halfpenny, an attractive and imaginative house of stone in course of erection for a retired farmer.

STRICKLAND KETEL

The adjoining parishes of Strickland Ketel and Strickland Roger originally formed one manor in the ownership of Ketel, grandson of the first Baron of Kendal. Around the 12th century Ketel granted a portion to Roger, thought to be a soldier of Norman descent. In the Domesday Book the district is recorded as *Stircaland*, a name denoting a pasture for cattle, this becoming *Strickland* in medieval times. The latter name is preserved in *Stricklandgate*, Kendal (the way to Strickland) but the destination-boards of omnibuses bound thereto say not Strickland but *Burneside* or *Bowston* and the parish names are rarely used except in affairs of administration.

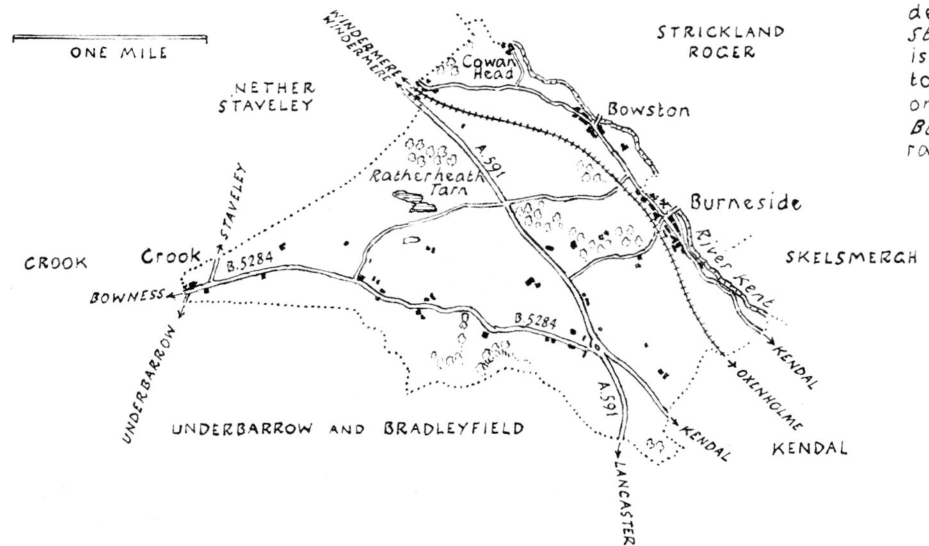

The River Kent divides the two parishes, which share also the industrial village of Burneside, a good example of community development around a place of work, for here is the large paper mill of the firm of James Cropper and Co. Ltd., a family concern that has given employment for over a century, provided accommodation and amenities for its workers and their families and in general played a major role, and a benevolent one, in the life and welfare of the village. Croppers and Burneside are almost synonymous names. Think of one and you think of the other.

Strickland Ketel has the church, the inn and the railway station of Burneside; the mill and the ancient Hall are across the Kent in Strickland Roger; the houses of the village extend along both sides of the river and are growing in numbers. The mill workers are not alone in finding Burneside good to live in. Outside the busy village, Strickland Ketel is a pleasant rural area, most of it farmed but having also some elegant residences in spacious parklands and small communities at Bowston and Cowan Head. The main road A.591 and two other classified roads run through the parish, as does the branch railway to Windermere, Ketel being much better served than Roger in the matter of communication with the world beyond its boundaries. Unlike Roger, too, very little of Ketel's acreage is rough land, but a small patch has escaped cultivation at Ratherheath, where there is an attractive tarn on which many Kendal people have learned to skate. But for 'outsiders' coming from the south along the new Kendal bypass, the A591, Strickland Ketel means only the start of heaven, for at its boundary the Lakeland fells suddenly appear.

Strickland Ketel

The parish church of St Oswald

The parish church of St Oswald was founded as a chapel of Kendal, the early records being obscure although it is known that a building occupied a nearby site from 1717 until 1826 when a new church was erected, the latter in turn being considerably enlarged to its present proportions in 1881. There are good stained windows, and carved oak fittings are a feature of the neat interior. Until 1972 a small spire crowned the tower, having been transferred from the 1826 structure, but was then dismantled because of defects, the appearance of the church being enhanced by its removal.

The church serves the two parishes of Strickland Ketel and Strickland Roger

Strickland Ketel

Houses of distinction

left: *Ellergreen*
bottom left: *Bannel Head*
below: *Tolson Hall*

Strickland Ketel

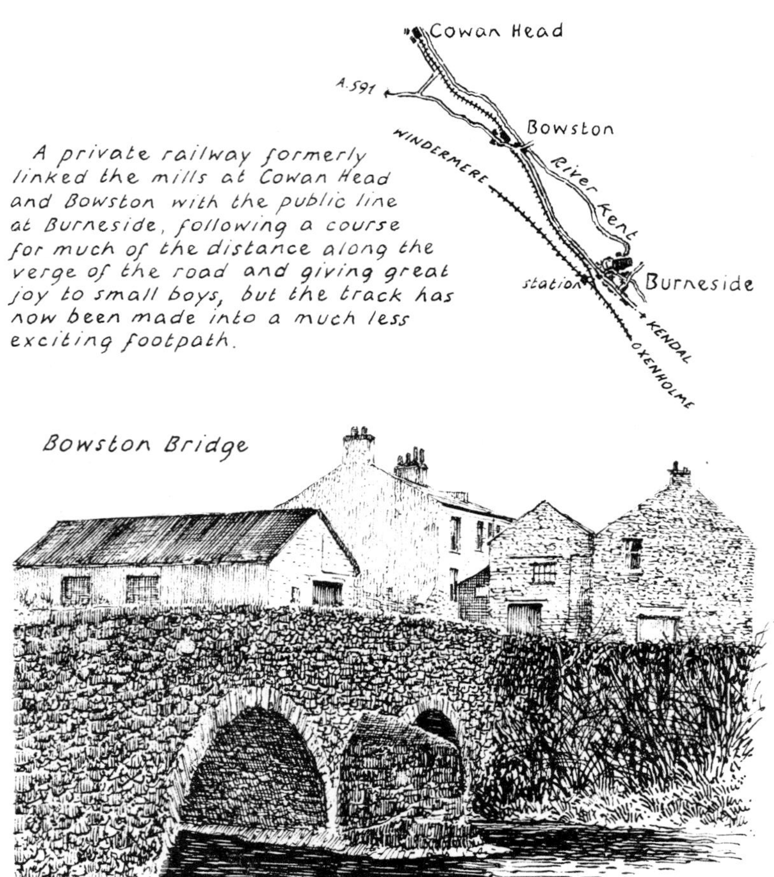

A private railway formerly linked the mills at Cowan Head and Bowston with the public line at Burneside, following a course for much of the distance along the verge of the road and giving great joy to small boys, but the track has now been made into a much less exciting footpath.

Bowston Bridge

Bowston and Cowan Head

Both Bowston and Cowan Head may be said to be largely by-products of the papermaking industry.

The mill at Cowan Head started operating around the middle of the 18th century, being subsequently taken over by James Cropper and Co. Ltd., and has worked consistently since. The Bowston mill, which was closed and demolished recently, was erected by that firm in 1874.

Cowan Head

Strickland Ketel

The Elba Monument, a landmark on a hill overlooking the A.591.

Whale Jaw Bones, also a familiar sight on the A.591. During recent improvements to this road the bones suffered damage, the present display being merely an abridged version of the more impressive originals.

Ratherheath Tarn — where many Kendal folk learned to skate and many didn't.

Cottages at Plumgarths

Gateside Farm

Garnett House

STRICKLAND ROGER

The valley boundaries of Strickland Roger are formed by the rivers Kent and Sprint, and from their junction at Burneside green pastures rise northwards to a tract of moorland crossed by a linking boundary a thousand feet higher. The Kent bisects the village of Burneside, the paper mill, many cottages, a new housing estate and the medieval Hall being within the angle formed by the confluence of the rivers and thus part of this parish. It is a busy corner, the large sheds of the mill giving it a strongly individual character, but beyond this centre of activity and in marked contrast is the field-patterned slope rising to the fell, wholly agricultural but with a few handsome residences, and above it the open moor of Potter Fell, a delightful maze of colourful undulations jewelled by a necklace of tarns and blessed with a commanding view of the Kent valley.

ONE MILE
LONGSLEDDALE
WHITWELL AND SELSIDE
LONGSLEDDALE
1250'
Potter Fell
1090'
Ulgraves
Gurnal Dubs
Garnett Bridge
KENDAL
OVER STAVELEY
Potter Tarn
652'
River Sprint
STAVELEY
River Kent
GARTH ROW
Gurnal Bridge
Bowston Bridge
Sprint Mill
STRICKLAND KETEL
paper mill
SKELSMERGH
Hall
KENDAL
Burneside

Sprint Mill and cottages

Sprint Mill is, alas, typical of almost all of the little Westmorland riverside mills that, last century, were milling corn or making bobbins or woollens. Those that survive stand derelict or have been put to other use. In either case they have lost their character.

Strickland Roger

17th century houses

left: *High Hundhowe*

bottom left: *Mire Foot*

below: *Godmond Hall*
(added to a medieval
pele tower)

Burneside Hall

Burneside Hall, built mainly in the 14th century, was originally the manor house of the family of Burneshead (the name from which *Burneside* is derived)

It is a splendid example of a defensive house of that period, being embattled and surrounded by a moat and having a walled enclosure for cattle. The ruined north tower, which has a double-vaulted basement, was ivy-covered, but in 1974 the stonework was cleaned and repaired. The gatehouse, still intact, was added in the 16th century.

Chimney detail

Strickland Roger

Potter Fell

The rough upland of Potter Fell rises to over 1200 feet, having splendid views and a fine cairn on Ulgraves; it is a popular resort of local people, the main attraction being the lovely tarn of Gurnal Dubs in a surround of heather and bracken. This is an industrial reservoir, formed by damming two natural tarns, and supplies water to the paper mill at Burneside, as do also two other reservoirs nearby, Potter Tarn and Ghyll Pool, the firm having exclusive water rights on the fell. Ghyll Pool was formerly the source of supply for the village of Burneside. A series of smaller tarns, hidden from each other by rocky hummocks, add further distinction to the fell.

Garnett Bridge is a hamlet romantically situated at the narrow entrance to Long Sleddale. The River Sprint, here confined in a rocky channel, formerly powered a corn mill.

Gurnal Dubs

The cairn on Ulgraves, looking up Long Sleddale

TEBAY

A tour of the villages of Westmorland gives a general impression of quiet wellbeing and prosperity. Almost everywhere rural and depending mainly on agriculture, the little communities in the valleys and nestling among the fells have an air of peace and contentment. The natives, often occupying the family home of generations and proud of their traditions, seem to suffer nothing from their denial of urban excitements and their tranquil lives in pleasant environments are reflected in a satisfaction with their lot and a happy acceptance of things as they come. Few emigrate from Westmorland villages.

Unhappily, Tebay is an exception. This is a place of great antiquity, having been populated for as long as records exist, and it emerged from medieval times as a hamlet engaged mainly in farming the fertile lands of the Lune and rearing sheep on the fells. A sudden importance was thrust upon it by Victorian enterprise, changing its economics profoundly, with the coming of the railway: the main line north from Euston was laid through the Lune Gorge, and because of its strategic position a branch line to Darlington connected here. The maintenance of the tracks, in particular those on the long gradient on Shap Fells, and the administration of a large station — Tebay Junction — and sidings, required much local labour. There was work for all and additional recruitment was induced by the provision of terraced houses for the staff. It was as though the Klondyke had come to Tebay. But sadly, within the past two decades, a hundred years of industrial prosperity ended with the closure of the station and the abandonment for ever of the branch line. Trains no longer halt here for refuelling or to take on an extra engine for the long climb to Shap: they race through powered by electricity. The station has been demolished and not a trace of it remains. The terraced houses overlook a desert of ashes.

The railway today has little need of Tebay. After creating here an animated business complex it has left behind an industrial skeleton.

Tebay has been cruelly mutilated, but, given time and an infusion of new activity, it will recover.

The parish church of St James was erected in 1880, largely at the expense of both the railway companies and their workers.
It is of neat and unusual design, having a circular tower and an interior faced with brick.

Tebay

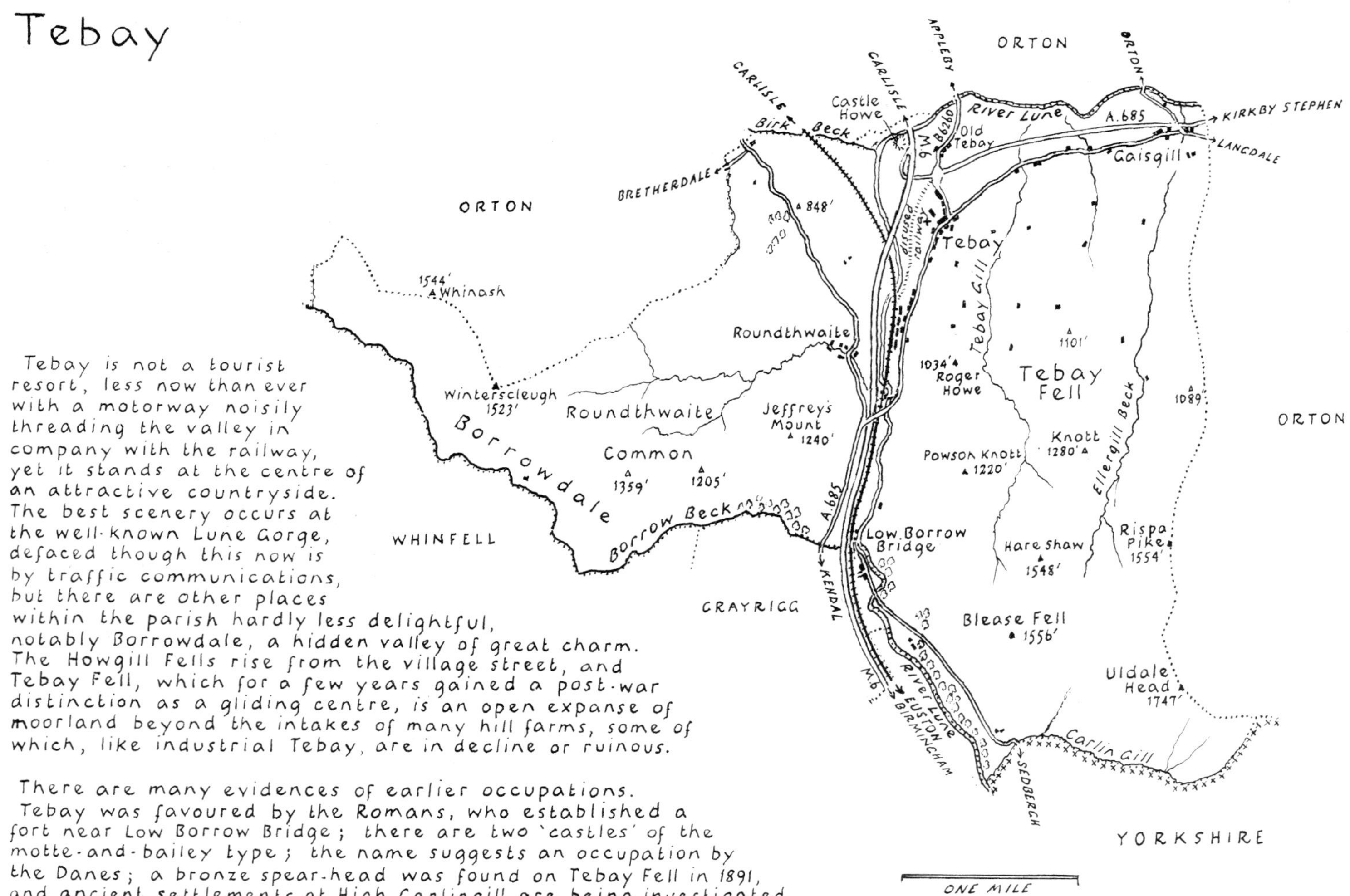

Tebay is not a tourist resort, less now than ever with a motorway noisily threading the valley in company with the railway, yet it stands at the centre of an attractive countryside. The best scenery occurs at the well-known Lune Gorge, defaced though this now is by traffic communications, but there are other places within the parish hardly less delightful, notably Borrowdale, a hidden valley of great charm. The Howgill Fells rise from the village street, and Tebay Fell, which for a few years gained a post-war distinction as a gliding centre, is an open expanse of moorland beyond the intakes of many hill farms, some of which, like industrial Tebay, are in decline or ruinous.

There are many evidences of earlier occupations. Tebay was favoured by the Romans, who established a fort near Low Borrow Bridge; there are two 'castles' of the motte-and-bailey type; the name suggests an occupation by the Danes; a bronze spear-head was found on Tebay Fell in 1891, and ancient settlements at High Carlingill are being investigated.

Tebay

*Farmhouses:
at Roundthwaite (left)
at Gaisgill (above)*

Old Tebay

*Railway houses
at Tebay*

Tebay

Borrowdale:
a treasure of Westmorland
that may soon be robbed of its beauty

below: *the lower reaches of the valley*

right: *from Powson Knott, Tebay Fell*

bottom right: *High Borrowdale (ruinous)*

Borrow Beck

Carlin Gill

Tebay

The River Lune near High Carlingill

In a curve of the River Lune and now partly concealed by the motorway is the artificial earthwork of Castle Howe, a motte-and-bailey castle, reputed to have been, in its prime, the ancient seat of the family of Tibbay.

This unusual cold store (or ice-house) is in the grounds of Town Head, Roundthwaite, but is thought to have served Roundthwaite Abbey, an older farm nearby, which despite its name had no known monastic connections.

Tebay

Gelstone

Overcluegill (ruinous)

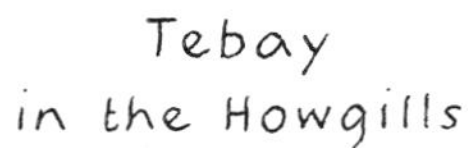

Carlingill Bridge

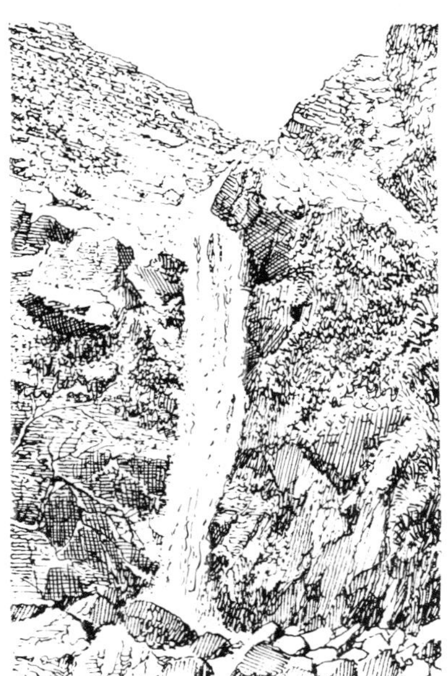

The Spout, Carlin Gill

Tebaygill Beck

The Lune Gorge from Fairmile Road, with the "parallel roads" of the railway and the motorway on the left

Tebay

Bridges

Tebay Bridge, on the road to Orton

Lune's Bridge

Low Borrow Bridge, seen through an arch of the railway viaduct. The 17th century bridge, once alone, is today one of four crossing Borrow Beck within a furlong's distance.

TEMPLE SOWERBY

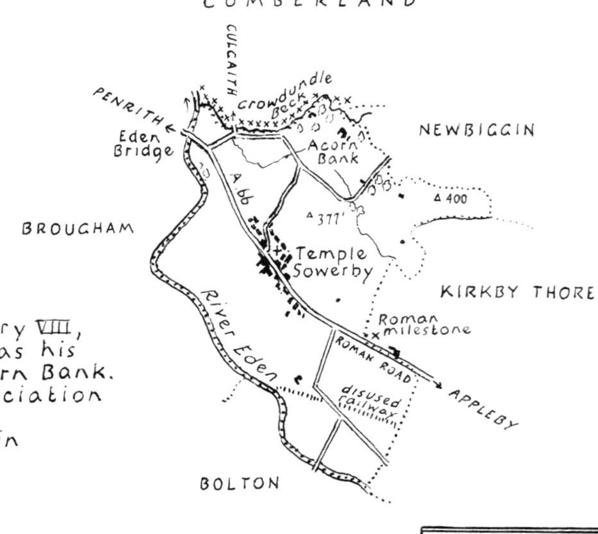

Temple Sowerby's distinctive name and dignified appearance suggest a proud history; examination of the record of events reveals a history perhaps better described as out of the ordinary.

The Romans knew the place and the Danes probably settled here and named it *Saurby*, but these visitors were no strangers elsewhere in the district and the sequence of developments became unusual only when the manor was given in the Middle Ages to the Order of Knights Templars, a crusading military and religious organisation suppressed in 1312 and succeeded in ownership by the Knights Hospitallers, who in turn were deposed by Henry VIII, the manor being granted in 1543 to a Thomas Dalston, and it was his descendants who in 1656 built the splendid manor house of Acorn Bank. *Temple* was added to the name of the manor because of its association with the Knights Templars.

Until 1880 the township of Temple Sowerby was subservient in administrative and ecclesiastical matters to the neighbouring parish of Kirkby Thore, of which it was part, but in that year obtained separate parochial status.

The village, partly bordering the A.66 and plagued by continuous traffic but mostly grouped around an open green away from the main road, is attractive, the church, of red sandstone, being a feature. A maypole survives.

Temple Sowerby parish adjoins Cumberland. Its west boundary is the Eden, grown to a stately river during its long journey from Mallerstang, and just north of Eden Bridge, where Crowdundle Beck joins, this lovely watercourse passes out of Westmorland, the county of its birth — a little sadly, surely?

Eden Bridge

Temple Sowerby

The parish church of St James, a handsome structure in local red sandstone, is a 1770 rebuilding of a 14th century chapel and was further restored in 1873, the principal feature of a pleasing interior being an elegant arcade.

Visitors entering the church are given the secular information at the doorway, by a carved message accompanying a benchmark of the Ordnance Survey, that the height above sea level at this point is 348¾ feet.

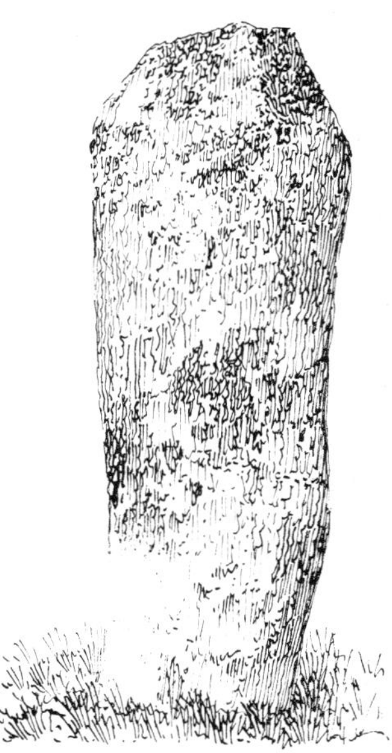

The A.66 road through Temple Sowerby is laid on the site of a Roman road (from York to Brougham). A Roman milestone, 4½ feet high and now enclosed by a fence, stands at the side of the road on the boundary with Kirkby Thore parish.

Temple Sowerby

Acorn Bank, an imposing mansion in red sandstone, is the manor house of Temple Sowerby and beautifully situated in spacious grounds. Parts of the building date from 1656, but extensive additions were effected in the 17th and 18th centuries. Now owned by the National Trust, the gardens are open to the public in the summer months. There is a current proposal to use the house as a convalescent home.

This ancient sundial standing in the grounds was discovered last century at Fallowfield nearby. It has a curious inscription in the form of a dialogue.

Acorn Bank

Temple Sowerby

Village scenes

Temple Sowerby is one of the few Westmorland villages retaining a maypole

Acorn Bank corn mill (disused)

THRIMBY

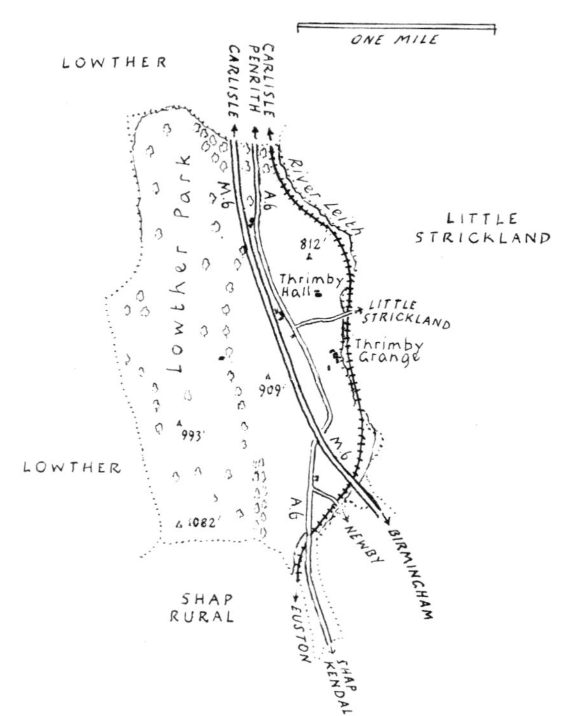

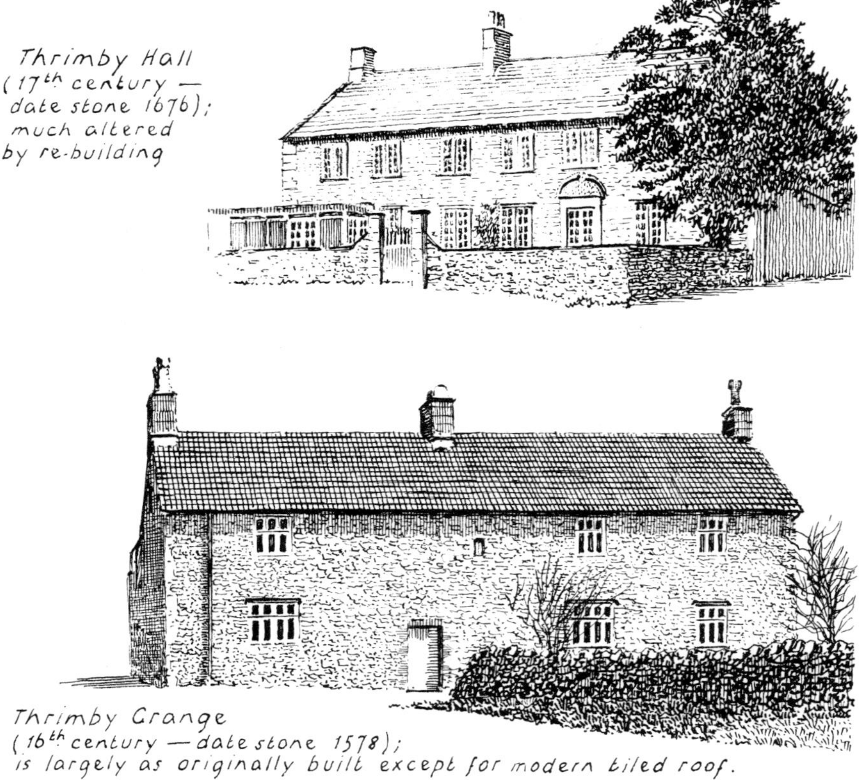

Thrimby Hall (17th century — date stone 1676); much altered by re-building

Thrimby Grange (16th century — date stone 1578); is largely as originally built except for modern tiled roof.

With no more than half a dozen houses Thrimby is the least-populated of Westmorland's parishes, nor is any further residential development likely, for this is a place butchered by important and noisy lines of communication, and not the setting for a peaceful rural existence. The main-line railway runs along the eastern boundary and the A.6 and the M.6 slice through the heart of it. The scenery is spoiled by traffic, but partially redeemed by the beautiful and expansive private parkland of Lowther, which covers the western half of the parish.

There are two old houses of great character, reminders of the days when Thrimby's sphere of influence went further afield and included both Great and Little Strickland, now separate parishes. The church of St Mary, at Little Strickland, is still regarded as the parish church of Thrimby — a deference to its long-suffering pride.

Thrimby

Emperor's Lodge stands at the south entrance to Lowther Park, where the Emperor's Drive starts its two-and-a-half miles approach to Lowther Castle; they were so named to commemorate a visit by the German Emperor in 1895. The Drive has been obstructed by the motorway just inside the Park grounds, a new entrance having been constructed nearby to take a diversion under the motorway by a bridge.

An old bridge near the railway line indicates the route of the former highway out of Shap to the north. In the background is the motorway.

Thrimby Farm

Old settlements at Thrimby

In the field opposite to Thrimby Farm, on the east side of the A.6, and in adjoining fields, are many unnatural undulations believed to be the earthworks of ancient village settlements, an opinion supported by old maps and aerial photographs. The site has not been fully investigated as yet, nor have excavations been made.

TROUTBECK

The Troutbeck valley is familiar to all habitual visitors to the Lake District. Its stream flows into Windermere after a long journey from the high fells east of Kirkstone, and it is a journey of loveliness, entering, from the bleak uplands where its initial waters assemble, a region of rich pastures and woodlands.

The parish boundary runs mainly around the watershed of the valley, enclosing a village of considerable charm with buildings of strongly individual character in traditional styles of the 17th century forming picturesque groups, happily little spoiled by the intrusion of new dwellings. Its attractiveness, however, proves a magnet for summer visitors and campers, whose weight of numbers is often a torment to the residents. A very large camp and caravan site chokes the narrow throat of the valley, serving a useful and necessary purpose but marring the visual amenities. Troutbeck, at least in summertime, is not the rural retreat it once was.

Native customs die hard here. The division of the township into three 'hundreds', the election (not too solemnly) of a Mayor, the Shepherds' Meets, and their associated legends, testify to the sturdy independence always exercised. Antiquities are present in the upper parts of the valley, where the Roman Road can be seen slanting up to High Street along what is known as Scot Rake; there are ancient cairns on the Tongue, an upthrust of land that effectively divides the higher dale into two branches; an old village settlement is nearby.

Troutbeck's worst day within living memory occurred in June 1953, when severe flooding was caused by a cloudburst on Wansfell. But most of its days are good. Really good.

Troutbeck's church has the distinction, a most unusual one, of having the name Jesus Church, formerly Jesus Chapel, since its consecration in 1562. The structure then existing became in a ruinous condition and was rebuilt in 1736, major restorations and alterations following in 1861, but the original beams, a notable feature of the interior, were retained.

Troutbeck

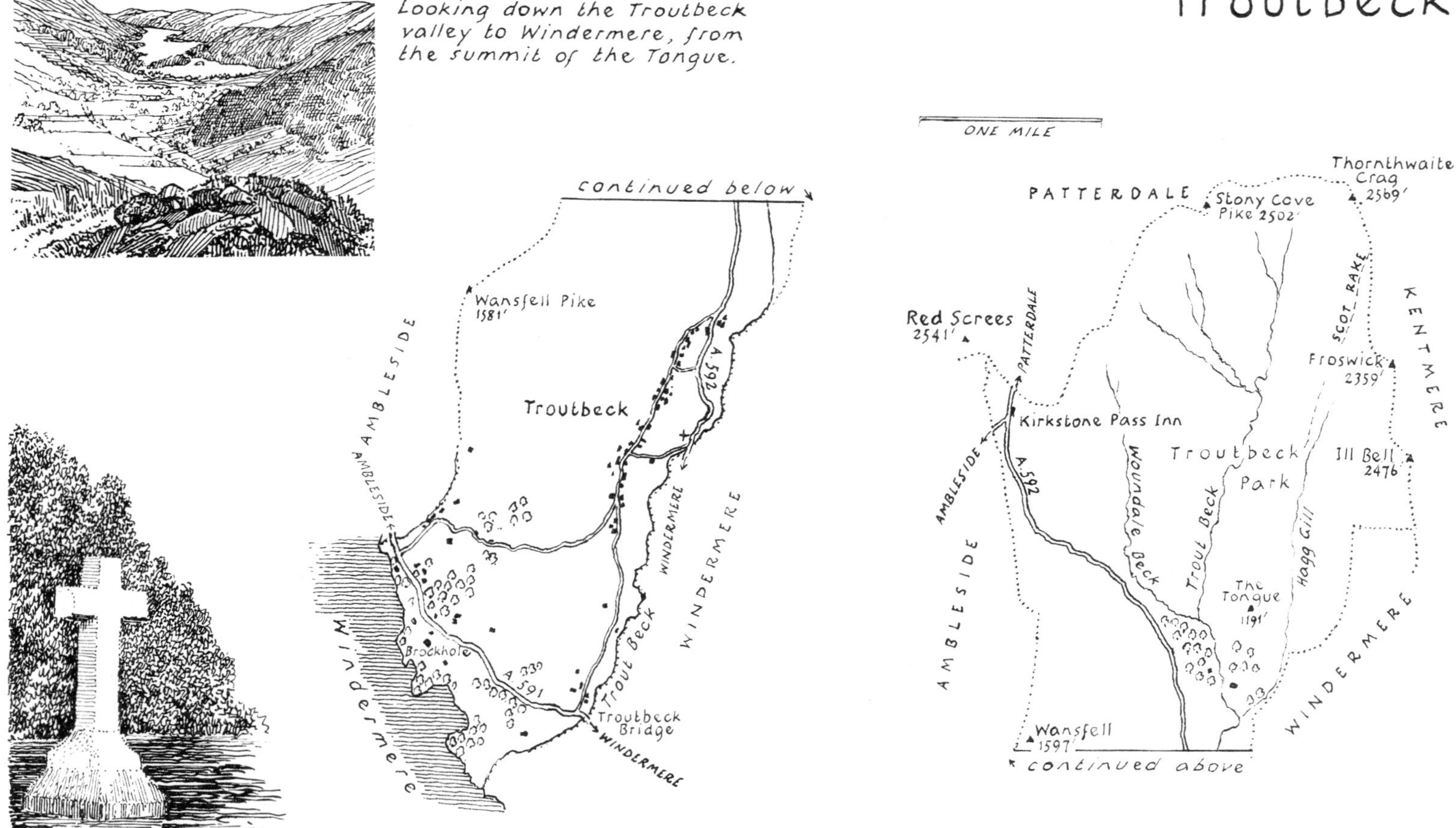

The name of White Cross Bay, Windermere, derives from a stone cross erected on the bed of the lake a few yards offshore as a memorial to two young men who lost their lives by drowning in 1853.

Troutbeck

Town End dates from 1623, when it succeeded another house on the same site. It was built as the family home of the Brownes and so occupied through to 1947, when it was acquired with its splendid furnishings by the National Trust. The oak woodwork is of outstanding excellence and much of the furniture is unique. This beautiful example of a 'statesman's' home is open to the public.

Brockhole, built as a private residence about 80 years ago, is now the property of the Lake District Planning Board and has been adapted imaginatively as a National Park Centre providing information and educational services relating to the district — an innovation that has proved very popular with visitors. Spacious grounds give public access to the shore of Windermere.

Troutbeck

Architectural styles
(mainly 17th century),
Troutbeck village

Troutbeck

Troutbeck

Troutbeck Park

Thornthwaite Crag

Stony Cove Pike

Thornthwaite Crag is distinguished by the tallest column of stones, 14' high, on any Lakeland fell. This very prominent landmark is shown on Ordnance maps as a beacon.

17th century bridge, Trout Beck

Troutbeck

The Troutbeck valley

Troutbeck

Kirkstone Pass

left: Approaching the pass on the road from Troutbeck, with Red Screes in the background

looking down to Kirkstone Pass from Red Screes

Kirkstone Pass Inn

UNDERBARROW AND BRADLEYFIELD

The parish church of All Saints was erected in 1869 to replace a church of 1708, which itself succeeded an earlier structure on the same site.

Sheltered by lofty limestone cliffs yet open to the sun, the lovely tract of country at the head of the Lyth Valley, where the alluvial flats end in undulating hillocks, where sheep and cattle graze in undisturbed peace, is perhaps more typically Westmorland than the upland fells and mountains. This is a region of damson blossom, honeysuckle and wild roses; of ivygrown walls; of whitewashed cottages and farmsteads: a tranquil place indeed. In the village of Underbarrow modern bungalows mix, none too harmoniously, with 17th century buildings but elsewhere the traditional scene changes only with the seasons.

Dominating all is the white escarpment of Scout Scar (properly but seldom referred to as Underbarrow Scar), a classic viewpoint with a twin in Cunswick Scar, beyond which, to the east, gradual slopes decline to the farmlands of Bradleyfield and then to urban Kendal.

The shelter on Scout Scar, locally known as the Umbrella or the Mushroom, was erected in 1912 as a memorial to King George V. An ingenious view indicator originally provided therein has been robbed of its details by vandals, and abandoned.

Underbarrow and Bradleyfield

at Tullythwaite

Chimneys of Hollin Bank

Underhill

Cairn on Cunswick Scar

Cunswick Hall

Cunswick Hall is the oldest house in the parish, the date of the original building, the seat of the Leyburne family being in some doubt, but it is known that a pele tower formerly existed. The house has been rebuilt but the gateway remains undisturbed. On the approach from the north there appears to be traces of an ancient settlement.

The gateway, thought to be 15th century, has a panel, re-set, bearing the Tudor Royal Arms.

WAITBY

Waitby parish extends north from the limestone heights of Ash Fell to the softer scenery and patterned fields of the Scandal Beck valley: a landscape of contrasts, everywhere attractive but comparatively little known and rarely visited, only the Ash Fell road carrying any volume of traffic; local needs are served by narrow lanes of single track width. Yet, until recently, three railways crossed this quiet countryside, only one of which survives as a passenger line. There are two small hamlets: Waitby and Smardale, the latter place having a splendid Hall and formerly a railway station and being situated at the portals of a wooded valley of great charm and outstanding interest. There is no church, no inn, no shop; the old school has locked doors and a silent bell. Today the parish is quieter than ever, in decline, and its dependency on nearby Kirkby Stephen is absolute.

The future may hold little for Waitby, but the past held much. The parish is rich in antiquities. Although within its boundaries there are few dwellings and a population insignificant in numbers, evidences of early occupations at different ages of man are profuse, occurring moreover in all parts of the area, and there is no doubt that during the periods before history began to be recorded Waitby had a succession of residents and was a place of greater importance than it is today.

Smardale Hall

The old school

Smardale Hall is of unusual design, the residential part being a long narrow rectangle, 86' x 27', with round towers at the four corners. The building is ascribed to the 16th century and succeeded another on the same site. The fabric is in good condition; in appearance the structure is out of the ordinary and impressive. It is now occupied as a farmhouse.

Waitby

Waitby

Smardale Viaduct

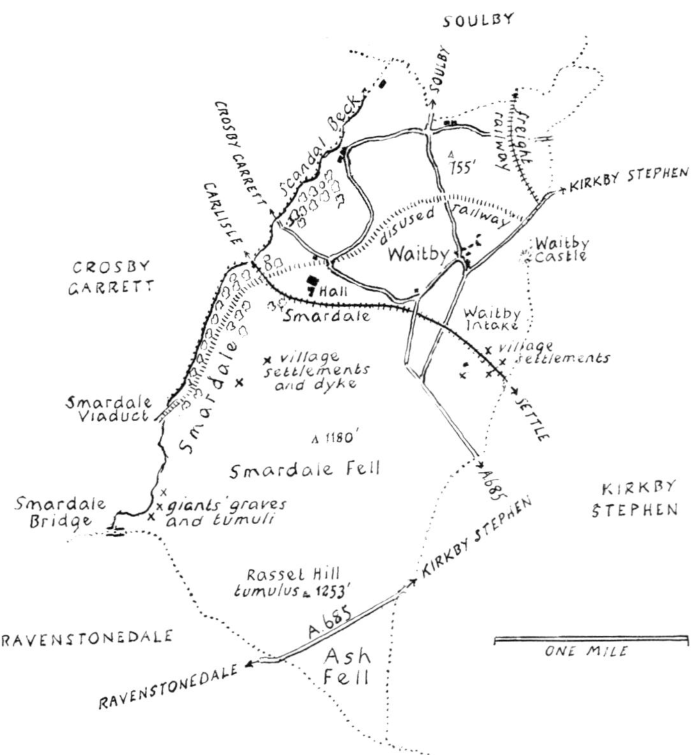

The elegant Smardale Viaduct carried the now-defunct branch railway between Tebay and Darlington over Scandal Beck. North of it for a mile the line ran through a wooded defile, with the beck far below, before being crossed by the still-active Settle-Carlisle line at another viaduct — a spectacular example of railway engineering. The abandoned track has become a botanists' delight, many uncommon varieties of flowers being rampant here in Arcadian surroundings.

The antiquities of Waitby

The origins of the archaeological antiquities in Waitby parish are obscure: they are older than recorded history and take many forms. There are several ancient village settlements, represented by enclosures and hut circles, on the slopes above Scandal Beck at Smardale and in Waitby Intake; dykes, although now intermittent, can be followed for two miles, linking the principal settlements; "giants' graves" are profuse in the vicinity of Smardale Bridge; a tumulus on Rasset Hill produced the interred bones of a cremated adult; on a hilltop near Waitby the site of a castle can be identified; and around the present hamlet are obvious lynchets or cultivation terraces used by early settlers.

Tourists concerned only with the 20th century should pass by Waitby. Imaginative seekers after the secrets of the past would do well to linger.

Waitby Castle occupies the crest of a low hill, and, although disturbed, the earthworks can be seen in the form of an oval enclosure surrounded by a ditch and rampart (similar to the better-preserved Croglam Castle at Kirkby Stephen).

Of the many village settlements the best known and most conveniently accessible are those situated in Waitby Intake, occurring on both sides of the railway in four groups of earthworks, the two adjoining on the east having been damaged during the construction of the permanent way embankment. Railway engineers were no respecters of ancient monuments.

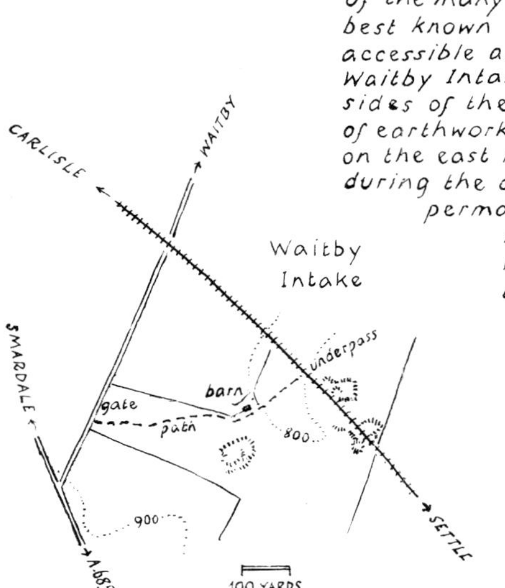

Giants' Graves, Smardale

Opinions differ as to the purpose of the pillow-mounds recorded on Ordnance maps as giants' graves (a name given to them locally). Some authorities say these were artificial warrens made for rabbits, as a food supply; others that they were platforms for the drying of bracken; all agree that they were not burial mounds. The proximity of those at Smardale to the village settlements, however, suggests some association with the culture of the villagers and therefore dates them to the same period of prehistory — long before rabbits were introduced to this country.

WARCOP

Warcop, once a quiet agricultural district in the Eden Valley with an extensive and uninhabited moorland bordering the highest, loneliest, and most remote part of Yorkshire, is quiet no more. Established here is an Army training camp and the whole of Warcop Fell is now a target range for heavy guns: a no-man's-land indeed, a dead wilderness. Intruders venture at their peril. Written permission, not lightly given, is needed before human foot can be set there.

The village of Warcop, however, inbetween the bangs of the guns is delightful, straggling the roads and open greens by the river and presided over by a venerable church. Through the parish runs the former Kirkby Stephen-Carlisle railway line but since its closure to passengers its use has been restricted to the conveyance of freight from the quarries at Hartley to the main line at Appleby. The Roman road that became the A66 also bisects the parish and is notoriously busy but happily it bypasses the village, which has only one classified road.

The early history of Warcop, anciently Warthecoppe, is largely based on legend and assumption, but traces of old settlements in various parts of the parish confirm a prehistoric occupation. At Howgill Fold, now out of bounds, is an old village complex; near the church are the earthworks of dykes and camps; Castle Hill was named after a fortress that once stood there, and monastic cells are known to have been formed at Sawbridge and Burton.

A mile west of the church is the cul-de-sac village of Sandford, with an inn.

The parish church of St Columba

The parish church of St Columba has an endearing quaintness, the result of many alterations and extensions to the original 12th century structure, parts of the fabric of which remain.

Traditions are maintained by an annual Rushbearing ceremony and procession of children.

Warcop

Warcop's lovely 16th century bridge across the Eden is narrow, taking single traffic only. It has been saved from 'improvement', probably merely because it carries a quiet minor road.

Roman Fell,
from the ruins of Burton Hall

Burton

Within easy memory, Burton Hall was a large and elegant mansion with several ancient features and three fishponds. It has been demolished entirely and the site is now within the target area of the Army guns. Burton has (to quote an apt and obvious colloquialism) gone for a Burton.

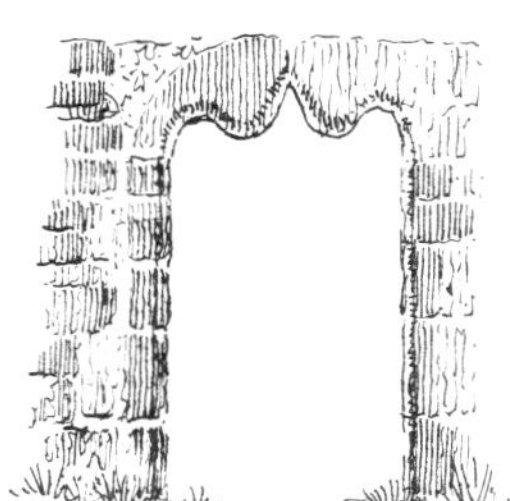

This old doorway was saved from Burton Hall and re-erected in the churchyard of St Columba's

The facade of Warcop Hall clearly displays the three periods of its architecture — the Elizabethan manor house, a formal Georgian extension and a fanciful Victorian wing.

Warcop Hall

The maypole stands on the base of the old village cross

Warcop

continued below
Warcop Fell
1838'
Tarn Gill
1919'
Longfell Pike
1898'
Dogber Tarn
ONE MILE
MURTON
HILTON
APPLEBY
APPLEBY
site of Roman fort
Espland
Howgill Fold
ancient settlement
ruins of Burton Hall
A.66
654'
MUSGRAVE
ROMAN ROAD
Black Hill
803'
Highclose Sike
freight railway
687'
Mire Sike
Sandford Mire
Hayber Beck
Clump Hill
833'
Sandford
B.6259
ORMSIDE
River Eden
Hall
635'
A.66
BROUGH
Warcop
630'
559'
B.6259
KIRKBY STEPHEN
KIRKBY STEPHEN
APPLEBY
Black Sike
Bleatarn
610'
Waterhouses Beck
Sawbridge Hall
GREAT MUSGRAVE
ASBY
SOULBY
MUSGRAVE
ASBY
MURTON
YORKSHIRE
2211'
Little Fell
2445'
2123'
Burton Fell
MURTON
MUSGRAVE
Roman Fell
1946'
Warcop Fell
continued above

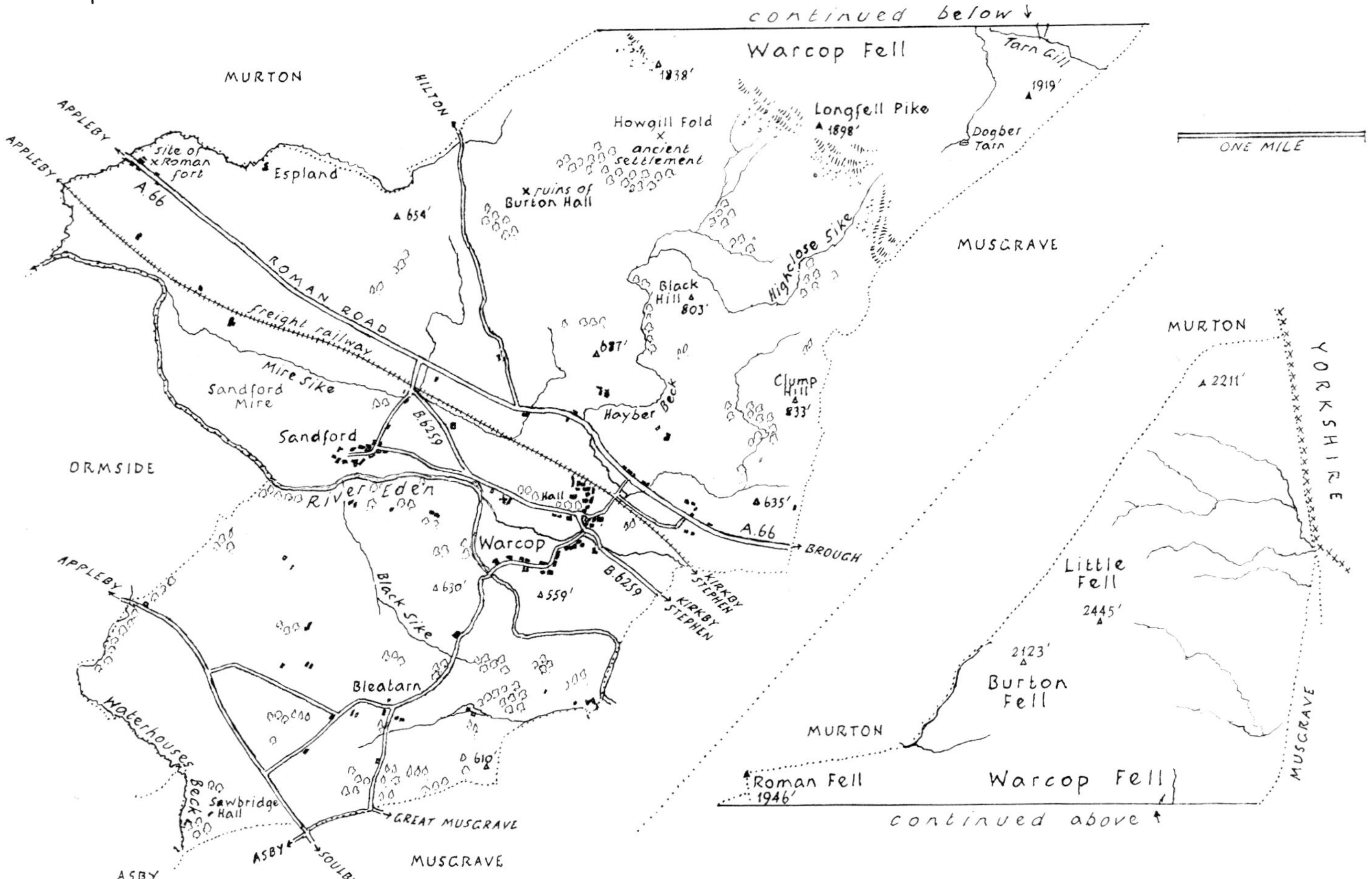

WHARTON

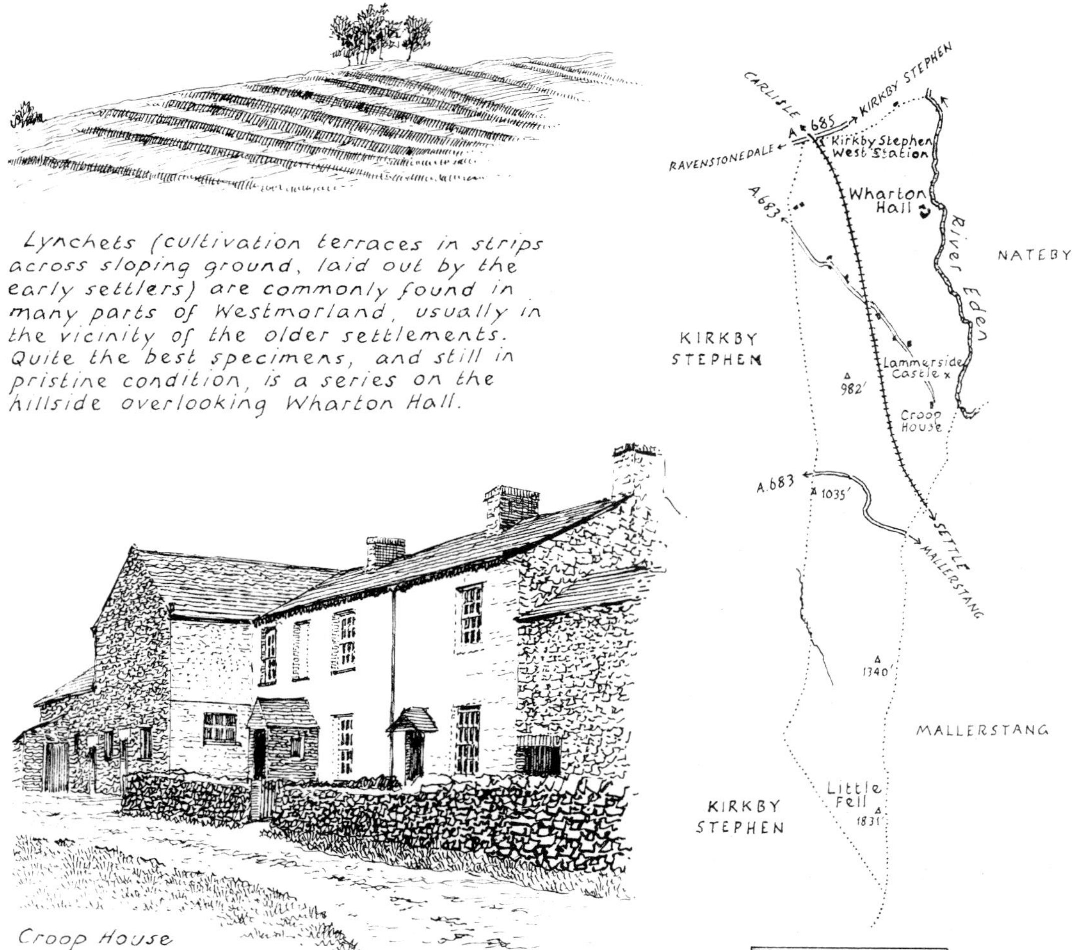

Lynchets (cultivation terraces in strips across sloping ground, laid out by the early settlers) are commonly found in many parts of Westmorland, usually in the vicinity of the older settlements. Quite the best specimens, and still in pristine condition, is a series on the hillside overlooking Wharton Hall.

Croop House – a Wharton farm

Wharton parish comprises a long narrow corridor of ground on the west bank of the River Eden as it leaves Mallerstang and its boundaries extend in the south over rough terrain almost to Wild Boar Fell. It consists of a few farmhouses: there is no village, no church or school, no inn or shop, no petrol pump or signposted through road. The reason for its proud status as a separate township is found in the long history of the family of Wharton, whose estate it was as long ago as the reign of King Edward I and who, for military exploits, attained noble rank.

Although its buildings are few they include two monuments of extraordinary interest: (a) the ruined Lammerside Castle with origins lost in antiquity, and (b) Wharton Hall, once in ruins too but largely restored and today a most impressive sight on its eminence overlooking the Eden.

Trains rushing along the Settle to Carlisle line are reminders of the world outside the parish but pass unheeded by the few human beings and their many animals. They are of no concern. The birth of a calf is far more important in Wharton.

Wharton

Lammerside Castle

Lammerside Castle, long derelict and partially destroyed, has only a ruined 14th century tower left standing, but of this sufficient remains to indicate the plan of the passages and rooms, the arched doorways being a feature. The original structure covered an adjoining area also. Some field walls in the vicinity appear to have been built of facing stones stripped from the castle.

Exterior and interior doorways

Wharton

The old hall
(in course of restoration)

Wharton Hall

Wharton Hall is one of the county's best surviving examples of a late medieval house built for defence, the buildings being ranged around a courtyard and access gained only through a gatehouse arch. Parts of the fabric are ruinous, but the 15th century block is intact and happily being restored externally to its original appearance by the present owner — a most commendable undertaking. A commodious range of farmbuildings, added later, adjoins the Hall.

The north-west range
and the gatehouse

WHINFELL

Whinfell is a parish without a grouped community, having only a score of farmhouses widely scattered along the valley formed by the River Mint; the greater part consists of a long bare ridge topping 1500′ and rising from the cultivated strath in smooth but unremitting slopes suitable only for sheep grazing; over the ridge the ground falls away more steeply into Borrowdale. The topography of the parish is simple, its boundaries being formed mainly by the watercourses that drain the ridge, which is itself the dominant feature. The highest point, Whinfell Beacon, has historic interest; this apart, the parish has had an uneventful past.

The area extends to the A.6 in the north, where, until it became a casualty of the motorway, the Leyland Clock was a familiar landmark; otherwise the road communications are confined to narrow lanes with many gates and flowery hedges, the district remaining very much as it was when first settled in the 17th century.

In a county where the fells are such a feature of the landscape it is remarkable that so few have given their names to the parishes. Commonly the parish names are derived from the valleys and the Viking and Danish settlements therein; or, also commonly, from the early lords of the manor. Whinfell is an exception.

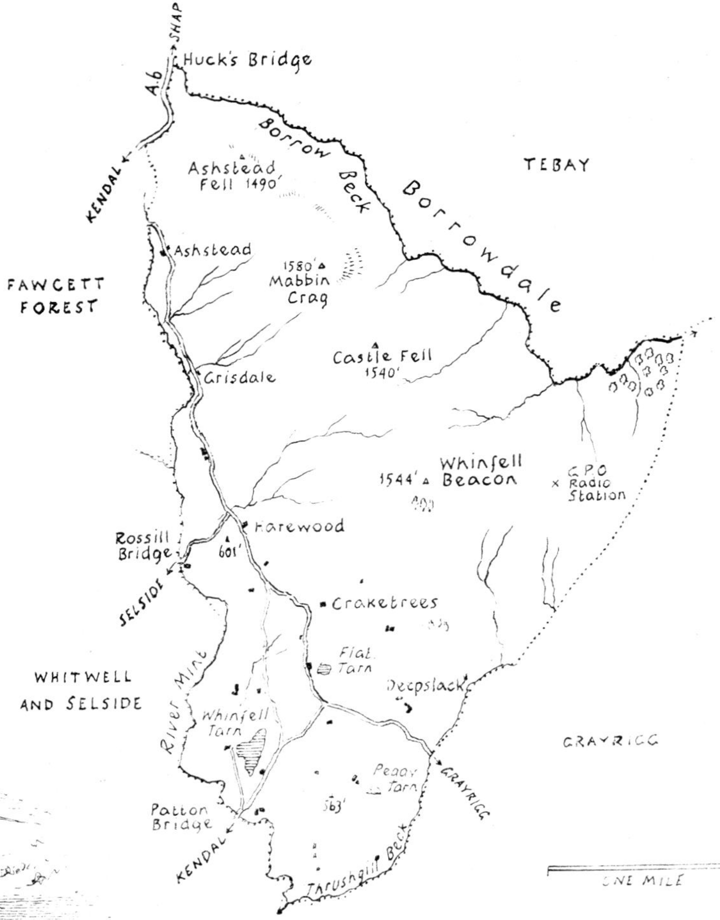

Whinfell Tarn

Borrans

Grisdale

The 17th century Rossill Bridge has a graceful single arch and no parapets. Its responsibilities have been taken over by a more recent and wider bridge nearby. The old has beauty, the new no beauty. It is a sad reflection on modern methods that men no longer build for beauty as well as utility. Very little of 20th century construction will be regarded with pleasure or pride by future generations.

Harewood

Borrowdale
from Castle Fell

Signal stations on Whinfell

15th century

20th century

The Monster of Whinfell

The burghers of Kendal, or those of them who turn their eyes to the hills, were shocked a few years ago by the sudden appearance on the Whinfell skyline of a G.P.O. radio repeater station.

Unfortunately this unsightly contraption must also be recorded as a part of Westmorland's heritage.

In the years of unrest along the Border, a system of beacons was installed on certain prominent heights to give warning, by fires, of the approach of invaders. One of the six 'statutory' sites in Westmorland, scheduled in a list dated 1468, was Whinfell Beacon. (The others were at Helton, Orton, Farleton, Barbon and Stainmore).

Local inhabitants were charged with the duty of maintaining the beacons, and the plantation near the top of Whinfell provided an easily accessible supply of firewood.

WHITWELL AND SELSIDE

The cairn on Whiteside Pike

The last area of cultivation before the A.6 starts the long climb from Kendal over the bleak wastes of Shap Fells is at Selside, where a few square miles of undulating country is wholly farmed, and, being used mainly for grazing, is a patchwork of green fields, a vivid emerald carpet set against a backcloth of sombre fells and a reward for good husbandry. In the midst is the splendid 14th century Selside Hall, the church, and a primary school that serves not only this but adjacent parishes also.

The A.6 bisects the parish, following a line that marks a difference in landscapes. South of it is the fertile Selside pasture bordered by the River Mint; north is a rising wedge of moorland between the valleys of Long Sleddale and Bannisdale, culminating in the prominent summit of Whiteside Pike, a place of rock and heather. On the fringe of this starker scenery is the secluded mansion of Lowbridge House in beautifully wooded grounds.

Although the name of Whitwell is preserved in the name of the parish, its significance has passed into history. In the middle ages Whitwell was a manor separate from Selside, becoming incorporated as the result of a marriage. Not a trace of Whitwell Hall remains.

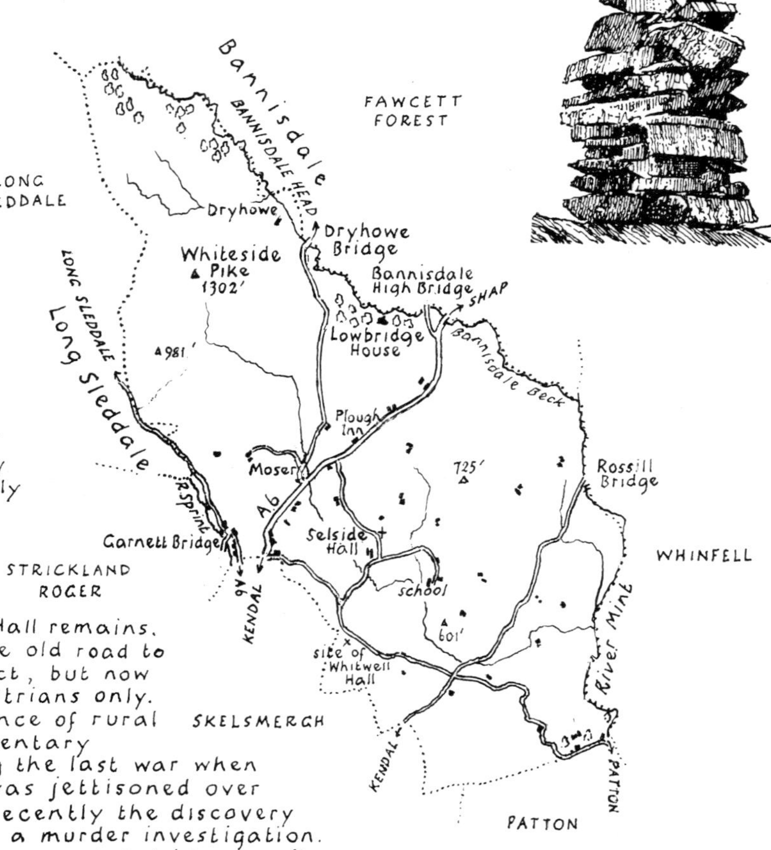

In this parish the old road to Shap is still distinct, but now accessible to pedestrians only.

Selside, the essence of rural peace, had a momentary excitement during the last war when a stick of bombs was jettisoned over its fields. More recently the discovery of a corpse led to a murder investigation. Some things *do* happen at Selside despite its seeming immunity from disturbance of any sort.

An inn sign for The Plough

Whitwell and Selside

The parish church of St Thomas was built in 1838, the massive tower being an addition in 1894 and unusually constructed over the nave, not adjoining it. A notice inside the church gives details of earlier churches on the site.

Selside Hall, parts of which are of the late 14th century, was the seat of the Thornburghs, who settled here from Yorkshire and remained until 1774. The house was built with a central hall (since altered) and two cross-wings, one of which has barrel-vaulted chambers. A massive beam supports the kitchen ceiling. This is a building that strongly reflects the past — a place of blocked doorways and suspected secret passages, of stories of ghosts and visible reminders of past occupiers. Human bones were found during alterations. The north wing, which retains a handsome window, was used as a chapel until the 18th century.

Whitwell and Selside

Lowbridge House

Built in 1837, and later enlarged, Lowbridge House is the family home of the Fothergills. It is a handsome mansion in lovely grounds, well screened by trees and having interesting garden ornamentations.

Bannisdale High Bridge carries a preserved section of the old Shap road (used now only for access) over Bannisdale Beck. It is probably of 17th century date.

Whiteside Pike

WINDERMERE

Windermere is probably the best known of all Westmorland place-names. It is memorised in schooldays — "the largest lake in England" — and later visited, occasionally or regularly, in adult life by those who seek renowned scenes of natural beauty. It is a lovely sheet of water, the most friendly of the lakes and the most frequented. In olden times it was named Wynandermere.

Windermere is also the name of a large village that likes to call itself a town and of an extensive parish that includes not only this urban community but reaches far into the hills above Troutbeck, taking in the the former township of Applethwaite, once of greater importance than Windermere Town when the latter was little more than a hamlet known as Birthwaite; indeed the full extent of the lake was annexed to Applethwaite before passing to Windermere parish by a merger of townships in 1894.

As Applethwaite diminished in significance, Windermere flourished exceedingly after, and because of, the coming of the railway in 1847, even though trains could go no further and here turned back. But most of the new visitors thus introduced to the district wanted to go no further: it was Windermere they wanted to see, having heard much of it, and popular railway excursions now made this possible. At Windermere they were in a new land, amongst beauty outside any previous experience. Windermere was a gateway to adventure and romance.... People came in droves, increasingly. Industrialists made their homes here — splendid homes, too — and laid out beautifully landscaped gardens. Tourists were catered for by modern hotels and guest houses and shops. The railway brought prosperity on an expanding scale, so that today Windermere, both town and lake, is a favourite holiday resort. Happily the seasonal influx of visitors has detracted little from the natural amenities, and Windermere's richly diversified landscape, blessed with delightful open spaces and viewpoints, remains an abiding joy.

The rapid growth of residential development in Victorian days led to the creation of an urban district council, which was amalgamated with Bowness, on the lakeside, in 1905. The railway, demoted to a single track and under threat of closure, is less popular nowadays but only because of the postwar fashions of transport, fast highways and motor cars bringing more visitors than ever before. All roads lead to Windermere.

Windermere, from Queen Adelaide's Hill

Windermere

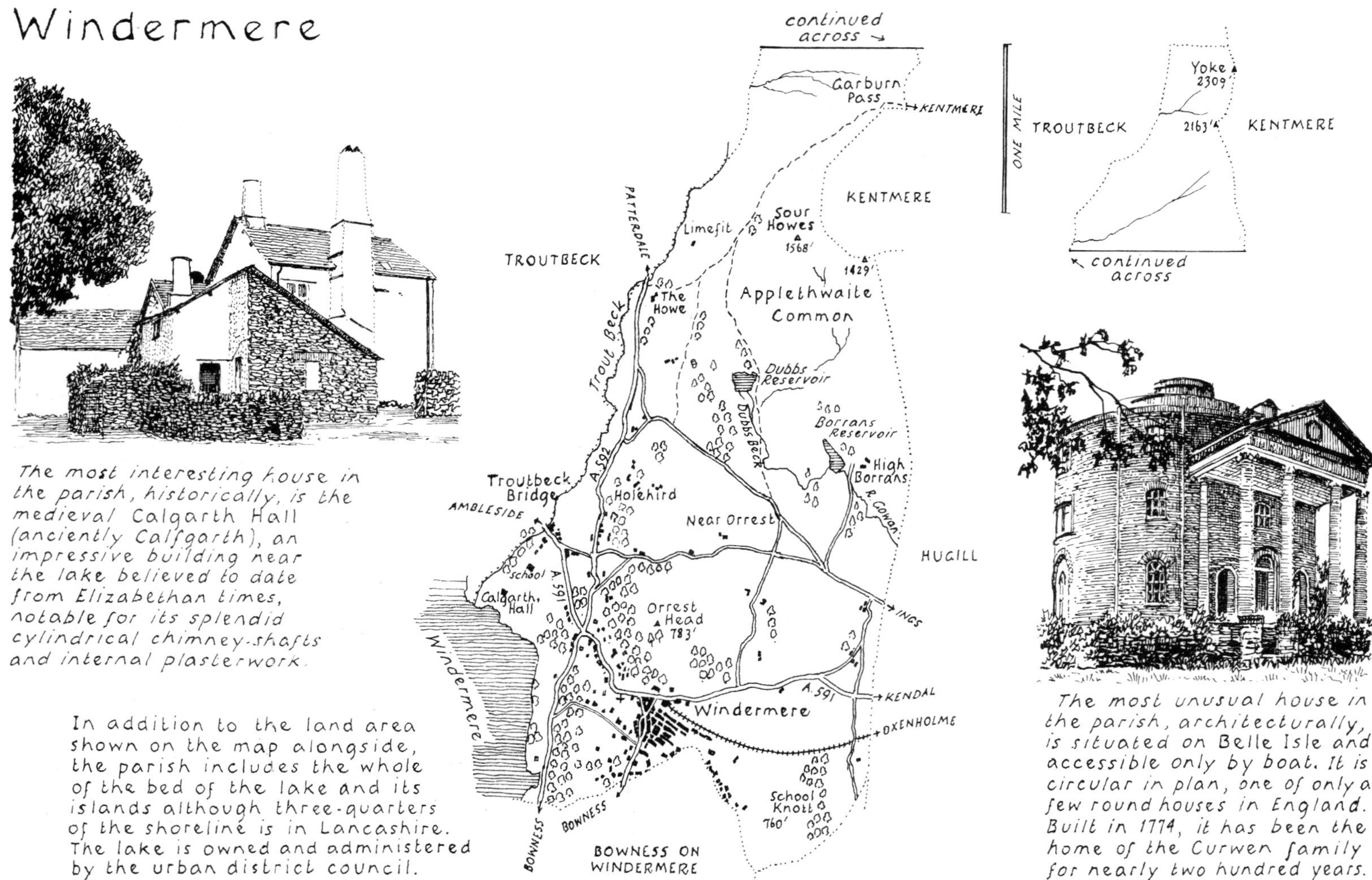

The most interesting house in the parish, historically, is the medieval Calgarth Hall (anciently Calfgarth), an impressive building near the lake believed to date from Elizabethan times, notable for its splendid cylindrical chimney-shafts and internal plasterwork.

In addition to the land area shown on the map alongside, the parish includes the whole of the bed of the lake and its islands although three-quarters of the shoreline is in Lancashire. The lake is owned and administered by the urban district council.

The most unusual house in the parish, architecturally, is situated on Belle Isle and accessible only by boat. It is circular in plan, one of only a few round houses in England. Built in 1774, it has been the home of the Curwen family for nearly two hundred years.

Windermere

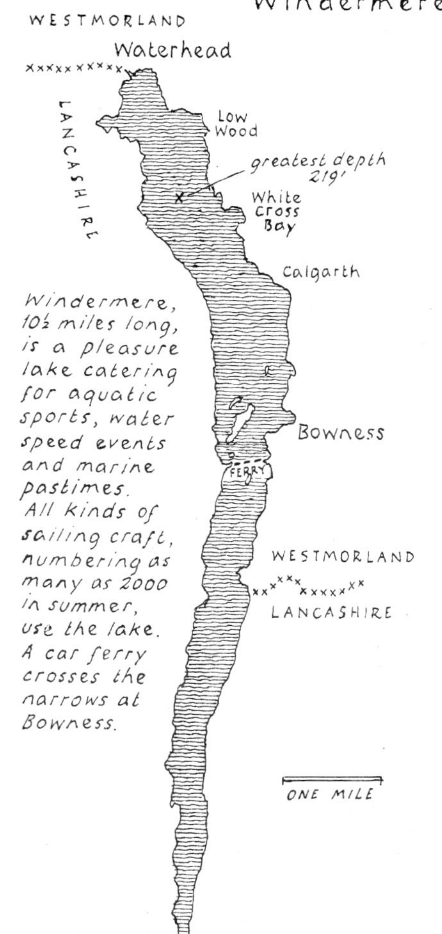

Windermere, 10½ miles long, is a pleasure lake catering for aquatic sports, water speed events and marine pastimes. All kinds of sailing craft, numbering as many as 2000 in summer, use the lake. A car ferry crosses the narrows at Bowness.

St Mary's Church, serving the ecclesiastical district of Applethwaite, was built in 1848 as a chapel to meet the needs of a fast increasing population following the coming of the railway. A quick succession of additions and alterations, and a major reconstruction in 1881-2, have completely changed the appearance of the 1848 chapel, and little of the original fabric remains.

Windermere

Although Windermere is commonly thought of as primarily a popular lakeside holiday resort, with many fine residences and landscaped open spaces and gardens, the area is predominantly agricultural and there are large tracts of rough ground within the parish suitable only for sheep grazing. Before tourists were numerous, farming was the main industry, the centres of activity being the several attractive farmhouses that still grace the rural scene. In the past century farming has given place to catering for visitors in economic importance but it continues to be a source of local employment, and those engaged in Windermere's favoured fields enjoy the bonus of a lovely environment all the year round.

Near Orrest, *built 1707, has a massive circular chimney*

Mislet,
17th century,
was used, in part, as an early Friends Meeting House

Longmire,
17th century, still has its original spinning-gallery

Some of the many houses of distinction in the parish

Hammar Bank

Not the least of the delights of Windermere is the fine array of elegant, often too ornate but generally handsome residences, standing in beautiful gardens, that have been contributed to the scenery by local men of substance and industrialists from the Lancashire towns. In spending their money thus, they have given pleasure not only to themselves.

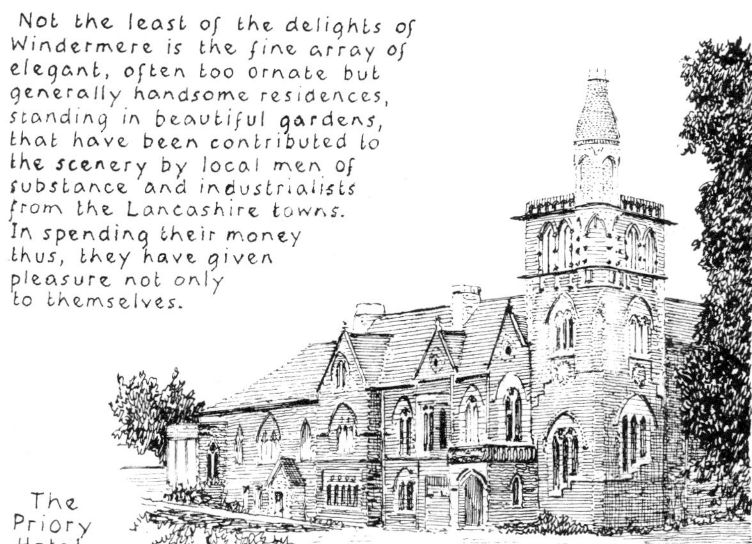

The Priory Hotel

Holehird, *beautifully situated in ornamental grounds, was the home of H. Leigh Groves, a generous benefactor prominent in local affairs, and bequeathed by him to the district council. Since 1961 it has been occupied as a Cheshire Home. Also in the grounds is a garden centre of the Lakeland Horticultural Society, a special feature being an extensive rock garden. Together, the house and grounds have been put to excellent and appreciative use.*

Windermere

View from Orrest Head

Cottages at Troutbeck Bridge

High Borrans, now a Field Study Centre for Tynemouth

Fusethwaite Yeat

Old Droomer

WINTON

The parish of Winton occupies an irregular strip of land extending southeast from the River Eden for seven miles, at first over lowland pastures but then inclining gradually over rough ground to reach, at an elevation of 2000 feet, a sterile wilderness adjoining the boundary with Yorkshire. The small village of Winton, sufficiently distant from the nearby A.685 to ensure its privacy and preserve its pleasant rural character, houses most of the sparse population of the parish, and there are a few farms, but the higher ground is entirely without habitations, rarely visited, a silent and lonely desert featureless except for the waterfall of Bleaberry Force and the remarkable array of cairns known as Nine Standards, which decorate the boundary with Hartley and dominate the whole parish, standing like sentinels on a rampart.

Contemporary authors, the Rev. John Langhorne and the historian Dr. Richard Burn, who achieved fame in the 18th century by their writings and other scholastic attainments, were natives of Winton.

The old corn mill, in an Arcadian setting, has been silent for 60 years but retains the skeleton of its water wheel.

Winton Hall has a stone tablet dated 1665 but the building is thought to be of much earlier period, an assumption supported by its medieval appearance. Massive buttresses, mullioned windows and heavy studded doors are features that impart a distinctive character. An addition on the south side of the Hall is 18th century.

Winton

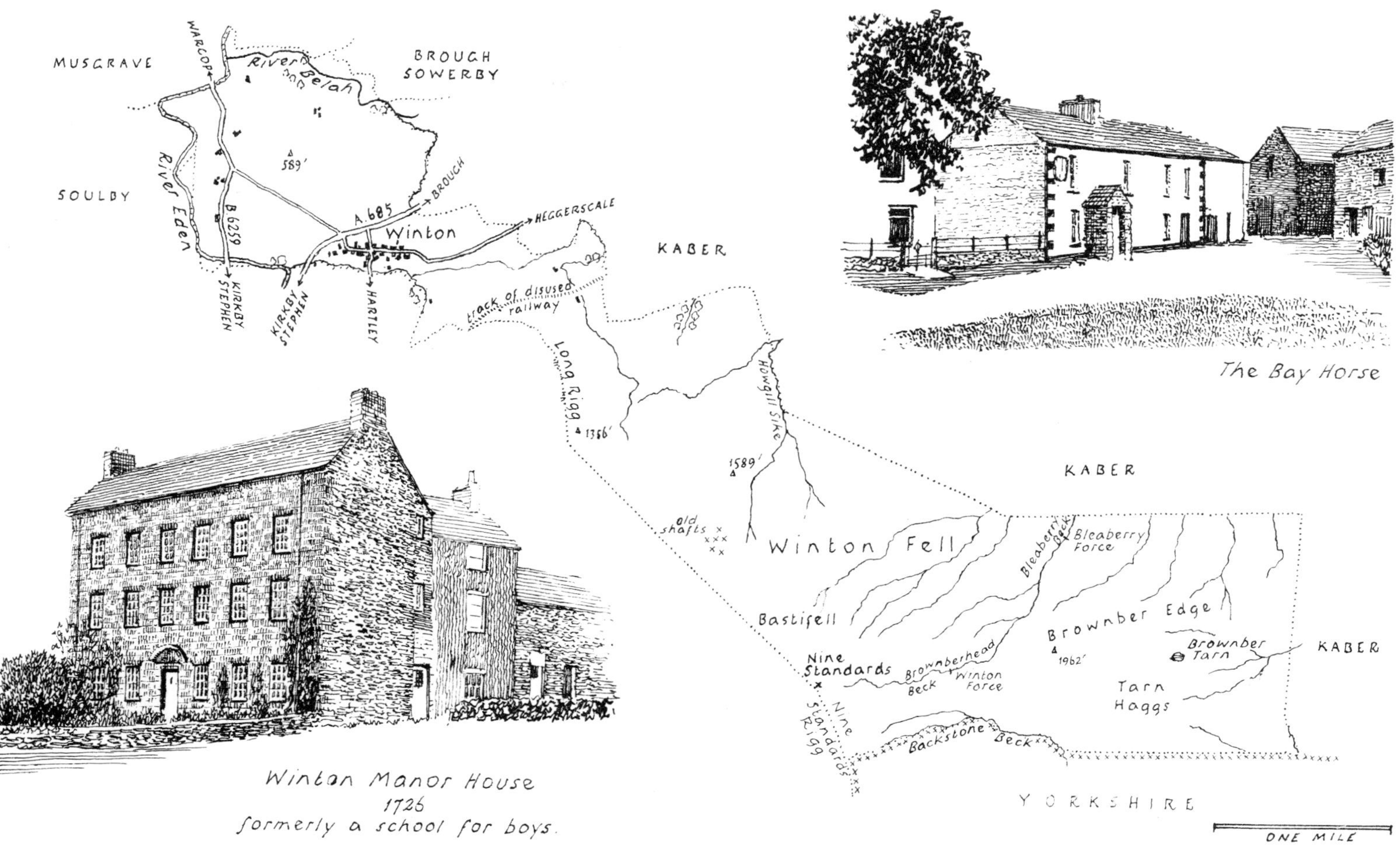

The Bay Horse

Winton Manor House
1726
formerly a school for boys.

WITHERSLACK

Many rural areas of Westmorland have a soothing effect on visitors from the towns and, as an antidote to urban pressures, the demand for country weekend homes increases. Witherslack is typical of the sort of place most favoured. This is truly a delectable region, secluded from, but with convenient access to, the A.590 road; sheltered by elevated escarpments; embowered in dense woodlands and having the charms peculiar to a limestone bedrock.

The village is formed of groups of dwellings lining quiet leafy lanes, some of them of modern design but fitting harmoniously into the scene. There are two large mansions, also unobtrusive behind a screen of fine trees: these are the homes, past and present, of the Stanley family, with the title of Earl of Derby and a notable record of service both to country and county. The Derby Arms was long the venue of a manorial court.

The western boundary is formed by the River Winster, with Lancashire beyond; the eastern boundary runs along the edge of Whitbarrow Scar. They draw together in the south but their meeting is delayed by a further appendage to the parish, enclosing most of Foulshaw Moss and extending to the Kent Estuary, the landscape here — a flat salt marsh — being in complete contrast to the limestone hinterland.

The parish church of St Paul, founded by bequest as a chapel of Beetham in 1664 in succession to a smaller chapel at the old Hall, is notable for many interesting fittings and monuments that have survived the enlargements and alterations of the church in the 18th and 19th centuries. The handsome west tower is sadly marred by two full-height iron drainpipes, omitted from the drawing.

Witherslack

Chapel Head Scar

Beck Head

Mill Side

Witherslack

The old Hall

A model village in the garden of a roadside cottage

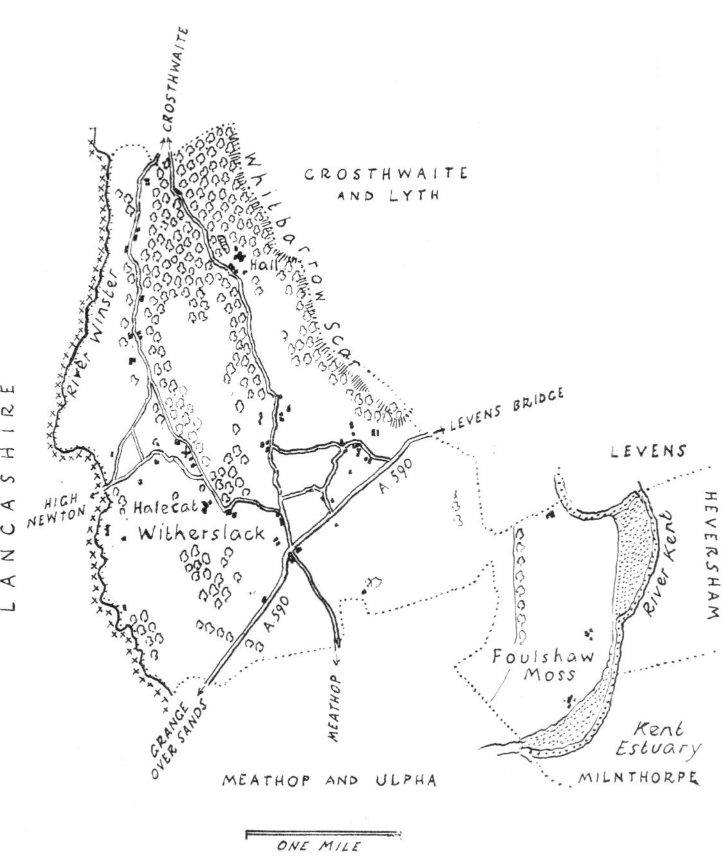

Witherslack

Halecat House

The Stanleys were granted the manor of Witherslack and the title of Earl of Derby by Royal favour in late medieval times and have always maintained a close interest in local and county affairs. The imposing Witherslack Hall was erected in 1874 as the family seat but since the last war has been occupied as a private school, Halecat House now being the principal residence.

Witherslack Hall

The entrance, Witherslack Hall

Witherslack

A : *A hamlet near the church*

B : *Nether Hall*

C : *Halecat Cottage*

D : *High Fell End*

B

C

A

D

YANWATH AND EAMONT BRIDGE

Yanwath, bordering on Cumberland, is a place deep-rooted in history, a history so old that it is almost forgotten; and only place-names on Ordnance maps and a few stones and earthworks remain to support the researches of learned scholars, who have identified Neolithic monuments and early village settlements that indicate primitive communities living here long before events began to be recorded. The Romans were here, too, and after them the Normans, who created the manor of Yanwath. Of later vintage, the medieval Hall is a reminder of the troubled years of the border raids.

Yanwath, linked with Eamont Bridge in one parish, today is a place burdened with heavy traffic. The main railway to the north cut through its fields last century, since when the development of road transport caused the promotion of the old turnpike through the parish to main artery status, and this, the A6, in turn became inadequate to cater for a fast increasing weight of traffic and had to be relieved a few years ago by a modern motorway. The old monuments remain, no longer solitary but sandwiched between noisy highways. Few passers by stop to look, and wonder.

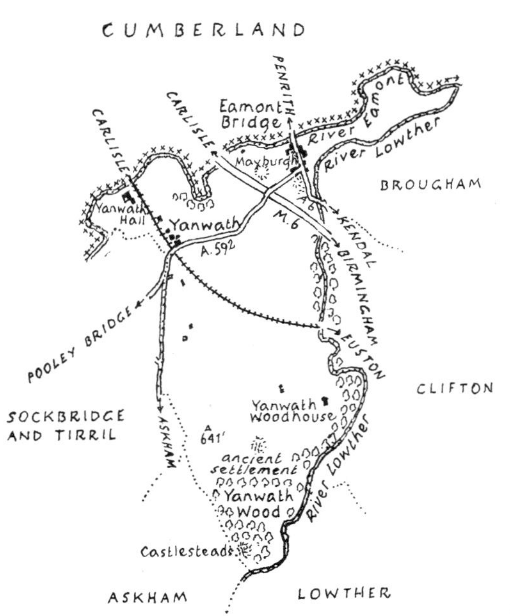

Two rivers, the Eamont and the Lowther, which at least have not changed with the times, form the northern and eastern boundaries, but the single ford of the early Britons, the Yamon Wath, from which the parish got its name, has been replaced by three bridges.

Yanwath today is crowded with new monuments.

Maybrugh is an impressive example of a henge monument and possibly 4000 years old. A flat area of 1½ acres is enclosed by a rampart of pebbles 15' high. Only one standing stone, 9' high, is left of an original group.

Maybrugh

Yanwath and Eamont Bridge

King Arthur's Round Table

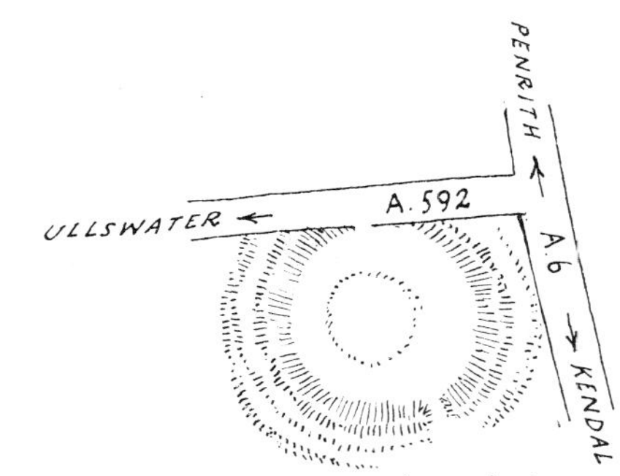

A smaller but similar earthwork, still indicated on Ordnance maps as Little Round Table (site of) was destroyed in the construction of an entrance to Lowther Park.

The field in the angle formed by the junction of two busy roads, the A6 and the A592, contains obvious earthworks in the form of a circular entrenchment around a raised platform, and a noticeboard of the Department of the Environment, in whose care it is, announces the site as King Arthur's Round Table, a name derived from a legendary association with that king and a supposition that the amphitheatre was used for knightly combats and feats of strength. Sir Walter Scott refers in a poem to "...... *red Penrith's Table Round*
For feats of chivalry renowned."

It is now accepted, however, that this is a henge monument, like Maybrugh nearby, and that the two sites were contemporaneous and probably of Neolithic period.

The Mansion House, formerly named Eamont Bridge Hall, was built in 1686 as a private residence, later served as a workhouse and was subsequently converted for use as tenements.

Yanwath and Eamont Bridge

A little known bridge
— and a well known one;
A bridge that has no traffic
— and a bridge that has too much

Eamont Bridge *has stood since the 16th century, succeeding earlier bridges and a still earlier ford. This is a long-established crossing of the river and an important stage on the old trade route between north and south. The bridge, despite a widening, is inadequate to carry a double line of vehicles and traffic lights are in operation, while pedestrians no longer use the refuges above the massive cutwaters and are diverted to a footbridge alongside. Relief from traffic congestion has now been provided by the motorway.*

Low Gardens Bridge *spans the River Lowther in a single graceful arch, a thing of beauty. It is not accessible to motorists, being in the private grounds of Lowther Park.*

Yanwath and Eamont Bridge

Yanwath Hall, an imposing domestic stronghold, overlooks the boundary with Cumberland, standing on the steep south bank of the River Eamont, which added a natural defence. It has been splendidly preserved and its original appearance is little changed. The turreted pele tower and adjoining range of buildings were built in 1322, and extended in the following century to form three sides of a courtyard. In the 16th century the Hall was partly ruinous but careful renewal restored the dignity of the structure and subsequent maintenance has preserved it.

It is fitting that the book should end with Yanwath Hall, for this is a typical, and excellent, example of a medieval semi-fortified manor house in Westmorland at the most turbulent period of the county's history, when Border warfare was a cause of general unease and insecurity.

The Hall stands today as a symbol of defiance against invasion, of determination to fight for independence.

The threat from over the Border has passed, but what the Scots could never do in centuries of strife has been accomplished by anonymous clerks in a Whitehall office overnight, on 31st March 1974, by an act of legislative surgery, thereby proving the pen of the Establishment to be mightier than the sword. They have robbed Westmorland of its name and independence; what they have not done, nor could ever do, is to rob Westmorland folk of their sentimental regard for the county, and of their pride in its manifold and characteristic delights.

New generations, with diminished local patriotism, may have little thought for the past, but it is earnestly to be hoped that the birthright bequeathed to them will always be revered and treasured as precious. It is Westmorland living on after being pronounced dead. While its heritage remains there can be no requiem for Westmorland.